Linguistics: The Cambridge Survey

Volume IV
Language: The Socio-cultural Context

Linguistics: The Cambridge Survey

Editor-in Chief
Frederick J. Newmeyer University of Washington

Editorial Board
Stephen Anderson The Johns Hopkins University
John Baugh University of California, Santa Cruz
William Bright University of Colorado
Janet D. Fodor Graduate School and University Center, City University of New York
Victoria A. Fromkin University of California, Los Angeles
Ruth Kempson School of Oriental and African Studies, Universtiy of London
Wayne O'Neil Massachusetts of Technology
Henk Van Riemsdijk Tilburg University
Arnold M. Zwicky The Ohio State University and Stanford University

Executive Editor
Robert N. Ubell Robert Ubell Associates, New York

Linguistics: The Cambridge Survey

Edited by Frederick J. Newmeyer

University of Washington

Volume IV
Language: The Socio-cultural Context

CAMBRIDGE
UNIVERSITY PRESS

Published by the Press Syndicate of the University of Cambridge
The Pitt Building, Trumpington Street, Cambridge CB2 1RP
40 West 20th Street, New York, NY 10011-4211, USA
10 Stamford Road, Oakleigh, Melbourne 3166, Australia

First published 1988
First paperback edition 1989
Reprinted 1990, 1993, 1995

Printed in Great Britain by Athenæum Press Ltd, Gateshead, Tyne and Wear

British Library cataloguing in publication data

Linguistics: the Cambridge survey.
Vol. 4: Language; the socio-cultural context
1. Linguistics
I. Newmeyer, Frederick J.
410   P121

Library of Congress cataloguing in publication data

Language: the socio-cultural context.
(Linguistics, the Cambridge survey; v. 4)
Includes indexes.
1. Sociolinguistics.   2. Language and culture.
I. Newmeyer, Frederick J.   II. Series.
P121. L567 vol. 4 [p40] 410 s [401′.9] 87–23876

ISBN 0 521 30834 8   hardback
ISBN 0 521 37583 5   paperback

Contents

Contributors to Volume IV

John Baugh Department of Linguistics, University of California, Santa Cruz
Diane Blakemore Department of French, University of Southampton
Donna Christian Center for Applied Linguistics
Wolfgang U. Dressler Institut für Sprachwissenscshaft, University of Vienna
Alessandro Duranti University of California, San Diego
William A. Foley Department of Linguistics, University of Sydney
Gregory R. Guy Department of Linguistics, Stanford University
Jane H. Hill Department of Anthropology, University of Arizona
Beatriz R. Lavandera University of Buenos Aires and CONICET
Sally McConnell-Ginet Department of Modern Languages and Linguistics, Cornell University
David Sankoff Centre de recherches mathématiques, University of Montreal
Deborah Schiffrin Department of Linguistics, Georgetown University
Bernard Spolsky Department of English, Bar-Ilan University
Keith Walters Department of Linguistics, University of Texas, Austin

Preface

Language: the socio-cultural context is the last of four volumes comprising *Linguistics: the Cambridge survey*. The first three volumes of the series are entitled *Linguistic theory: foundations, Linguistic theory: extensions and implications*, and *Language: psychological and biological aspects*. Their common thread is the treatment of language as a mental or biological entity. Thus they are devoted primarily to presenting the constructs of theoretical linguistics and to probing the evidence for their psychological reality, as well as to sorting out the implications that their reality may have for diverse areas of investigation. But language, of course, is more than a mental phenomenon. Indeed, many would say that such a function is secondary to its role in *social* interaction, i.e. to its function in communication and as the principal agent for the transmission of cultural and social values.

The point of departure of the chapters in this volume is the socio-cultural aspect of language; each explores a different dimension of this aspect. The volume begins with a critical overview by Beatriz R. Lavandera of studies of language in its socio-cultural context. She contrasts three different orientations guiding such studies: one in which the investigator's attention is focussed on practical goals, without challenging any of the precepts of normal mainstream linguistics; one which takes the position that most traditional problems of mainstream linguistics admit of a solution once social variables are incorporated; and a third which attempts to reconstitute linguistics itself to provide a theory of language in its social context. Lavandera shows that the radical differences of opinion within sociolinguistics and allied fields derive primarily from the adoption of one of these three orientations.

Chapter 2, 'Language, culture, and world view' by Jane H. Hill, discusses the difficult question of the relationship between the forms that a particular language may manifest and its speakers' perception of reality and the nature of their cultural institutions. Hill focusses on the well-known 'linguistic relativity hypothesis' advocated by Edward Sapir, Benjamin Whorf, and others, and provides a detailed discussion of one particular area that lends itself to investigation along these lines, namely that of a language's selection of color terms.

In the third chapter, 'Language and social class,' Gregory R. Guy addresses the question of how and why social classes differ in their use of language, and argues that this issue has significance for the field of linguistics. He takes up topics such as those sociosymbolic aspects of language that identify the speaker as having a particular social identity; the social class that most characteristically produces linguistic innovations; and the relationship of class membership and style shifting in discourse.

The fourth chapter is John Baugh's 'Language and race: some implications for linguistic science.' The principal implication that Baugh draws is that linguistics can be an important weapon in the war against racism, in particular by exposing the flimsy theoretical basis of a number of ill-conceived remedial language programs designed for minority school pupils.

Chapter 5, 'Language and gender' by Sally McConnell-Ginet, addresses the broad spectrum of issues surrounding the different linguistic productions by and about men and women and the encoding of gender in the linguistic signal itself. Among many other topics, McConnell-Ginet discusses some of the mechanisms through which male social privilege leads to a kind of linguistic privilege and reviews the research on gender and conversational interaction.

In his opening remarks to Chapter 6, 'Bilingualism,' Bernard Spolsky points out that the topic can be approached from many different vantage points, including that of sociolinguistics, neurolinguistics, grammatical theory, bilingual education, and language planning. Spolsky focusses in particular on language spread, i.e. the increase in the use of a particular language variety for a given communicative function, and language choice, i.e. the bilingual's decision (conscious or unconscious) to use one language rather than the other.

In Chapter 7, Keith Walters surveys the field of 'Dialectology,' which has undergone a marked change of orientation in the past few decades. Originally the field had a rural and regional focus; now the orientation is much more toward the socially stratified speech of urban centers. This change has brought the study of dialect differentiation head-to-head with sociology, anthropology, and psychology, as well as with numerous branches of sociolinguistics.

In 'Sociolinguistics and syntactic variation' (Chapter 8), David Sankoff's goal is to ground the study of variation in a synthesis of the Labovian quantitative paradigm and a Habermasian critical approach to understanding. He argues that such an approach is superior to that provided by either generative grammar or experimental models, and he disputes claims that the study of syntactic variation requires fundamentally different methods from that of phonological variation.

The ninth chapter is William A. Foley's 'Language birth: the processes of pidginization and creolization.' Foley shows how pidgins characteristically originate in 'foreigner talk' and outlines the stages from stable pidgin to expanded pidgin to creole. Much of the chapter is devoted to two case studies of pidgins indigenous to New Guinea: Yimas Pidgin and Police Motu.

Chapter 10, 'Language death' by Wolfgang U. Dressler, discusses the conditions surrounding the extinction of a minority language as a result of its replacement by a dominant majority language. Dying languages characteristically manifest similar changes at all levels of grammatical structure (lexical, phonological, morphological, and semantic). Sociolinguistic factors also accompany the terminal decay of a language, including the lack of puristic reactions against the massive interference from the dominant language and a tendency towards monostylism.

In 'Language planning: the view from linguistics,' Chapter 11, Donna Christian addresses the issues involved in organized attempts to influence the way language is used. As she notes, strictly linguistic factors are almost always outweighed by political, social, and cultural ones. Nevertheless, linguistics can play a role in language planning, especially those branches of the field that are devoted to the study of language in its socio-cultural setting. Christian cites language planning attempts from many parts of the world, giving special attention to the situation in Singapore and Canada.

The field of ethnography of speaking probes the relationship between language use and local systems of knowledge and social conduct; it views discourse as one of the main loci for the transmission of cultural patterns of knowledge and social action. Put more simply, its subject matter is the role of speaking in shaping people's lives. Alessandro Duranti in Chapter 12, 'Ethnography of speaking: towards a linguistics of the praxis,' contrasts this approach with that taken by generative grammar and by most sociolinguists and conversation analysts.

The last two chapters are devoted to the linguistic interactions of speakers and hearers. The field of discourse analysis is covered in Chapter 13, Diane Blakemore's 'The organization of discourse.' Blakemore discusses the conditions under which a text is judged coherent and cohesive, and argues that the principles governing such matters are fundamentally distinct from those proposed within grammatical theories. The second half of the chapter is devoted to motivating a relevance-based account of discourse.

Chapter 14 by Deborah Schiffrin presents the field of 'Conversation analysis,' which typically focusses more on the social setting of verbal interchanges than does discourse analysis. Schiffrin addresses such questions as the nature of the appropriate transcription to be used and the selection of the relevant corpus. The chapter treats in some detail two particular areas of interest in conversation analysis: the coordination of turn-taking and dialogic pairs, i.e. questions and their answers and compliments and their responses.

Frederick J. Newmeyer

1 The study of language in its socio-cultural context

Beatriz R. Lavandera

1.0. Introduction

It does not seem far-fetched to hold Chomsky indirectly responsible for the accelerated development of sociolinguistics and ethnolinguistics at the end of the 1960s and for the emphasis laid upon pragmatics and discourse analysis in the mid 1970s. Paradoxical as it may seem, his revival of the Saussurean *langue–parole* dichotomy (under the names 'competence' and 'performance'), and, even more important, his assertion of the autonomy of syntax, sparked a renewed interest in the study of language in its socio-cultural context. Both these twin pillars of Chomskyan linguistics seemed to many to shut out most of the more interesting questions about language, in particular those relating to its functioning in society. As a consequence, a sizeable number of linguists struck out on their own, as it were, and devoted themselves to building alternative conceptions of language, in which its social function was regarded as paramount.

The reaction to Chomsky's position that the systematicity of language is confined to competence took a number of different forms. Some, seeing systematicity outside of competence in Chomsky's narrow use of the term, attempted to extend the notion of competence to cover most of the aspects that Chomsky ascribed to performance. An example is Hymes's (1972) 'communicative competence,' which he defined as the knowledge of the abstract rules of a language required to produce sound/meaning correspondences, and the ability to use those correspondences between sound, meaning, and form in socially and culturally appropriate ways. On the other hand, some saw system in performance as well as in competence and began to develop theories specifically of the former (e.g. Labov 1969, 1972a). But whichever path was taken, a growing core of investigators was united in the conviction that the Chomskyan paradigm was too narrow to accommodate most of the interesting questions about language.

In the following pages, I will survey and comment upon the principal trends in the study of language in its socio-cultural context. I do not aim at exhaustive coverage of the topic, nor do I plan to conduct a survey of the chapters of this volume (a survey of surveys hardly seems like a useful enterprise!). Rather, I will here and there refer briefly to the chapters to illustrate general points and to use their content as a sounding board for my own views on the general problem of language and social context.

1.1. Some dimensions of the study of language and socio-cultural context

Approaches to socially oriented linguistics do not pigeonhole themselves into neat divisions, each of which is distinct from the others in terms of its subject matter, goals, methodology, and so on. The situation is much more complex: we find among the various parts of the field considerable overlapping along many dimensions, so that two areas that share the same basic subject of investigation may disagree on methodology, while the methodology of one of them may be shared by researchers in an entirely different area of investigation. The following subsections outline what I feel are the three most important dimensions along which approaches to language in its socio-cultural context may be described: their basic subject matter, i.e. their conception of what is meant by 'language use' (1.1.1); their fundamental goals (1.1.2); and their willingness to employ formal methods of analysis (1.1.3).

1.1.1. Language use

All of the subfields represented in this volume share a common feature – their aim is to study language in use. Yet 'use' is understood in deeply divergent senses, each of which for all practical purposes defines a semi-independent discipline. For example, in the area known as 'ethnography of speaking,' which was pioneered by John Gumperz and Dell Hymes (see Gumperz 1971; Gumperz & Hymes 1972; Hymes 1974) and is represented by Duranti's chapter (12) in this volume, 'use' refers to the use of the linguistic code or codes in the conduct of social life. Studies in this area are dynamic and interactional and, in most recent work, adopt Goffman's theory of social order (1971, 1974, 1981). The data of analysis in the ethnography of speaking tend to be utterances or collections of utterances, features of the speaker, hearer, and speech situation, and the presumed purpose of the speech.

The 'quantitative paradigm' shares with the ethnography of speaking a body of data defined on the basis of produced utterances. However, in this area, which originated in work by William Labov and his collaborators, the *object* of analysis is no longer an utterance or collection of connected utterances. Rather it is the 'aggregate statistical data' that result from quantifying linguistic variables and correlating them with external variables in all the utterances of the corpus, which itself is obtained from a socio-economically representative sample of speakers (cf. Labov 1972a). Three chapters in this volume deal with the quantitative paradigm from different angles: Guy's 'Language and social class' (3) relates it to the hard issue of appropriate social theories for sociolinguistics; Walters's 'Dialectology' (7) presents the practitioners of this model as modernized urban dialectologists; and Sankoff's 'Sociolinguistics and syntactic variation' (8) advocates this paradigm in the strongest terms and endows it with (I think questionable) social goals.

Other areas focus on the utterance as well, but typically at an interpersonal level, abstracted to one degree or another away from the social context. This is the case for most work in discourse analysis and to a lesser extent in conversation analysis, represented in this volume by the chapters (13 and 14) by Blakemore and Schiffrin, respectively. Of all the subdisciplines covered in this volume, discourse analysis shares in its methodology and results the greatest number of features with Chomskyan linguistics. While its subject matter may be real speech used in real speech situations, it tends to approach this subject matter in the autonomous way that generative grammarians approach the patterning of grammatical elements.

Finally, there is an approach to language use that is very different from those just described. This approach (or, more properly, set of approaches) falls under the heading 'macro-sociolinguistics.' Here the data are not utterances, but systems, in particular languages or language varieties that occur within the same community. The task of the linguist becomes to study and analyze the relationships among such systems. Some branches of macro-sociolinguistics represented in this volume are bilingualism (Chapter 6), dialectology (Chapter 7), language planning (Chapter 11), language birth (Chapter 9), and language death (Chapter 10).

1.1.2. Goals of the study of language in context

While approaches differ in their subject matter, they also differ in their ultimate objectives. Not surprisingly, in an area as diverse and far-ranging as that of the study of language in its social context, we find widely diverging goals. Dell Hymes, in a 1972 address at a Georgetown Round Table (published in Hymes 1974), outlined what he saw as the three most important distinct goals of practitioners of sociolinguistics (in the widest sense of the term). Since I find Hymes's trichotomy a useful one, I will present it in this section.

Hymes referred to the first orientation as 'the social as well as the linguistic.' This category involves socially oriented work whose immediate goals are practical ones, such as that involving language as it relates to education, to minority groups, and to language policies. To pursue such goals one need not challenge normal mainstream linguistics. Indeed, as Hymes pointed out, such luminaries of grammatical research as Sapir, Bloomfield, and Swadesh involved themselves in practical concerns. Work in this tradition continues today, and is represented in this volume by the chapters by Baugh on 'Language and race,' (4) by Christian on 'Language planning,' (11) by Dressler on 'Language death,' (10) and by McConnell-Ginet on 'Language and gender' (5).

Hymes called the second orientation 'socially realistic linguistics.' This orientation, represented in the 1970s especially by the work of Labov and his colleagues, challenges existing linguistics by drawing on data from the speech community itself and by developing new methodologies which in turn result in new findings about language. Nevertheless, Hymes did not see its goals as deviating significantly from those of normal linguistics, in that it has typically addressed itself to very traditional problems: the nature of linguistic rules, the nature of sound change, and so on.

Hymes saw the third orientation, 'socially constituted linguistics,' as possessing goals fundamentally different from those of the first two. In his words, it represents

> the fundamental challenge to whose threshold we have come; [it] expresses the view that social function gives form to the ways in which linguistic features are encountered in actual life; [it] must begin by identifying social functions, and discover the ways in which linguistic features are selected and grouped to serve them . . . it shares a concern for social realism and validity . . . A socially constituted linguistics is concerned with social as well as referential meaning, and with language as part of communicative conduct and social action. (1974: 196)

Hymes, whose advocacy of this orientation toward language and society was explicit, saw as its most important distinguishing feature the fact that it strives toward a 'theory of language,' not a 'theory of grammar.' Normal linguistics has principally been involved in constructing the latter. That is, it has been concerned with the study of regularities in language that pertain solely to the relative frequency of occurrence or cooccurrence of various structures. Thus the quantitative paradigm is an example of an approach devoted to a theory of grammar.

A theory of language, on the other hand, studies the use of utterances in discourse within a communicative situation undivorceable from its social context. Thus the phenomena of social order are systematically incorporated into the linguistic analysis and priority is given to the social over the linguistic in order to achieve a better understanding of language. This orientation insists as well on the role of function in determining the distribution of linguistic forms.[1]

1.1.3. The question of formalization

A further important division among 'socially concerned' linguists, and one which does not dovetail with the first two, centers around the issue of formalization. Three important (and contrasting) positions are those of William Labov, Dell Hymes, and Teun van Dijk. Labov, for example, shares many of the assumptions about formalization inherent in mainstream generative grammar; indeed, he sees his own theory as not only compatible with that theory, but also contributing to it. Specifically, through the mechanism of the 'variable rule,' he incorporates social variables directly into already existing generative mechanisms. He has even expressed the hope that his variation theory might provide answers to all (or at least some) traditional questions that have occupied generativist theory. It is worth noting, however, that while Labov still sees variable rules as beneficial (as pointed out by the Walters chapter, 7, in this volume), he has backed off considerably in recent years in the degree of explanatory power he feels is attributable to them. Labov now states that 'Linguistic variables or variable rules are not in themselves a "theory of language." They are all heuristic devices . . . Thus a variable rule analysis is not put forward as a description of the grammar, but as a device for finding out about the grammar' (1978: 10–13).

Dell Hymes, on the other hand, has advocated formulating rules of speaking as a means of making an analysis precise, but has cautioned his readers that when dealing with the understanding of human purposes and needs, formal analysis might be indispensable, 'but [it is] only a means, and not that understanding itself' (1974: 64–5).

Hymes, while he talks of 'rules' and 'knowledge of rules,' does not appear to consider them to be the sort that could be incorporated into an algorithm for producing appropriate utterances or for relating utterances to context. Actually, Hymes has never made explicit the form of the rules that he sees in the communicative competence of the speaker–hearer that would represent his or her ability to use utterances in socially and culturally appropriate ways.

Finally, van Dijk's work (1977) is representative of a trend that extends rule formulation to cover many aspects of pragmatics, in particular to account for the specific functions of discourse types in certain contexts and social situations. While for Hymes, human needs and intentions seem to be irreduc-

---

[1] Sankoff's chapter in this volume credits variation theory for the interest within sociolinguistics in function and interpretation, without acknowledging earlier proponents of the use of these concepts in the study of variation, e.g. Hymes (1974), Lavandera (1978, 1982).

ible to formal analysis, van Dijk extends formal analysis to cover these areas and to speakers' and hearers' knowledge, beliefs, and preferences as well.

While van Dijk and others refer to 'pragmatic rules,' one must not be misled into thinking that such rules are highly formalized within an axiomatized system like the rules of generative grammar. In most cases, they tend to be fragmentary or isolated, and used rather loosely, e.g. in the way that Labov (1972b) refers to 'rules for ritual insults.' Such 'rules' are better termed 'statements,' 'conditions,' 'principles,' 'maxims,' 'strategies,' and so on, rather than rules. And to be sure, such terms have often been employed (cf. Grice's 1975 'maxims'; Gumperz's 1982a 'strategies'; and Searle's 1969, 1979 'conditions').

1.2. The need for a social theory

If one's sights are set on a theory of grammar rather than a theory of language, then it is not crucial which social theory the sociolinguist adopts. Such a theory, for example, is not crucial to the variationists, whose goal is to uncover quantitative patterns and correlations that reveal linguistic structures within performance. Indeed, variation theory does not even demand that the correlations be made with social or stylistic factors. As David Sankoff puts it in his contribution to this volume, 'the internal linguistic conditioning of interest to variationists . . . can be amply exemplified in the phonology of a single individual . . . without regard to social or stylistic factors' (p. 141). What could be farther from Hymes's notion of a socially constituted sociolinguistics?

On the other hand, the situation is quite different for those whose goal is to develop a theory of language in its social context, rather than a theory of grammar. The concern with the choice of a social theory becomes paramount, since one of the fundamental questions is which elements of the social context affect the production and understanding of language in natural settings.[2]

Gregory R. Guy's chapter (3) in this volume surveys the possible social theories that might be called upon to define the extralinguistic variables of concern to sociolinguistics. As he rightly points out, practically all work in this area to date has been carried out within Labov's model of social stratification. Guy also discusses, briefly and clearly, what would be involved in a sociolinguistic analysis from a Marxist outlook (see also Rickford 1986). (Marxist variation studies tend, unfortunately, to be highly inadequate. An example is Bordieu & Boltanski 1975, which never went beyond proposing a subjective method for constructing a more representative sample.)

---

[2] For an excellent example of how social divisions hinder communication, see Gumperz's studies of interethnic verbal exchanges (1982a, b).

I disagree with Guy's statement that a Marxist view of society as a conflict of social classes could coexist with Labov's (1972a) definition of a speech community in terms of a social norm imbued with prestige and shared by all social classes. Guy attempts to rephrase Labov's position in Marxist terms, but fails, in my view. Indeed, Labov himself believes that the choice of social theory is irrelevant to the linguistic result (personal communication, July 1986), and has written:

> As far as the synchronic aspect of language structure is concerned, it would be an error to put for [sic] much emphasis on social factors. Generative grammar has made great progress in working out the invariant relations within this structure, even though it wholly neglects the social context of language. (1970: 78)

Given such an attitude, it is not surprising that Labov could describe the English passive as a sociolinguistic variable even after having found that it cannot be correlated with social factors (see Labov & Weiner 1977 and, for discussion, Lavandera 1978).[3]

The lack of concern with social theory shown by many practitioners of the quantitative model has caused many sociolinguists to turn away from that model.[4] Others have divided their concerns: they continue quantitative formal studies, while at the same time devoting an important and successful part of their research to the use of linguistic evidence and argumentation to shed light on eminently social problems, as has Labov in much work (e.g. 1982).

My position is that any theory that aims at understanding social life and organization through a study of the principles governing verbal communication must grant first priority to the choice of social theory.

1.3. **The problem of context**

The diversity of goals and methodologies within the study of language and society and the lack of a consensus on an adequate social theory (or even on the need for one) has led to even greater diversity of opinion on what the relevant contextual features are for an adequate sociolinguistic analysis. The following two subsections review and comment upon some of the issues in this regard. In 1.3.1 I summarize the many aspects of context that have been

---

[3] Weiner and Labov later (1983) published a corrected version in which they reported the effect of some social factors, including sex, age, class, and ethnicity.

[4] To be fair to the variationists, many of them are now explicitly aware of the shortcomings in the methodology to which I alluded above and have broadened their base in a number of important ways. Also, variation theory is hardly homogeneous; for work within this general framework that introduced important modifications, see L. Milroy 1980, J. Milroy & L. Milroy 1985, and Guy 1979.

7

deemed relevant; 1.3.2 discusses the (dramatic) consequences of the choice of social versus interpersonal context as the more important for analysis.

1.3.1. A methodological issue: the actual choice of contexts

It is a highly controversial issue which contextual features are most relevant to the production and interpretation of speech, and we find different models stressing different features. This section outlines those that have been considered as having most important effects on the form and/or function of the string of speech under analysis.

Probably the leading factor cited has been the immediate communicative situation within which the speech act is performed (for extensive discussion, see Hymes 1972, 1974). However, there are many ways of looking at the communicative situation. Labov, for example, stresses large-scale factors that are properties of the participants in a communicative situation, like sex, age, race, socioeconomic status, and so on. Labov also includes 'style' as a major external variable, which he defines as 'the amount of attention paid to speech.' Ethnomethodologists, however, disagree, and claim that styles in particular, and institutional arrangements in general, are not associated with linguistic products; rather it is talk that helps to constitute or reinforce them. Hence, for them, 'self' (along with 'other' and 'situation') are themselves social contexts, which have symbolic meanings for participants. Furthermore, individual efforts at expression alone cannot create a self; rather 'those expressive meanings have to be understood and acted upon by the one to whom they are directed' (Chapter 14 below, p. 266).

Others, such as Gumperz (1982a, b) stress the larger noncommunicative situation in which the communicative event takes place and in which the speech act is embedded. Still others stress the divisions internal to the speech community, such as groups, networks, classes, etc., and those cultural patterns prevailing within it which affect the speech behavior of each of the participants in the analyzed speech event.[5]

Other contextual features that have been proposed within different models as being relevant to the production and interpretation of speech include shared knowledge, beliefs, intentions, presuppositions, inferences, and so on that may have a social or cultural basis; meaningful nonverbal action that precedes, accompanies, or follows the speech under analysis;[6] the characteristics of the existing relationships between speaker(s) and hearer(s),

---

[5] For a thorough review of the competing definitions of 'speech community,' see Guy's chapter in this volume and Rickford 1986.

[6] Goffman's theory places special stress on nonverbal modalities, which work in concert with the purely linguistic means towards achieving social organization. For a good selection of Goffman's most important statements about the problem of the relationship between language and social organization, see the Schiffrin chapter (14) in this volume.

whether symmetric or asymmetric; and the characteristics of the speaker(s) and hearer(s) that are used by members of the community in the laying down of norms, laws, and decisions, such as their sex, age, race, or educational level.

Despite this rather long list of contextual features that have been appealed to by various sociolinguistic models, it is my contention that the main difference among the different models does not reside in their choice of contexts *per se*, but rather in the hypotheses that they set up about the interrelationship *between* language and context, and whether they grant the social priority over the linguistic, as does Hymes, the linguistic priority over the social, as does Labov, or treat the two together, as I feel is correct.

1.3.2. Social context versus interpersonal context

So far in this overview I have used the term 'context' somewhat ambiguously to cover both social context and interpersonal context. Any comprehensive study of language use, needless to say, must appeal to both. Yet the subdisciplines represented by the chapters in this volume do not call upon them equally, as I shall now illustrate.

In the ethnography of speaking and in most branches of sociolinguistics, it is social context that is most relevant (though there are both ethnolinguists and sociolinguists who would reject this characterization). The context is 'social' in the sense that it encompasses the internal organization of a society, with its tensions, internal differences, subgroupings, and so on. Thus the study of language in a social context consists of the study of the linguistic material produced within the structure of the society. It pays special attention to the way in which particular characteristics of the society affect the structures of variation and change of the language spoken, and, conversely, to the way in which different uses of language and different attitudes about its varieties affect the internal dimensions and forces of the recipient community.

It is worth citing a couple of examples of the mutual influence between linguistic structure and social structure that forms a primary topic of investigation by ethnographers of speaking and sociolinguists. Take for example the adoption by increasingly large members of a speech community of a stigmatizing attitude toward the use of some particular linguistic variant, which in turn is likely to result in a linguistic situation affecting internal relations among groups. Another example might be the way in which upwardly mobile members of the lower middle class will manifest a concern for hypercorrection that is likely to have linguistic manifestations.

On the other hand, in subdisciplines such as pragmatics, discourse analysis, and conversation analysis, the interpersonal or 'interactional' context typically takes priority over the social. These areas are not devoted to understanding the interaction of the linguistic structure with the structure of the society; rather, the focus is devoted to (usually two) interacting individuals – a speaker and a listener. The context that is assumed to be essential to the understanding of the exchanged utterances or texts includes elements rooted in psychology, such as intentions, beliefs, and rationality. In these subdisciplines, even when social factors like 'power' and 'status' are appealed to (as in Brown & Levinson 1978), they enter the analysis through the psychological configuration of the individual. The kinds of acts described and explained by pragmatic theories in particular (those of Grice 1975 and Searle 1979 are good examples) are primarily oriented to the psychological setups of the interacting individuals.

To give an example, studies of politeness strategies tend to focus solely on the state of the relationship between the participants themselves, in particular to their state of psychological satisfaction or offence. The approach to personal relationships is thus a 'punctual' one: one or both of the participants are pleased or insulted by a single act. Yet they typically ignore the social fact that such strategies reflect the distribution of power in the society. How power is assigned and maintained linguistically in the society remains outside the scope of conversation analysis and pragmatics.

This is not to imply that all investigators who focus on participants in a speech event put forward the image of a thoroughly passive speaker–hearer. John Gumperz's 'discourse strategies' framework, for example (see Gumperz 1982a, b) upholds an active dynamic view of the speaker and hearer, in which the speech actors themselves can modify, and even create, many of the features of the social context of their speech. Some of these changes, which can be the result rather than the conditioning factor of the speech exchange, are easy to pinpoint, such as the formality of the situation and the symmetric or asymmetric character of the relationship between speaker(s) and hearer(s). Indeed, as Gumperz demonstrates, the power of both speaker and hearer to modify social contexts can go well beyond the rather obvious modifying factor just mentioned.[7]

1.4. Discourse analysis

This discussion will close with a more detailed look at an approach to the study of language use that typically appeals to the interpersonal rather than to the social context, namely discourse analysis. I hope to show that such an appeal, with its consequent exclusive focus on internal properties of discourse such as cohesion, coherence, and relevance is not mandatory. Rather, it is

[7] A large body of literature builds upon Gumperz's active view of the speaker and hearer (see especially Ervin-Tripp 1972). For an alternative view of politeness strategies, see Lavandera 1987.

possible to go beyond the interpersonal to the social and establish external connections with the social context within which discourse functions.

I should begin by pointing out that the term 'discourse' has been used in the literature of the last decade as the synonym of two terms with quite different meanings: 'situated speech' and 'text.' The former use can be found in research carried out in the ethnography of speaking, sociolinguistics, and (occasionally) pragmatics; the latter use is the one most commonly applied by the field of discourse analysis itself and the related field of text grammar. Indeed, 'discourse' (in the latter definition) constitutes the sole object of study of most work in discourse analysis, whose purpose (abstracting away from various differences among its practitioners) is to understand the difference between a collection of unconnected sentences and a well-formed text (for a good example, see van Dijk 1977).

Reading a representative paper from the field of discourse analysis as represented in the English-speaking countries ('Anglo-Saxon discourse analysis,' one might call it) is often a disappointing experience. Typically, such a paper will fall into one of two categories. In the first, the analyst deals with an antiseptic parceled text, cleansed of ideological load, and isolated from the chain of discourses of which it is part. In the second, the analyst keeps the text entirely on the mental level, and exemplifies the properties attributed to a well-formed discourse (cohesion, coherence, relevance, and so on) with little more than short sequences of two or three artificially constructed sentential sequences.[8]

Chapter 13 in this volume synthesizes the Anglo-Saxon tradition of analyzing 'discourses' outside of their social context of production and reception (though reference is made to van Dijk's rather different approach).

I see a much more fruitful approach to discourse analysis taking place outside the Anglo-Saxon tradition (for a good overview, focussing on French and Marxist approaches in particular, see Seidel 1985). This alternative tradition began more than fifty years ago with the work of Vološinov (1973) and Bakhtin (1981) (who in all probability were the same person), which has been described by Gill Seidel as having 'injected into pragmatics and linguistics a political awareness and a theory of social action, largely Marxist, that can be seen as part of the development of socially relevant and socially realistic linguistics' (1985: 44; see also Hymes 1977). It continues today in the work of the French discourse analyst Ducrot (1972, 1973, 1984) and in that of many others who see their work as part of the general study of communicative behavior and social action.

For this approach, which is the one that I advocate, the examination of

---

[8] Even such an exhaustive treatment of cohesion as that provided by Halliday and Hasan (1976) does not provide the elements with which to uncover the hierarchization of information within the text, which should certainly have priority over the issue of 'well-formedness.'

units like utterances, short exchanges, and speech acts and texts in isolation are but intermediate (though necessary) steps in the understanding of the social nature of speech. To obtain a full picture of language in context, we must study interdiscourse relations, in which several discourses are connected by their reference to the same topic with differences in their schematic organization; intertextual or sequential relations, i.e. where each discourse paves the way for the discourse that will follow it, produced by the same or by a different speaker; and how the social function of a discourse is altered by the ideology within which it is produced or received.[9]

[9] At the Instituto de Lingüística de la Universidad de Buenos Aires we are currently developing an approach to discourse such as I have just outlined. Our working paper series, *Análisis sociolingüístico del discurso político. Cuadernos del Instituto de Lingüística*, includes articles on internal hierarchization of information (Pardo 1986; Lavandera 1986b), interdiscourse relations (Lavandera *et al.* 1985), and intertextual relations (Raiter & Menéndez 1986; Lavandera 1985). An important research undertaking is an analysis of what is specific to discourse within the social functioning of language and an identification of the way in which discourse features respond to and, in turn, create functions of social scope, including the roles or symbolic loci of the participants in the *énonciation* (García Negroni & Raiter 1986). Others include the means of 'referred discourse' (Zoppi 1986) and mitigating resources (Lavandera 1986a).

REFERENCES

Bakhtin, M. M. 1981. *The dialogic imagination*. Ed. M. Holquist, trans. by C. Emerson & M. Holquist. Austin: University of Texas Press.
Bordieu, P. & Boltanski, L. 1975. Le fétichisme de la langue. *Actes de la recherche en sciences sociales* 4: 2–32.
Brown, P. & Levinson, S. 1978. Universals in language usage: politeness phenomena. In E. Goody (ed.) *Questions and politeness*. Cambridge: Cambridge University Press.
Dijk, T. van. 1977. *Text and context*. London: Longman.
Ducrot, O. 1972. *Dire et ne pas dire*. Paris: Hermann.
Ducrot, O. 1973. *La preuve et le dire*. Paris: Mame.
Ducrot, O. 1984. La notion de sujet parlant. *Recherches sur la philosophie et le langage* 2: 65–92.
Ervin-Tripp, S. 1972. On sociolinguistic rules: alternation and cooccurrence. In Gumperz & Hymes 1972.
García Negroni, M. & Raiter, A. 1986. Hacia un análisis de la dinámica del discurso: el discurso del Doctor Tróccoli. *Análisis sociolingüístico del discurso político. Cuadernos del Instituto de Lingüística*. Buenos Aires: Universidad de Buenos Aires.
Goffman, E. 1971. *Relations in public*. New York: Basic Books.
Goffman, E. 1974. *Frame analysis*. New York: Harper & Row.
Goffman, E. 1981. *Forms of talk*. Philadelphia: University of Pennsylvania Press.
Grice, H. P. 1975. Logic and conversation. In P. Cole & J. Morgan (eds.) *Syntax and semantics 3: speech acts*. New York: Academic Press.
Gumperz, J. 1971. *Language and social groups*. Stanford: Stanford University Press.
Gumperz, J. 1982a. *Discourse strategies*. Cambridge: Cambridge University Press.
Gumperz, J. 1982b. Language and social identity. Cambridge: Cambridge University Press.
Gumperz, J. & D. Hymes (eds.) 1972. *Directions in socio-linguistics: the ethnography of communication*. New York: Holt, Rinehart, & Winston.
Guy, G. 1979. Variation in the group and the individual. In W. Labov (ed.) *Locating language in time and space*. New York: Academic Press.
Halliday, M. & Hasan, R. 1976. *Cohesion in English*. London: Longman.
Hymes, D. 1972. Models of the interaction of language and social life. In Gumperz & Hymes 1972.

Hymes, D. 1977. *Foundations in sociolinguistics: an ethnographic approach*. Philadelphia: University of Pennsylvania Press.

Labov, W. 1969. Contraction, deletion, and inherent variability of the English copula. *Language* 45: 715–62.

Labov, W. 1972a. *Sociolinguistic patterns*. Philadelphia: University of Pennsylvania Press.

Labov, W. 1972b. Rules for ritual insults. In D. Sudnow (ed.) *Studies in social interaction*. New York: Free Press.

Labov, W. 1978. Where does the sociolinguistic variable stop? A reply to B. Lavandera. *Texas Working Papers in Sociolinguistics* 44. Austin: SW Educational Development Laboratory.

Labov, W. 1982. Objectivity and commitment in linguistic science: the case of the Black English trial in Ann Arbor. *Language in Society* 11: 165–202.

Labov, W. and Weiner, J. 1977. Constraints on the agentless passive. University of Pennsylvania: ms.

Lavandera, B. 1978. Where does the sociolinguistic variable stop? *Language in Society* 7: 171–82.

Lavandera, B. 1982. Le principe de réinterpretation dans la théorie de la variation. In N. Dittmar & B. Schlieben-Lange (eds.) *La sociolinguistique dans les Pays-Bas de langue romane*. Tübingen: Narr.

Lavandera, B. 1985. Intertextual relationships: 'missing people' in Argentina. In R. Shuy (ed.) *Georgetown University roundtable on languages and linguistics*. Washington: Georgetown University Press.

Lavandera, B. 1986a. Decir y aludir: una propuesta metodológica. *Filología* 20: 21–31.

Lavandera, B. 1986b. Textual analysis of a conditional utterance. *Linguistische Berichte* 102: 155–70.

Lavandera, B. 1987. The social pragmatics of politeness forms. In U. Ammon & N. Dittmar (eds.) *Sociolinguistics: an international handbook of the science of language and society*. Berlin: de Gruyter.

Milroy, J. & Milroy, L. 1985. Linguistic change, social networks, and speaker innovation. *Journal of Linguistics* 21: 339–84.

Milroy, L. 1980. *Language and social networks*. Baltimore: University Park Press.

Pardo, M. 1986. Hacia una redefinición de las nociones de tema y rema de la oración al discurso. *Filología* 21: 59–93.

Raiter, A. & Menéndez, S. M. 1986. El desplazamiento de un signo ideológico (análisis lingüístico del discurso político) in *Análisis sociolingüístico del discurso político*. *Cuadernos del Instituto de Lingüística*.

Rickford, J. 1986. The need for new approaches to social class analysis in sociolinguistics. *Language and Communication* 6.3: 215–21.

Searle, J. 1969. *Speech acts*. Cambridge: Cambridge University Press.

Searle, J. 1979. *Expression and meaning*. Cambridge: Cambridge University Press.

Seidel, G. 1985. Political discourse analysis. In T. van Dijk (ed.) *Handbook of discourse analysis*, Vol. 4: *Discourse analysis in society*. New York: Academic Press.

Vološinov, V. N. 1973. *Marxism and the philosophy of language*. New York: Seminar Press.

Weiner, I. & Labov, W. 1983. Constraints on the agentless passive. *Journal of Linguistics* 19: 29–58.

Zoppi, M. 1986. El discurso referido o en busca del contexto perdido. *Análisis sociolingüístico del discurso político. Cuadernos del Instituto de Lingüística*. Buenos Aires: Universidad de Buenos Aires.

2 Language, culture, and world view
Jane H. Hill

2.0. Introduction: the Whorf hypothesis

The human, social world is a meaningful one, and speech is the most important device by which humans create and distribute meaning. The determination of the constraints on this creation and distribution, and the role of language in the relationship between cognizing human beings and the cognized environment, are central concerns of scholars in many disciplines.

A thorough review would require attention at least to the literatures of philosophy, psychology, anthropology, and the literary theory of translation. The role of language as a map for social action is a practical as well as an intellectual concern, as evidenced in work by feminist scholars (see McConnell-Ginet, Borker & Furman 1980), to note only one example. The present review will concentrate primarily on the shapes that these concerns have assumed within anthropology during the last decade.

Modern anthropologists concerned with the relationship between language, culture, and world view trace their intellectual genealogy through a 'Whorf hypothesis': that the forms of meaning created in the syntactic, morphological, and phonological patterns of language can vary more or less without limit, and that these forms, which constitute reifications of the world, are powerful mediators of human understanding, which should in its own turn assume a more or less unlimited range of forms. Although the work of Whorf (1956) and his immediate intellectual ancestors Sapir and Boas has played a major role in defining the issues for anthropologists in this century, the 'Whorf hypothesis' was first posed in its modern form by Wilhelm von Humboldt. Von Humboldt in turn built upon the work of Kant, Herder, and Hegel in developing his notion of language as the embodiment of a *Weltanschauung* or world view, which mediates between the nature of reality and human understanding. Neo-Kantian philosophers like Cassirer, and semantic field theorists like Trier and Weisgerber, developed these lines of thought contemporaneously with American anthropo-

14

logists. The precise connections between thinkers on the two continents remain to be worked out. Recent work by Malkiel (1974), Rollins (1980), Heynick (1983), and Golla (1984) are contributions to the history of the issue in American anthropology. Schaff (1973) reviews the history of linguistic relativity in anthropology (including the post-Whorfian period in the 1950s and 1960s), psychology, and philosophy.

Students of linguistic relativity have been concerned to state the 'Whorf hypothesis' in a testable form. Whorf 1956, the major source for this scholar's views, is a miscellany, posthumously compiled, of published works, papers presented, and unpublished manuscripts, and, in addition to displaying a tendency toward hyperbole, provides no clear statement of any 'Whorf hypothesis.' Alford (1978) has emphasized that Whorf has been the victim of a good deal of misrepresentation. Nonetheless, scholars have adopted for discussion two 'Whorf hypotheses:' a strong linguistic determinism, and a weaker 'linguistic relativity.' Linguistic determinism is a hypothesis which proposes that the forms of language are prior to and determinative of the forms of knowledge and understanding. That is, human beings could not imagine a kind of knowledge which was not encoded in their language. Linguistic relativity suggests that there are no *a priori* constraints on the meanings which a human language might encode, and these encodings will shape unreflective understanding by speakers of a language. Fishman (1982) has noted the importance of a 'Whorfianism of the third kind:' an ethical linguistic relativism, which insists on the value of 'little languages' like Hopi as precious contributions to the totality of human understanding.

No strong form of linguistic determinism is supported either in the writings of Sapir or Whorf (with the exception of an occasional burst of hyperbole), or in the available data. It is often pointed out (Cole & Scribner 1974: 43) that statements in Whorf's writings which might be read as implying a linguistic determinism are contradicted by his own interpretive method, which aimed at the discovery and comparison of patterning in a variety of languages. Both Sapir – a published poet – and Whorf contrasted an individual potential for a reflective consciousness of language – found among poets, linguistic scholars, and bilinguals – with 'habitual' unreflective vernacular adherence to its patterns. Friedrich (1979) has explored the implications for linguistics of a 'Sapir hypothesis' on the relationship between language and individual imagination. Perhaps the clearest statement for linguistic determinism in Whorf's writings is found in 'The relation of habitual thought and behavior to language,' where Whorf remarks that, although language patterns and cultural norms influence each other,

> in this partnership the nature of the language is the factor that limits
> free plasticity and rigidifies channels of development in the more

15

autocratic way. This is so because a language is a system, not just an
assemblage of norms. Large systematic outlines can change to
something new only very slowly, while many other innovations are
made with comparative quickness. (Whorf 1956: 156)

The evidence does not support even this rather moderate statement of
linguistic determinism. Work on problems in intercultural communication
(Gumperz 1982; Scollon & Scollon 1981) shows that very different cultural
patterning can be expressed in the same language, so that Britons and
Indians, or Euro-Americans and American Indians, may experience consistent miscommunication in spite of the fact that they are employing the
same lexico-grammatical material. The patterns of language can be quite
flexible under contact. To cite just one of many convincing examples, Hollenbach (1977) has described the reversal of a temporal deictic system in
Copala Trique under the influence of Spanish.

2.1. **Linguistic relativity**

With linguistic determinism largely discredited, recent work has tested the
second type of Whorfianism, the claim for a linguistic relativity, including the
hypothesis that human languages are highly variable, and that this variability
will be reflected in nonlinguistic knowledge and behavior. The dominant
strategy has been to try to determine the limits on variation in the forms of
language through the exploration of linguistic universals, and to try to
constrain the possible variation in the forms of cultural representations by
developing a theory of cultural conceptualizations and their integration. The
first requirement for an anthropological study of linguistic relativity is to
develop accurate descriptions of language structures in accordance with the
best theoretical knowledge. These must be paired with equally accurate
ethnographies, for the relationship between language and nonlinguistic
knowledge and behavior is highly complex, and world view cannot simply be
'read off' linguistic structures. A number of classic descriptions of linguistic
structure have recently been shown to be faulty, and more recent work also
requires reevaluation in the light of new advances in the study of universal
grammar.

Among the most important classical claims about exotic language structure are those of Whorf for Hopi, and these must be substantially modified. A
number of years ago Longacre (1956) suggested that Whorf's grammatical
generalizations were often faulty, and recent work on Hopi has borne out his
suspicions. Whorf made far-reaching claims about the Hopi view of time,
which he represented as a 'becoming later,' and contrasted with a 'standard
average European' view of time as a number of little pieces of matter passing

out of the future and into the past. Whorf argued that the Hopi view was embodied in such habitual linguistic patterns as the absence of spatio-temporal metaphors, the impossibility of counting units of time, and the absence of tenses in the verb. Innumerable counterexamples to these claims can be found in the work of Gipper (1976), Voegelin, Voegelin and Jeanne (1979), and Malotki (1979, 1983). Specialists have also generally dismissed Whorf's claims about the representation of time in European languages. For example Joos (1968) shows that English tends to collapse the distinction between the past and the conditional, just as Hopi tends to neutralize the difference between the future and the conditional (to form what Whorf referred to as the 'manifesting' aspect). Such neutralizations are not at all unusual, as demonstrated in Dahl 1983. Even Whorf's most extensively documented claim for Hopi, that its series of 'punctual and segmentative' verb forms constituted an exhaustive and very accurate taxonomy of the forms of eventing in the universe which was closer to a physicist's view of reality than that embodied in 'standard average European,' has been invalidated. Voegelin, Voegelin and Jeanne (1979) find that the punctual–segmentative distinction is relatively unproductive and irregular in Hopi.

Whorf is not the only scholar of the 'classical' period of linguistic relativism to have made exaggerated and poorly documented linguistic claims. Hutchins (1980) has discredited Lee's (1949) claim that Kiriwina (a language of the Trobriand Islands) lacks terms which denote logical relations among propositions, and that this absence embodies a world view for which the relationship of cause and effect is 'of no significance.' Hutchins lists a number of Kiriwina logical connectives, and illustrates the devices which are used to accomplish conjunction (Kiriwina does lack a particle equivalent to English 'and').

Happily, some of the important classical examples in the literature of linguistic relativity have survived reinspection. Sapir's claim that a number of indigenous languages of the Pacific Northwest lacked a distinction between nouns and verbs has withstood the test of time (see Kinkade 1983). In contrast to her claims about Kiriwina, made without any foundation in fieldwork, Lee's claims about the structure of Wintu, a California language which she studied at first hand, have largely been sustained in a new grammar by Pitkin (1985), although Pitkin is silent on the relationship between the structure of Wintu and the world view of its speakers.

Keesing (1972) has pointed out the tendency for linguistic anthropology to lag behind developing theories about language, and a number of recent proposals in the literature of linguistic relativity require reassessment in the light of new knowledge about language universals emanating both from autonomous syntax (Chomsky 1982) and functional grammar (see Nichols 1984 for a good review of recent work). An excellent case in point is

Kearney's (1984) claim that the appearance of surface personal pronouns in European languages reflects the evolution of an individualist view of the self. Latin (presumably pre-individualism) had *sum* 'I am,' without a pronoun, while modern French and German have *je suis* and *ich bin*, respectively, with pronouns. Kearney ignores the fact that in Italian and Spanish, languages spoken in societies which were surely not exempt from the rise of capitalism and the increasing importance of the individual, we find the equivalent expressions without pronouns: *sono, soy*. Chomsky (1982) has discussed this variation. He proposes a universal phrase structure condition, #Subject, INFL, VP#, which claims that every sentence in a human language must have a subject. However, there are variants or 'parameters' of this condition, one of which is the possibility for 'pro-drop,' which is seen in Spanish and Italian. Chomsky considers the setting of the parameter to be quite independent of nonlinguistic factors, and apparently random distribution of pro-drop in closely related languages would appear to support this proposal. However, there may be constraints on pro-drop associated with context of situation. An account of these constraints depends on knowing the markedness of pro-drop in the particular language, so the parameter may take the form of setting marking. For instance, in Spanish the pro-dropped sentences are the unmarked expressions, with *yo* (or other pronouns) being added for emphasis or disambiguation. In English, where the presence of the pronoun appears to be the unmarked case, Philips and Renolds (1987) have noted that pro-drop occurs in contexts such as the responses by prospective jurors to *voir dire* questioning, where it appears more frequently in male than in female usage. The linguistic literature (and simple attention to the facts) suggest a less sweeping and more complex claim about the 'meaningfulness' of pro-drop than that made by Kearney. The pro-drop variable appears to be available to all human languages; in some languages, the choice can become meaningful and express a view of the world. The mere presence of one or another kind of form, however, does not allow the inference of a particular concept of the self.

2.1.1. Animacy hierarchies

A second example of an account of the relationship between language and world view which requires reevaluation in the light of recent work in universal grammar is that by Witherspoon (1977, 1980) of the Navajo animacy hierarchy. Animacy hierarchies appear to be quite widespread in human languages (Silverstein 1976b). Functional grammarians believe that they reflect a universal human capacity, undoubtedly of adaptive importance, to conceive of the world as organized into more or less animate entities. This conception is reflected in grammatical patterning in most human languages.

For instance, entities higher on the animacy hierarchy are more likely to be the subjects of passives, are more likely to be permitted as the agents of transitive verbs, and are more likely to be topicalized than entities which are lower on the animacy hierarchy. In Navajo, a verb-final language, a pair of prefixes *yi-* and *bi-* mark the case relationships between two nouns preceding a transitive verb. If the prefix is *yi-*, the first noun is acting upon the second, as in (1):

    (1) MAN HORSE *yi*-KICK 'The man kicked the horse'

If the prefix is *bi-*, the second noun acts upon the first:

    (2) MAN HORSE *bi*-KICK 'The horse kicked the man'

Witherspoon (1977) has pointed out that while (1) and (2) are grammatical in Navajo, (3) and (4) are not.

    (3) *HORSE MAN *yi*-KICK 'The horse kicked the man'
    (4) *HORSE MAN *bi*-KICK 'The man kicked the horse'

Explanation of the ungrammaticality of (3) and (4), according to Witherspoon, requires an account of Navajo world view. Witherspoon argues (1977, 1980) that the *bi-* prefix should be translated as 'allows itself to be acted upon,' while the translation of the *yi-* prefix should be something like 'as the entity with the higher potential for control, in this context, acts . . .'. Sentence (3) is ungrammatical because the horse is inherently a less potent controller than a man; the proper expression is (2) where the man, although object, remains in control. Sentence (4) is ungrammatical because the horse is again represented as the controlling entity. Since this is absurd, one must say (1) instead. Witherspoon has found that a careful investigation of quartets of sentences of this kind reveals a very complex ordering of the Navajo universe in terms of potential for motion, which seems to control Navajo judgements about the grammaticality of sentences with the *bi-/yi-* object prefixes. The principle of 'potential for motion' is central to an integrated and uniquely Navajo vision of the universe. However, functionalist grammatical theory suggests that we should place less emphasis on the uniqueness of the Navajo system. It is true that the Navajo language exhibits an unusually elaborate animacy hierarchy, particularly in the complex rankings among inanimates such as water, trees, stones, and the like. One can argue, however, that this represents a secondary elaboration within Navajo thought and language of a very general tendency in human cognition. The notion of a universe ordered in terms of 'potential for motion' is latent in all human languages, and indeed evidences of such an order can be found even in English. Cooper and Ross (1975) have pointed out that it can be seen in the order of nouns in 'frozen' English expressions such as 'men and machines' and 'animal, vegetable, or mineral.' Another excellent test for animacy in English is the frame 'hit against,' where expressions such as *He hit the stick against the tree* are acceptable, while *He hit the stick against the horse* is a bit odd, as is *He hit the stick against the feather* – but not *He hit the feather against the stick*. The last pair is highly reminiscent of the complex Navajo ordering of inanimates.

2.1.2. Language, knowledge, and vision

Another example of an ethnolinguistic finding which requires reevaluation in light of recent work on language universals is Tyler's (1984) claim that the sensory modality of vision is the preferred way of knowing for speakers of 'standard average European' languages. He finds that the assimilation of knowledge to vision is a 'pervasive trope' in Western languages, and contrasts this with Dravidian languages, where the master trope for knowledge is *to say* or *to do*, not *to see*. However, Viberg (1983) has summarized work which suggests that Tyler's linguistic evidence for this trope is simply one manifestation of a universal implicational hierarchy for verbs of perception which can be identified in human languages, in which *to see* is the left-most verb. That is, the meaning of *see* can almost universally be extended to include other perceptual concepts (as in English *Let me see how that tastes, Let me see how that sounds, Let me see how that feels*, etc.). Viberg observed that 'Especially *see* and *know* seem to be covered by one word in a number of languages' (1983: 157). He cites examples from Australia, New Guinea, and the Pacific, as well as from Indo-European languages. Thus, English and other Western languages seem to reflect a general tendency in the languages of the world to have vision as the prototypical sensory modality, rather than representing a unique (and, Tyler seems to think, dangerous) development.

2.2. Meaning, expression, and the 'unsaid'

While much recent grammatical theory has emphasized language universals, generative grammarians do continue to debate whether different languages exhibit different expressive power. Katz (1978) has claimed that natural languages are 'effable' – any proposition can be uttered in any human language. However, E. L. Keenan (1978) has noted that translatability between languages may be constrained by an 'efficiency requirement': 'A human language must permit the communication of thoughts in a way that is reasonably efficient, relative to the lifespan and cognitive abilities of human beings' (1978: 160). Keenan finds that languages differ in logical power in a number of subtle ways, such as their capacity to relativize arguments, or to promote them to subject position in the passive. While many of these differences seem to be distributed over universal implicational hierarachies (see Comrie 1979 for a review), the relationship between these distributions and world view has not been explored. In general, language differences do not seem to be related to differences in logic in the narrow sense. Scribner (1977) summarizes a number of studies which suggest that differences in the handling of syllogisms are not related to language structure, but instead seem to be correlated with schooling. Hamill (1978, 1979) and Galda (1979) have reported the same result. In addition Hamill and Galda have both pointed out that careful probing of apparently 'illogical' responses to syllogistic problems by speakers of non-Western languages will almost invariably reveal that the respondent has changed the major premise, and that the reasoning does follow appropriately from this changed form.

Central concerns for recent investigators of the relationship between language form, knowledge, and cultural life are the facts that meaning resides not simply in the material of the linguistic forms, but in the distribution of this material across the field of the 'unsaid' (Tyler 1978), and that referential meaning is everywhere confounded with pragmatic or interpersonal force in speaking. Silverstein (1976a, 1985), McLendon (1977), Keesing (1979) and Colby (1985) have emphasized that our ability to comprehend language is inextricably intertwined with encyclopedic cultural knowledge. An example of the complex exegesis which is required in order to account for usage can be seen in Quinn's (1982) analysis of the denotative scope of the term 'commitment' used by American English speakers discussing marriage. Empson (1951) has shown how 'complex words' can contain in implicit structure a very large range of possible connotations. Speakers are capable of many kinds of inferences from the 'said' to the 'unsaid,' including lexical inference or presupposition (Miller 1979), practical inference (Miller 1979) (also known as inference from conventional implicature, Grice 1975), and inference from conversational implicature (Grice 1975). While E. O. Keenan (1976) has questioned the universality in human speech communities of the Gricean maxims, which are the source of conversational inference in Grice's theory, it seems likely that in fact they are everywhere applicable, even where some highly valued styles of speech depend on directness and elaboration. Brown and Levinson (1978) have pointed out that indirectness and elaboration can be understood as conversational strategies, such as 'being polite,' only if we imagine that something like the Gricean maxims lies behind hearer inference. Even in quite formal argumentation a substantial 'unsaid' component may be present, as Hutchins (1980) has shown in his discussion of land litigation in the Trobriand Islands. When the background cultural knowledge which speakers can be presumed to share is incorporated into the structure of argumentation, it can be shown that the vernacular logical system which governs argument is highly rule-governed and 'logical.'

The realm of the 'unsaid,' a vast and unspoken source of human cultural meaning derivable primarily only by inference, lies not only in the conditions of pragmatic interaction, but in the patterning of grammar itself. Linguists of every theoretical persuasion have pointed out that the surface representation of any sentence inevitably leaves out a great deal of semantic detail. Langacker (1984) has suggested that not only is this 'sparseness' of the linguistic code inseparable from the pragmatic phenomena noted above, but that grammarians should treat as identical phenomena the fact that in the sentence *She heard the piano* there is likely to be a piano player who is not mentioned, and the fact that in *John is likely to succeed* the subject of *to succeed* is represented by what Chomsky (1982) has called an 'empty category.' For Langacker, an important goal of grammar is the specification of how such grammatical 'images' (which he believes may be quite different from language to language: see Langacker 1976, Casad & Langacker 1985) might be related to conceptual structure, a specification which must be achieved within a theoretical framework where all meaning is linguistic (that is, linguistic meaning is of an 'encyclopedic' rather than a narrowly 'semantic' character, cf. Haiman 1980).

Even in the realm of the lexicon itself, the 'unsaid' surfaces in the form of what Berlin, Breedlove and Raven (1973) called 'covert categories.' In a study of Tzeltzal plant names, these authors found that unlabeled categories yielded the same kinds of behavior, such as the ability to sort exemplars reliably, as labeled categories. In a recent study of the lexicon of fishing techniques among the Sinama of Mindanao, Randall (1985) has found that covert categories function as 'script headers' – labels which access scripts or scenarios which allow inferences about the meaning of sentences. Randall comments that 'Some scripts are identified not just from an instrumental [i.e. type of hook used] script header but also from *assumptions* about what the speaker would have added if they had any other script in mind' (1985: 259). That is, covert categories have the same kinds of cognitive power as labeled categories. Atran (1983), in a study of the emergence of the level of the 'family' in scientific taxonomy, has found the origins of these categories in covert European folk taxa which emanate from 'common sense' noticing of the world.

Students of the relationship between language and knowledge must cope not only with the 'unsaid,' but with the fact that a great deal of speech does not seem to convey any referential meaning. Malinowski (1923) long ago pointed out the significance of 'phatic communion' – language uttered only to mark the presence and existence of the speaker, rather than to convey information. Lehrer (1983) has shown that much of the English language vocabulary for the description of the taste and odor of wines does not seem to have any fixed meaning, even among experts, but seems to function primarily in constructing a vague tone of knowledgeableness and concern about wine among a group of speakers. Gatewood (1983) has pointed out the importance of 'loose talk': people are able to discourse upon complex issues without a firm referential foundation. The inverse of the 'loose talk' phenomenon is that people often learn complex knowledge without much in the way of linguistic input, and that knowledge thus acquired (Gatewood's example is how to catch Pacific salmon with purse seines) is often unspeakable, consisting primarily of 'flows, contours, intensities, and resonances' and not 'ideas, concepts, categories, and links' (1985: 216). When both the non-referential 'said' and the encyclopedic 'unsaid' are taken into account, it is clear that the relationship between the totality of knowledge and the representational capacity of any particular human language is a question which is entirely open to empirical exploration, and the lists of kinds of human knowledge which are not closely related to language must be expanded beyond the war-horse repertoire of art and music to include a great deal of technical knowledge that might seem, at first blush, to be highly linear and codable.

2.3. **Culture and cognition**

If, taking into account the problems outlined above, we continue to explore the relationships between the forms of language and what D'Andrade (1981) has called the 'cultural part of cognition,' other problems arise. If there is, in fact, a 'cultural part of cognition,' how can we separate it from, on the one hand, innate computational processes which limit the range of variation in the structure of human language and in the forms of human cognition, and, on the other hand, the idiosyncratically patterned residues of individual experience, which may remain forever ephemeral and private? Those culture theorists who have been concerned with the relationship between language and culture tend to share a 'cognitive' paradigm, in which culture is seen as a set of 'complexly rational' mental phenomena (Dougherty 1985: 3). A number of cultural theorists, such as Keesing (1974), Crick (1976), Hutchins (1980), and D'Andrade (1984), seem to concur that these 'mental phenomena' are a hierarchy of rules for the construction of propositions, which may be very far-reaching and are likely to be 'referentially transparent' and essentially undiscussable by natives of the culture, and a set of descriptive and normative propositions which may be explicitly represented in language or other media. For instance, D'Andrade (1984) distinguishes between 'constitutive rules,' which tend to be organized hierarchically and create complexes of cultural entities, and 'regulatory rules,' which constrain action in reference to entities created by constitutive rules through a set of 'norms.' Among the cultural entities

created by constitutive rules are 'meaning systems,' which have representational, constructive, directive, and evocative functions, these functions
being differently elaborated in different meaning systems (D'Andrade 1984:
96).

2.3.1. Discussive constraint

An important consequence of a culture theory which sees culture as including a set of rules for the construction of meaning systems is that among the
meaning systems constrained by these rules will be those of language.
Hymes (1966) has reviewed this consequence with great clarity: although
human languages are potentially infinite in their expressive power, constitutive cultural rules will constrain the deployment of this expressive power in
discourse, and speaking may have different functions in different societies.
Ochs and Schieffelin (1984) have shown that profound differences in the
way human communities deploy linguistic resources begin at the earliest
stages of language acquisition. Hymes's proposals for an ethnography of
speaking constitute a program for the investigation of discursive constraints
in any society, but examples of constraints on discourse which have been
reviewed for Western cultures include the epistemes of Foucault (1972) and
the paradigms of Kuhn (1970). Hymes himself was influenced by the critical
theory of Kenneth Burke, who has developed a theory of symbolic action in
which the fundamental units of discursive constraint are 'terministic
screens' which shape rhetoric (Burke 1966), and a five-term dramatistic
framework, including scene, act, agent, agency, and purpose, which constrains the possible foci of discourses both at the micro-level of the literary
work and at the macro-level of 'attitudes toward history' (Burke 1955,
1966).

The relationship between the many levels of discursive constraint, from
the 'attitudes toward history' to the sentence itself, are of great interest. If,
as Langacker has proposed, the 'empty' agent in *She heard the piano* is
parallel to the empty subject of *to succeed* in *John is likely to succeed*, then
are both of these phenomena connected to the rarefaction of meaning at the
epistemic level? Hymes (1966), in his original discussion of the cultural
limits on discursive practice, noted an attitude of 'seriousness' and 'perfec-
tivity' in Wishram, an American Indian language of the Pacific Northwest,
and showed how this practice could be identified at all levels of the deployment of discourse, from the level of the distribution of speech events across
lifetimes to the level of the sentence itself, where it regulated the choice of
verb tense. An important direction in the investigation of high level discourse constraints has developed in the study of metaphor. Lakoff and
Johnson (1980) have suggested that an important type of discursive con-

straint may be constitutive metaphors of the type UP IS GOOD, or ARGUMENT IS WAR, which will produce a wide range of appropriate sub-metaphors in usage. That metaphoric systems of the type pointed out for English by Lakoff and Johnson should be considered as high order 'constitutive rules' is suggested by the fact that native speakers are usually quite unconscious of them. Important studies of the essentially 'figurative' nature of the language of linguistic science itself have been published by Reddy (1979) and Silverstein (1979). Studies of metaphoric systems in non-Western languages include work by Rosaldo (1972, 1975) on Ilongot, K. Basso (1976) on Western Apache, and Bierhorst (1985) on Nahuatl, as well as the several papers in Sapir & Crocker 1979. Brown and Witkowski (1981) have suggested that some metaphors are found in many languages, and may reflect universal and innate knowledge structures.

2.4. **Anthropology and world view**

The theory of world view in anthropology includes at least two major subdivisions. One, which considers world views as systems of cultural adaptation, has received thorough review recently in the work of Kearney (1975, 1984); C. Brown (1984b) has criticized Kearney for his lack of attention to language. A second, more linguistic body of work descends from work of Sapir, Benedict, Radin, and Bateson on cultural knowledge systems. Many recent studies in this tradition do not distinguish the 'propositional' content of language and world view from their affective or emotive content; Rosaldo (1984) has emphasized that to separate propositional 'cognition' from affective 'emotion' may be a Western bias, for emotion is also a form of understanding. Thus, for instance, studies by E. Basso (1985) on Kalapalo, a Brazilian tribe, and by Feld (1982) on the Kaluli of New Guinea emphasize the affective power of sound. K. Basso (1984) has described the power of Apache stories to invest the landscape with a deep moral content. Friedrich's (1978) study of the system of lexicon and symbolic meaning surrounding the goddess Aphrodite in the ancient world combines propositional and affective aspects of meaning, as does the work of A. Becker (1975, 1979, 1984) on Burmese and Javanese. The work of Rosaldo (1972, 1973, 1975, 1980, 1984) on Ilongot emphasizes the very complex interplay between proposition and affect. Studies by Calame-Griaule (1970) on the Dogon of West Africa, by Witherspoon (1977) and Pinxten, van Dooren, and Harvey (1983) on Navajo emphasize propositional content of world views.

While the degree of coherence of cultural meaning systems remains a question for empirical study (Levine 1984: 72), the studies noted above join a tradition which holds that at the highest level of organization, cultural meaning systems will tend toward a high degree of what Kearney (1984) calls 'logico-structural integration,' both internally and in relation to he environments which they represent. Witherspoon (1977) has even suggested that each culture's world view is reducible to a single fundamental principle which organizes all thought; Witherspoon's analysis of the role of the concept of 'potential for motion' in grammatical judgements by Navajos, reviewed above, is an example of such a fundamental principle and the scope of its application. Pinxten *et al.* (1983), in their treatment of the Navajo natural philosophy of space, have suggested that Navajo thought may owe its integration to its basic circularity. Rather than a system of primitive and derived notions, the components of the Navajo world view are all connected in a complex network, which lacks linear relations such as causality. Another example of a proposal for a very high degree of integration of world view which encompasses discursive practice in language is found in A. Becker's (1984) work on Burmese. Becker identifies a root metaphor of 'integrity' which is highly productive in Burmese 'ways of speaking' about the organization of language and the organization of the world. This metaphor can be identified in contexts ranging from Buddhist theology to the forms of the Burmese writing system. According to Becker, this metaphor contrasts with a root metaphor of 'linearity' in English-speaking usage. For Javanese, A. Becker (1979) and J. Becker (1979) have emphasized the principles of cyclicity and coincidence as pervasive in Javanese music and drama, contrasted with English linearity and causality. Highly coherent systems of constraints on discourse have been described which are based on cultural practices which are quite widespread in modern human societies, such as the presence of money (Crump 1978, 1981), literacy (Goody 1977), differences between the strategies of dominant and dominated classes (Bisseret 1979, Bourdieu & Passeron 1977, Bernstein 1972), and combinations of the above (Washabaugh 1980).

2.5. Studies of cognitive processes

In contrast with very broad studies of the role of language in world view of the type noted above, which are based on extensive long-term participant observation in the communities under study, much recent work within the framework of questions posed in terms of linguistic relativity has dealt with very limited sub-systems of representation which are considered in isolation, not only from the totality of a world view, but even from the context of discursive deployment of their contents. These studies emphasize a relatively narrow system of relationships between meaning in the lexicon, perception, and a limited range of 'cognitive' processes such as recall and sorting. ('Cognition' is a much more fashionable term in today's anthropology of language than 'world view.') The flavor of this work, which shares the universalist and experimental biases of cognitive science, can be appreciated by examining the directions which have been taken in the investigation of color terminologies and folk taxonomies.

2.5.1. Color terms

Berlin and Kay (1969) startled students of the structure of terminological systems with their work on color terminologies. While color had been the domain *par excellence* for demonstrations of linguistic relativity, Berlin and Kay showed, through a survey of the color term systems of the world combined with laboratory experiments on color naming behavior, that human languages exhibited a very limited range of terminological systems in this domain. These derived from an innate human capacity to perceive organization in the color spectrum. The 'focality' of a stimulus color was a principal manifestation of this innate perceptual organization, and was a much more powerful predictor of such phenomena as color memory and sorting than the linguistic coding of the color field.

Relatively few exceptions to the constraints on color terminologies proposed by Berlin and Kay have been identified; an example is the system described by Hardman (1981) for Jaqaru, an Aymaran language of Chile, where, among eight basic terms, four are for various kinds of red (shocking pink, burgundy, reddish brown, and wine red). Alongside the basic eleven terms reviewed in Kay & McDaniel 1978 (the most recent of several updatings of the original 1969 proposals by Berlin and Kay) there appears to exist at least one other system, a contrast of 'warm' and 'cool' color categories, identified by Dougherty (1977) in West Futunese (a Polynesian language) and by Berlin and Berlin (1975) in Aguaruna, an indigenous language of eastern Ecuador. In addition to the delimitation of the range of possible terminological systems, a great deal of work has been devoted to the description of what is represented by color terms. Here, color terminology research has become involved in the debate between 'check-list' theorists of lexical representation, prototype theorists, and exemplar theorists (Smith & Medlin 1981), and between proponents of categorical perceptions which represent natural discontinuities (Mervis & Roth 1981) and proponents of 'fuzzy' accounts of representation (Kay & McDaniel 1978, Coleman & Kay 1981). In addition to debates over the broad structure of color knowledge there are discussions of alternative possibilities for focal colors. For instance, while originally Berlin and Kay believed that focal GRUE (a basic color category in systems which have only one term covering the colors labeled 'green' and 'blue' in English) was always identical with focal GREEN, Aguaruna was shown to have focal GRUE in BLUE (Berlin & Berlin

1975). Burgess, Kempton and MacLaury (1985) have explored GRUE in Tarahumara, a Uto-Aztecan language of northern Mexico in which color term stems must always appear with suffixes which indicate the closeness to the prototype of the color in question. This lexical peculiarity enabled a detailed exploration, both at the group and individual level, of the lexical representation of the color field among Tarahumara speakers.

Lucy and Shweder (1979) have argued against claims that superior recall and sorting efficiency for colors is conditioned largely by innate cognitive organization of color categories around natural foci, rather than around linguistically imposed categories. They found that when the Munsell color chart (the elicitation instrument used in nearly all studies of color terminology) was adjusted to eliminate a bias toward focal colors, recall and sorting seemed to be more responsive to the linguistic factor of 'communicability' – the ability of native speakers to describe a particular color so that another speaker could recognize it – than to focality. Lucy and Shweder argued that their results supported a 'Whorfian' view of the relationship between cognition and the color lexicon. Kay and Kempton (1984), in a study comparing English speakers (who distinguish GREEN and BLUE) with Tarahumara speakers (who have GRUE), have claimed that this 'Whorfian' effect can be eliminated if experimental procedure blocks a 'naming strategy.' However, their procedure can be interpreted as imposing a very powerful naming influence, which blocks the strategy indigenous to the respondent's native language. While such an effect hardly argues for the unbreakable bonds of native-language patterning, it is certainly a 'Whorfian' effect, and not a demonstration of the power of color focality.

Where ethnographic materials, particularly with historical depth, are available for the role of color in a society, the relationship between this and color terminology has been shown to be tenuous. Baines (1985) has reviewed the relationship between color terminology and the decorative and symbolic use of color in ancient Egypt. He shows that for thousands of years the ancient Egyptian language exhibited a four-term system – Stage IIIa in the Kay & McDaniel 1978 system. However, over the same period painters employed a seven-color system, corresponding to Kay & McDaniel Stage V in the earlier period up to about 1500 BC. By the time of the Greek period this system included nine colors, corresponding to Kay & McDaniel Stage VII (without grey). Although the ancient Egyptian 'basic color terms' never included BLUE, blue as a paint color carried a very significant symbolic load, and was 'the most prestigious painted color . . . employed in the most obviously nonrealistic way' (Baines 1985: 288). Baines's result, which suggests the detachment of basic color terminology from color usage, is supported by a study by Bender (1983). Bender found that in Sudanese Arabic an important skin color was lexicalized as GREEN. Examining the history of color terminology in Arabic, Bender concludes that the GREEN color term is a modern reflex of an ancient term for 'macro-BLACK.' Bender's study suggests that usages established at one stage of a development of a terminological system can be extremely conservative, surviving in specialized domains even though the dominant terminological system may change substantially.

The experimental paradigm and the narrowly constrained definition of 'basic color terms' in research deriving from the original results of Berlin and Kay (1969) have been frequently criticized. Friedl (1979) provides an all-too-rare glimpse of what really happens in field research with the Munsell color chart. Her respondents, weavers of the Luri in southwestern Iran, who recognized the most subtle distinctions between dye lots, found the Berlin–Kay paradigm of investigation simply absurd; Friedl observes that her attempts to employ it compromised her hard-won *rapport* with her subject population. Sahlins (1976) has pointed out that the relationship between universal constraints on color perception and the cultural representations which exploit colors is far more complex than suggested in most publications on color terminology. Bousfield (1979) has criticized the 'epistemological chauvinism' of the Berlin–Kay paradigm, in particular its reduction of the color lexicon to a system of 'basic terms' and its use of ostensive definition in color naming and recognition tasks. Mathiot (1979) has proposed a procedure for the study of color nomenclature which will allow greater cultural sensitivity than the Berlin & Kay techniques.

2.5.2. Folk taxonomies

In spite of criticism of the Berlin–Kay paradigm, its major emphases – the definition of universal constraints on possible terminological systems in the form of implicational scales, and the use of an experimental approach as opposed to an emphasis on participant observation – have dominated studies of other terminological domains. The study of folk taxonomies exemplifies this paradigmatic hegemony. Here, the constraints on possible terminologies include Berlin's (1972, 1976, 1977) theory of a limitation on the possible depth of taxonomic systems, and C. Brown's several proposals for implicational constraints on the repertoire of terminologies at the level of the 'life form' rank (see C. Brown 1984a for a summary of the work of C. Brown and his colleagues during the previous decade). C. Brown *et al.* (1976) proposed that the constraints on folk taxonomy applied to both biological and non-biological classification; this point has been challenged by Stanlaw and Yoddumnern (1985) and by M. Brown (1985). Lancy and Strathern (1981) have proposed that some societies may not exploit taxonomic ordering; they present evidence that the Melpa of highland New

Guinea are a 'low-taxonomizing' group, preferring to order the world by a pairing strategy. Melpa do not do well on experimental tasks which require hierarchical sorting.

The universalist thrust in the study of terminological systems has been sustained even in connection with affective dimensions of meaning, even in lexical domains which would appear to be highly susceptible to cultural differentiation. Osgood, May & Miron (1975) reported cross-cultural universals of affective meaning. White (1980) has used multidimensional scaling techniques to show that terminologies for the description of personality pattern according to similar evaluative factors in a number of unrelated languages and societies.

There is a good deal of debate in the literature about whether the structure of lexical systems derives more from cultural salience and function or from the lexical copying of natural discontinuities. Berlin and Kay (1969), Kay (1977) and C. Brown (1979) have all proposed that there is a relationship between cultural complexity and the structure of lexical systems. Hunn (1976, 1979) has argued that lexical distinctions replicate natural discontinuities, but has recently (1982) suggested that there may be kinds of taxa which reflect special purposes and knowledge, which will have to be distinguished from 'core taxa' based on morphological differences. Randall and Hunn (1984) have argued that 'functional' categories may be sufficiently important that C. Brown's (1984a) proposed bio-taxonomic universals must be abandoned. Wierzbicka (1984) has pointed out that the literature on folk taxonomy is riddled with confusion between formal and functional categories.

A second area of debate in the study of folk nomenclatural systems has to do with interinformant diversity. Gardner (1976) and Gatewood (1984) have argued that interinformant diversity is substantial enough that great caution should be used in claiming that a lexical system is 'cultural.' Boster (1985), however, has suggested that a 'cultural' level of the lexicon can be located in the usage of experts in particular domains; expert informants exhibit high levels of agreement.

The cognitive paradigm in the investigation of structures of lexical meaning in anthropology has clearly been a very productive one. Most cognitive anthropologists now believe that, in a variety of lexical domains, including color terminology, personality and emotion words, kinship terminologies, and folk biological taxonomies, the possible forms of lexical systems are highly constrained. Sperber (1985b) has proposed an enthusiastically rationalist account of cultural concepts, suggesting that human beings are prone to accept certain kinds of concepts which are 'catching' (his paper is subtitled 'Towards an epidemiology of representations'). For Sperber, the anthropological study of non-literate societies is crucial to the development of a rationalist theory of the constraints on cultural representations, because literate societies can sustain rather marginal representative structures. Without literacy, only the most basic and 'catching' representations will survive.

A universalist approach, which suggests that linguistic relativity is quite limited and that apparently linguistically imposed differences in cognition may be derivable from much more general universal constraints on human cognitive variation, has dominated recent work. However, within the systems of universal constraints, changing and inherently variable human languages do provide a great deal of material which can be made meaningful by cultural processes of the type Boas called 'secondary rationalizations.' The tendency of constitutive rules of culture toward logico-structural coherence will yield correlation between language usage and world view, which is the result of historical interchange between the secondary rationalization or reification of linguistic patterning and reification processes in other components of world view. These coherent systems of reification clearly do have the power to shape our 'habitual thought and behavior.' The original demonstrations by Boas (1889) and Sapir (1925, 1933), that the sound patterning of our languages constrains our perception of speech sounds, have never been refuted. Whorf's examples of the power of labels to affect behavior, which came not from his study of exotic languages but from his work as an insurance adjuster, remain convincing. The structures of discourse characteristic of our native language constrain our ability to comprehend text. Boas showed this in his discussion of the assimilation of the journey of a Russian explorer to the frame of the Raven myth cycle by the Tlingit Indians of the Pacific Northwest (Boas 1905). Rice (1980) has shown that American English speakers have great difficulty comprehending and remembering Eskimo stories, and invariably assimilate these to American English schemata when they are asked to repeat them. While the study of linguistic relativity is a complex and difficult area, the implications of hypotheses about the influence of our languages on our 'habitual thought and behavior' are very serious ones. While there is much evidence that the range of variability of human language is less than was once thought, the study of linguistic relativity must remain central to the linguistic enterprise, for it is only through such study that we can rise above 'habitual thought and behavior' to the level of reflective consciousness and appreciation of the patterns and possibilities of our own language, and an understanding of the full range of the richness of human thought reflected in the languages of the world.

REFERENCES

Alford, D. K. H. 1978. The demise of the Whorf hypothesis. *Proceedings of the Fourth Annual Meeting of the Berkeley Linguistics Society*: 485–99. Berkeley: Berkeley Linguistics Society.

Atran, S. 1983. Covert fragmenta and the origins of the botanical family. *Man* 18: 51–71.

Baines, J. 1985. Color terminology and color classification: ancient Egyptian color terminology and polychromy. *American Anthropologist* 87: 282–97.

Basso, E. 1985. *A musical view of the universe*. Philadelphia: University of Pennsylvania Press.

Basso, K. H. 1976. 'Wise words' of the Western Apache: metaphor and semantic theory. In Basso & Selby 1976.

Basso, K. H. 1984. Stalking with stories: names, places and moral narratives among the Western Apache. In Plattner & Bruner 1984.

Basso, K. H. & Selby, H. A. (eds.) 1976. *Meaning in anthropology*. Albuquerque: University of New Mexico Press.

Becker, A. L. 1975. A linguistic image of nature: the Burmese numerative classifier system. *International Journal of the Sociology of Language* 5: 109–21.

Becker, A. L. 1979. Text-building, epistemology, and aesthetics in Javanese shadow theatre. In Becker & Yengoyan 1979.

Becker, A. L. 1984. Biography of a sentence: a Burmese proverb. In Plattner & Bruner 1984.

Becker, A. L. & Yengoyan, A. A. (eds.) 1979. *The imagination of reality*. Norwood: Ablex.

Becker, J. 1979. Time and tune in Java. In Becker & Yengoyan 1979.

Bender, M. L. 1983. Color term encoding in a special lexical domain: Sudanese Arabic skin colors. *Anthropological Linguistics* 25: 19–27.

Berlin, B. 1972. Speculations on the growth of ethnobotanical nomenclature. *Language in Society* 1: 51–86.

Berlin, B. 1976. The concept of rank in ethnobiological classification: some evidence from Aguaruna folk botany. *American Ethnologist* 3: 31–40.

Berlin, B. 1977. Speculations on the growth of ethnobotanical nomenclature. In Blount & Sanches 1977.

Berlin, B. & Berlin, E. A. 1975. Aguaruna color categories. *American Ethnologist* 2: 61–87.

Berlin, B., Breedlove, D. & Raven, P. 1973. General principles of classification and nomenclature in folk biology. *American Anthropologist* 75: 214–42.

Berlin, B. & Kay, P. 1969. *Basic color terms*. Berkeley: University of California Press.

Bernstein, B. 1972. *Class, codes, and control*. New York: Schocken Books.

Bierhorst, J. 1985. *Cantares mexicanos*. Stanford: Stanford University Press.

Bisseret, N. 1979. *Education, class language and ideology*. London: Routledge & Kegan Paul.

Blount, B. & Sanches, M. (eds.) 1977. *Sociocultural dimensions of language change*. New York: Academic Press.

Boas, F. 1889. On alternating sounds. In Stocking 1974.

Boas, F. 1905. The mythologies of the Indians. In Stocking 1974.

Boster, J. S. 1985. 'Requiem for the omniscient informant:' there's life in the old girl yet. In Dougherty 1985.

Bourdieu, P. & Passeron, J. -C. 1977. *Reproduction in education, society and culture*. Beverley Hills: Sage Publications.

Bousfield, J. 1979. The world seen as a color chart. In Ellen & Reason 1979.

Brown, C. 1979. Folk zoological life forms, their universality and growth. *American Anthropologist* 81: 791–817.

Brown, C. 1984a. *Language and living things*. Rutgers: Rutgers University Press.

Brown, C. 1984b. World view and lexical uniformities. *Reviews in Anthropology* 11: 99–112.

Brown, C., Kolar, J., Torrey, B. J., Tru'o'ng-Quang, T. & Volkman, P. 1976. Some general principles of biological and non-biological folk classification. *American Ethnologist* 8: 73–86.

Brown, C. & Witkowski, S. 1981. Figurative language in universalist perspective. *American Ethnologist* 8: 596–615.

Brown, M. 1985. Individual experience, dreams, and the identification of magical stones in an Amazonian society. In Dougherty 1985.

Brown, P. & Levinson, S. 1978. Universals of language usage: politeness phenomena. In E. Goody (ed.) *Questions and politeness*. Cambridge: Cambridge University Press.

Burgess, D., Kempton, W. & MacLaury, R. E. 1983. Tarahumara color modifiers: individual variation and evolutionary change. *American Ethnologist* 10: 133–49.

Burke, K. 1955. *A grammar of motives*. New York: Braziller.

Burke, K. 1966. *Language as symbolic action*. Berkeley: University of California Press.

Calame-Griaule, Geneviève. 1965. *Ethnologie et langage*. Paris: Gallimard.

Casad, E. H. & Langacker, R. W. 1985. 'Inside' and 'outside' in Cora grammar. *International Journal of American Linguistics* 51: 247–81.

Chomsky, N. 1982. *Lectures on government and binding*. Dordrecht: Foris.

Colby, B. N. 1985. Toward an encyclopedic ethnography for use in 'intelligent' computer programs. In Dougherty 1985.

Cole, M. & Scribner, S. 1974. *Culture and thought*. New York: Wiley.

Coleman, L. & Kay, P. 1981. Prototype semantics: the English word *lie*. *Language* 57: 26–44.

Comrie, B. 1979. *Language universals and linguistic typology*. Chicago: University of Chicago Press.

Cooper, W. E. & Ross, J. R. 1975. Word order. In Robin S. Grossman *et al.* (eds.) *Papers from the parasession on functionalism*. Chicago: Chicago Linguistic Society.

Crick, M. 1976. *Explorations of language and meaning*. New York: Wiley.

Crump, T. 1978. Money and number: the Trojan horse of language. *Man* 13: 503–18.

Crump, T. 1981. *The phenomenon of money*. London: Routledge & Kegan Paul.

Dahl, O. 1983. Temporal distance: remoteness distinctions in tense–aspect systems. *Linguistics* 21: 105–22.

D'Andrade, R. G. 1981. The cultural part of cognition. *Cognitive Science* 5: 179–95.

D'Andrade, R. G. 1984. Cultural meaning systems. In Shweder & Levine 1984.

Dougherty, J. W. D. 1977. Color categorization in West Futunese: variability and change. In Blount & Sanches 1977.

Dougherty, J. W. D. (ed.) 1985. *Directions in cognitive anthropology*. Urbana: University of Illinois Press.

Ellen, R. F. & Reason, D. (eds.) 1979. *Classifications in their social context*. New York: Academic Press.

Empson, W. 1951. *The structure of complex words*. London: Chatto & Windus.

Feld, S. 1982. *Sound and sentiment*. Philadelphia: University of Pennsylvania Press.

Fishman, J. A. 1982. Whorfianism of the third kind: ethnolinguistic diversity as a worldwide societal asset. *Language in Society* 11: 1–14.

Foucault, M. 1972. *The archaeology of knowledge*. New York: Pantheon.

Friedl, E. 1979. Colors and culture change in southwest Iran. *Language in Society* 8: 51–68.

Friedrich, P. 1978. *The meaning of Aphrodite*. Chicago: University of Chicago Press.

Friedrich, P. 1979. Poetic language and the imagination: a reformulation of the Sapir hypothesis. In *Language, context, and the imagination*. Stanford: Stanford University Press.

Galda, K. 1979. Logic in non-Indo-European languages: Yucatec Maya, a case study. *Theoretical Linguistics* 6: 145–60.

Gardner, P. M. 1976. Birds, words, and a requiem for the omniscient informant. *American Ethnologist* 3: 446–69.

Gatewood, J. B. 1983. Loose talk: linguistic competence and recognition ability. *American Anthropologist* 85: 378–87.

Gatewood, J. B. 1984. Familiarity, vocabulary size, and recognition ability in four semantic domains. *American Ethnologist* 11: 507–27.

Gatewood, J. B. 1985. Actions speak louder than words. In Dougherty 1985.

Gipper, H. 1976. Is there a linguistic relativity principle? In R. Pinxten (ed.) *Universalism versus relativism in language and thought*. The Hague: Mouton.

Golla, V. (ed.) 1984. *The Sapir–Kroeber correspondence*. Survey of California and Other Indian Languages, Report No. 6.

Goody, J. 1977. *The domestication of the savage mind*. Cambridge: Cambridge University Press.

Grice, H. P. 1975. Logic and conversation. In P. Cole & J. Morgan (eds.) *Speech acts*. New York: Academic Press.

Guenther, F. & Guenther-Reutter, M. (eds.) 1978. *Meaning and translation*. New York: New York University Press.

Gumperz, J. (ed.) 1982. *Language and social identity*. Cambridge: Cambridge University Press.

Haiman, J. 1980. Dictionaries and encyclopedias. *Lingua* 50: 329–57.

Hamill, J. F. 1978. Transcultural logic: testing hypotheses in three languages. In M. D. Loflin & J. Silverberg (eds.) *Discourse and inference in cognitive anthropology*. The Hague: Mouton.

Hamill, J. F. 1979. Syllogistic reasoning and taxonomic semantics. *Journal of Anthropological Research* 35: 481–94.

Hardman, M. J. 1981. Jaqaru color terms. *International Journal of American Linguistics* 47: 66–8.

Heynick, F. 1983. From Einstein to Whorf: space, time, matter, and reference frames in physical and linguistic relativity. *Semiotica* 45: 35–64.

Hollenbach, B. 1977. Reversal of Copala Trique temporal metaphors through language contact. *International Journal of American Linguistics* 43: 150–4.

Hunn, E. 1976. Toward a perceptual model of folk biological classification. *American Ethnologist* 3: 508–24.

Hunn, E. 1979. The abominations of Leviticus revisited: a commentary on anomaly in symbolic anthropology. In Ellen & Reason 1979.

Hunn, E. 1982. The utilitarian factor in folk biological classification. *American Anthropologist* 84: 830–47.

Hutchins, E. 1980. *Culture and inference, a Trobriand case study*. Cambridge, MA: Harvard University Press.

Hymes, D. H. 1966. Two types of linguistic relativity. In W. Bright (ed.) *Sociolinguistics*. The Hague: Mouton.

Joos, M. 1968. *The English verb*. Madison: University of Wisconsin Press.

Katz, J. J. 1978. Effability and translation. In Guenther & Guenther-Reutter 1978.

Kay, P. 1977. Language evolution and speech style. In Blount & Sanches 1977.

Kay, P. & Kempton, W. 1984. What is the Sapir–Whorf hypothesis? *American Anthropologist* 86: 65–79.

Kay, P. & McDaniel, C. K. 1978. The linguistic significance of the meanings of basic color terms. *Language* 54: 610–46.

Kearney, M. 1975. World view theory and study. *Annual Review of Anthropology* 4: 247–70.

Kearney, M. 1984. *World view*. Novato: Chandler & Sharp.

Keenan, E. L. 1978. Some logical problems in translation. In Guenther & Guenther-Reutter 1978.

Keenan, E. O. 1976. On the universality of conversational implicatures. *Language in Society* 5: 67–80.

Keesing, R. 1972. Paradigms lost: the new ethnography and the new linguistics. *Southwestern Journal of Anthropology* 28: 299–332.

Keesing, R. 1974. Theories of culture. *Annual Review of Anthropology* 3: 73–97.

Keesing, R. 1979. Linguistic knowledge and cultural knowledge. *American Anthropologist* 81: 14–36.

Kinkade, M. D. 1983. Salish evidence against the universality of 'noun' and 'verb.' *Lingua* 60: 25–40.

Kuhn, T. 1970. *The structure of scientific revolutions*. Chicago: University of Chicago Press.

Lakoff, G. & Johnson, M. 1980. *Metaphors we live by*. Chicago: University of Chicago Press.

Lancy, D. F. & Strathern, A. J. 1981. 'Making twos': pairing as an alternative to the taxonomic mode of representation. *American Anthropologist* 83: 773–95.

Langacker, R. W. 1976. Semantic representations and the linguistic relativity hypothesis. *Foundations of Language* 14: 307–57.

Langacker, R. W. 1984. Active zones. *Proceedings of the Tenth Annual Meeting of the Berkeley Linguistic Society*: 172–88.

Lee, D. D. 1949. Being and value in a primitive culture. *Journal of Philosophy* 48: 401–15.

Lehrer, A. 1983. *Wine and conversation*. Bloomington: Indiana University Press.

Levine, R. A. 1984. Properties of culture, an ethnographic view. In Shweder & Levine 1984.

Longacre, R. E. 1956. Review of *Language and reality* by Wilbur M. Urban and *Four articles on metalinguistics* by Benjamin Lee Whorf. *Language* 32: 298–308.

Lucy, J. A. & Shweder, R. A. 1979. Whorf and his critics: linguistic and non-linguistic influences on color memory. *American Anthropologist* 81: 581–615.

McConnell-Ginet, S., Borker, S. & Furman, N. 1980. *Women and language in culture and society*. New York: Praeger.

McLendon, S. 1977. Cultural presuppositions and discourse analysis: patterns of presupposition and assertion of information in Eastern Pomo and Russian narrative. In M. Saville-Troike (ed.) *Linguistics and anthropology*. Washington: Georgetown University Press.

Malinowski, B. 1923. The problem of meaning in primitive languages. In C. K. Ogden & I.A. Richards (eds.) *The meaning of meaning*. New York: Harcourt Brace.

Malkiel, Y. 1974. Editorial comment: a Herder–Humboldt–Sapir–Whorf hypothesis? *Romance Philology* 28: 199.

Malotki, E. 1979. *Hopi-Raum*. Tübingen: Gunter Narr Verlag.

Malotki, E. 1983. *Hopi time*. Berlin: Mouton.

Mathiot, M. 1979. Folk-definitions as a tool for the analysis of lexical meaning. In M. Mathiot (ed.) *Ethnolinguistics: Boas, Sapir, and Whorf revisited*. The Hague: Mouton.

Mervis, C. & Roth, E. M. 1981. The internal structure of basic and non-basic color categories. *Language* 57: 384–405.

Miller, G. A. 1979. Practical and lexical knowledge. In E. Rosch & B. B. Lloyd (eds.) *Cognition and categorization*. Hillsdale: Erlbaum.

Nichols, J. 1984. Functionalist theories of grammar. *Annual Review of Anthropology* 13: 97–117.

Ochs, E. & Schieffelin, B. B. 1984. Language acquisition and socialization: three developmental stories and their implications. In Shweder & Levine 1984.

Osgood, C. May, W. H. & Miron, M. S. 1975. *Cross-cultural universals of affective meaning*. Urbana: University of Illinois Press.

Philips, S. U. & Reynolds, A. 1987. The interaction of variable syntax and discourse structure in women's and men's speech. In S. U. Philips, S. Steele & C. Tanz (eds.) *Language, gender, and sex in comparative perspective*. Cambridge: Cambridge University Press.

Pinxten, R., van Dooren, I., & Harvey, F. 1983. *Anthropology of space: explorations into the natural philosophy and semantics of the Navajo*. Philadelphia: University of Pennsylvania Press.

Pitkin, H. 1985. *Wintu grammar*. University of California Publications in Linguistics 94.

Plattner, S. & Bruner, E. M. (eds.) 1984. *Text, play, and story*. Washington: American Ethnological Society.

Quinn, N. 1982. 'Commitment' in American marriage: a cultural analysis. *American Ethnologist* 9: 775–98.

Randall, R. A. 1985. Steps toward an ethnosemantics of verbs and complex fishing technique: scripts and the 'unsaid' in listener identification. In Dougherty 1985.

Randall, R. A. & Hunn, E. J. 1984. Do life-forms evolve or do uses for life? Some doubts about Brown's universals hypothesis. *American Anthropologist* 11: 329–49.

Reddy, M. J. 1979. The conduit metaphor: a case of frame conflict in our language about language. In A. Ortony (ed.) *Metaphor and thought*. Cambridge: Cambridge University Press.

Rice, G. E. 1980. On cultural schemata. *American Ethnologist* 7: 152–71.

Rollins, P. C. 1980. *Benjamin Lee Whorf: lost generation theories of mind, language, and religion*. Ann Arbor: Popular Culture Association/University Microfilms International.

Rosaldo, M. Z. 1972. Metaphors and folk classification. *Southwestern Journal of Anthropology* 28: 83–99.

Rosaldo, M. Z. 1973. I have nothing to hide: the language of Ilongot oratory. *Language in Society* 2: 193–223.

Rosaldo, M. Z. 1975. 'It's all uphill': the creative metaphors of Ilongot magical spells. In M. Sanches & B. Blount (eds.) *Sociocultural dimensions of language use*. New York: Academic Press.

Rosaldo, M. Z. 1980. *Knowledge and passion*. Cambridge: Cambridge University Press.

Rosaldo, M. Z. 1984. Toward an anthropology of self and feeling. In Shweder & Levine 1984.

Sahlins, M. 1976. Colors and cultures. *Semiotica* 16: 1–22.

Sapir, D. & Crocker, C. (eds.) 1977. *The social use of metaphor*. Philadelphia: University of Pennsylvania Press.

Sapir, E. 1925. Sound patterns in language. In Sapir 1949.

Sapir, E. 1933. The psychological reality of phonemes. In Sapir 1949.

Sapir, E. 1949. *Selected writings of Edward Sapir*. Berkeley: University of California Press.

Schaff, A. 1973. *Language and cognition*. New York: McGraw-Hill.

Scollon, R. & Scollon, S. B. 1981. *Narrative, literacy, and face in interethnic communication*. Norwood: Ablex.

Scribner, S. 1977. Modes of thinking and ways of speaking: culture and logic reconsidered. In P. C. Wason & P. N. Johnson-Laird (eds.) *Thinking*. Cambridge: Cambridge University Press.

Shweder, R. A. & Levine, R. A. (eds.) 1984. *Culture theory: essays on mind, self, and emotion*. Cambridge: Cambridge University Press.

Silverstein, M. 1976a. Shifters, linguistic categories, and cultural description. In Basso & Selby 1976.

Silverstein, M. 1976b. Hierarchy of features and ergativity. In R. M. W. Dixon (ed.) *Grammatical categories in Australian languages*. New Jersey: Humanities Press.

Silverstein, M. 1979. Language structure and linguistic ideology. In P. R. Clyne, W. F. Hanks & C. L. Hofbauer (eds.) *The elements: a parasession on linguistic units and levels*. Chicago: Chicago Linguistic Society.

Silverstein, M. 1985. The functional stratification of language and ontogenesis. In J. V. Wertsch (ed.) *Culture, communication, and cognition: Vygotskian perspectives*. Cambridge: Cambridge University Press.

Smith, E. E. & Medlin, D. L. 1981. *Categories and concepts*. Cambridge, MA: Harvard University Press.

Sperber, D. 1985. Anthropology and psychology: towards an epidemiology of representations. *Man* 20: 73–89.

Stanlaw, J. & Yoddumnern, B. 1985. Thai spirits: a problem in the study of folk classification. In Dougherty 1985.

Stocking, G. W. Jr (ed.) 1974. *The making of American anthropology 1881–1911*. New York: Basic Books.

Tyler, S. A. 1978. *The said and the unsaid*. New York: Academic Press.

Tyler, S. A. 1984. The vision quest in the west, or what the mind's eye sees. *Journal of Anthropological Research* 40: 23–40.

Viberg, A. 1983. The verbs of perception: a typological study. *Linguistics* 21: 123–62.

Voegelin, C. F., Voegelin, F. M. & Jeanne, L. M. 1979. Hopi semantics. In A. Ortiz (ed.) *Handbook of North American Indians*, Vol. 9: *Southwest*. Washington: Smithsonian Institution.

Washabaugh, W. 1980. The role of speech in the construction of reality. *Semiotica* 31: 197–214.

White, G. M. 1980. Conceptual universals in interpersonal language. *American Anthropologist* 82: 759–81.

Whorf, B. 1956. *Language, thought, and reality*. Cambridge, MA: MIT Press.

Wierzbicka, A. 1984. Apples are not a 'kind of fruit': the semantics of human categorization. *American Ethnologist* 11: 313–28.

Witherspoon, G. 1977. *Language and art in the Navajo universe*. Ann Arbor: University of Michigan Press.

Witherspoon, G. 1980. Language in culture and culture in language. *International Journal of American Linguistics* 46: 1–13.

3 Language and social class

Gregory R. Guy

3.0. Introduction

In all human societies individuals will differ from one another in the way they speak. Some of these differences are idiosyncratic, but others are systematically associated with particular groups of people. The most obvious of these are associated with sex and developmental level: women speak differently from men, and children differently from adults. These two dimensions of social variation in language are in part biologically determined (e.g. differences in laryngeal size producing different pitch levels for adult men and women), but in most societies they go beyond this to become conventional and socially symbolic. Thus men and women differ by far more in language use than mere pitch. (In fact, even their pitch differences are more pronounced than can be anatomically explained.) Such sociosymbolic aspects of language use serve an emblematic function: they identify the speaker as belonging to a particular group, or having a particular social identity.

In many societies some of the most important of these sociolinguistic divisions are associated with differences in social prestige, wealth, and power. Bankers clearly do not talk the same as busboys, and professors don't sound like plumbers. They signal the social differences between them by features of their phonology, grammar, and lexical choice, just as they do extralinguistically by their choices in clothing, cars, and so on. The social groups at issue here may be harder to define than groups like 'men' and 'women,' but they are just as real. They are the divisions of a society along lines of SOCIAL CLASS.

Class divisions are essentially based on status and power in a society. Status refers to whether people are respected and deferred to by others in their society (or, conversely, looked down on or ignored), and power refers to the social and material resources a person can command, the ability (and social right) to make decisions and influence events. Differences of status and power are the essence of social class distinctions, and it is these that we

37

will have to examine in order to understand class differences in the use of language.

The questions we will be addressing deal mainly with how and why social classes differ in their use of language. Such questions are often considered to be interdisciplinary, in that they involve concepts and problems from more than one traditionally defined academic field: class is the province of sociology and political science, while language belongs to linguistics. A common response to such interdisciplinary issues is to define them out: some linguists will say these questions do not fall within linguistics because they are primarily concerned with social structure, or because they appeal to extralinguistic explanations, or, more subtly, because they involve performance rather than competence. While such views may rightly be considered narrow and sectarian, it is nevertheless incumbent upon us to show the relevance of these problems to linguistic science and its theoretical concerns, and also to other disciplines, and to society at large.

Writing as a linguist, I will focus primarily on the first issue, significance for linguistics, but the general social relevance of these questions seems substantial. The linguistic data will help illuminate the structure of our society and identify social divisions and points of conflict and convergence. They will illustrate the class-based nature of standard varieties of language and the subjective nature of linguistic prejudice. And they will help reveal the sources of social innovation and the motivations of the innovators. The questions of what we as a society have in common, what things divide us, and where we are going are vital ones for any human society, and linguistic answers to these questions should be a very useful source of insight.

The significance of class for linguistics is rooted in the fundamentally social nature of language: language exists so that people can communicate, not for private, individual pursuits. So language is quintessentially a social product and a social tool, and our understanding of any tool will be immeasurably enhanced by a knowledge of its makers and users and uses. If class is one of the main organizing dimensions of society, then this fact should be reflected in the evolution and utilization of language. And if the task of linguistics is to describe and explain language in all of its aspects, then the issue of class will loom large in a number of ways, as we shall see below.

3.1. **Central problems**

There are four central problems underlying current work on language and class. One of these, the definition of class, is specific to this field, and will be discussed at length in the next section. But the other three each reflect general problems for linguistics. They are: the description of language use, the explanation of language change, and the construction of linguistic theory.

Class is involved in the description of language use for the most obvious of reasons: the existence of social variation in language. Linguists have not yet achieved even a minimal observational level of adequacy in respect of sociolinguistic variation, and class will be an important dimension in the organization and explanation of these facts. Class is involved in the study of language change because of the long-recognized link between social change and linguistic change. Many linguistic innovations can now be shown to have been socially motivated, to have originated in a particular class, and to have spread through society along predictable social lines. And class is relevant to the construction of linguistic theory because of the relevance of sociolinguistic variation to the definition of the object of study and the competence–performance distinction. The 'orderly heterogeneity' which appears in class variation in language use reveals a communicative competence which must be incorporated in our theoretical accounts. These three areas, each a central problem for modern linguistics, will be the focus of the last three sections of this chapter.

3.2. Defining class

One of the problems facing researchers dealing with these issues is the definition of class. While our social intuitions about differences in status and power may enable us to distinguish professionals from unskilled laborers, or white-collar workers from blue-collar, they are not adequate for empirical research. More objective definitions of the categories are required. While such definition is fundamental to our enterprise, it is hardly uncontroversial. A variety of approaches to the problem have been taken, using as measures of class such things as wealth, income, education, occupation, place of residence, and so on. We cannot hope to represent the full range of scholarly thinking on this subject, but let us briefly survey two major approaches.

3.2.1. Marxism and class conflict

One of the most influential thinkers on the subject of social class is of course Karl Marx (1906). Marx's theory of class and political economy is a rich and complex one, which we cannot hope to do justice to here, but no discussion of class and language would be complete without at least a brief consideration of some important points.

In Marx's view, the basic dynamic of human history is conflict between classes. Classes are groups of people who share common economic interests; that is, they are defined by their common role in the economic system, their 'relationship to the means of production.' In a capitalist economy, the principal class division is between those who own productive capital (the capitalists or bourgeoisie) and those who do not (mainly the workers). Capitalists can live off the earnings of their capital – profits, rents, interest – while workers can support themselves only by their own labor. The conflict between the two arises from exploitation: the capitalists' earnings constitute an expropriation of some of the value produced by the labor of workers.

The Marxist definition of class thus focusses on conflicting interests and differences in power, and not on status. The bourgeoisie do not constitute a class because they occupy some uniformly high position of status and esteem in society, but rather because of their common economic interests through the private ownership of capital, and their social and political power to maintain and defend those interests against the conflicting interests of the many who do not gain similar benefits from the system.

Although the basis of the class system is thus seen as economic, it has direct ramifications in the non-economic social 'superstructure,' including things such as public mores and standards, religion, and status. Generally these areas of public life will reflect the taste and ideology of the dominant classes. This is where the issue of language enters. While a given sound, sign, or syntactic structure clearly bears no intrinsic relationship to class or the organization of the economy, the *social evaluation* of language differences between people obviously depends directly on differences of power, status, and class. The clearest instance is in the notion of a 'standard.' The belief in the existence of some 'inherently good' variety of their language is one of the most deeply held tenets of public ideology in most Western countries. Yet a cursory inspection of the facts will reveal that these standard varieties are nothing more than the social dialect of the dominant classes.

Beyond the fundamental class division in Marxist thought between owners and workers, other important distinctions are made which will be relevant in interpreting sociolinguistic differentiation. One is that people's conditions of work deeply affect their ideology and social outlook. 'Conditions of work' refers to such things as whether one works in isolation or as part of a group, whether one is relatively autonomous or closely supervised, and whether one's daily work routine is fixed and regimented or varied and flexible. In the Marxist view, industrial workers in modern factories are at an extreme on all of these counts: they work together with hundreds of others, following a rigidly prescribed and closely supervised routine. These life experiences should engender class consciousness and an ideology of solidarity and cooperation. But the same cannot be said of certain other groups who are neither capitalists nor industrial workers: managers, professionals, clerical workers – the groups that are commonly called the 'middle class.'[1] These groups benefit more from the system as it is, have more autonomy and flexibility at work, and work in relative isolation. Hence they value an ideology of individualism, and are politically more conservative.

How does such a view of class relate to language? Many of the findings and debates of sociolinguistics are illuminated by these concepts, as we will see below. An example is the very existence of social dialects. These are not an *a priori* given of linguistics; in fact, Chomsky and many others assume that the development of linguistic theory can proceed as if they do not exist. But sociolinguistic studies reveal them wherever we look. This needs explanation. From a Marxist viewpoint the existence of class dialects is a consequence of the divisions and conflicts between classes. Social barriers and social distance give rise to class differences in language in the same way that geographic barriers and spatial distance generate geographic dialects.

Other problems which the Marxist view of class illuminates are the social motivation of linguistic change, the continued existence of nonstandard forms, and the unity or disunity of the speech community. Generally, the important aspect of this theory for linguistics is the emphasis on class interests and class conflict. It sometimes provides a more coherent explanation of language phenomena arising from social division than the alternative definitions of class, to be discussed below, which tend to emphasize social unity.

3.2.2. Class and status

The major alternative to a Marxist definition of class focusses on social unity and status more than on conflict and power. This view sees class as a relatively continuous scale on which individuals are ranked according to assorted personal characteristics such as level of education, income, occupation, etc., which collectively imply a certain degree of social esteem. Since the one status hierarchy encompasses all of society, this viewpoint emphasizes social unity, implying that all groups share common social evaluations in terms of prestige and behavioral norms, and perhaps even common goals and aspirations, in the sense that everyone knows what it means to get ahead (principally to make more money) and how one is supposed to go about doing so (work hard, save money, etc.). Class conflicts are minimized, individual competition is emphasized. The distribution of socially symbolic characteristics such as sociolinguistic variables should, from this standpoint, be relatively gradient, finely stratified, without the sharp breaks in the social fabric that Marx perceives.

---

[1] In a Marxist analysis an important distinction would be made between 'white-collar' workers and the petty bourgeoisie, or small capitalists (shopkeepers and small businessmen), although both would probably be lumped together as 'middle class' on the status scales discussed here.

This approach is common in Western sociology, and has been a major influence in sociolinguistics. Methodologically it has one clear attraction: it facilitates the development of objective, quantifiable measures of social class, and allows us to rank everyone in an empirical study on such a scale. Such methods were first introduced in linguistics (as far as I am aware) by Labov in his classic pioneering study of the '*Social stratification of English in New York City*' (*SSENYC*, 1966).

In this work Labov relies extensively on the class rankings developed by Michael (1962) for a sociological survey called the 'Mobilization for Youth' (MFY), which was conducted in the same area that Labov studied about one year before he began his research. Labov and Michael thoroughly discuss the problem of defining social class, and emphasize the importance of using criteria based on production rather than consumption. But most of Labov's linguistic analysis utilizes Michael's linear scale of social rank – a hierarchy of status rather than a dichotomy of power and interest: 'most of the approaches which we will attempt will involve the matching of linguistic variables against a linear social ranking' (1966: 208). As the title of the work states, *SSENYC* deals with SOCIAL STRATIFICATION: the fine-scale linguistic layering of people along the 'linear social' scale which in this book is usually termed 'socioeconomic class' (SEC).[2]

SEC is quantified by Labov on the MFY scale by means of 'a ten-point socioeconomic index' which combines 'three objective characteristics – occupation, education, and family income – into a single linear scale' (1966: 171). Each individual studied was classified into one of four ranks on each of the three dimensions mentioned. Thus on the education scale a person is at step 0 if he or she completed only primary school, step 1 for part of high school, step 2 for completing high school, and step 3 for any college-level education. The individual's SEC score is simply the sum of the rankings on the occupation, education, and income scales. SEC can thus range from a low of 0, for those who rank at the bottom of all three scales, to a high of 9, for those with the highest rankings in occupation, education, and income.

Labov does not always attempt to discriminate all ten points of this index in his analysis of the linguistic data in *SSENYC*. Classes 7 and 8 are usually combined (due to the paucity of informants in class 8), and various other combinations are used, according to whether they illuminate or obscure aspects of the overall structure of the data. The most common groupings used are 0–1, sometimes labeled 'lower class'; 2–5, labeled 'working class'; 6–8, labeled 'lower middle class'; and 9, the 'upper middle class.' Furthermore, he also uses another 4-point scale called 'social class' (SC, contrasting with the 10-point SEC), based only on education and occupa-

---

[2] A common variant used in other studies is SES – socioeconomic status.

tion, and not income. For some purposes Labov contends that this organization of the data reveals regularities that the finer scale obscures. To some
extent this kind of redefinition of the groupings from figure to figure can be
criticized as forcing a desired result from the data, but in the main it
represents an admirable attempt to explore the major social correlates of
linguistic variation.

For Labov, the question of whether class divisions are dichotomous or
continuous is reducible to the empirical problem of fine versus sharp
stratification:

> If we think of class as a rigid series of categories, in which the marginal
> cases are rare or insignificant, then a proof of class correlation with
> language would require equally discrete categories of linguistic
> behavior (in our terminology, *sharp stratification*). Language traits
> characteristic of Negro and white groups in the United States, for
> example, would [show this pattern]. If, on the other hand, we think of
> class as a continuous network of social and economic factors, in which
> every case is marginal to the next one, we would expect that language
> would also show a continuous range of values, and the number of
> intermediate points of correlation would be limited only by the
> consistency and reliability of the data (in our terminology, *fine
> stratification*). . . . It is clear that class and language relationships will
> be somewhere between these two extremes. . . . The cutting points
> where the linguistic evidence shows the greatest internal agreement
> will be indicated as the most natural divisions of the class continuum –
> to the extent that language is a measure of class behavior. (1966:
> 235–7)

In his quantitative analysis of the New York City data Labov finds both
kinds of stratification: post-vocalic /r/, and the vocalic variables (eh) and (oh)
show relatively fine stratification, while the interdental fricatives are fairly
sharply stratified: stop articulations are overwhelmingly confined to the lower
and lower-working classes. The interesting social difference between the two
types of cases is that (r) and the vowel variables show evidence of being
changes in progress, while the variation between stop and fricative articulations of (th) and (dh) is a long-standing one found in many English dialects.
This correlation is an interesting one which finds some support in other
studies as well: changes in progress in Norwich (Trudgill 1974: 104–10) and
Australia (Guy *et al*. 1986: 37) also show relatively fine stratification.[3] If this is

---

[3] There are cases in the literature of stable sociolinguistic markers showing relatively fine stratification –
see for example Trudgill's study of (-ing) and (t) (1974: 92–6). But what seems to be lacking are
changes in progress showing relatively sharp stratification, although the fronting of the nucleus of (aw)
in Philadelphia, reported in Labov 1980, may be an example of this. It might be necessary to distinguish
between changes from above, such as NYC (r), and changes from below, as this could certainly
influence the type of stratification which emerges.

a general pattern, it may shed some light on the nature of class relations. Newly emerging variables might separate people finely according to their social status, but when the dust settles after the long haul, sharp and fundamental class divisions emerge. The long-established form acquires a firm, even indexical, class identity, while the new form may be merely trendy.

Most sociolinguistic studies of the last two decades rely on some kind of scalar index like Labov's for their operational definition of social class. Labov himself has continued to use this kind of approach in his work in Philadelphia and elsewhere. Trudgill (1974) uses an even finer scale in Norwich: a 30-point composite of 6 separate scales (Labov's three plus locality, father's occupation, and housing). The scale used in Sydney by Horvath (1986) and Guy *et al.* (1986) is simpler, however, involving just a 3-point scale (MC, UWC, LWC) defined exclusively in terms of occupation, using, as is standard practice in such studies, a sociological scale of occupational prestige, in this case Congalton 1962. This is clearly the minimum scale for useful work on language and social class; a scale which distinguishes only two groups is to be avoided, as it will not address many of the important questions to be discussed below.

3.2.3. The linguistic marketplace

No matter what approach we use to define class, there is one way in which it does not correlate simply and directly with linguistic variation along the standard/nonstandard dimension. That is that people in certain occupations tend to use more standard varieties of language than other people at the same level of status, income, or education. The occupations in question are ones such as teacher, journalist, or receptionist, which involve two kinds of activities: projecting a public image, and linguistic socialization (promulgating norms). This has been clear in sociolinguistic studies since Labov's department store survey, which showed that behind-the-scenes employees like stockboys used far fewer prestige variants than employees who dealt with the public (1966: 63–89). Furthermore, the same study showed that speakers use of prestige variants also correlated with the prestige of the store they worked in, even among employees doing the same kind of job and earning about the same income! Facts like these suggest that the type of linguistic demands an individual faces at work may involve other factors beyond the ones we have used to define class.

Considerations such as these have led to the development by some scholars of a concept known as the *linguistic market*, which is operationalized by Sankoff and Laberge as 'an index which measures specifically how speakers' economic activity, taken in its widest sense, requires or is necessarily associated with competence in the legitimized [or] standard . . . language' (1978: 239). This index was a composite of the subjective rankings which eight judges (all trained sociolinguists) assigned to speakers based on descriptions of their 'socioeconomic life histories.' While open to some criticism on methodological grounds,[4] this approach nonetheless represents an interesting attempt to modify the definition of social class so as to take into account these partly independent sociolinguistic requirements of occupation.

3.2.4. Defining class in nonindustrial economies

The studies we have cited so far deal with speech communities in advanced industrial countries, all characterized by similar capitalist economies and class systems in which the major actors are an urban working class, a professional/managerial/white-collar middle class, and a capitalist upper class. What about countries with different economies and class profiles? How is class to be defined there and what relationship does it have to language? These problems are not as well understood, but some relevant work has been done.

The social and economic structures of the nations of the 'third world' show several important differences from those that we have been considering. One is that most have a comparatively tiny industrial sector, and a proportionately much larger agricultural sector. Socially this means there is a large class of peasants and landless agricultural laborers (most with little or no formal education), and a relatively small industrial working class. It also means that until quite recently most of the population has lived in the countryside. In the last two decades many third world countries have undergone explosive urbanization, but there is still a much larger fraction of the population living on the land than in the USA or Europe.

Linguistically these facts have a number of implications. In the first place, the number of 'nonstandard' speakers is vast, typically constituting a large majority of the population. Second, urbanization is bringing together people who speak many different dialects (or even different languages), creating a linguistic cauldron unparalleled in the industrial world. Thirdly, the extremes of class (wealth and poverty) and the ethnic diversity of many areas means that the range of sociolinguistic variation (the degree of difference between standard and nonstandard varieties) is much greater than we are accustomed to working with in the more homogeneous industrial nations.

These facts challenge some of our fundamental sociolinguistic notions. For example, based on his work in the USA, Labov defines the speech

---

[4] For example, the descriptions of speakers' life histories, on which judges based their evaluations of a speaker's standing in the linguistic market, were not strictly comparable across speakers, and could conceivably have been written so as to bias the judges' rankings.

community partly in terms of shared linguistic norms. If we look at cities like São Paulo, Lagos, or Jakarta, where perhaps a majority of the present population was born elsewhere, and many may not even speak the official language, let alone the standard dialect, it seems unlikely that they will constitute speech communities in the same sense as New York City. Like the community as a whole, the social classes might be expected to be less cohesive, because of these pronounced ethnic and regional divisions.

Another challenge is to our theories of language change. As we shall see in section 3.4, Labov, Kroch, and others emphasize the role of the working class in linguistic innovation in industrial countries. Is this also true in nations where industrial workers are a tiny minority of the population? Studies of sociolinguistic variation in the third world suggest a somewhat different picture. For example, research in Rio de Janeiro (Guy 1981) and Brasilia (Bortoni-Ricardo 1985) suggest that the main ongoing change for working class speakers is one of increasing standardization: they are becoming more like the dominant social groups rather than innovating and moving away from them. Bortoni-Ricardo demonstrates that this results from urbanization; rural immigrants to Brasilia acquire more and more features of the urban standard the longer they are there. This would seem to be a general consequence of the early stages of industrialization, urbanization, and improved education, all of which should have standardizing effects. But other studies reveal that standardization is not the only kind of change occurring. Cedergren's data (1972) on the lenition of /tʃ/ in Panama show a change that has moved away from the historic norm, beginning in the working class and lower middle class – the type of class distribution that Labov considers typical of change in progress.

One overriding aspect of the social history of most of the third world which has had great impact on class and language is colonialism. The language problems of newly independent, mostly multilingual countries have received a great deal of attention from linguists (Fishman, Ferguson & Das Gupta 1968), and class issues are inherent in these problems.

Under colonial regimes the 'ruling classes' in these countries were foreigners, who spoke a language unrelated to those of the indigenous peoples. These colonialists drew national boundaries at their own convenience, creating multilingual states, in which all administrative, legal, and educational functions were normally carried out in the European language of the rulers. Among the virtues of this arrangement was that it centralized power in the hands of this social and linguistic elite, and excluded the other classes from access to even the most elementary tools of political debate and institutional change: a common language, literacy, education, etc. Interestingly, after independence this situation was often maintained, in that the emerging indigenous elite adopted the language of the ex-colonial power and maintained it in most of its previous social functions. In class terms the colonial language serves the same exclusive purpose for the domestic dominant class as it did for the foreign one. As long as organizing and governing is seen to demand fluency in a foreign language such as French or English, how can mere peasants and workers hope to achieve even a modicum of political power?

3.2.5. Pidgins, creoles, and class

One area in which all of these issues come together is the study of pidgin and creole languages. The very existence of such languages is derived from class conflict and the capitalist economy: most arose from the enslavement of African or Melanesian peasants by European capitalists to produce sugar and other crops for the markets of an industrializing Europe. Slave societies started out as multilingual and multiethnic communities *par excellence*, in which a 'standard language' and the development of a speech community were imposed by force. Modern societies with this history still exhibit the most extreme kind of sociolinguistic variation: the post-creole continuum.

As for the social origins of change, in their formative days such languages were changing at a phenomenal rate, and most of the changes originated with the slaves, who constituted the working class in these communities. But from the standpoint of the speakers, the general direction of change has been towards the European standard, which makes it a kind of targeted change in which the highest status 'acrolectal' speakers are in the lead.

One scholar in this field whose work has led to substantial insights into the problem of language and class is Rickford. In his work on Guyanese creole, particularly in the village of Canewalk (1979, 1986), he has pointed out the inherent limitations of the multiscale index approaches to social class, and emphasized the necessity of 'emic' (i.e. locally meaningful) definitions of class. In a small Guyanese village like Canewalk the classificatory scales of occupational status, education, and income that were discussed above are basically irrelevant; if applied unaltered they would probably put everyone together in one of the lowest categories. But this does not mean that local class distinctions do not exist. On the contrary, Rickford demonstrates that people in Canewalk have a lively awareness of class distinctions, and identify two principal local groups, which he calls the Estate Class (EC), who are mostly cane-cutters on the local sugar plantation or 'estate,' and the non-Estate Class (NEC) made up of shop-owners and tradesmen of the village, plus the estate's foremen and drivers.

Membership in these classes is thus defined in part by income, occupation, and so on, but also by rather dramatic differences in social attitudes and ideology. One instance is their views of standard language: the NEC views language in a normative way, believing that use of standard English helps one get ahead, while the EC members 'see the assigned value of English as just another aspect of ruling class ideology' (1986: 218), which is irrelevant to self advancement since the system is stacked against them in any case.

These class differences are dramatically reflected in linguistic usage. For example, the two groups show virtually non-overlapping distributions in their use of acrolectal (standard English) varieties of personal pronouns. Overall, EC speakers use only 18% of such pronouns, while the NEC uses 83%. If we view this in stratificational terms, as a community with shared norms but different levels of prestige or achievement, we would obscure the fundamental conflict of goals and interests which obtain in this community.

Findings of this nature lead Rickford to call for increased attention in sociolinguistics to conflict models of class such as those of Marx and Weber. The issue is more than just a distinction between 'fine' and 'sharp' stratification; the whole assumption of fundamental unity and shared norms in a speech community is questioned by the fact of class differences in ideology, especially their ideology of language.

3.2.6. Class and other social dimensions

Another challenge that confronts us in defining class is the interaction between this and other social dimensions, such as race, ethnicity, and sex. Class involves differences in prestige and power. If men and women, or blacks and whites, are differentiated by prestige and power by virtue of their sex or race, then separating these effects may be difficult.

A number of studies now exist showing that men and women at the same social class level do not necessarily behave linguistically in parallel ways. For example, in Guy *et al.* 1986, which describes the social distribution of an intonational change, there is a sharp split between men and women in the lower working class (illustrated in Figure 2, see below, p. 59). Women at this level show the highest rate of use of this innovation, higher than any other portion of the sample population, while their male counterparts show a very low rate of use – not only less usage than any of the female groups, but also substantially less than upper working class men.

Just assigning a class ranking may require different procedures for men and women. The criteria used in an index scale – occupation, income, education, etc. – would often assign very different class levels to husband and wife in the same family, if applied individually. It would not be the least unusual to find a doctor at the top of all three scales whose wife had only a moderate level of education and had no occupation or income outside of the home (which in these scales is usually taken as no occupation or income at all). The normal solution to this problem is to assign the class ranking of the head of the family (usually the husband) to all members of the family, including spouse and children. So for many married women, their class ranking on one of these scales does not depend on their individual achievements, but instead is a family attribute. Defining the class of two-income families, or of women who enter and leave the labor force repeatedly due to childbearing, is still more complicated. In any case it is clear that class and sex cannot be treated as entirely orthogonal social dimensions.

Similar problems arise in connection with race and ethnicity. Where racism and prejudice exist, the power and status of an individual may depend more on color or nationality than on personal achievements. In fact, one's occupational and educational prospects may be greatly circumscribed by race. In the United States, as in many Western countries, the class distribution of races is markedly skewed: blacks are far more likely to be found at the bottom of the scale. And linguistically, many Afro-Americans are set clearly apart from surrounding white communities by the way they talk. So to try to treat race and class as independent phenomena clearly misses some fundamental truths, as well as some obvious historical facts. Under slavery Africans were forcibly assigned a position at the very bottom of society by virtue of their race, regardless of individual characteristics, and this situation continues, at least in part, because of ongoing racism. The linguistic differences, the existence of Black English, reflect this history.

3.3. **Class and language use: current trends**

One of the principal concerns of sociolinguistics over the past decades has been describing language in use. The study of sociolinguistic variation is essentially the description of the differential use of language by different social groups – particularly social classes. A number of important concepts and findings have emerged from this work on class and the use of language which now form part of the basic currency of the discipline. Accordingly we will begin this section with a rapid survey of some of these basic notions.

One of the most fundamental is the concept of the *speech community*. This is the basic unit or object of study for a linguistics that is cognizant of the social setting of language. It has been given many different definitions by linguists going back to Bloomfield 1933 and beyond, but these generally converge on two main defining characteristics: density of communication and shared norms. By *density of communication* is meant simply that members of a speech community talk more to each other than they do to outsiders; the boundaries of communities will normally fall at troughs in the pattern of communication. This is a commonplace observation in dialect geography: mountain ranges, dense forests, and other barriers to communication are often the boundaries of dialect regions.

The other, equally important, criterion – *shared norms* – refers to a common set of evaluative judgements, a community-wide knowledge of what is considered good or bad and what is appropriate for what kind of (socially defined) occasion. Such norms may exist for all aspects of social behavior, but our interest of course is in linguistic norms.

One reason that shared norms form part of the definition of the speech community is that they are required to account for one of the principal sociolinguistic findings regarding variation by class and style, namely that the same linguistic variables are involved in the differentiation of social classes and speech styles. Study after study has shown that variables stratified by class are also the object of *style shifting*: a variant favored by high status speakers is used more by everyone in the community in their careful styles. These points are illustrated in Figure 1, showing Labov's data on the pronunciation of post-vocalic /r/ in New York City (1966: 240). A consonantal realization of this variable is used more by the higher classes, and by all classes in their more formal styles. (The (r) index equals the percentage of consonantal pronunciations, and the class groups are defined according to the SEC scale explained above, p. 42.)

How can we account for this uniformity of behavior except by some community-wide interpretation of the social meaning of this variable, a shared norm? In this case the norm assigns high status to consonantal pronunciations of (r). This has consequences in two dimensions at once: high status people talk this way all the time, and all strive to talk this way when they are on their 'best linguistic behavior.' Of course this means that a given level of consonantal pronunciation of (r) does not equate directly to a speaker's class; some lower class (SEC 1) speakers use this variant about as

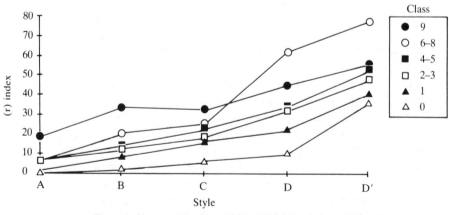

Figure 1. Class stratification of (r) in NYC (after Labov 1966).

much in reading wordlists as the upper middle class (SEC 9) does in casual speech.

The pronunciation of (r) is thus a *social marker* for this community: an arbitrarily defined feature of language that indicates something about the social status of speakers and the situational context in which they are speaking. Knowledge of these social facts marks membership of the speech community; the social significance of a New Yorker's pronunciation would be totally lost on Chicagoans (although they might be able to locate it geographically).

But one question arises immediately: if everyone in the community knows the norm, knows the high-prestige forms and can use them in style shifting, why don't they all adopt them completely, and thus acquire for themselves the implied cachet of status? This harks back to the problem of social unity versus social conflict we discussed in connection with defining class. A linguistic norm is a unifying feature of a community: everyone knows it and knowing it sets insiders apart from outsiders. But even though everyone may know what the high-status variants are, it is not necessarily true that all would want to adopt them in their everyday speech. For working class people with no expectation of achieving higher social status, the use of such variants may be considered snobbish, effete, and an act of hostility to one's family, friends, and neighbors. A number of studies have shown that subjective reactions to sociolinguistic variables are thus differentiated by class, and involve more than just a single scale of prestige (e.g. Labov 1972b; Guy & Vonwiller 1984).

Labov (1972a: 249) makes a distinction between overt and covert norms. The high-status variants we have referred to possess *overt prestige*: they are associated with the undeniable social power of upper class speakers, may be required for higher-status jobs and upward mobility, and are promulgated by the agents of standardization in society, such as the mass media and school teachers. But for many working class or lower middle class speakers, the 'nonstandard' linguistic variables associated with their groups may also possess *covert prestige*. The basic social significance of these covertly prestigious variables is one of solidarity: a person who uses them is considered to belong, to be 'one of the boys,' to be suitable as a friend, etc. Also for certain groups these forms may signify toughness or masculinity: nonstandard speakers were considered more likely to win a street fight by respondents in Labov 1972b.

Emphasizing the unifying norms that appeal to overt prestige may thus obscure important conflicts in the speech community. The fact that nonstandard speakers have not historically rushed to adopt the dominant linguistic norms shows that these do not have the same force for all classes, and that different classes may have different social and linguistic goals.

51

The kind of systematic patterning of linguistic usage that we have seen in Figure 1 is also an example of another important finding of sociolinguistics, which Labov has termed *orderly heterogeneity*. Viewed from the standpoint of an asocial and categorical linguistics, these data would constitute nothing but messy alternation between two realizations of a single systematic unit – /r/. No rule could be given predicting which variant would be used when, so the best one could do would be to call such cases 'free variation' or 'optional rules,' and leave them alone. But it is clear from the figure that the variation is highly structured and systematic, albeit in a quantitative, probabilistic way. Different classes and different styles are finely differentiated, and bear stable, uniform relationships to one another. These facts can be discerned only by systematic study of the community, and of language in use, and would seem to form part of the linguistic competence of each speaker. The implications of this for linguistic theory, for the competence/performance distinction and so on, will be discussed in section 3.5.

3.3.1. Stratification studies

What may be considered the 'mainstream' of work dealing with language and class are the studies that look at the social stratification of particular speech communities. The classic, seminal work of this type is Labov's monumental study of New York City (1966). This work is far too multifaceted for us to do it justice here. As can be gathered from the foregoing discussion, Labov pioneers in it many of methods that are now considered fundamental in this field, and discovers or defines many basic concepts and findings. We have already discussed a number of these issues, so for the moment we will confine ourselves to two further points regarding class differentiation of English in New York City, referring again to Figure 1.

The first point is that 'stratification' is an apt term for the pattern. Distinguishing 6 class groups here, we find that they maintain discrete non-overlapping levels of (r) use across all but the most casual speech styles. Only in style A is there convergence, and even here 3 discrete levels can be distinguished. This implies a remarkable fine tuning in people's linguistic behavior, an extraordinary sensitivity to the self-identifying social symbolism inherent in the pronunciation of this variable, and the contextual constraints of different speech situations.

The second point about this graph is the one deviation from regular ordering of the groups: the crossover by the second highest group in the most formal styles. Labov has termed this 'hypercorrection by the lower middle class' (1972a: 122ff.), and demonstrates that it is associated with a high level of linguistic insecurity. These are people who aspire to social and linguistic upward mobility, are very conscious of their own linguistic 'shortcomings' (in terms of use of prestige variants), and overdo their attempts to remedy them. Such a pattern is often repeated in this and other studies.

Since *SSENYC*, Labov has gone on to do a number of other studies bearing on the question of language and social class. His work in Harlem on Black English (Labov *et al.* 1968, Labov 1969, 1972b) explores questions of class, status and race. His work on sound change (Labov, Yaeger & Steiner 1972, Labov 1980, 1981) illuminates the role of class in language change, as will be discussed below. And his long-term study of the Philadelphia speech community has revealed important new insights into internal divisions in the speech community, social networks, and the interaction between class and sex and race. A number of works (including several already cited) by Labov and his associates and students draw on this research, but the definitive work has yet to appear.

Since Labov's pioneering work, many stratification studies of other speech communities have been carried out by other linguists. We have space here to cite only a few of the most significant in regard to language and class. One of these is Trudgill's 1974 study of Norwich, which, as we have seen, incorporates a very fine measure of class. It also looks at several different neighborhoods, and so explores the interaction between class and residence patterns. Another major study is the one of Montreal French, undertaken by G. Sankoff, D. Sankoff, Cedergren, and a number of associates (G. Sankoff & Cedergren 1971, D. Sankoff & Laberge 1978, G. Sankoff, Kemp & Cedergren 1980). This is important for being one of the first in-depth studies of a language other than English, and for examining what was historically the low-status language in a bilingual country. Significantly for the development of sociolinguistic theory, this work confirms the major findings we have cited above, such as orderly heterogeneity, style shifting, etc., despite the different social and linguistic history of this community. Further work of similar significance is being conducted by Poplack in Ottawa (to appear).

The work of Horvath and her associates in Sydney breaks important new ground in dealing with problems of class, ethnicity, and nonnative speakers (Guy *et al.* 1986, Horvath 1986). It includes a large corpus of recent (first and second generation) immigrants and examines their linguistic impact on the sociolinguistic structure of the community.

Moving out of the industrialized world, we have already had occasion to mention the significant work done by Cedergren in Panama and Rickford in Guyana, both of which shed new light on the class situation in those countries. Other work of importance in the third world includes a number of studies in Brazil (Lemle & Naro 1977, Scherre 1978, Guy 1981, Naro 1981, De Oliveira 1982), Modaressi's work in Teheran (1978), and a number of studies of creole speaking communities (e.g. Bailey 1966, Bickerton 1975).

3.3.2. Network studies

A somewhat different approach to the problem of language and social groups is found in a body of studies focussing on personal networks. Labov used this approach with adolescent peer groups in Harlem (Labov *et al.* 1968), and has continued to use it in studying adult networks in Philadelphia, especially interracial ones. The method has been particularly emphasized by Milroy (1980) in her work in Belfast. At first glance these works might seem in opposition to the class approach to sociolinguistic differences, in that they emphasize the uniqueness of each individual's life experiences and contacts. But I would suggest that in fact the difference is merely one of scale. Network studies are microsociological in focus, while class studies are macroscopic. Across a class there are incontrovertible similarities in economic circumstances and linguistic behavior, but within it there are individual differences in experience and activity which, if properly described, may lead to important new insights into social processes in language, especially the process of linguistic change.

3.3.3. Bernstein

One scholar who has had a great deal to say about language and class is Bernstein (1964, 1971), who is also one of the most controversial figures in this field. He attempts to account for the linguistic differences between social classes in terms of his concept of 'code,' which encompasses many features of language but is essentially a kind of semantic and pragmatic style. There is an 'elaborated code,' relatively independent of context and social roles and relatively explicit, and a 'restricted code,' which is high in context dependency and leaves more meaning implicit in social relationships and situation. The basic difference Bernstein sees between social classes is the range of codes they command: working class people, he thinks, tend to be confined to the restricted code, whereas middle class speakers are also versatile in using an elaborated code. Since the elaborated code is required for writing (because of its decontextualized nature), and since it is also the variety preferred by the schools, working class children start out in these arenas at an inherent disadvantage, which might explain their relative lack of success in school, and in subsequent social advancement.

This theory has proven to be open in a number of ways to both misuse by its supporters and criticism by its detractors. Misuse of the theory often begins by equating elaborated with 'good' and restricted with 'bad,' and by losing track of the distinction between what people do and what they can do. From there it is a short step to labeling working class people linguistically and intellectually deficient, incapable of an elaborated code, and perhaps incapable also of the logical and rhetorical clarity of thought which is presumed to require the elaborated code for its expression. Such propositions are rejected by Bernstein himself, but they are not uncommon in work inspired by his ideas (for a survey see Dittmar 1976, Chapters 1–3).

Criticism of Bernstein follows several lines. First, he appears to accord a rather exalted status to the social consequences of linguistic differences. It seems a perverse logic to imply that the class system is maintained by code differences between speakers; the reverse is far more plausible. Secondly, the theory overlooks the importance of class conflict in linguistic differentiation. Bernstein implies that the restricted code of the working class arises from the role-oriented social psychology and family relationships he assumes characterize working class people. But as we have seen, language attitude studies show evidence (such as covert prestige, the solidarity semantic of working class linguistic markers) suggestive of class conflict, which would provide a far simpler, more straightforward explanation of class differences in language. Finally, the whole theory is essentially based on a middle class ideology. Learning the elaborated code is portrayed as the ticket out of the working class. This depends on two patronizing and erroneous assumptions: first, that everyone in their right mind would want to move out of the working class, if they could; and second, that individual action is the way to achieve this. The first is contradicted by a mass of evidence showing that most people have a strong allegiance to their network, neighborhood, and class, and the second is disputed by the historical fact that the lot of workers has mainly been improved by collective action (strikes, unions, political parties and campaigns). So in conclusion, although Bernstein has been an influential thinker on language and class, his motives and methods have been questioned by many scholars in the field.

3.4. Class and language change

One of the most important areas in class and language studies is the description and explanation of linguistic change. Some of the oldest questions in linguistics are how and why languages change, and the best answers often come from outside a language, from the social history of its speakers. The history of English cannot be understood without reference to the Norman Conquest, nor the genesis of creoles without reference to slavery. Thus in so far as class is an issue in social change, it is an issue for historical linguistics.

In linguistic theory, twentieth-century scholars have generally separated historical questions from the problem of synchronic description and explanation. Following Saussure, the synchronic and diachronic perspectives have been considered diametrically opposed. While this division has led to great advances in our understanding of language, it leaves unresolved the problem of integration. Most of our synchronic theories are structural and static, and not very compatible with what we know about language change. If we conceive of language structurally, as an edifice built of phonemes and lexemes, features and rules, it is hard to see how and why it could change. Buildings do not evolve into other buildings, but languages change all the time, primarily because of changing social conditions within their communities of speakers. In order to heal the Saussurean division of our discipline and construct a dynamic or organic theory of language accommodating both structure and change, we must address issues of social class and sociolinguistic variation.

3.4.1. Change in progress

Broadly speaking, social change seems to give rise to language change. But the details of this historical interplay between language and society are not fully understood. One reason for this is that traditionally historical linguistics has been concerned more with the broad sweep of linguistic evolution across the centuries, rather than with studying the social spread of particular innovations. Indeed the latter is nearly impossible to do given the usual limited data of historical linguistics: a small selection of written documents surviving from earlier periods. To adequately trace the social origins and motivations of linguistic innovation requires looking at change *in progress*, preferably in an environment where our access to data is, at least in principle, unlimited. Thus such studies are ideally done on the language of the present, using spoken data gathered from the community around us, rather than on earlier stages of the language using written materials. Until this century such research was difficult or impossible, but with the invention of sound recording devices, and modern developments in sociolinguistic survey methodology, we are now in a position to address these questions empirically.

The essential questions are: 'Which social groups originate changes?' and 'What is their motivation for doing so?' The first question presupposes one fact which should perhaps be made explicit: namely that innovations are not adopted uniformly and simultaneously across society; rather, some groups are innovators or early adopters, while others lag behind. This clearly means that linguistic change involves social variation: at a given point in time in the course of a change there will be some members of the speech community using the new form and some using the old form.[5] In fact, it is likely that many individuals will vary in their usage, alternating between old and new forms, perhaps influenced by audience, social context, etc.

Given these facts, who are the innovators? Most answers to this question have been phrased in terms of social class. One idea that received a certain currency was that members of the dominant class originate innovations, motivated by an elitist desire to set themselves apart from the masses (the 'flight of the elite'). Such changes would spread because people with the highest status are the ones that others are most likely to emulate. This theory may account for some historical changes, such as the spread of innovations from dominant social centers in medieval European languages (e.g. the spread of Parisian French – the language of the French court – across France). But in modern sociolinguistic work one striking fact emerges: not a single case has been recorded of untargeted innovation originating in the highest social class! Those few cases identified in the literature of changes in progress starting at the top all involve the borrowing of some external prestige norm, i.e. *targeted change*. An example of such a targeted change introduced from the top is the consonantal pronunciation of post-vocalic /r/ of New York City, discussed above, which is being imported into NYC English from the socially dominant 'General American' dialect. The agents of this change are the upper classes. The important thing to notice is that this 'innovation' does not bring anything new into the language, but just involves dialectal redistribution of variants.

Untargeted changes, on the other hand, internally developed and not borrowed, do bring in something completely new, and tend to originate among the working class. Accounting for them has been a major concern of linguistics throughout its history. Modern studies of change in progress appeal mainly to social class dynamics as the driving force of such innovation. Two main theories have been proposed, one focussing on active innovation and the other on resistance to change.

The first of these theories is Labov's, developed in a number of works (1966, 1974, 1980, 1981, Labov, Yaeger & Steiner 1972). He calls this 'change from below the level of conscious awareness,' and in a series of studies of changes in progress has found a social class distribution that he believes characterizes this type of innovation. This is the *curvilinear pattern*, in which the innovation peaks in the 'interior' groups (the working class or lower middle class), and falls off at either extreme. These interior groups

---

[5] Of course it should be emphasized that sociolinguistic variation does NOT necessarily imply change in progress. Many stable sociolinguistic variables appear to have persisted in certain languages for generations without one form winning out over the other.

are the innovators, and in Labov's view they have a positive social motivation to innovate, which is group solidarity or 'local identity.' As a sociosymbolic device, a marker of belonging to their locality, their community, perhaps their class, emerging distinctive characteristics of their local dialect are favorably evaluated and adopted and extended by these groups. The changes serve a positive function of contrastive self-identification: members of the group have them, and outsiders are marked by their absence.

We might ask why just these groups are so motivated; why don't other classes innovate to mark their identity? In his early work Labov allows such a possibility, but from his Philadelphia studies a more precise account has emerged: the interior groups lead because they are the ones for whom this local solidarity is strongest. The lowest class (the chronically unemployed, the homeless, etc.) have little or no local ties or group allegiance, and the highest classes do not depend on locality or group for their identity, but move in national or international circles.[6] We might note that although Labov does not use these terms, this interpretation is in tune with the Marxist concept of class ideology: the solidary, cooperative ideology of the working class versus the competitive, individualistic ideology of other classes.

The other principal theory of class and language change has been articulated by Anthony Kroch (1978). Whereas Labov focusses on the question of why some people are motivated to innovate, Kroch asks why others RESIST innovation. He suggests that change is the natural condition of language, but that some social groups avoid or suppress innovation. The motivation for this linguistic conservatism is the same as for political conservatism: a favorable position in the existing *status quo*. In other words, linguistic change should correlate directly with position in the class hierarchy, generally beginning at the bottom and being adopted only late, or never, at the top. This theory also has an interpretation in Marxist terms. The conservatism of dominant groups stems from a need to defend their favorable position against democratic demands, and in so far as their conservative standards for language use are publicly accepted, their social status and power will be enhanced by their possession of this 'social capital.'

The one substantial difference in these theories is in their predictions about what should happen at the lower end of the class hierarchy. In Labov's view, as we have seen, the lower class lags in sound change, but according to Kroch these people have the least investment in the *status quo* and should innovate freely, probably even more so than the working class. These are empirically testable claims: what do the facts show? In fact they show both patterns. A number of studies cited by Kroch show a simple

---

[6] This account arises primarily from the network and neighborhood studies in Philadelphia cited previously, and is in part my own interpretation based on personal communications.

linear pattern with peak use of a new form at the bottom, whereas Labov relies on another, quite substantial, body of work showing his curvilinear pattern. How can we resolve this contradiction?

The answer appears to lie in the difference in focus of the two theories. They are looking at different sides of the innovation issue, Labov asking what motivates people to innovate, and Kroch asking what motivates them to resist an innovation. So the two theories are not inherently contradictory, but rather complementary. The study of intonational change in Australian English, mentioned above (Guy *et al.* 1986), makes this point clearly. The social class distribution of this innovation, reproduced here as Figure 2, shows both the curvilinear and the linear pattern separated by sex. Both men and women show higher use in the working class than in the middle class, but in the lowest class the men slope down while the women go even higher. Subjective reaction studies in this community also show that the innovation in question has both kinds of social significance: it is perceived as being unsuitable for high-status occupations – the negative evaluation accorded the innovation by the dominant classes, but simultaneously given favorable rankings on solidarity scales such as friendliness – the positive symbolism of the 'interior' groups.

This suggests a synthesis of the theories of Labov and Kroch, in which conflicts over the sociosymbolic significance of linguistic innovations are seen as a consequence of the conflicting interests of different social classes. The working class (broadly defined to include the lower-paid and lower-status levels of the middle class such as secretaries, clerical workers, book-keepers, etc.) are the basic source of untargeted innovations, and for many of them these new forms will acquire a positive symbolic value as markers of

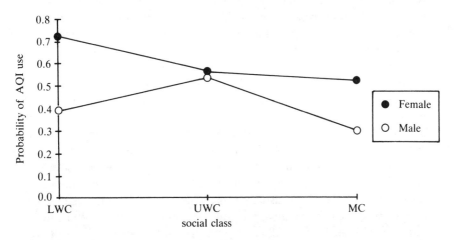

Figure 2. Australian questioning intonation by class and sex. (Guy *et al.* 1986)

group solidarity. Higher-status groups however, not belonging to the working class and wishing to defend their social position, will naturally resist and denigrate such innovations. The ultimate outcome for any particular change will depend on the balance of these social forces. In the end this comes down to a common sense view of social change. In our own everyday experiences no doubt we have all encountered situations where some people attach themselves to an innovation and actively promulgate it, while others, perhaps with something to lose, resist the change. While perhaps greatly simplified, this would seem to be a basic dialectic of human societies.

3.5. Class and linguistic theory

Class differentiation of language is ultimately of great importance for linguistic theory. It is true, of course, that much of modern linguistic thought has disputed this position, taking as its object of study a hypothetical object wildly at odds with linguistic reality. As Chomsky formulates it: 'linguistic theory is concerned primarily with an ideal speaker–listener, in a completely homogeneous speech community, who knows its language perfectly . . .' (1965: 3) But if we wish to achieve even a minimal level of adequacy for our theories, it is necessary to move beyond this imaginary monostylistic idiolect and confront the problem of sociolinguistic variation. There are three principal areas where this will be an issue for linguistic theory. First, there is the form of the grammar, which should be designed so as to accommodate systematic lectal differences. Second, there is the problem of variation in meaning. And finally, there is the fundamental distinction between *langue* and *parole*, or competence and performance, which is called into question by some of the basic findings of sociolinguistics.

One of the basic concerns of modern linguistics is writing grammars. A grammar is supposed to be a formal account of the structure and workings of some language. An adequate grammar must address the question of the scope of its object of description, the language, in that it will have to define the limits of the language community it is attempting to account for, and to accommodate, at least some kinds of social differences in language. We cannot write a grammar of English unless we are prepared to say what is and is not English, or perhaps what is only partly English, and to account for the linguistic differences which this great abstraction encompasses.

Studies of language and social class help us to do this in several ways. First, they help delimit the language by identifying speech communities, dialects and sociolects. An instance is the behavior of different social classes within one speech community that we have considered above. While these classes may differ linguistically in many respects, they do so in an orderly, systematic fashion, all sharing the same norms for language use, and all shifting the same way in more formal contexts. Findings such as these are vital for the task of identifying the unity of a language from among the enormous diversity of dialects (and idiolects?) that we find in the world. If a group of lects displays this kind of 'orderly heterogeneity,' if a group of speakers displays this kind of common attitudes to language use, in a way that other lects and speakers do not, then we have begun to identify the limits of what our grammar must account for.

Furthermore, the very form of the grammar should be partly determined by the nature of such variation. As an example, suppose that we had two competing theories of the syntax and semantics of negation in English, both of which adequately account for the common intuitions of their upper middle class authors, who only use single negation. Suppose further that one of these theories fails completely if applied to structures involving multiple negation (perhaps because it assumes that multiple negatives cancel each other out, as in symbolic logic), while the other theory, via some simple alternative setting of a parameter or feature, provides a straightforward account of multiple negation. Given our knowledge of class dialects of English, which tells us that multiple negation is used every day by most working class speakers of English, the latter theory is obviously to be preferred, although a linguist who postulates a fictional homogeneous speech community might easily choose the inadequate alternative.

The second problem for linguistic theory is variation in the meaning systems of language. Studies have shown class differences in syntax (Lavandera 1975, 1978), lexical choice (Sankoff, Thibault & Bérubé 1978), discourse (Horvath 1986), and intonation (Guy & Vonwiller 1984) which could all affect the meaning of a text. This presents a challenge for our theories of semantics and communication. Do such mismatches in semantic systems lead to ambiguity and miscomprehension? If not, is there some higher level analysis which allows people to interpret semantic systems different from their own? Such questions can be addressed only by looking at class differences.

Finally there is the problem of *langue* and *parole*, recast by Chomsky as competence and performance. *Langue* and competence are supposed to incorporate the features of a language common to all speakers, the knowledge they must share in order to use the language appropriately. But as we have seen, speakers share more than mere grammaticality judgements. They also have a passive knowledge which allows them to recognize and interpret other social class varieties of the language, and an active knowledge which allows them to adapt their own syntax, phonology, and lexicon to different situations, audiences, topics, etc. In other words they have a *communicative competence*, common to all members of a speech community, which encompasses sociolinguistic variability. An adequate linguistic theory should be able to account for this ability of native speakers.

Ultimately this calls into question the very utility of the competence–performance, *langue–parole* distinction. If these are oppositions between unity and diversity, between design and execution, then they are difficult to maintain in the face of two fundamental findings of sociolinguistics. On the one hand we have orderly heterogeneity, which identifies *unity and system within parole/performance*, and on the other hand we have inherent variability, which is *diversity within langue/competence*. Thus the study of language and class may lead the way to an ultimate synthesis of the second great Saussurean dichotomy.

REFERENCES

Bailey, B. 1966. *Jamaican creole syntax*. Cambridge: Cambridge University Press.
Bernstein, B. 1964. Elaborated and restricted codes: their social origins and some consequences. In J. Gumperz & D. Hymes (eds.) *The ethnography of communication*. American Anthropologist 66 (6.2).
Bernstein, B. 1971. *Class, codes, and control*. London: Routledge & Kegan Paul.
Bickerton, D. 1975. *Dynamics of a creole system*. New York: Columbia University Press.
Bloomfield, L. 1933. *Language*. New York: Holt.
Bortoni-Ricardo, S. M. 1985. *The urbanization of rural dialect speakers: a sociolinguistic study in Brazil*. Cambridge: Cambridge University Press.
Cedergren, 1972. The interplay of social and linguistic factors in Panama. Doctoral dissertation, Cornell University.
Chomsky, N. 1965. *Aspects of the theory of syntax*. Cambridge, MA: MIT Press.
Congalton, A. A. 1962. *Social standings of occupations in Sydney*. Kensington, NSW: University of New South Wales School of Sociology.
De Oliveira, M. A. 1982. Phonological variation in Brazilian Portuguese. Doctoral dissertation, University of Pennsylvania.
Dittmar, N. 1976. *A critical survey of sociolinguistics*. New York: St Martin's.
Fishman, J. A., Ferguson, C. & Das Gupta, J. (eds.) 1968. *Language problems of developing nations*. New York: Wiley.
Guy, G. R. 1981. Linguistic variation in Brazilian Portuguese: aspects of the phonology, syntax, and language history. Doctoral dissertation, University of Pennsylvania.
Guy, G. R., & Vonwiller, J. 1984. The meaning of an intonation in Australian English. *Australian Journal of Linguistics* 4.1: 1–17.
Guy, G. R., Horvath, B., Vonwiller, J., Daisley, E. & Rogers, I. 1986. An intonational change in progress in Australian English. *Language in Society* 15.1: 23–51.
Horvath, B. 1986. *Variation in Australian English: a sociolinguistic study of English in Sydney*. Cambridge: Cambridge University Press.
Kroch, A. 1978. Towards a theory of social dialect variation. *Language in Society* 7: 17–36.
Labov, W. 1966. *The social stratification of English in New York City*. Washington: Center for Applied Linguistics.
Labov, W. 1969. Contraction, deletion, and inherent variability of the English copula. *Language* 45: 715–62.
Labov, W. 1972a. *Sociolinguistic patterns*. Philadelphia: University of Pennsylvania Press.
Labov, W. 1972b. *Language in the inner city*. Philadelphia: University of Pennsylvania Press.
Labov, W. 1974. Linguistic change as a form of communication. In M. Silverstein (ed.) *Human communication: theoretical explanations*. Hillsdale: Erlbaum.

Labov, W. 1980. The social origins of sound change. In W. Labov (ed.) *Locating language in time and space*. New York: Academic Press.

Labov, W. 1981. What can be learned about change in progress from synchronic description? In D. Sankoff & H. Cedergren (eds.) *Variation omnibus*. Edmonton: Linguistic Research.

Labov, W., Cohen, P., Robins, C. & Lewis, J. 1968. *A study of the non-standard English used by Negro and Puerto Rican speakers in New York City*. Report on Co-operative Research Project 3288. New York: Columbia University.

Labov, W., Yaeger, M. & Steiner, R. 1972. *A quantitative study of sound change in progress*. Report on National Science Foundation contract GS–3287. Philadelphia: US Regional Survey.

Lavandera, B. 1975. Linguistic structure and sociolinguistic conditioning in the use of verbal endings in *si* clauses (Buenos Aires Spanish). Doctoral dissertation, University of Pennsylvania.

Lavandera, B. 1978. Where does the sociolinguistic variable stop? *Language in Society* 7: 171–82.

Lemle, M. & Naro, A. 1977. *Competências básicas do português*. Rio de Janeiro: MOBRAL.

Marx, K. 1906. *Capital: a critique of political economy*. New York: Random House.

Michael, J. 1962. The construction of the social class index. *Codebook for the Mobilization for Youth*. Appendix A. Mimeo. New York: Mobilization for Youth.

Milroy, L. 1980. *Language and social networks*. Oxford: Blackwell.

Modaressi, Y. 1978. A sociolinguistic analysis of modern Persian. Doctoral dissertation, University of Kansas.

Naro, A. 1981. The social and structural dimensions of a syntactic change. *Language* 57: 63–98.

Poplack, S. to appear. The care and handling of a megacorpus: the Ottawa–Hull French project. In R. Fasold & D. Schiffrin (eds.) *Language function and use*.

Rickford, J. 1979. Variation in a creole continuum: quantitative and implicational approaches. Doctoral dissertation, University of Pennsylvania.

Rickford, J. 1986. The need for new approaches to social class analysis in sociolinguistics. *Language and Communication* 6.3: 215–21.

Sankoff, D. (ed.) 1978. *Linguistic variation: models and methods*. New York: Academic Press.

Sankoff, D. & Laberge, S. 1978. The linguistic market and the statistical explanation of variability. In D. Sankoff 1978.

Sankoff, D., Thibault, P. & Bérubé, H. 1978. Semantic field variability. In D. Sankoff 1978.

Sankoff, G. & Cedergren, H. 1971. Some results of a sociolinguistic study of Montreal French. In R. Darnell (ed.) *Linguistic diversity in Canadian Society*. Edmonton: Linguistic Research.

Sankoff, G., Kemp, W. & Cedergren, H. 1980. The syntax of *ce que/qu'est-ce que* variation and its social correlates. In R. Shuy & J. Firsching (eds.) *Dimensions of variability and competence*. Georgetown: Georgetown University Press.

Scherre, M. M. P. 1978. A regra de concordância de número no sintagma nominal em português. MA dissertation, Pontifícia Universidade Católica do Rio de Janeiro.

Trudgill, P. 1974. *The social differentiation of English in Norwich*. Cambridge: Cambridge University Press.

4 Language and race: some implications for linguistic science*

John Baugh

4.0. Introduction

The relationship between language and racial groups has both a biological and a political dimension. The biological dimension first emerged historically as distinct genetic characteristics evolved among various human tribes in relative geographical isolation. Thus, in the typical case, language and race were originally correlated directly. But throughout history, linguistic change has been both rapid and drastic in comparison with the stability of the distinct racial groups. Thus the relative status and life expectancy of a language have come to be much more a function of the political and economic circumstances of its speakers than of their race *per se*. Indeed, the speech communities of influential world languages like English and Russian are *multi*racial, a fact that reflects their global expansion and great political and economic influence.

Whatever the evolutionary correlation may be between race and language, linguists hold all races – and the languages of their speakers – to be equal. Franz Boas and his student Edward Sapir eloquently stated the case for the equality of race and language respectively:

> I believe the present state of our knowledge justifies us in saying that, while individuals differ, biological differences between races are small. There is no reason to believe that one race is by nature so much more intelligent, endowed with great will power, or emotionally more stable than another that the difference would materially influence its culture. (Boas 1940: 13–14)

> When it comes to linguistic form, Plato walks with the Macedonian swineherd, Confucius with the head-hunting savage of Assam. (Sapir 1921: 219)

* The Black English interviews reported herein were made possible by a grant-in-aid from the American Council of Learned Societies. Additional support has been provided by the Policy Research Institute of The University of Texas at Austin. I am indebted to C. Larrimore, Frederick Newmeyer, and Anthony Woodbury for helpful suggestions on earlier versions of this paper. I take ultimate responsibility for all observations and conclusions.

This linguistic ideal of equality among languages and the various races has never been reflected in social terms. Domination of some groups over others has been the rule rather than the exception throughout history. We know all too well that some languages or dialects have come to be associated with the social status of the people who employ them. Bloomfield's observations regarding different groups within a speech community are as relevant now as they were a half-century ago:

> We shall examine first the simpler case, as it appears in the United States. The most striking line of cleavage in our speech is one of social class. Children who are born into the homes of privilege, in the way of wealth, tradition, or education, become native speakers of what is known as 'good' English; the linguist prefers to give it the noncommittal name of Standard English. Less fortunate children become native speakers of 'bad' or 'vulgar' or, as the linguist prefers to call it, nonstandard English. (Bloomfield 1933: 48)

The social division of dialects, particularly along racial lines, is obviously not unique to the United States. Other examples abound from around the globe – legacies of the incontrovertible political and economic dimensions of post-colonial racism, among other pertinent factors. Racism has a linguistic aspect, of course; racists believe that their language (and most other aspects of their culture) is superior to those of the 'inferior' races. Such an attitude, if supported by political domination, whether overt or covert, is used to justify attempts to impose various doctrines on racially subordinate groups. Ironically, these policies are usually offered in the name of 'improving' the plight of less fortunate peoples.

4.1. Jensen's hypothesis and the LSA response

Our science is uniquely equipped to redress the linguistic dimension of morally indefensible racist ideologies wherever they are found. While linguists, of course, have no special expertise on the political factors that support racism, they are in a unique position to expose racially loaded fallacies about language and mind. The most notorious is Arthur Jensen's claim (1969) that black children are intellectually inferior to white children on *genetic* grounds. Since Jensen's notions were based in part on fallacies about black language, linguists were ideally suited to combat them. And they did just that. The Linguistic Society of America in 1972 endorsed a widely publicized resolution by Anthony Kroch and William Labov that exposed the flimsy intellectual basis of Jensen's ideas. Given its importance and the fact that it can serve as a model for future struggles against overtly racist ideas, it is worth citing in full:

The writings of Arthur Jensen which argue that many lower class people are born with an inferior type of intelligence contain unfounded claims which are harmful to many members of our society. Jensen and others have introduced into the arena of public debate the theory that the population of the United States is divided by genetic inheritance into two levels of intellectual ability: one defined by the ability to form concepts freely, the other limited in this area and confined primarily to the association of ideas.

Because this theory, if accepted, would necessarily alter educational policy and seriously affect the lives of many of our fellow citizens, and because linguists are familiar with a large body of evidence which bears on the question, the Linguistic Society of America issues the following statement and resolution, representing the considered professional opinion of scientific linguists. The following conclusions are based on facts generally known to linguists:

1. By an early age, children learn without direct instruction, on the basis of the speech that they hear, the largest part of the grammar of their native language. This grammar is the knowledge of a hierarchically structured set of relations, used by the speaker to produce and understand an unlimited number of simple and complex sentences.

2. No one language or dialect, standard or non-standard, is known to be significantly more complex than another in its basic grammatical apparatus. Linguists have not yet discovered any speech community with a native language that can be described as conceptually or logically primitive, inadequate or deficient.

3. The non-standard dialects of English spoken by lower class families in the inner cities of the United States are fully formed languages with all of the grammatical structure necessary for logical thought. Statements to the contrary by some educational psychologists are misinterpretations of superficial differences in the means of expression between these dialects and standard English.

4. No theory yet developed by linguists or psychologists can account satisfactorily for children's language learning ability. It is generally agreed that the mere association of ideas is not sufficient. The minimal ability necessary to learn and to speak any human language includes native skills of much higher order of magnitude than those used in the laboratory tests offered in evidence for Dr. Jensen's view.

On the basis of these generally recognized conclusions of linguistic investigation, linguists agree that all children who have learned to speak a human language have a capacity for concept formation beyond our present power to analyze; that language learning abilities indicate that the nature and range of human intelligence is not yet understood or well-measured by any current testing procedure; that tests which may have some value in predicting later performance in school should not be interpreted as measures of intelligence in any theoretically coherent sense of the word; that to attribute a limited level of 'associational intelligence' to a sizable section of our population is a serious misconception of the nature of human intelligence. (Kroch & Labov 1972: 17–18)

4.2. **Farrell's reinterpretation of Jensen's hypothesis**

Misconceptions about language, race, and intelligence are not in general as blatant as Jensen's. But even where such misconceptions lend inadvertent credence to racist myths and ideologies, linguists can – and I believe should – devote the necessary time to dispelling these errors.

To illustrate this point, we will consider a case from the United States, where some well-intentioned scholars have advocated ill-conceived language policies in an effort to help black children improve their IQ scores. Thomas J. Farrell (1984a) advocates that we revive the old McGuffy readers to help black Americans attain higher degrees of literacy, and proposes as well a series of audio-visual exercises and platitudes about how blacks need to apply themselves to study in order to learn. But Farrell's suggestion ignores the differences between standard and nonstandard English as contributing to the black students' lower test scores. Farrell, like so many others, appears to be laboring under the misconception that language differences are irrelevant in the testing situation, and thus implicitly supports the idea that blacks are intrinsically 'less intelligent' than whites.[1]

The most insidious aspect of Farrell's work, particularly his 1983 paper 'IQ and standard English,' is his resuscitation of many of the misconceptions found in Jensen's original hypothesis. Farrell, to be sure, does not posit genetic deficiencies. In their place, he finds 'literacy deficiencies.' For example, he finds that literacy and the attainment of certain grammatical structures found in Standard English are required for abstract thought.[2] Only then does

---

[1] Farrell ignores cultural and economic factors as a determinant of IQ scores. Yet, as we have seen, even Bloomfield was aware that whether one is 'privileged' or 'less fortunate' is a major determining factor in academic success. Furthermore, the same black students who get low scores on standardized IQ tests score much higher on the alternative tests developed by black psychologists that are biased in favor of black culture.

[2] Readers who are unfamiliar with the history of this thesis are encouraged to read Farrell (1978, 1983, 1984a, 1984b). Detailed commentary on Farrell's hypotheses can be found in Greenberg 1984. Hartwell 1984, Himley 1984, and Stratton 1984. Sledd (1983, 1984) and Farrell (1984b debate the pedagogical dimensions of the hypotheses.

the cognitive transformation take place that allows speakers to move from an 'oral mentality' to a 'literate mentality.'

4.3. The linguist's response to Farrell

Many of the assumptions that Farrell draws upon to support this hypothesis are incompatible with established principles of linguistic science. Consider, for example, the following passage from his 1983 paper:

> The development of abstract thinking depends on learning (1) the full standard deployment of the verb 'to be' and (2) embedded modification and (3) subordination. Historically these are the three features of language that developed as the ancient Greeks moved from oral to literate composing, which resulted in the development of abstract thinking. IQ test scores reveal that black ghetto children have not developed the power of abstract thinking, and they do not speak standard English. (481)

He sees rational thought essentially as a gift of the Greek alphabet: 'Abstract thinking did not develop with the all-consonant alphabet; it developed only with the Greek alphabet . . . the development of letters for vowel sounds was important for the development of abstract thinking' (1984a: 475). How does Farrell measure abstract thinking? His debt to Jensen is explicit: 'IQ tests used by Jensen and other educational psychologists [are] "valid" and "reliable" measure of abstract thinking' (1983: 471).

Confusions about language permeate Farrell's work. For example, he expresses some skepticism about currently prevailing views in linguistic theory:

> I know that one theory of linguistics postulates that meaning is conveyed through so called deep structures, not surface forms. But I for one do not believe this is true because I have known too many people who are very poor readers and who also do not know standard English. Conversely, I have not encountered any good readers who do not know standard English. (1984b: 822)

Such opinions confuse very different cognitive processes and do not take functional (ethno)linguistic considerations into account. For example, speech and writing involve radically different neurological processes, each of which is dependent to varying degrees on a set of unpredictable communicative events. It would seem, then, that Farrell compounds Jensen's errors by adding a set of misconceptions about language and cognition.

The assumption that literacy deficiencies are at the heart of the issue is tenuous at best. Contrary to Farrell, substantial evidence exists that abstract thought was available to humans long before the representation of vocalic phonemes in the Greek alphabet. For example, primitive tool and meta-tool[3] making represent incontrovertible evidence of abstract thought among early humans. No one can deny the importance of writing in various cultures around the world. Yet literacy is distributed according to capricious political and economic variables that are subject to constant changes, while the cognitive interplay of *langue* and *parole*, so central to abstract thought, is available to all normal children in language acquisition. In fact, it is the miracle of language acquisition itself that distinguishes our species most strongly from all others. While all normal children learn to talk, only some are provided with adequate opportunities to master literacy. Opportunity, or lack thereof, is the critical factor. In cognitive terms, literacy is more comparable to other skilled behaviors, like artistic talent, that develop and improve with the right combination of time, training, and economic support. Without the proper opportunity, children will not become literate, because literacy is not inherent or innate. This contrasts sharply with oral language development among normal children, which is universal regardless of race, creed, or national origin.

Linguists recognize the cognitive differences between speech and writing, and handle the studies comparing them with ethnographic sensitivity and, if possible, strict experimental controls (see Chafe 1981; Tannen 1982). These differences have implications at many levels of analysis. For example, Ochs (1979) introduces the distinction between planned and unplanned discourse, which divides along the axis of written versus spoken modes of discourse – a division observed in Tannen 1982 to be complementary to the traditional division between formal and informal discourse. Thus any hypothesis that attempts to link race, language, and abstract thought will be further biased by neglecting the fundamental differences in the possible modes of discourse.

The likelihood of an American child's success in education and in standardized IQ tests tends to correlate not only with his or her wealth and privilege, but also with which of the following three groups he or she falls in: (1) children who learn standard English as their native dialect; these are typically children with well-educated parents; (2) children who learn a (stigmatized) nonstandard variety of English as their native dialect, including many nonwhites and poor whites; (3) those children who did not learn

---

[3] Thomas Sebeok, in the course of a lecture on the history of communication presented at the University of Texas at Austin on 28 October 1985, stressed the history of 'meta-tool' making as a uniquely human behavior, which represents further evidence of detailed abstract thought among preliterate humans. While humans are not the only species to make tools, they are the only meta-tool makers. There is substantial archaeological evidence to support the early existence of meta-tools among all races prior to the classical period in Greece. Such 'meta-tools' are tools that are created for the express purpose of producing other tools: one must produce a meta-tool in order to make the tool that is desired.

69

English as their first language. These divisions are linguistic, and clearly have nothing intrinsic to do with race.

Farrell, to be sure, attempts to disassociate himself from the racial foundations of Jensen's views by stating: 'There are educated blacks who speak standard English, and their children generally score better than most of their black ghetto peers on IQ tests. This paper is obviously not about them' (1983: 479). Thus, while Jensen's original hypothesis was directed at all blacks, due to its strict genetic interpretation, Farrell's revised hypothesis is limited to those less fortunate blacks who have not mastered literacy. But there is no mention of the white illiterate population, or of the generally declining rates of literacy in the United States. Since Farrell thus makes it appear that the problem is racial rather than social, he perpetuates the initial racial bias in Jensen's work.

Farrell places enormous stress on the surface distribution of the verb 'to be,' and its usage among blacks who do not speak standard English. But in the light of my own detailed analysis of the (black) English copula, as well as research by other linguists (see Labov 1972; Wolfram 1974; Baugh 1980, 1983; Holm 1984), the assumption that 'surface forms are significant in cognitive development' (Farrell 1984a: 474) is simply not supported by the best empirical evidence. If anything, the surface distribution of *to be* in black vernacular English is more concise, in purely logical terms, than the archaic preservation of the full forms of *is* and *are* in formal written prose.

To be specific, black vernacular English optionally omits present tense forms of the English copula as the unmarked case. There is a sound semantic justification for this, since the present tense forms of *to be* are semantically vacuous. They convey no meaning and are preserved largely due to prescriptive convention, not logical necessity. It is just for this reason that nonstandard dialects, such as black vernacular English, have the capacity to prune this optional auxiliary verb in the unmarked (present) tense. Future and past tense marking of the auxiliary is preserved in this dialect. Thus, a close examination of the empirical evidence repudiates the claim that Black English is less logical than standard English or is incapable of abstractions.

To illustrate still further the point that Black English can be put to sophisticated logical use, consider the following transcription from my field-work in Los Angeles. The speech reflects many nonstandard characteristics, including the strongly vernacular use of 'ain't' for 'didn't' and many other variables that will be apparent. The informant is a 25-year-old black male who is an active participant in vernacular black culture. He works as the night manager at the local bowling alley and is employed as a door-man (guard) at the public pool during the day. Here he recounts an incident with a police officer that reflects both logic and abstract thought:

J (interviewer) O.K., so what happened?

DJ (informant) Oh, yeah, now, check it out. I'm riding down the street, (al) right? I got me a blue Monza, and my lady by my side. We pull up to a stop sign, you know, and I stop. Y'know? I look both ways and then I starts to go, well, midway up the next block, up slides this policeman . . . tells me, 'pull over!' Y'know, like, he pulls up along side of me and then parks his bike in front of my car.

J: Uh huh.

DJ: So, he gets off the ol' bike and starts walkin' back to my car, and I'm sayin' to myself, 'Why me?' So, he tell me, 'You ran the stop sign back there and your brake light's out.' I said, 'I ain't run the stop sign,' and he said, 'You ran it!' So he take my license and proceeds to start writin' up this ticket when it dawns on me what's happenin'. I said, 'Well, wait a minute man; if I didn't stop at the stop sign and you came from 'round the corner, then you've never seen the back of my car; you pulled in front of me. So how can you tell me my brake light is out 'less I stepped on the brake for the stop sign?' (Imitating the officer's voice) 'Well, you just a smart [MF] ain't ya kid?'

The logic is impeccable; one cannot confirm what one has not seen. However, this logical demonstration cost the informant two additional citations for unrelated (minor) vehicle violations that were detected after a time-consuming search by the officer.

The preceding example is of great linguistic importance as an answer to Farrell and his cothinkers; it illustrates that one must examine the logical content of discourse case by case. It shows that logical discourse is not inherently seated in writing as opposed to speech. But a moment's thought should be enough to convince anybody that it could not be: Stonehenge, hieroglyphics, the Aztec calendar, and many artifacts from preliterate cultures provide countless examples of abstract thought. To determine the logical content of a discourse one must examine the particular content and channel of communication, among other factors, for the specific communicative event (for discussion, see Hymes 1962).

We must therefore dismiss from serious consideration any interpretation that links literacy and abstract thought. In spite of the tremendous time and effort invested in the topic, there has never been a viable shred of evidence to demonstrate the linguistic superiority of some races over others. Attempting to salvage this idea by attaching it to the invention of writing and the politicized spread of literacy is both intellectually pretentious and ludicrous. It should be dismissed from serious scholarly consideration.

4.4. **Conclusion: linguistic science versus racist myths about language**

In closing, I would like to share a few personal observations, because as a black child I encountered some teachers who shared the philosophy of Jensen and Farrell. I did not have the wisdom or sophistication to challenge the foundations of the linguistic chauvinism that I and other minority students experienced at the hands of a few racist teachers. While it should be a truism that students need support and genuine encouragement from their teachers, I had some who were so flagrant with their bigotry that they would openly chastise and humiliate minority students. One teacher in junior high school informed me that there was nothing I could do to get a passing grade in his course, a required course in state history. To add further insult to this educational injury, the portrayal of minority Americans during this class was either malicious or ignored altogether.

I was not alone in undergoing this type of experience, and although bigoted teachers are rare exceptions, it is almost impossible for the minority student to complete an education without encountering discrimination to some degree. These bitter pills of humiliation and degradation thrive on ignorance – the kind of ignorance that is perverse and mendacious by nature. Education has always been the best cure for ignorance, and linguists can add vital insights to the educational process. The black parents that I have interviewed in several years of fieldwork in black American communities categorically want the best possible education for their children. By this they mean a traditional education, in which teachers will help all students master the required standard literacy skills, regardless of their race or personal background.

I share the desire to see blacks and other nontraditional students achieve higher levels of educational success, but I disagree with many that the accomplishment of this entails the denial of cultural pluralism. We should continue to support innovative and effective educational policies that are sensitive to cultural and, ultimately, individual educational needs.

This chapter has focussed on the American context, and examples of the situation in the United States have been given as illustration. But it need not have; a similar story could be told in many countries, where race and language correspond to social stratification. Many of the same arguments that have been raised to 'prove' that black vernacular English is an inferior (i.e. less logical or abstract) representation of standard English have been raised to make the same point about the languages or dialects of other racially oppressed groups. Armed with the conviction that racism is immoral, linguists must be willing to continue to provide objective scientific insights about language that will expose incontrovertible flaws in the untenable linguistic views that leach on racism (for more discussion, see Labov 1982). Linguists have an especially important role to play whenever linguistic differences among socially disparate racial groups are seen as the cause, rather than the symptom, of limited academic performance among members of such groups. That linguists should be called upon to play a socially active role should not be surprising – from time to time, the direct expertise of scientists is required for influencing the events of the day. During World War II, for example, physicists were called upon by their respective nations to help 'win the war.' Linguistics (which often compares itself with physics, on theoretical grounds), as we have seen, can be an important weapon in the war against racism.

REFERENCES

Baugh, J. 1980. A reexamination of the black English copula. In Labov 1980.
Baugh, J. 1983. *Black street speech: its history, structure and survival.* Austin: University of Texas Press.
Bloomfield, L. 1933. *Language.* London: Allen & Unwin.
Boas, F. 1940. *Race, language and culture.* New York: The Free Press.
Chafe, W. L. 1981. Integration and involvement in speaking, writing and oral literature. In Tannen 1981.
Farrell, T. J. 1978. Differentiating writing from talking. *College Composition and Communication* 29: 346–50.
Farrell, T. J. 1983. IQ and Standard English. *College Composition and Communication* 34: 470–84.
Farrell, T. J. 1984a. Reply by Thomas J. Farrell. *College Composition and Communication* 35: 469–78.
Farrell T. J. 1984b. Comment on James Sledd's 'In defense of the students' right.' *College English* 46: 821–2.
Givón, T. 1979 (ed.) *Discourse and syntax.* New York: Academic Press.
Greenberg, K. 1984. Response no. 1 to Thomas J. Farrell. *College Composition and Communication* 35: 455–60.
Hartwell, P. 1984. Response no. 2 to Thomas J. Farrell. *College Composition and Communication* 35: 461–5.
Himley, M. 1984. Response no. 3 to Thomas J. Farrell. *College Composition and Communication* 35: 465–8.
Holm, J. 1984. Variability of the copula in Black English and its creole kin. *American Speech* 59: 291–309.
Hymes, D. 1962. The ethnography of speaking. In T. Gladwin & W. C. Sturtebant (eds.) *Anthropology and human behavior.* Washington: Anthropological Society of Washington.
Jensen, A. 1969. How much can we boost IQ and scholastic achievement? *Harvard Educational Review* 39: 1–123.
Kroch, A. and Labov, W. 1972. Linguistic Society of America: resolution in response to Arthur Jensen (1969). *Linguistic Society of American Bulletin* (March). Washington: Linguistic Society of America.
Labov, W. 1972. *Language in the inner-city: studies in the Black English vernacular.* Philadelphia. University of Pennsylvania Press.
Labov, W. 1980. (ed.) *Locating language in time and space.* New York: Academic Press.
Labov, W. 1982. Objectivity and commitment in linguistic science: the case of the Black English trial in Ann Arbor. *Language in Society* 11: 165–201.
Ochs, E. 1979. Planned and unplanned discourse. In T. Givón (ed.) *Discourse and syntax.* New York: Academic Press.
Sapir, E. 1921. *Language.* New York: Harcourt, Brace and World.
Sledd, J. 1983. In defense of the students' right. *College English* 45: 667–75.

Sledd, J. 1984. James Sledd responds. *College English* 46: 822–9.

Stratton, R. E. 1984. Response no. 4 to Thomas J. Farrell. *College Composition and Communication* 35: 468–9.

Tannen, D. (ed.) 1981. *Spoken and written language: exploring orality and literacy*. Norwood: Ablex.

Tannen, D. 1982. Oral and literate strategies in spoken and written narratives. *Language* 58: 1–21.

Wolfram, W. 1974. The relationship of white southern Speech to vernacular black English. *Language* 50: 498–527.

5 Language and gender

Sally McConnell-Ginet

> ... Why can't a woman talk more like a man?
>
> (H. Higgins, phonetician)

5.0. Introduction

Questions of gender are now seen as a major challenge in almost every discipline that deals with human behavior, cognition, institutions, society, and culture. Within linguistics, however, sex/gender studies have played a relatively minor role: 'feminist linguistics' is far better known in literary than linguistic circles (see e.g. Ruthven 1984, Chapter 3). There are, of course, occasional publications in linguistics journals and papers at linguistics meetings. It is fair to say, however, that the recent 'feminist intervention,' which is largely responsible for the increased attention to gender in so many areas of intellectual inquiry, has been little felt by most linguists, many of whom have scoffed at claims (e.g. in Spender 1980) that language is 'man made.'

Why have linguists been relatively inactive in the rapidly growing area of research on language and gender? One reason is that most of the initial impetus for investigation of this area derived from feminist thinkers' concern to understand gender, especially the mechanisms that create and maintain male dominance, and not from interest in language as such. This emphasis made the early research of limited professional interest to linguists though often of considerable personal and political interest to many of us as participants in the women's movement.

In fields like anthropology and literature, however, many leading non-feminist scholars soon saw gender studies as of great potential theoretical significance, whereas linguistic theoreticians (correctly) saw gender as irrelevant to the questions of formal grammar that have been center stage in mainstream linguistics. Many linguists do not see how to combine their linguistic interests and their feminism. Can sex and gender function as central analytical categories in linguistic thought? Can a feminist linguistics profitably interact with mainstream linguistic research traditions? Must we swim against that mainstream to explain the language component of gender phenomena? For those of us whose intellect and passion have been fired by recent feminist thinking but who are also engaged by questions in linguistic theory, there is real urgency in the project of connecting issues of gender to some of the issues we care about as linguists.

Much recent linguistics has as its primary concern the principles that constrain the possible structure of *languages* – linguistic systems represented by grammars. Formal linguistics has little to say directly about *language* – the practice of using a language (i.e. a linguistic system) or languages in a community and the relation of individuals to such systems and their use. Nonetheless, the systematic study of possible properties of languages is necessary for illuminating work on language; conversely, any adequate theory of languages and grammars must ultimately be able to support or be compatible with an account of language.

The critical distinction between systems – languages – and their situated uses and relations to users – language – is often ignored by those whose main interest is gender (or more generally, society and culture). (I adopt Lewis 1975's use of the court versus mass distinction – *language* versus *a language* or *languages* – as shorthand for the 'system versus uses and users' distinction.) The distinction has been challenged by linguists whose primary concern is language function rather than form. But to understand just how function and form connect, and how gender systems shape and are shaped by language, I find it very useful to consider both language and languages, while keeping sight of the difference between them. The sexual politics of language can be played out, for example, in struggles over which system(s) a community should use. (See Valian 1977 and Black & Coward 1981 for discussion of the limitations of gender studies that conflate the linguistic system and its uses.)

The word *gender* in the title of this chapter refers to the complex of social, cultural, and psychological phenomena attached to sex, a usage common in the behavioral and social sciences. The word *gender* also, however, has a well-established technical sense in linguistic discussions. Gender in this technical sense is a grammatically significant classification of nouns that has implications for various agreement phenomena. In the familiar Indo-European languages for which gender noun classes were early recognized, there is some connection, albeit highly attenuated, between gender of nouns and sex of their referents. The connection is shown not only by the class labels *feminine* and *masculine* but also by the fact that gender 'agreement' can depend on sex of a deictically given referent rather than on gender class of an antecedent. Many languages, however, show a similar agreement-based categorization of nouns where the nominal classes show no connection at all to sex. Thus as a technical linguistic notion *gender* has virtually severed the connections to sex it had when first introduced to describe languages like Latin and German.

Gender is a useful term for present purposes precisely because it suggests an arbitrariness or conventionality in the socio-cultural construction of the (non-sexual) significance of sex and sexuality not unlike that involved in the construction of Indo-European grammatical gender classes with weak connections to sex. (McConnell-Ginet 1983a, Section 4 and Smith 1985, Chapter 2 discuss the relevance for language studies of the cultural construction of sexual difference.) In the title of this chapter, ambiguity does not really arise, since *gender* in its grammatical sense does not conjoin any more happily with *language* than does *ablaut* or *adjective* or *anaphora: language and x* suggests that *x* designates something considered separate from language – the law, race, literature – not a linguistic component or concept.

Gender studies can illumine some important questions of potential linguistic relevance, especially for understanding the connection between language and languages. How do grammars, mental representations of linguistic systems, connect to other modules of the mind (e.g. those involved in social cognition, in person perception, in the planning of intentional action)? How do minds connect to each other through language use? What do rules of phonetic realization look like and how can they vary within a speech community and from context to context? How are social and linguistic change connected to one another? What role does language use play in social categorization and cultural evaluation of its users? More generally, to what extent are patterns of language use reflective of social structure and of cultural values, of inequality and oppression? Can language be in part constitutive of culture and society, of women and men and their relationships? If so, how? Gender-focussed studies shed some light on these and other questions, although we are still a long way from providing satisfactory answers.

Gender studies have made it quite clear that language users have a wide range of beliefs and knowledge about language that go beyond the rules and representations specifying grammars. There are, for example, gender-related norms as to who should use which expressions in particular social contexts, gender differentiation in access to rules for special genres of language use such as lamentations or ritual insults, and gender-related 'frozen' patterns of expression (English *man and wife, #husband and woman* versus Spanish *marido y mujer, #hombre y marida*). Are all such pragmatic beliefs and knowledge governed by principles common to other kinds of social cognition or do some have a distinctive structure because they are about linguistic expressions and actions? How are they represented and how do they connect to grammars?

More generally, a focus on gender raises forcefully some fundamental questions about the links between language and social and cultural patterns.

How are linguistic forms endowed with significance? How do the meanings a grammar associates with an expression interact with contextual factors in constraining what speakers mean and what hearers understand them to have said by uttering that expression? What is the role of power and of conflict in constructing interpretations and in choosing among competing interpretations? Do our linguistic practices tend to sustain existing gender arrangements, to avert fundamental challenges to those arrangements? ('Obviously,' says the feminist. 'But tell me how,' says her other self, the linguist.)

Gender is of special theoretical interest because it is so pervasive. Gender is implicated not only in race relations, in social stratification, in legal codes and practices, in educational institutions (language in academia is thoughtfully discussed in Treichler & Kramarae 1983) but also affects religion, social interaction, social and cognitive development, roles in the family and the workplace, behavioral styles, conceptions of self, the distribution of resources, aesthetic and moral values, and much more. And gender is of special practical interest because it is the focus of a widespread struggle to change the material conditions and the ideological frameworks of women's (and men's) lives.

Rather than attempt a comprehensive (and necessarily sketchy) survey, I have chosen to emphasize a particular theoretical perspective on language/ gender studies. Recent books in this area with some sort of linguistic orientation (and with their own rather different emphases and limitations) include Kramarae 1981; Vetterling-Braggin 1981; Thorne, Kramarae & Henley 1983; Cameron 1985; Shibamoto 1985; Baron 1986; Frank & Treichler (forthcoming); Philips, Steele & Tanz (1987); Thorne et al. also includes an invaluable annotated bibliography that updates and extends the useful bibliography in Thorne & Henley 1975. The newsletter *Women and Language*, now edited by Paula Treichler and Cheris Kramarae at the University of Illinois, is a useful guide to ongoing research not only in America but also elsewhere (see e.g. the Winter 1984 'multicultural issue'), citing work in many different disciplines.

Language (use) involves the *production* by linguistic agents (speakers or writers) of linguistic forms; in using these forms, agents are *meaning* to express content and to present themselves as social beings and actors in the world. I discuss first production and then meaning.

5.1. Production: patterns of linguistic forms

How does gender interact with patterns of linguistic expressions produced (spoken or written)? This is often construed as a question about how the sex or gender of the linguistic agent, the speaker or writer, affects which linguistic forms are produced. Moving from sex to gender can make the investigation more subtle: gender categories are not restricted to the male/female dichotomy, females need not be feminine, and femininity can be a matter of degree.

Nonetheless, focus on gender as just involving properties of individual linguistic agents can obscure important insights into how gender affects language production. For example, there might be no connection at all between agent's sex or gender and patterns of language produced but significant interactions between forms produced and sex or gender of the audience (Brouwer, Gerritsen & de Haan 1979 discusses one such case). Production patterns might show systematic dependence on the sex/gender relations between agents and their audience, e.g. same-sex versus cross-sex situations of language use, or the Yana data reported in Sapir 1929 in which what mattered was whether or not the group was male only. Or they might show dependence on other features that make gender more or less salient in particular situations of language use, e.g. my colleague Eleanor Jorden reports that a Japanese woman can use a relatively low level of so-called 'feminine' speech markers when speaking to a male classmate about their studies but a much higher level when talking with that same classmate at a party. In a real sense, agents are responsible for what is produced. But this does not mean that it is only through agents' sex or other individual gender characteristics that sex/gender systems can affect linguistic production.

There are two reasons why we might tend to view the study of linguistic production as the study of speakers. The first is a general psychological phenomenon observed in our strongly individualistic culture. Language production is a form of behavior, and the 'ultimate attribution error' (Pettigrew 1979) is to explain a person's behavior as due to intrinsic properties of the person – e.g. her grammatical knowledge or her intellectual capabilities – without reference to contextual factors that might play a role. Those involved in language/gender studies have not been immune to this error. The second reason lies in linguistics itself. Linguists have primarily studied grammars, systems instantiated in the minds of the linguistic agents. Linguistic production is *prima facie* evidence only for the grammar (or grammars) in the mind of the agent responsible for the production. For many linguistic purposes (e.g. writing grammars), there is little reason to look beyond the speaker to her audience or her situation. But to look at language in interaction with gender (or with other socio-cultural phenomena for that matter), it is not enough to observe how features of linguistic production connect to characteristics of the producers. The study of how gender affects linguistic production is not exhausted by the study of how the gender characteristics of speakers affect their speech (of writers their writing). Yet this is all that the prevalent sex-difference approach considers.

Even where linguistic production patterns do covary systematically with gender characteristics of speakers (e.g. with speaker sex), there are still important questions to be asked about what explains this covariation. It might be evidence of (1) gender differentiation in the grammars or systems of linguistic knowledge that underlie speakers' uses (this is what phrases like 'women's language' and 'genderlect' seem to suggest), (2) grammaticized gender display, which I discuss and illustrate below under the rubric 'gender deixis,' (3) pragmatic systems and expectations about how the grammar is or should be used ('nice girls don't say *what the fuck!*'), (4) favored linguistic strategies for achieving given aims ('get him to think it was really his idea to do what you want done'), (5) emphasis on particular aims or goals ('what's really important is sharing feelings'), or (6) some combination of two or more of the above.

Most contemporary linguists would expect no sexual differentiation in the acquisition of grammars UNLESS there were differences in the grammatical systems underlying the language usage that girls and boys encounter. This is because we take core linguistic capacity to be a species-universal biological characteristic. To put it slightly differently, gender interacts with linguistic knowledge only to the extent that it interacts with linguistic exposure. Children might, of course, be exposed to multiple systems, to which they might attend somewhat differently. For example, in developing their own grammars, girls might attend specially to the linguistic productions of their older female playmates, their mothers, and other female models. It is theoretically even possible that sex has some connection to certain details of what Chomsky calls the 'language organ,' although there is no evidence that this is so (a few papers concerned with neurolinguistic investigations and sex differences appear in Philips *et al.* 1987). But one thing that makes gender especially interesting is that in most cultures there is significant cross-sex linguistic communication at all stages of the life cycle, suggesting that there must be considerable linguistic knowledge shared by the sexes.

What I call *gender deixis* provides the most explicit link between gender and linguistic units produced; here the particular form of some linguistic unit *expresses* or *means* something about gendered properties of the circumstances of language production, the gendered perspective from which an utterance is produced. Like person or social deixis (see Levinson 1983, Chapter 2), gender deixis is in some sense grammaticized, part of the language system. One clear example of gender deixis can illustrate the kind of phenomena involved. Ekka (1972) reports that in Kŭṟux, a Dravidian language, 'feminine' conjugations of verbs signal that the speaker is speaking 'as a woman among women;' apparently, these verbal forms linguistically express the 'femininity' of the conversational group. In contrast, *gender stereotypes* (models 'of') and *gender norms* (models 'for') incorporate respectively the community's views about how gender *is* related to language and how it *ought* to be. The English *-fuckin-* infix (as in *absofuckinlutely*) provides an example of a gender stereotype, useful to film-makers for evoking a certain 'macho' image, whether or not the 'macho' types in question actually are the main users of these forms; a gender norm preaches that such forms aren't to be used by women or 'in mixed company.' *Gender markers* represent actual associations between occurrence of linguistic units and gender phenomena that are informative for (and thus potentially manipulable by) community members, even though the association might not be a matter of conscious knowledge. In Montreal French the use of *tu/ vous* rather than *on* for indefinite reference is strikingly sex-differentiated among younger speakers (Laberge & Sankoff 1980); this is one of many examples of a gender marker. (Smith 1979 discusses mainly what are markers in this sense, ranging over a variety of ethnographic situations.) Gender-deictic expressions will, of course, be gender markers (because of the connections between linguistic meaning and language use discussed in section 5.2), though the converse does not hold (e.g. the use of indefinite *on* in Montreal, though strikingly associated wth female speakers does not 'mean' anything about gender and thus is not gender-deictic). Gender stereotypes, norms, and markers are matters of language and not part of a language; thus they involve production frequency, not just categorical production or non-production. (Bodine 1975 distinguishes sex-preferential or sex-exclusive distributional patterns, an important distinction but limited to surface occurrence data that do not directly indicate gender significance.)

Gender deixis is also direct, whereas stereotypes, norms, and markers may all involve either a direct or an indirect connection between linguistic phenomena and gender. For example, people might associate utterance of 'Let's wash yourself now, honey' (at least preferentially) with female speakers, but make the association through a primary link with child tending and additional background beliefs about the connections between child care and women. In fact, it can be argued that most links between language production patterns and gender characteristics of producers are indirect (Brown & Levinson 1979, McConnell-Ginet 1985a), many both a reflection and a component of male dominance (O'Barr & Atkins 1980 put it in almost these terms). Finding a correlation between a language feature (e.g. frequency of tag questions with a final rising intonation) and a gender phenomenon (e.g. sex of speaker) does not in itself tell us anything about the social and cultural contexts, the mechanisms, that produce the correlation.

So-called 'women's language' has often involved (pervasive) gender deixis rather than the gender-differentiated grammars suggested by this phrase. (See e.g. Sapir 1929, Haas 1944, and Flannery 1946 – recently reviewed in Taylor 1983 – for Amerindian situations in which gender deixis was apparently enforced and pervasive.) Among the languages of the world, however, gender deixis is apparently rare: i.e. we fairly seldom find distinct ways of saying the same thing where the difference between the two means something about gender properties of the context-of-utterance. Rarer still are situations where agents *must* express something about gender in the context (as English-using communities enforce the use of first person forms for agent reference in speech) or where such expression is pervasive (like social deixis in Japanese), affecting so many forms that few utterances will not express gender meaning.

Furfey (1946) argued that in none of the then reported cases of gender-differentiated speech did the sexes have distinct codes or grammars; more recent assessments of different ethnographic situations support that claim (in addition to references already cited, see Philips 1980, Borker 1980, Sherzer 1983, and Philips *et al.* 1987). Where quite distinct language systems are in a community's repertoire, gender is often implicated in their use (see e.g. Gal 1978 for Hungarian/German contact and many other references in Thorne *et al.* 1983). Languages reserved for ritual use or other specialized functions are generally accessible only to participants in these rituals and functions, such participation being frequently gender-differentiated (medieval Latin, for example, was almost exclusively 'men's language'). And Hakuta (1986) reports that among some Amazon Indians, marriage partners must be selected from a different (home or first) language group, a situation where there is universal multilingualism.

What did Lakoff (1975) mean when she spoke of 'women's language' (WL) among English speakers? Was she claiming gender deixis in English? Certainly some people took her to be claiming that, for example, *magenta* 'means' that its user is speaking 'as a woman,' feminine or effeminate. What Lakoff actually did was simply to identify a number of features as constitutive of American English WL: tag questions (in certain contexts), a set of positive evaluative adjectives, certain specialized color words, 'question' intonations on declaratives, euphemisms, hedges, indirect request forms and other 'polite' expressions (*could you perhaps manage to pass the salt?*), prescriptively sanctioned forms (*To whom do you wish to speak?*), and others. Her method was essentially that used in grammatical investigations: elicitation of 'acceptability' judgements from herself and other native speakers. The difference was that her data involves judgements not just of a linguistic form but of that form *as produced* by a certain kind of speaker. She does note that not all women use these forms and that men sometimes do, but she does not say exactly what meaning should be attached to their presence or absence or relative frequency in someone's speech. In contrast, she does explicitly speak of women as compelled to become bilingual if they want to function in the public 'men's' world, suggesting that she is assuming (perhaps only a normative or stereotypical) dual system or 'genderlect' model. (See McConnell-Ginet 1983a for further discussion of that model.)

Whether Lakoff intended to be understood as saying that WL features involved gender deixis or constituted some sort of genderlect is not really clear. What is clear from her explicit denials, however, is that she was not proposing an account of the distribution of WL features in actual women's and men's speech. Most readers nonetheless supposed that she was claiming that her WL features were (also) what I have called gender markers, significantly gender-differentiated in their actual distribution. Lakoff herself was not unaware that acceptability judgements might well reflect systematic beliefs about how gender does (stereotype) or should (norm) affect speech better than they reflect actual usage. Edelsky (1976, 1977), Haas (1979), Kramer (1974, 1978), Siegler and Siegler (1976) and others offer evidence that certain elements of the picture Lakoff detailed have some reality as stereotypes. But even as stereotype, Lakoff's WL seems most relevant for the WASP middle class populations that American researchers have mainly studied. Middle class black women, for example, do not find 'coherent images of themselves in the contemporary literature on language and gender' (Stanback 1985: 177). And one woman complained to Barrie Thorne (personal communication): 'I'm tired of being told that I talk like a man. I talk like a Jew.' As a normative model, the WL features have rather limited support, even among mainstream white women.

Although actual distribution of WL features was not what Lakoff was interested in, actual distribution is of considerable interest not only for learning whether gender-differentiated systems exist in a community but also for exploring other ways in which gender may affect production. Lakoff's ideas about WL inspired many quantitative descriptive studies of women's speech (especially in American English – see Thorne *et al.* 1983 for references), some of which failed to find the differences that stereotypes suggest (e.g. Dubois & Crouch 1976). Other studies find some of the suggested differences but only in certain contexts (e.g. Crosby & Nyquist 1977, Jay 1980) or connected with gender through other intervening variables like power (e.g. O'Barr & Atkins 1980). Such findings suggest that the phenomena involved are situationally sensitive rather than attributable simply to speakers' gender. There has also been recent linguistic research on the WL question in other languages (see e.g. Light 1982 on Chinese, Shibamoto 1985 on Japanese, and a number of the papers in Philips *et al.* 1987).

Frequential gender markers that are not generated by strategic choices or tied to other intervening variables like social status generally indicate gender-differentiated social networks. Do such markers, which are found,

demonstrate the existence of 'genderlects'? There have been some sophisticated quantitative studies that find low level phonetic and morphosyntactic
variation statistically linked to speaker sex (see e.g. Nichols 1983; Trudgill
1983, Chapters 9 and 10) within particular communities. Syntactic variation
has been studied less often than phonological, in part due to greater difficulties in defining the unit that 'varies.' (See Lavandera 1978; the crucial
point is that different syntactic constructions often differ in function, unlike
alternative phonetic realizations of a single underlying phonological segment.) Some evidence has been offered, however, of statistically significant
links between syntactic variants and speaker sex both in English (e.g.
Philips 1983) and in other languages (e.g. Japanese, as reported in
Shibamoto 1985). And Guy (Chapter 3 in this volume) provides other
examples of quantitative studies of systematic variation correlated with
speaker sex, including lexical and intonational variants as well as differences
in segmental phonology and syntax.

When systematic variation is found, some theorists incorporate it into a
grammar with variable rules. Though language users clearly are capable of
regulating their speech to achieve a certain frequency of realization of
variable units, showing sensitivity to and tacit knowledge of statistical
regularities, what underlies this capability seems to me cognitively quite
distinct from what underlies (categorical) grammatical knowledge. But even
if we do take frequencies of alternative variants to be specified by the
linguistic system, to be part of what an individual knows (perhaps a distinct
'variable rule' module in her grammar), it would be appropriate to speak of
'genderlects' only if the frequency setting of *individual* grammars were
directly linked to gender; to the extent that variationists focus on *group* data
within a community they show us nothing about what I would call
'genderlects,' individual gender-conditioned grammars.

Much of the empirical research on WL, not only in English but also in
other languages, suffers from the absence of any principled theory of how
and why gender phenomena might or might not interact with language
production. It can be useful to count surface structural features of actually
occurring corpuses and correlate these with gendered properties of the
speech situation: sex and (perceived) gender of speaker, sex and
(perceived) gender of hearer, gender relations of participants, gender
salience of situation. The more difficult and interesting step is explaining
correlations that do occur, detailing the mechanisms that produce them, and
it is this step that some investigators refuse to attempt, since in doing so they
would have to move beyond what is directly observable. (Hiatt 1977 is an
ambitious computer study of written texts that I criticize in McConnell-
Ginet 1979 for such limitations.) A recurring suggestion has been that
women tend to adopt the 'prestige' variant in their community more often

than men, but matters are more complicated than this (see e.g. Nichols 1980, 1983, 1984 for useful discussion); explanations of this putative tendency are at best limited (Trudgill's, 1983, is one of the more interesting).

One of the reasons Lakoff's work has been of continuing interest is that she does link her proposals to some kind of theory of why language use might show gender differentiation, proposing that WL signals womanliness through its connections with deference and unwillingness to assume responsibility for one's assertions. There are, of course, other interpretations of the features Lakoff associates with deferring and abrogating responsibility, as I and others have pointed out many times (see e.g. McConnell-Ginet 1983a for some alternatives that present a more positive view of women as linguistic agents), but what I want to emphasize here is the importance of Lakoff's recognition of the fact that investigations limited to what is directly observable and easy to count cannot explain how gender affects production.

Brown (1976, 1980) has contributed to development of a theoretical perspective on language and gender by proposing explicit links between micro-level linguistic variables and macro-level strategic patterns of language use involved in politeness and connecting those patterns to gender-differentiated social networks and relations in a particular ethnographic setting. Brown and Levinson (1978) develop a general theory of linguistic politeness as involving attention to both positive and negative 'face needs' of conversational interactants. Positive face is connected to being identified with others and their interests and social connections. Negative face is tied to respect for others' rights, individual integrity or autonomy. It is possible to show concern for both positive and negative face (which is what the Mexican women whom Brown studied did with other women and with men), although there is tension between them. Certain forms can be seen as indicative of the agent's attending to positive-face needs of the audience (e.g. Brown so categorized a Tzeltzal diminutive particle in the Mexican community she studied) and others as indicative of attention to negative-face needs (e.g. certain adverbial modifiers that 'soften' or ameliorate directives). Given a functional analysis of the forms, counting them *can* provide information about strategies. The change of emphasis from a system one acquires simply by virtue of one's social identity to a set of strategies one develops to manage social interactions is one of the most promising developments in research on language production and producer's gender.

Looking at the significance of the forms produced, especially those whose function is primarily to handle social relations, can put WL questions in a different light. Brown and Levinson's politeness model suggests some useful hypotheses as to why and how forms produced might both reflect and maintain male dominance. In egalitarian relations, negative politeness shows mutual respect, tending to suggest distance, and positive politeness suggests intimacy or affection, associated with closeness. To give negative politeness attests to the recipient's independence, whereas to give positive politeness can imply the recipient's vulnerability to the giver's good offices. In stratified relations, the inferior is generally constrained to give (the semblance of) negative politeness and receive (the semblance of) positive, which explains, I think, why we find again and again that the form used in situations of distance between equals (e.g. German *Sie*) is required usage from the inferior speaking 'up,' the one used in situations of closeness (e.g. German *du*) is freely permitted to the superior speaking 'down.' Brown and Gilman's classic study (1960) of the 'pronouns of power and solidarity' notes this conjunction but does not really show why it is so pervasive and useful to those who want to mask coercive power relations as ordinary social relations of interdependence. McConnell-Ginet (1978) and Wolfson and Manes (1980) study the sexual politics of address in light of this 'ambiguity.' What we have is less an ambiguity than a form whose linguistic significance – perhaps in this case something like attention to positive face – does not say what particular aims and motives speakers have in producing it. That is, the (very) general content is compatible with a variety of different, more specific, interactional moves. You may consider your address form or your compliment an act of friendship, but I may hear it as condescending or manipulative; I may intend my rising intonation to encourage you to continue, but you may hear it as insecure or deferential (McConnell-Ginet 1983b). The linguistic forms themselves support such sharply divergent functions. Goffman (1977) notes that 'the arrangement between the sexes' in our culture is constructed on the model of that between parents and their children, involving *both* affection and asymmetrical control; this observation helps explain the ambivalence of what we say to one another, the complex significance of cross-sex power and solidarity.

5.2. Meaning: expressing content and announcing attitudes

Research on gender and language production focussed initially on two issues. How do women (and men) speak? How are they spoken (or not spoken) of? My first course on language and gender was organized around these headings, with little connection between them. We have seen above that the first question is only one small part of a much larger one: how does gender affect language production? The second question raises issues of 'sexist language'; see e.g. Schulz 1975, Stanley 1978, the papers in Vetterling-Braggin 1981, and many other sources for documentation of the derogation, sexualization, and homogenization of female reference, the universalization of male reference, and other aspects of the expression of misogynistic and sexually biased content. But the second question is also ultimately unduly restrictive. Rather than focussing just on how we are spoken of (or not spoken of), I want to draw attention to a more general question: how does gender affect what (and how) agents *mean* by their linguistic productions?

In meaning, agents are both *expressing content* and *announcing themselves and their attitudes*, roughly the functions Brown and Yule (1983) dub *transactional* and *interactional*, respectively. Languages, interpreted systems, assign content or content structures; we present ourselves and convey our attitudes only in situated language use. Content is the message: its expression is accompanied by meta-messages that situate the content in particular social contexts, provide guides to how that expression should be understood and acted upon, announce the agent's stance towards the message.

Attitudes ('women are the eternal mystery') and self-presentation (e.g. certain kinds of gender perspectives) may themselves actually be part of content, of what the speaker expresses. Content, however, is never a component of interactional meaning, an asymmetry which partly explains the focus of linguistic semantics on content. Nonetheless, the content one expresses is a powerful indicator of attitudes and the act and form of its expression often an important element in the construction of social relations. Van Dijk (1984) notes, for example, that expression of negative attitudes towards ethnic minorities by white Dutch 'majority' speakers (whose audience is also from the same group though an unknown interviewer rather than a friend) frequently involves strategies designed to forestall negative judgements of the expresser as racist. Thus content and social significance interact.

Many analysts assume that the 'illocutionary attitudes' the agent means (e.g. whether she is performing the speech act of asserting or one of inquiring) belong to content. To mean a particular illocutionary attitude, however, is to mean the expressed content to have a particular sort of effect on the context: conveying illocutionary attitudes involves conveying a 'meta-message' about where this particular content is to fit in the whole transaction. The same linguistic expression can be used with radically different illocutionary 'forces,' but such multiple functioning seems less like ordinary content ambiguity than like the tension noted above between whether the expression of familiarity stems from closeness or from disrespect. (Like any other attitudes, the illocutionary ones may themselves be part of expressed content: e.g. 'I claim that . . .'). Illocutionary meaning, however, is different from other kinds of interactional meaning in being a virtually ubiquitous accompaniment of the expression of content and essential to an agent's meaning anything at all. It is like them in being radically underdetermined by linguistic form and thus heavily context-dependent.

Genderized expression of meaning and interpretive conflicts emerge often in interactional meaning, where assumptions about goals and about one another's personal positions are especially critical. Tag questions and rising intonations on declaratives, for example, are primarily of interactional significance and have multiple functions (e.g. indicating willingness to engage in further talk or a relatively low commitment to one's assertion); it is not surprising that the meaning recipients assign them does not always coincide with what their producers intend to convey.

Meaning and language production are, of course, intimately connected to one another: in order to mean anything at all, a person must become an illocutionary agent, a producer of linguistic expressions endowed with significance, with meaning. The basic conception of what it is for an agent, a speaker or writer, to mean something by producing some linguistic expression directed towards some potential recipient(s), hearers or readers, I draw from Grice (1957). My reformulation goes like this:

> Agent A means utterance U to express content C and a particular attitude towards that content to recipient(s) R just in case (i) A intends U to direct R's attention towards C and to give grounds for R to think that A has the attitude in question towards C, and (ii) A intends this effect on R to be produced by virtue of R's recognizing that A does so intend.

There are problems with this (and with other formulations), but it retains Grice's two central ideas. First, the agent's intentions are of crucial importance: to mean is to engage in a certain kind of intentional action. Second, however, what the agent can mean, can intend to express by some utterance U, is constrained by what effects she can reasonably expect (or hope) to produce in the recipient(s) by virtue of his (their) recognition of her so intending: to mean is to engage in a social action.

Intentions to mean – 'illocutionary' aims (Austin 1962) – are fulfilled simply in being recognized, in being comprehended. In contrast, intentions to persuade, dissuade, comfort, impress, delight, frighten, or amuse – 'perlocutionary' aims – are easily recognized without being fulfilled. We are not surprised, therefore, to find sexual bias affecting accomplishment of these perlocutionary aims, a bias often reflected in evaluations of women's language productions. (Baron 1986 provides historical perspective on how women's speech has been evaluated, and Ostriker 1986 examines the genderized language of critical discourse about women's poetry.) It may be somewhat more surprising to discover that women can suffer discrimination even in obtaining understanding, in conveying what they mean, quite apart from how people judge its efficacy or the quality of its expression. We might want to say that to ensure understanding, an agent need only say exactly what she means, i.e. choose words and syntactic constructions whose linguistic meaning expresses exactly the content she seeks to convey.

My Gricean-type definition of what the speaker means makes no reference to linguistic meaning at all, says nothing about what linguistic expressions –as opposed to language producers – mean. Grice (1982) identifies linguistic meaning with social norms that regulate what agents are to mean in their productions of particular expressions. Familiar approaches to linguistic meaning analyze a language as assigning semantic values of some appropriate type to linguistic expressions, with recursive principles for combining word and phrasal meanings to yield sentential content. The Gricean definition is sometimes thought of as just delineating how agents can mean more than what they explicitly say (indirectness as in 'would you happen to know what time it is?' as a request that the addressee tell the speaker what time it is) or even something different (nonliteralness of various kinds or even mistakes). But even when the agent's intentions are to say exactly what she means, the Gricean account still does some work; the agent can be said to intend to invoke mutual knowledge of the language system assigning the desired interpretation. In fact, it will generally be presumed that the linguistically assigned meaning is part of common background (cf. the 'linguistic presumption' discussed in Bach & Harnish 1979) and that this linguistic meaning is intended to play a role in identifying what the speaker means.

The fundamental aim an agent must have in her act of meaning is to be understood, to communicate – and to direct this act (at least potentially) to an audience beyond herself. This is built into the Gricean definition. Sometimes communication of content is most crucial, whereas at other times adopting a social stance is what has primacy. But to get started at all, one must be able to speak or to write, to produce linguistic expressions for apprehension (and in the happy case, comprehension) by others. This can be problematic.

Conversation is not an equal-opportunity activity. For example, West and Zimmerman (1983) find men pushing women off the conversational floor, taking longer turns and more of them in cross-sex conversations and even disrupting the turn-taking system by interruptions that 'violate' the current speaker's rights to sole occupancy of the conversational floor until the end of her current unit. On the basis of detailed analysis of conversations of three heterosexual couples, Fishman (1983) argues that women bear a disproportionate share of the maintenance work in cross-sex conversations, helping men develop their topics through providing minimal encouraging responses (*mmhmm*), asking questions, and listening. In contrast, the men did not so help their female conversational partners, whose attempts to develop their own topics tended quickly to run out of steam through the men's nonresponsiveness. Interruptions and topic control typically mark the dominant person in overtly stratified pairs: doctor–patient, employer–employee, parent–child.

Still what happens is not fully explained by pointing to male privilege and dominance. Edelsky (1981) has proposed that women fare much better when conversationalists suspend the 'one at a time' rule that usually prevails in favor of a 'shared floor.' Her analysis found some instances of mutual talk that was not interruptive; this occurred when participants knew one another well and were very much engaged in the conversation. Under such conditions, women and men produced roughly the same amounts of talk. There has been relatively little of this kind of analysis of single-sex conversations, although Goodwin (1980a) compared boys' and girls' play groups, with particular focus on the form in which directives were cast, finding that the boys tended to use bald imperatives whereas the girls tended to use forms like *let's* and *why don't we*.

Maltz and Borker (1982) draw from this and related research two different normative models of conversation, which, they hypothesize, girls and boys develop in their (mainly single-sex) peer groups. The boys learn to use language to create and maintain dominance hierarchies; the girls create horizontal ties through their words and negotiate shifting alliances. Drawing on Maltz and Borker's analysis, Tannen (1986, Chapter 8) suggests that adult women and men bring different expectations of their conversational partners to cross-sex conversations, that we come from different 'cultures' that have shaped our views of conversation.

This picture of gender-differentiated conversation models is based on limited populations and does not address the influence of ethnicity, social class, or the demands of particular situations. Nonetheless, there seems to be some support for the notion that middle class American women and men typically learn, in their childhood social groups, to structure discourse in different ways. This may explain some of the prevalent patterns of cross-sex conversational problems. Especially suggestive is Tannen's (1986) claim that 'women are more attuned than men to the meta-messages of talk,' by which she means what is 'implicated' over and above what is explicitly said. Meta-messages frequently (though not exclusively) involve social and interpersonal dimensions of meaning; analysts have suggested that those dimensions often also enter into women's messages, are part of their overtly expressed content (see e.g. Harding 1975, Goodwin 1980b, Hughes 1985, Cazden & Michaels 1985).

Two main suggestions of the research on gender and conversational interaction are relevant for present purposes. First, in trying to mean, 'she' may pay more attention than 'he' to whether her intentions can be expected to be recognized by their intended recipient: she tends to be more attuned to the social dimensions of her acts of meaning and the attendant potential problems. Her cultural experience provides a less individualistic view of the world and recognizes more social interdependence. Second, to the extent that men dominate language production where audiences include both sexes – not only cross-sex conversations but also public speaking to mixed-sex audiences and writing for mixed-sex readership – a 'woman's eye' view of the world will be less familiar to the general (mixed-sex) public than a 'man's eye' view. There is not *a* view of the world common to members of each sex. The point is rather that men (and dominant groups generally) can be expected to have made disproportionately large contributions to the stock of generally available background beliefs and values on which speakers and writers rely in their attempts to mean and which are particularly critical in attempts to mean to an unfamiliar audience.

These observations may help us to understand charges of sexism in language and, more generally, claims that women are a 'muted' group, denied the 'power of naming' and linguistically alienated (see e.g. Spender 1980, Kramarae 1981 and from the perspective of literary theory, Showalter 1982). My aim is to suggest something of the mechanisms through which social privilege leads to a kind of linguistic privilege, making it appear that the language itself supports the interests and reflects the outlook of those with privilege (by virtue of sex or class or race), that the language itself resists threats to that privilege. The appearance is not illusory, although it is not a language (an interpreted system) but language (use) that helps subordinate women (and other dominated groups).

Socially directed intentions play a role both in cases where what is *meant* is different from what is *said* (linguistically assigned meaning) and in cases where the two coincide. To succeed in meaning more than what one's sentences themselves express, an agent relies on general principles (e.g. that utterances will be assumed 'relevant') plus whatever can be taken as part of the mutually accessible background. For example, precedent and assumed accessibility of negative appraisals of women's intellectual powers make it easy for someone to mean to insult by an utterance of 'you think just like a woman,' harder to do so by an utterance of 'you think just like a man' (though with the right audience, the second sentence might be the more powerful insulter). What is successfully conveyed implicitly by uttering an expression can eventually, by virtue of precedents, become conveyed explicitly by that very same expression: this has apparently happened to *sissy* and *hussy*, for example (see McConnell-Ginet 1984). To understand 'you think like a woman' as an insult a hearer need only recognize the general accessibility of devaluation of women's thinking; she need not accept it. On the other hand, a speaker who means to insult through uttering 'you think like a woman' and succeeds in so doing may (perhaps mis-

91

takenly) take his success to signal his hearer's agreement with the negative appraisal he depends on. Since she sees that he intends to insult, she might respond with 'no, I don't' and simply mean thereby 'no, I am not shallow, irrational, etc.' He, on the other hand, might take her to accept his implicit negtive evaluation of women's thinking but to be dissociating herself from the general run of women. Because that negative evaluation remains implicit when she replies 'no, I don't,' it is likely to go unchallenged, and the subsequent discussion may even reinforce its hold.

The general point is that in order to mean, agents presuppose, take things for granted, and that what can be taken for granted depends on what has been (often and audibly) expressed and can be assumed to be readily accessible. Views that are little heard, that are not common currency, can reliably function as background only in linguistic exchanges between familiars. Such views will not contribute to general patterns of meaning more than what is said and thus they will not leave their mark on standard interpretations (the *hussy* case). Lewis (1979: 172) claims that there is a rule of accommodation for presupposition; namely, that 'if at time t something is said that requires presupposition P to be acceptable, and if P is not presupposed just before t, then – *ceteris paribus* [unlikely in a world of unequal speakers] and within certain limits – presupposition P comes into existence.' But not all speakers are assumed to be saying something acceptable, and accommodation is especially unlikely if what is said is in conflict with what might generally be thought presupposed. Views that are common currency cannot easily be ignored, even by those who challenge or disavow them. To devise reasonable strategies for being understood, agents must take account of what their audience is likely to take for granted – not necessarily to believe, but to treat as the 'unmarked' opinion.

In attempting to speak literally and directly, agents must presuppose access to an *interpreted* language system, must take for granted standard assignments of semantic value. For words, semantic values are sometimes thought of as feature sets or 'definitions' in terms of necessary and sufficient conditions for application of the word. On this view, we can count on others to understand because we can count on their assigning the same features or applying the same definition as we do. Definitions or feature sets in individual agents' heads 'regulate' their (literal) usage of expressions. But there are problems of several kinds with this picture, among which are vagueness and instability of criteria for using expressions.

The alternative view that I want to sketch here is the radical one, developed in several of the articles in Putnam 1975, that 'meanings [of syntactically simple expressions] ain't in the head,' which is to say that we can't always regulate our usage for communicative purposes by reference to our individual cognitive constructs. People use many words for which they have at best limited knowledge of criterial features, words for which they lack a definition. What guides the ordinary person in using the word *gold*, for example, is what Putnam calls a stereotype of gold, a set of widely held beliefs or presumptions about gold, that may sometimes lead to labeling as gold what is really pyrites. This doesn't mean that in the ordinary person's language, what *gold* means allows it to be applied to pyrites; it just means that the ordinary person talks about gold without being able to tell definitively what is and what is not gold, and thus can sometimes misapply the word. Suggestively, Putnam speaks of a 'linguistic division of labor': there is a scientific theory that distinguishes gold from pyrites, which some scientists know. The rest of us intend to use *gold* to speak about the same 'natural kind' of stuff that the scientific experts call gold, though we are sometimes fooled by the superficial appearance of pyrites.

Expertise seems straightforward in the case of identifying gold. It becomes problematic, however, when we turn to words and concepts that play a role in our informal, everyday theories of ourselves and our social world, our values and our ideologies. A fairly simple case that has been much discussed is that of the pronoun *he*, over whose interpretation there has been considerable dispute. In contexts of reference to a specific person, *he* unambiguously conveys maleness: 'someone$_i$ is at the door but I don't know who he$_i$ is' implies the maleness of the unknown person. In contexts where femaleness has been made explicit or is especially salient, it is difficult to use *he* even where there is no reference to a specific individual: *any boy or girl who thinks that !? he knows the answer . . .*' is generally judged bizarre. Yet prescriptive grammar enjoins English users to use *he* when the antecedent is a sex-indefinite generic: *when the child is around two, he will . . .* is a familiar kind of example.

Martyna (1980, 1983) has investigated *he–man* language. One thing she has shown is that women and men tend to produce *he* in somewhat different contexts, with men more likely than women to adopt the so-called masculine generic uses. On the other hand, women interpreting *he* in such contexts are a bit less likely to infer that maleness is somehow meant. Why might it matter what interpretations are assigned to pronouns? Because the interpretations assigned play a role in what speakers can do by means of uttering sentences containing those pronouns. Allowing the same form to be interpreted so that it presumes maleness in the case of specific reference makes it problematic to connect that form to cases where maleness is ostensibly not presumed. For such connections to work reliably requires tacit appeal to a theory that people are male unless proven otherwise, that femaleness is contrasted with maleness in being a special and distinctive form of humanness, a marginal condition. That such a theory does still operate was made clear to me once again when I heard a radio commentary on the November 1984 Mondale–Ferraro defeat. Some Democrat suggested that the party should draw the moral that it can not identify with 'marginal' and 'special interest' groups – blacks, the handicapped, union members. Rather, this man went on, we must recognize that the 'average voter is a white middle class male.' Given that more women are registered and vote than men, we know this politician must mean 'average' in a quite special normative and not a statistical sense. In other words, this man made explicit the semantic connection between typicality and maleness which I have suggested is implicit in norms that urge us to use *he* when presumptions are not being made about sex.

The challenge to the prescriptively endorsed 'meaning' of *he* is a challenge to a view of the world in which human beings are presumed to be male unless proven otherwise, which helps us understand why it is resisted so vigorously. In principle, one can learn to apply *he* in the generic cases without accepting the theoretical perspective that connects those uses with those in which *he* refers to a specific individual. Still, it is rather difficult to *mean* a genuinely sex-indefinite *he*, simply because one can not rely on audiences to recognize that one does not intend to suggest maleness.

I want to reemphasize that I am not suggesting monolithic women's and men's views of the world. In McConnell-Ginet 1985b, I discussed how a large body of feminist discourse has been structured around the essentially semantic question of what being a lesbian means. Should we define 'lesbian' as a matter of psychosocial orientation towards women, as a 'continuum' of concern with and interest in women, as a political stance in opposition to patriarchy, as an erotic choice? Women writing in the past decade or two have urged these and other meanings. Feminism has assigned multiple meanings to lesbianism, but it is not just a matter of 'ambiguity.' Much of this discourse *proposes* meanings, *urges* them, as part of constructing a theory and politics of sexuality, sexual oppression, desire. These are couched as questions of semantics but they are not thereby insubstantial.

Given that a 'question of semantics' is often a 'question of values and action,' we can see that linguistic agents cannot always take shared access to a particular interpreted language for granted. Indeed, one thing linguistic agents and their interpreters do is negotiate some kind of accord on interpretation, choose among what we can think of as alternative interpretations of the (underinterpreted) system they do share. I suggest that it is precisely because natural languages are themselves so relatively empty of meaning, so 'formal,' that language users are able to do so very much with their words, indeed are forced to interpret those words actively. Expressions in formal systems are uninterpreted; it is their multiple interpretive possibilities that make them so useful for modeling diverse domains. Similarly, it is the multiple interpretive possibilities afforded us by natural languages that allow us to use those languages in developing our common thoughts, shaping our desires, and planning what we will do. Interpretation of natural language systems, endowing linguistic forms with significance, is not primarily a matter of identifying form–meaning links, of encoding and decoding. Interpretation is much more an active process, a socially situated and sometimes socially divisive construction of meaning.

The Gricean definition assigns the agent authority over what is meant; after all, it is agentive intentions that are crucial. But since those intentions are directed towards a recipient and are reflexive in the sense that the recipient is intended to recognize them and intended to recognize that he is intended to recognize them, the agent is not free to intend any meaning whatsoever. I might want to mean just something about humanity in my use of *he*, but I now have substantial reservations about the possibility of so meaning, reservations that block my forming certain intentions. And of course people can be less than candid about their intentions, sometimes even deceiving themselves. In many cases, there are established conventional meanings for linguistic expressions and often acknowledged 'experts' whom we depend on for regulating usage. What it is important to remember is that (1) those meanings are typically supported by background beliefs or 'theories,' often implicit and sometimes ungrounded and biased, and (2) their being 'conventional' is a matter of social prescription to use only certain interpretations of a language system, to use only certain 'languages,' prescriptions enforced by social privilege. The agent who challenges such prescriptions can only succeed where she is empowered by alternative *socially* endorsed practices (see Scheman 1980 on a new conception of anger arising in consciousness-raising groups).

In what ways does language shape the message(s), what agents mean? How do meanings get 'authorized,' inscribed in the culture's collective repertoire? Is there a politics of meaning? Which messages are conveyed to whom? How is gender implicated in what is meant? In what sense does language 'construct' gender? Does language 'define' women as unimportant, properly subservient to men? If so, what are the mechanisms? Frank and Treichler (forthcoming) include discussion of these issues (see especially Treichler's contribution). Kramarae and Treichler (1985) present some 'women's words,' which offer alternative perspectives on human beings and their relations (and also on language itself). And Trömmel-Plötz (1982, discussed in Mey 1984), proposes a vision of women using language to 'change the world,' especially the world of women's oppression. I have been able only to hint at the richness of these issues and some ways they can be fruitfully addressed.

In conclusion, three points should be emphasized. First, gender is not simply a matter of individual characteristics (e.g. sex) but also involves actions and social relations, ideology and politics. Second, patterns of language production depend on more than just the agent's intrinsic characteristics, her sociolinguistic 'identity:' they also reflect her assessment of social situations and her choice of strategies for the linguistic construction of her social relations (not just to men but to other women as well). Third, meaning interacts with gender because it links the social/psychological phenomenon of language with the abstract formal notion of a language, an interpreted linguistic system. The individual (what she means, her intentions) is also here inextricably enmeshed in the social (the constraints on the intentions she can have recognized and thereby realized, the social support required for invoking interpretations). In sum, a theory that accommodates the dual psychological and social nature of language and its relation to languages can help further understanding of gender and language.

REFERENCES

Abel, E. (ed.) 1982. *Writing and sexual difference*. Chicago: University of Chicago Press.
Austin, J. L. 1962. *How to do things with words*. Cambridge, MA: Harvard University Press.
Bach, K. & Harnish, R. M. 1979. *Linguistic communication and speech acts*. Cambridge, MA: MIT Press.
Baron, D. 1986. *Grammar and gender*. New Haven: Yale University Press.
Black, M. & Coward, R. 1981. Linguistic, social and sexual relations. *Screen Education* 39: 69–85.
Bodine, A. 1975. Sex differentiation in language. In Thorne & Henley 1975.
Borker, R. A. 1980. Anthropology: social and cultural perspectives. In McConnell-Ginet, Borker & Furman 1980.
Brouwer, D., Gerritsen, M. & de Haan, D. 1979. Speech differences between women and men: on the wrong track? *Language in Society* 8: 33–50.
Brown, G. & Yule, G. 1983. *Discourse analysis* (Cambridge Textbooks in Linguistics). Cambridge: Cambridge University Press.
Brown, P. 1976. Women and politeness: a new perspective on language and society. *Reviews in Anthropology* 3: 240–9.
Brown, P. 1980. How and why are women more polite: some evidence from a Mayan community. In McConnell-Ginet, Borker & Furman 1980.
Brown, P. & Levinson, S. 1978. Universals of language usage: politeness phenomena. In E. Goody (ed.) *Questions and politeness: strategies in social interaction* (Cambridge Papers in Social Anthropology 8). Cambridge: Cambridge University Press.
Brown, P. & Levinson, S. 1979. Social structure, groups, and interaction. In Scherer & Giles 1979.
Brown, R. & Gilman, A. 1960. The pronouns of power and solidarity. In T. Sebeok (ed.) *Style in language*. Cambridge, MA: MIT Press.
Cameron, D. 1985. *Feminism and linguistic theory*. New York: St Martin's Press.
Cazden, C. B. & Michaels, S. 1985. Gender differences in sixth grade children's letters in an electronic mail system. Paper presented at Boston University Child Language Conference, October 1985.
Crosby, F. & Nyquist, L. 1977. The female register: an empirical study of Lakoff's hypotheses. *Language in Society* 6: 313–22.
Dijk, T. van. 1984. *Prejudice in discourse*. (*Pragmatics and beyond*, Vol. 3.) Amsterdam: Benjamin.
Dubois, B. L. & Crouch, I. 1976. The question of tag questions in women's speech: they don't really use more of them, do they? ↓ *Language in Society* 4: 289–94.

Edelsky, C. 1976. Subjective reactions to sex-linked language. *Journal of Social Psychology* 99: 97–104.

Edelsky, C. 1977. Acquisition of an aspect of communicative competence: learning what it means to talk like a lady. In S. Ervin-Tripp and C. Mitchell-Kernan (eds.) *Child discourse*. New York: Academic Press.

Edelsky, C. 1981. Who's got the floor? *Language in Society* 10: 383–421.

Ekka, F. 1972. Men's and women's speech in Kũrux. *Linguistics* 81: 25–31.

Fishman, P. M. 1983. Interaction: the work women do. In Thorne, Kramarae & Henley 1983.

Flannery, R. 1946. Men's and women's speech in Gros Ventre. *International Journal of American Linguistics* 12: 133-5.

Frank, F. W. & Treichler, P. A. (eds.) forthcoming. *Language, gender and scholarly writing: MLA guidelines for nonsexist usage*. New York: Modern Language Association Publications.

Furfey, P. H. 1944. Men's and women's language. *The American Catholic Sociological Review* 5: 218–23.

Gal, S. 1978. Peasant men can't get wives: language change and sex roles in a bilingual community. *Language and Society* 7: 1–16.

Goffman, E. 1977. The arrangement between the sexes. *Theory and Society* 4: 301–31.

Goodwin, M. H. 1980a. Directive–response speech sequences in girls' and boys' task activities. In McConnell-Ginet, Borker & Furman 1980.

Goodwin, M. H. 1980b. He-said-she-said: formal cultural procedures for the construction of a gossip dispute activity. *American Ethnologist* 7: 674–95.

Grice, H. P. 1957. Meaning. *Philosophical Review* 66: 377–88.

Grice, H. P. 1982. More on meaning. In N. V. Smith (ed.) *Mutual knowledge*. New York: Academic Press.

Haas, A. 1979. Male and female spoken language differences: stereotypes and evidence. *Psychological Bulletin* 86: 616–26.

Haas, M. R. 1944. Men's and women's speech in Koasati. *Language* 20: 142–9. Reprinted in D. Hymes (ed.) 1964. *Language in culture and society*. New York: Harper & Row.

Hakuta, K. 1986. *Mirror of language: the debate on bilingualism*. New York: Basic Books.

Harding, S. 1975. Women and words in a Spanish village. In R. Reiter (ed.) *Towards an anthropology of women*. New York: Monthly Review Press.

Hiatt, M. 1977. *The way women write*. New York: Teachers College Press.

Hughes, L. A. 1985. How girls play the game. Paper presented at the Annual Meetings of the Association for the Anthropological Study of Play and The Society for Applied Anthropology.

Jay, T. B. 1980. Sex roles and dirty word usage: a review of the literature and a reply to Haas. *Psychological Bulletin* 88: 614–21.

Kramarae, C. 1981. *Women and men speaking: frameworks for analysis*. Rowley: Newbury House.

Kramarae, C., Treichler, P. A. with assistance from A. Russo. 1985. *A feminist dictionary*. Boston and London: Pandora Press (Routledge & Kegan Paul).

Kramer, C. 1974. Stereotypes of women's speech: the word from cartoons. *Journal of Popular Culture* 8: 624–30.

Kramer, C. 1978. Male and female perceptions of male and female speech. *Language and Speech* 20.2: 151–61.

Laberge, S. & Sankoff, G. 1980. Anything *you* can do. In G. Sankoff (ed.) *The social life of language*. Philadelphia: University of Pennsylvania Press.

Lakoff, R. 1975. *Language and woman's place*. New York: Harper & Row.

Lavandera, B. 1978. Where does the sociolinguistic variable stop? *Language in Society* 7: 171–83.

Levinson, S. C. 1983. *Pragmatics* (Cambridge Textbooks in Linguistics). Cambridge: Cambridge University Press.

Lewis, D. 1975. Languages and language. In K. Gunderson (ed.) *Language, mind, and knowledge: Minnesota studies in the philosophy of science 3*. Minneapolis: University of Minnesota Press.

Lewis, D. 1979. Scorekeeping in a language game. In R. Bäuerle, U. Egli & A. von Stechow (eds.) *Semantics from different points of view*. Berlin: Springer Verlag.

Light, T. 1982. On being *deing*: how women's language is perceived in Chinese. *Computational Analyses of Asian and African Languages* 19: 21–49.

Maltz, D. N. & Borker, R. A. 1982. A cultural approach to male–female miscommunication. In J. J. Gumperz (ed.) *Communication, language, and social identity*. Cambridge: Cambridge University Press.

Martyna, W. 1980. The psychology of the generic masculine. In McConnell-Ginet, Borker & Furman 1980.

Martyna, W. 1983. Beyond the he/man approach: the case for nonsexist language. In Thorne, Kramarae & Henley 1983.

McConnell-Ginet, S. 1978. Address forms in sexual politics. In D. R. Butturff & E. J. Epstein (eds.) *Women's language and style*. Akron: University of Akron Press.

McConnell-Ginet, S. 1979. Review of Hiatt 1977. *Language in Society* 8: 466–9.

McConnell-Ginet, S. 1983a. Review of Orasanu, J., Slater, M. K. & Adler, L. L. (eds.) 1979. *Language, sex and gender: does 'La différence' make a difference?* and Vetterling-Braggin 1981. *Language* 59: 373–91.

McConnell-Ginet, S. 1983b. Intonation in a man's world. In Thorne, Kramarae & Henley 1983.

McConnell-Ginet, S. 1984. The origins of sexist language in discourse. In S. J. White & V. Teller (eds.) *Discourses in reading and linguistics*. New York: Annals of the New York Academy of Sciences.

McConnell-Ginet, S. 1985a. Feminism in linguistics. In Treichler, Kramarae & Stafford 1985.

McConnell-Ginet, S. 1985b. 'It's just a question of semantics.' Paper delivered at the Annual Meetings of the Anthropological Association of America, Session on Interpretation.

McConnell-Ginet, S., Borker, R. A. & Furman, N. (eds.) 1980. *Women and language in literature and society*. New York: Praeger.

Mey, J. 1984. Sex and language revisited: can women's language change the world? *Journal of Pragmatics* 8: 261–83.

Nichols, P. 1980. Women in their speech communities. In McConnell-Ginet, Borker, and Furman 1980.

Nichols, P. 1983. Linguistic options and choices for black women in the rural South. In Thorne, Kramarae & Henley 1983.

Nichols, P. 1984. Networks and hierarchies: language and social stratification. In C. Kramarae, M. Schulz & W. M. O'Barr (eds.) *Language and power*, Beverly Hills: Sage.

O'Barr, W., Atkins, B. K. 1980. 'Women's language' or 'powerless language'? In McConnell-Ginet, Borker & Furman 1980.

Ostriker, A. S. 1986. *Stealing the language: the emergence of women's poetry in America*. Boston: Beacon Press.

Pettigrew, T. F. 1979. The ultimate attribution error: extending Allport's cognitive analysis of prejudice. *Personality and Social Psychology Bulletin* 5: 461–76.

Philips, S. U. 1980. Sex differences and language. *Annual Review of Anthropology* 9: 523–44.

Philips, S. U. 1983. The interaction of variable syntax and discourse structure in gender-differentiated speech in the courtroom. Paper presented at NEH Conference on Sex Differences in Language, University of Arizona. Revised version in Philips, Steele & Tanz forthcoming.

Philips, S. U., Steele, S. & Tanz, C. (eds.) 1987. *Language, gender and sex in comparative perspective*. Cambridge: Cambridge University Press.

Putnam, H. 1975. *Philosophical paper II: mind, language and reality*. Cambridge: Cambridge University Press.

Ruthven, K. K. 1984. *Feminist literary studies: an introduction*. Cambridge: Cambridge University Press.

Sapir, E. 1929. Male and female forms of speech in Yana. In D. G. Mandelbaum, (ed.) 1951. *Selected writings of Edward Sapir*. Berkeley: University of California Press.

Scheman, N. 1980. Anger and the politics of naming. In McConnell-Ginet, Borker & Furman 1980.

Scherer, K. R. & Giles, H. (eds.) 1979. *Social markers in speech*. Cambridge: Cambridge University Press.

Schulz, M. R. 1975. The semantic derogation of women. In Thorne and Henley 1975.

Sherzer, Joel. 1983. Ethnography of speaking and men's and women's speech differences. Paper presented at the NEH Sex Differences in Language Conference, University of Arizona, January 1983. Revised version in Philips, Steele & Tanz forthcoming.

Shibamoto, J. S. 1985. *Japanese women's language*. New York: Academic Press.

Showalter, E. 1982. Feminist criticism in the wilderness. In Abel 1982.

Siegler, D. M. & Siegler, R. S. 1976. Stereotypes of males' and females' speech. *Psychological Reports* 39: 167–70.

Smith, P. M. 1979. Sex markers in speech. In Scherer & Giles, 1979.

Smith, P. M. 1985. *Language, the sexes and society*. Oxford: Blackwell.

Spender, D. 1980. *Man made language*. London: Routledge & Kegan Paul.

Stanback, M. H. 1985. Language and black woman's place: evidence from the black middle class. In Treichler, Kramarae & Stafford 1985.

Stanley, J. 1978. Sexist language. *College English* 39: 800–11.

Tannen, D. 1986. *That's not what I meant!: how conversational style makes or breaks your relations with others*. New York: Morrow.

Taylor, A. R. 1983. 'Male' and 'female' speech in Gros Ventre. *Anthropological Linguistics* 24: 301–7.

Thorne, B. & Henley, N. (eds.) 1975. *Language and sex: difference and dominance*. Rowley, Newbury House.

Thorne, B., Kramarae, C. & Henley, N. (eds.) 1983. *Language, gender and society*. Rowley: Newbury House.

Treichler, P. A. forthcoming. From discourse to dictionary: how sexist meanings are authorized. In Frank & Treichler forthcoming.

Treichler, P. A. & Kramarae, C. 1983. Women's talk in the ivory tower. *Communication Quarterly* 31: 118–32.

Treichler, P. A., Kramarae, C. & Stafford, B. (eds.) 1985. *For Alma Mater: theory and practice in feminist scholarship*. Urbana: University of Illinois Press.

Trömmel-Plötz, S. 1982. *Frauensprache – Sprache der Veränderung*. Frankfurt-am-Main: Fischer.

Trudgill, P. 1983. *On dialect: social and geographical perspectives*. Oxford: Blackwell.

Valian, V. 1977. Linguistics and feminism. Reprinted in Vetterling-Braggin 1981.

Vetterling-Braggin, M. (ed.) 1981. *Sexist language: a modern philosophical analysis*. Totowa: Littlefield, Adams & Co.

West, C. & Zimmerman, D. 1983. Small insults: a study of interruptions in cross-sex conversations between unacquainted persons. In Thorne, Kramarae & Henley, 1983.

Wolfson, N. & Manes, J. 1980. 'Don't "dear" me.' In McConnell-Ginet, Borker & Furman 1980.

6 Bilingualism

Bernard Spolsky

6.0. Introduction

The topic of bilingualism (a term that generally includes multilingualism; cf. Weinreich 1953: 1) fits appropriately under many headings in a taxonomy of linguistic fields such as the one that forms the basis for this Survey. That people can and do know and use more than one language sets interesting and critical challenges to numerous subfields of the language sciences. One could therefore expect to find it treated in chapters dealing with neurolinguistics (are bilingual brains different?), with language processing (when a person is bilingual, are the two languages stored and processed separately?), with second language learning (by definition the study of how some people become bilingual), with pidgin studies (for speakers of pidgins are bilingual), with language death (as bilinguals give up on the use of one language in favor of another), and with language and education (for the usual aim of language education is to add control of one or more extra varieties of language).

The importance of the topic also means that there is a vast literature to review. Anyone seeking such an overview might safely start with any one of a number of reviews of the field: those which shaped its study, such as Weinreich 1953 or Haugen 1956, or which have charted its progress since then, such as Haugen 1973, Mackey 1976, Spolsky 1976 or, most recently, Grosjean 1982.

Definitions of the field naturally abound; just as even non-normativist linguists prefer not to accept the most popular meaning for the name of the profession, so we are unhappy with the common meaning ascribed to the term *bilingual*; as Haugen (1973) points out, if we count as a bilingual only someone with equal and native command of two or more languages, we exclude the vast majority of cases and are left with the least interesting. In practice, then, scholars in the field treat bilingualism as a relative rather than an absolute phenomenon, and consider anyone able to produce (or even understand) sentences in more than one language as the proper object of their study; the explanation of different levels of control of the two or more languages (or varieties) then becomes an issue of central theoretical concern.

The focus of interest varies from scholar to scholar. Neurolinguists find bilingualism a challenging phenomenon for speculating on differential localization of language and its parts. General and comparative linguists, following on Weinreich's point that language contact takes place in the head of a bilingual, have been concerned about the resulting relationships between the two languages. Psycholinguists (following Leopold's pioneering work) have concentrated on the ontogeny of bilingualism. Educational linguists have found a major field of application in the general problem of language education in multilingual settings and the specific solutions associated with the term *bilingual education*. Language planners study and try to control the political, social and economic effects of the creation and existence of linguistic minorities who are usually forced to bilingualism and often to language shift. Amidst this plethora, a simple listing of the names of researchers (let alone a short bibliography) would quickly exhaust my space limitations and the reader's patience. I will therefore, arbitrarily, limit this review to a brief account of two topics (language spread and resulting patterns of national and societal multilingualism, and bilingual education), and devote the remainder of my space to a consideration of one topic of perhaps more theoretical interest, language choice.

6.1. Language spread

One of the best-established fields of linguistics has been the study of the nature of language change; one strong tradition focusses on changes in the distribution and function of languages in a society. Scholars interested in societal bilingualism and multilingualism are constantly forced to deal with the complex relations between synchronic and diachronic facts; just as sociolinguists have shown ways of studying sound changes in process, so students of societal multilingualism see it as their task not just to survey and describe existing situations, but also to look at the forces and processes that explain changes in the patterns of language use over time. Various terms have been used for the many approaches to this phenomenon: language loyalty (or, more mundanely, language maintenance); language loss (or more dramatically, language death); language shift; and, most recently, language spread (or diffusion). As has been true of so many fields of sociolinguistics, language spread also was crystallized as a field at a conference sponsored by the Ford Foundation (in Aberystwyth in 1978) and the resulting volume of papers (Cooper 1982) has started to delimit and exemplify the field.

Language spread is defined by Cooper (1982: 6) as 'an increase, over time, in the proportion of a communication network that adopts a given language or language variety for a given communicative function.' It is thus essentially a study of an increase in the amount of bilingualism in a community. It draws, Cooper has suggested, on three separate research traditions. First, it aims to add language to the set of material and non-material items treated within the sociological study of the diffusion of innovation, making another attempt to bridge the gap between the sociology of language and general sociology (see Fishman 1978). Secondly, it builds on and continues work in language maintenance and shift, with the key difference that its focus is on the waxing rather than the waning language. Thirdly, it adds social context to studies of language change.

The quality and nature of work in language spread can best be captured by looking briefly at some recent representative studies. Mahmud (1982) uses the results of questionnaires administered to nearly 3000 students in all the schools (from primary to senior secondary) and to a number of their parents in the city of Juba, southern Sudan, in order to analyze the spread of Arabic and the consequent development of bilingualism in Arabic and one of a large number of vernacular languages. The children report some 50 different first languages (mother tongues), 9 of which are claimed by over 75 children. Just under a third report Arabic as a mother tongue, but for some of them it is probably one of two languages they acquired while very young. Arabic is more likely to be the mother tongue of younger than of older children: 45% of the 10–13-year-olds claim it, compared with 25% of 17–19-year-olds. However, this figure masks a demographic complexity, with recent immigrants to the city claiming less Arabic. When the child's two parents are from different tribes, the child is more likely to have Arabic as a mother tongue; other demographic factors leading to Arabic are the father's occupation and the place of birth (urban versus rural). Two-thirds of the children reporting Arabic as their mother tongue also claim that they can speak a vernacular. Analyzing language use within the single domain of the home, Mahmud finds variation by age: grandparents are the most likely, and young children the least likely, to use only the vernacular. Closer analysis of individual families shows different rates of diffusion for each generation. Mahmud shows the usefulness of the wave theory proposed by C.-J. Bailey (1974) for describing these results, and concludes that

> it seems that language diffuses through the different functions in a
> gradual time-governed process in a manner similar to the process of
> 'lexical diffusion,' whereby a linguistic change propagates itself
> gradually across the lexicon . . . (Mahmud 1982: 181)

In another study of language diffusion, Kachru (1978) looks at the development of South Asian varieties of English as a result of the spread of bilingualism in English and other languages in the region. English was brought to the area by missionaries who used it for proselytizing. In the early nineteenth century, its use was encouraged by a small group of Indians who saw its value. The main force for spread was the result of political decisions by the British governments. By the early twentieth century, the use of English as the official and academic language had established its prestige and led to English–vernacular bilingualism becoming the norm among the educated classes. Since the various countries of South Asia have become independent, the importance of English as a second language has continued. Kachru also shows the way in which the local varieties of English have developed distinctive linguistic features.

Other important studies have looked at the spread of Russian in the Soviet Union (Lewis 1972), of Spanish in Central and South America (Heath 1972, Heath & Laprade 1982), and of English in the world (Fishman, Cooper & Conrad 1977). Underlying them is an assumption of a functional or domain-related view of bilingualism; under appropriate conditions, a speaker of one language may be encouraged or constrained by social, economic, political, or religious pressures to add another variety to his or her communicative repertoire for certain specific functions and in certain domains. A diffusion model can account for this addition; thus diffusion studies can help integrate sociolinguistic studies into other studies of social change.

6.2. Bilingual education

As Haugen (1973) pointed out, the definition of a bilingual as someone with equal competence in two languages excludes from attention the specific groups that give rise to most practical and political concern, those bilinguals whose limitations in one of their languages (usually the standard but sometimes the mother tongue) lead to the apparent need of educational intervention. The fact that most children in the world do not come to school already controlling the language or variety that the school itself values and teaches means that most education has a large component of language teaching in it (Spolsky 1974). While it is true that other institutions are often more successful in producing functional bilingualism, it is almost always the case that schools have as their central task the increase in the proportion of members of a communication network who can use a given language or variety for specific functions. Whether we are talking of immigrants to Britain or the USA, of immigrant workers in EEC countries or refugees from Asia, of indigenous or urbanized populations in the Soviet Union or the South Pacific, the issue of language education in multilingual settings has been the focus of a great deal of debate, research, innovation, and evaluation. To the extent that sociolinguistics may be considered to have a specifically applied side (see Shuy 1984, Trudgill 1984), the problem to which it has been most applied is that of the language education of linguistic minorities.

The educational problem of the linguistic minority child is easily characterized, as Lewis (1980: 322) has shown. At a minimum, such a child needs to be able to speak two languages, the home language and the school language. At a maximum, there would be obvious benefit from a rich and full education in each of the languages. There is an intermediate possibility of varying amounts of initial education in the home language accompanied or followed by education in the standard language in order to guarantee equal educational opportunity. The pedagogical implications of these choices are reasonably clear; so are the costs (in terms of student suffering) of failing to provide even a minimum, and the resources required (such as teachers, materials, curricula) to provide programs of each kind. Confusions in levels of analysis cloud most debates, however, and studies; scholars themselves are likely to have firm positions (see Skutnabb-Kangas 1986) on the relative desirability of giving priority to the needs of the individual student (for the minimum or intermediate approach) or of the minority language community (for a language maintenance or enrichment program). Such confusions lead to programs with serious inconsistencies: Lewis (1980) shows how this works in practice in the USSR, USA and the United Kingdom. Bilingual education programs can be no more than attempts to teach the school language or to revive a dying language, or they can be programs carefully tailored to the needs of the local community and its children.

As is generally the case in applied studies, the development of a field is strongly influenced by the very political trends it aims to study. This may be seen in the work of Joshua A. Fishman, who in the mid 1970s was able to present an optimistic account of international bilingual education (Fishman 1976); a couple of years later, he looked at the role of English as a key component of international societal bilingualism (Fishman, Cooper & Conrad 1977); most recently, he has been mapping the petering out of the ethnic revival efforts that were basic to the development of enthusiasm for bilingual education in the USA (Fishman *et al.* 1985). In all of this work, Fishman's goal has been to give both a parsimonious account of the data he gathers and a theoretically motivated understanding of the social forces underlying language use.

Another important student of bilingual education has been William Mackey, whose influential typology (Mackey 1970) continues to be cited and refined; he has also described some important cases (Mackey 1972, Mackey & Beebe 1977), and has integrated the study of the bilingual school into a general description of bilingualism (Mackey 1976).

While most published work in the field of bilingual education tends to be attacks on one form of it (e.g. Epstein 1978), advocacy of it in one form or another (see the review in Edwards 1981), or descriptions of programs (see for example Spolsky & Cooper 1978, or more recently a wide range of articles in *Journal of Multilingual and Multicultural Development*), there have been a number of attempts to clarify the underlying dimensions of the field. Apart from those cited already, one should mention influential work on cognitive effects of education in mother tongue or second language by Cummins (1977, 1979, 1980, 1984a, 1984b) and work on the relation between political and ethnic conflicts and bilingual education by Paulston (1980, 1982, 1986).

6.3. **Language choice**

One of the central goals of the study of bilingualism is a theoretical model that will account for the bilingual's unconscious or conscious decision to use one language rather than the other. If we accept that all normal speakers, even monolinguals, have similar problems in deciding which variety, register, or style to use, the matter is of wider theoretical interest. The general issue of language choice then subsumes within it such topics as code-switching (there is ambiguity as to whether this term refers to changing from language to another in the midst of a discourse unit or only when a situation changes), stylistic variation, audience design, and language shift and spread (the long-term socialized result of a pattern of individual language choices).

In tackling this issue, we need first to consider the level of our analysis, as Breitborde (1983) expressed it. The choice (as in most language study) is the difficult one between performance and competence, however defined. Attractive as might seem the challenge to build a process or performance model that can account for every behavioral decision, there are a number of sound reasons to tackle first the still difficult (but hopefully manageable) task of developing a competence model; of trying to find the underlying system that informs and constrains (if it doesn't always actually govern) choice. First, as Jackendoff (1983) argues, just as a model of process necessarily includes a theory of storage and of what is stored, so a performance model necessarily involves a view of the underlying knowledge system or competence, while the opposite is not true. Second, principles of uncertainty appear to be as relevant in human behavior as in physics; a performance model will thus end up only with probabilities. Third, a process or performance model makes overoptimistic claims about the completeness of the model. For these reasons, it is at the very least a useful first step to attempt to define the underlying system, the rules or competence of a bilingual speaker.

This approach also has the advantage of clarifying another aspect of the issue, the social versus individual perspective argued by Breitborde (1983). Studies of individual bilingualism tend to be located naturally within psychology, while those of societal multilingualism fall under sociolinguistics. There is a not unnatural tendency in psychological studies to look at individual factors and ignore the social forces that account for them; thus a social psychologist might talk of integrative motivation or accommodation without accounting for the balance of social groups that explain individual values; similarly, sociologists might lack a method of showing how a social force enters into an individual case. As we shall see, when one tries to determine a grammar (set of rules) underlying language choice, one is forced to consider both these aspects; just as *langue* is a social fact present in individual speakers, so a competence model of language choice is a social phenomenon expressed in and derived from individual bilinguals.

How formal we choose to make our model is obviously also a matter to be decided. At the most informal, we might be satisfied as a first step with listing all the factors that affect language loss or maintenance (as Kloss 1966) or that influence language choice (as Grosjean 1982; see for instance his list on page 136). Kloss divides his factors up according to their direction and degree of influence. Grosjean (1982) classifies his according to a simple taxonomy: participant factors, situation, content of discourse, and function of interaction. Noting that it is rare for a single factor to be decisive, he briefly considers the potential weighting of the various factors, but concludes that it varies in different circumstances and communities.

One model that Grosjean describes favorably is that used by Rubin in her study of Spanish–Guarani bilingualism in Paraguay. Rubin (1968: 109) presents a decision tree to explain the choice between Guarani and Spanish. In a rural location, people choose Guarani; in a nonrural location, for formal speech, they select Spanish; for nonformal speech, if the situation is not intimate, Spanish is used; if it is intimate, and not serious, they choose Guarani; otherwise, the choice depends on the first language learned, the predicted language proficiency of the interlocutor, and whether the interlocutor is of the same sex or different. While this is presented as a decision tree, there is no claim that it is a formal stochastic model of the decision process; it completely ignores, for instance, a fact tht Rubin herself points out: that Spanish is used in school even in rural areas. We are probably better therefore considering it as an informal listing of factors to be included in a competence model with a tentative ranking of the order in which they apply or the weight to be attached to them.

Another way of representing the choice process is a statistical model. In the classic study of language choice in a bilingual community, Fishman and his colleagues presented the notion of domain as a construct that underlies appropriate language choice, and showed the statistical probability of domain accounting for performance. The notion of domain was proposed originally by Fishman (1964) and elaborated in Fishman 1972 as an explanation of normative language views that underlie language switching. In the Jersey City study (Fishman, Cooper & Ma 1971: 251), domains are empirically established 'higher-order generalizations' that are derived from 'congruent situation': situations in which role relations, locales, and topics are all in agreement. For the Puerto Rican Barrio, five domains were established: family, friendship, religion, education, and employment. Using self-report in congruent and partially congruent situations, Fishman showed that use of Spanish was most likely to be claimed in the domain of family, less in the domains of friendship and religion, and least in the domains of education and employment.

In an important consideration of language choice (which he calls code-switching), Breitborde (1983) asks one central question that is relevant to our concern:

> whether language use in a situation can be explained solely by components which comprise that event, or if there are not in addition certain societal regularities that must be incorporated in an understanding of situated language use. (1983: 5)

He sees in approaches by Blom and Gumperz (1972) and Scotton (1980) a tendency to focus on the individual choice in a micro-sociolinguistic situation rather on the wider macro-sociolinguistic background: Blom and Gumperz are thus forced to postulate a difference between situational switching and metaphorical switching. Breitborde himself prefers the macro-sociolinguistic approach through domains proposed by Fishman (1972), but offers a model that reinterprets domains, following Fortes (1969), as wider clusters of social factors which determine statuses. Scotton (1983a: 123) points out that her model, while seeing linguistic choice as 'individually motivated negotiations of identity' (1980: 360) assumes that this negotiation depends for its success on taking advantage of 'the communally recognized norms' that establish the meaning of the choices.

Scotton's model (1983b) is a 'social process' model that is based on a natural theory of markedness. In conventional situations, the unmarked choice is followed; a marked choice can be made to challenge the *status quo*; an exploratory choice is made in nonconventional situations to claim multiple identities. A conventionalized talk situation is one where societal norms specify clearly the meanings of choices; a nonconventionalized exchange is one where there is not agreement about the markedness of choices. The fundamental message being signaled is a 'rights-and-obligations set' accepted as appropriate by speaker and hearer.

Another important attempt to account for the social forces underlying language selection and code-switching is provided through a study of bilingual Austria by Susan Gal (1979). Looking at the behavior of people who are bilingual in German and Hungarian, Gal discovers that the best predictor of language choice is social network. Lesley Milroy (1980), in a study of vernacular maintenance in Belfast, develops a method of measuring network 'strength'; speakers with more dense and multiplex network ties are most likely to maintain the vernacular.

A somewhat more elaborate but ultimately very similar approach is provided from a social psychological perspective in the work of Giles and his colleagues on accommodation theory. The work is difficult to summarize without trivializing, for it consists of a large number of general statements about tendencies of speakers to modify (or not modify) their style of speaking (including code choice) in order to move towards (or, if appropriate, away from) that believed to be used by the addressee. A good number of papers elaborate on this basic concept, detailing the probable effect of various choices. Speech accommodation theory was developed to attempt to account for changes in speech style in the course of conversations: it thus deals directly with the issue of intraspeaker variation, and is easily seen to be applicable to a bilingual's choice between two languages. As summarized most recently (Beebe & Giles 1984, based largely on Street & Giles 1982), it has the following half-dozen basic propositions:

> 1. People will attempt to converge linguistically toward the speech pattern believed to be characteristic of their recipients when they (a) desire their social approval and the perceived costs of so acting are proportionally lower than the reward anticipated; and/or (b) desire a high level of communicative efficiency; and (c) social norms are not perceived to dictate alternative speech strategies . . .
>
> 2. The magnitude of such linguistic convergence will be a function of (a) the extent of the speakers' repertoires, and (b) factors (individual difference and environmental) that may increase the need for social approval and/or high communicational efficiency . . .
>
> 3. Speech convergence will be positively evaluated by recipients when the resultant behavior is (a) perceived as such psychologically (i.e. as integrative); (b) perceived to be an optimal sociolinguistic distance from them; and (c) attributed to positive intent . . .
>
> 4. People will attempt to maintain their speech patterns, or even diverge linguistically away from those believed characteristic of their recipients, when they (a) define the encounter in intergroup terms and desire a positive ingroup identity, or (b) wish to dissociate personally from another in an individual encounter, or (c) wish to bring another's speech behaviors to a personally acceptable level . . .

5. The magnitude of such divergence will be a function of (a) the extent of the speakers' repertoires, and (b) individual differences and contextual factors increasing the salience of the cognitive or affective functions in (4) . . .

6. Speech maintenance and divergence will be negatively evaluated by recipients when the acts are perceived as psychologically diverging (i.e. dissociative), but favorably reacted to by observers who define the interaction in intergroup terms and who share a common, positively valued group membership with the speaker . . .

In a recent attempt to blend the various approaches together into a single model, Bell (1984) has proposed the concept of audience design: a speaker modifies his or her style of speaking according to a present (or absent but salient) audience. Bell points out that recent analyses of language variation have shown it to be accounted for on two dimensions, linguistic (e.g. phonological or other constraints on the operation of a variable rule) and extralinguistic. This second dimension is divided into the social axis, dealing with variation between speakers, and the stylistic, dealing with variation within a speaker. The first of these has been extensively investigated, showing correlation of linguistic variation with the class, sex, age, and social level of the speaker. Put another way, one's language experience from birth provides one with a personal repertoire of language varieties, choice among which has still to be accounted for. In the literature, style has generally been assumed to be a matter of attention: in Labov's words: 'Styles can be ranged along a single dimension, measured by the amount of attention paid to speech' (1972: 208). There is, Bell points out, very little empirical support for this claim. In the study most commonly cited in its support, Bell himself notes that the speaker's inability to monitor his interviewer was more important than his inability to monitor his own production. Bell argues then that attention is at most a mechanism; the critical dimension is more likely to be concerned with the social situation and in particular the audience.

The model that Bell proposes has what he calls a style axiom:

> Variation on the style dimension within the speech of a single speaker derives from and echoes the variation which exists between speakers on the 'social' dimension. (1984: 151)

In certain situations, then, individuals shift styles (change varieties) to sound like other people; individuals also shift their speech pattern to sound like other people (when moving to a different region); and groups can shift their speech to sound like other people. The essential motivating force becomes the social value assigned to a given variety or feature and to the group which uses it. This permits Bell to show how intraspeaker variation (style) can be derived from interspeaker or social variation: each group has its own identity, which has value assigned by itself and others; as a result, the group differentiates its variety of language from others; its language is subsequently valued by itself and others; others can choose to shift towards the group's language.

In support of his model, Bell argues that stylistic variation appears always to mirror and never to exceed social variation; a feature that marks stylistic variation will generally be a less strong version of a feature that indicates social variation. The axiom has other important consequences: in language learning, for instance, the range of styles depends on the linguistic range to which a child is exposed. It thus presumably helps to account for the fact that foreign language learners are often limited to a single style. In language loss or death, the reduction of social variation leads to loss of stylistic variation. For the monolingual, style shift is analogous to code-switching for the bilingual.

Having established the basic match between intraspeaker stylistic variation and interspeaker social variation, Bell goes on to argue that both must have a similar explanation. He proposes the notion he calls 'audience design,' and suggests that there are four levels of hearer to be taken into account, ranging in salience from addressee through auditor and overhearer to eavesdropper:

> The proposed framework . . . assumes that persons respond mainly to
> other persons, that speakers take most account of hearers in designing
> their talk. The *speaker* is first person, qualitatively apart from other
> interlocutors. The first person's characteristics account for speech
> differences between speakers. However, speakers design their style
> for their audience. Differences within the speech of a single speaker
> are accountable as the influence of the second person and some third
> persons, who together compose the audience to a speaker's
> utterances. (1984: 159)

Bell proposes that just as the audience forms a continuum of salience, so their influence varies in strength. There are two confounding factors, the one (called initiative) dealing with attempts to redefine the social situation rather than respond to it, and the second concerning responses to non-audience factors such as topic and setting (the other components of Fishman's notion of domain). But audience is the main force, Bell argues.

The evidence supporting this notion can be divided into two parts, Bell suggests: part from the work on accommodation theory of Giles and others, described earlier in this paper, and part from recent variationist studies. There is a good body of empirical data supporting the main conclusions of accommodation theory, derived, as Bell complains, from studies that are linguistically somewhat naive in their use of such parameters as speech rate, utterance rate, and unsophisticated ratings of accent.

There is considerably more linguistic sophistication in a number of recent studies Bell cites of the effect of addressee on the speaker's style. The most comprehensive is that of Coupland (1980, 1984), who attempted to provide solid linguistic support for Giles's accommodation theory. For this study, Coupland collected tape-recordings of interviews of a clerk in a travel agency with 52 different local clients. Coupland showed that the occurrence of four regionally marked linguistic features was correlated with the social class of the client, and further that the rating for the clerk's own usage varied and correlated with the client she was addressing. Bell reanalyzes Coupland's data and shows that the convergence is consistent and massive towards lower class clients (on the average over half-way), but less consistent in the case of higher class clients.

Bell also considers the effect of non-audience features, in particular of setting and topic. There is good evidence that each has an effect, and their relation has been shown by Fishman's development of the construct of domain (Fishman *et al*. 1971; Fishman 1972). Bell argues interestingly that these two features might be considered to be derived from addressee; while they are, in specific cases, independent factors determining stylistic level, they may well gain their effect from their association with the personal factors. As Breitborde (1983) puts it: 'At a more abstract level topic and locale may themselves be manifestations or concomitants of a person's social status' (1983: 33).

A final dimension that Bell considers is the contrast between style design that is responsive to changes in the extralinguistic situation (audience or non-audience), and style design that itself initiates a change. As he points out, this is equivalent to the distinction between situational and metaphorical switching in Blom and Gomperz. It is also similar to the marked–unmarked situation in Scotton's model. Initiative design depends ultimately on the norms of responsive design; it is the marked case. It may also vary socially and personally. Initiative shift is interpretable (in terms of the normal system) but not predictable. One of the essential features of it is to address a person as though they were someone else. It is most obvious, Bell suggests, when the shift is towards an absent third person, labeled a referee: 'Referees are third persons not physically present at an interaction but possessing such salience for a speaker that they influence speech even in their absence' (1984: 186). In referee design, the speaker chooses a style as though the referee were an audience. The shift may be towards the speaker's own group (ingroup) or towards a group of which the speaker is not a member (outgroup). Ingroup referee design involves the social psychological surfacing of conflicting sociopolitical situations; examples Bell mentions are Wales and Montreal. It is essentially a short-term confrontation, a challenge that if successful will end the conversation. Outgroup referee design occurs when a speaker shifts to a prestigious style (or language) for a short time for an immediate purpose (rhetorical effect, for instance); it can also occur on a long-term basis and become institutionalized. This last is the case, Bell suggests, with diglossia, where an outgroup variety (geographically distinct in the case, for instance, of Haiti and Switzerland, and historically distant in the case of Greek and Arabic) forms the prestige variety. This kind of long-term pattern, though becoming the norm (and not the usual marked case of initiative behavior) is in every other way like the short term patterns:

> It involves divergence from the addressee; convergence to an absent referee, symbolic of identification with an outgroup; agreement by both speaker and addressee on the status of the outgroup and its language; inconsistent adoption of the forms of outgroup speech . . . and absence of feedback from outgroup speakers. (Bell 1984: 189)

We can see in Bell's work the close parallel between style shift and bilingual language choice. It seems to me useful to see as underlying both a set of norms for language or style choice which are themselves best represented as a preference model (Jackendoff 1983; Spolsky 1985; Schauber & Spolsky 1986) that includes rules that apply typically but not necessarily, and the weighting or salience of which is dependent on situations and attitudes. If we try to sketch how this might work, there appear to be at least two necessary conditions for choice of language for communication:

> Necessary condition 1: Use (speak, write) a language which you know.
> Necessary condition 2: Use (speak, write) a language which the person you want to communicate with knows.

While knowing a language is a gradient condition, that is to say it is measured on a continuum (or perhaps, rather, on a number of continua) and not a binary decision, the necessary condition for a well-formed linguistic interaction is that both speaker–writer and listener–reader can achieve a minimal threshold level of understanding. These two conditions explain why one of the first tasks that parents accept with a newborn child is teaching it their language, i.e. making sure that it can meet necessary condition 2. Similarly, these two conditions explain why the continued presence of a significant monolingual, such as an elderly grandparent, in the home will ensure that other members of the family will know that language. In communication with oneself (counting, dreaming, writing notes), it is obvious that the speaker–writer has the fullest freedom.

The typicality conditions that I list next can apply only where the two necessary conditions have been met, which means when the two interlocutors are (or can be expected to be) bilingual in the same two languages. The first pair relates to a preference according to how well the language is known by each of them.

> Typicality condition 1: Prefer to use the language you know best for the topic concerned.
> Typicality condition 2: Prefer to use the language that you believe the person you are addressing knows best for the topic being discussed.

Essentially, these two rules fall into two parts. First, they both assume that choice of language is influenced by the amount of knowledge and ease of expression, which themselves vary from topic to topic (perhaps domain to domain) depending on the experience of the speaker and, at another remove, on the experience (cultural history) of users of the language as a whole. The second part, equally pertinent to our concerns, is the question of whose preference is to count. Clearly, there will be cases where each user has (or can be assumed to have) equal and similar control of the two languages, but there will also be cases in which the two rules could lead to conflict. The resolution of this conflict is partly to be explained by the absolute and relative status of the two people concerned; it is partly to be explained by accommodation theory. The rules themselves are simple: the conditions that provide weighting for them are much more complex (see for instance Breitborde 1983; Genesee & Bourhis 1983).

The next condition is a conservative factor:

> Typicality condition 3: Prefer to use the language you used the last time you addressed this person.

To switch language use to a person you have regularly spoken to – a family member, a close friend – takes a major effort; thus, the weight of inertia favors linguistic conservatism: parents can be persuaded to speak a new language to their children more easily than they can be persuaded to use it to each other. The language first used by a couple with different mother tongues to speak to each other is most likely to be taught to their children, even though other pressures may lead it to play a minor role in family life.

> Typicality condition 4: Prefer a language that includes *or* excludes a third party.

There are conditions in which it is considered important to make it possible for a third party to be able to understand what one is saying or writing; similarly, there can be conditions that make it important to prevent a third party understanding. It is common to find children developing a passive

113

knowledge of the language their parents spoke for privacy; similarly, for servants to learn a language their employers used for secrecy.

The final condition is a complex and important one: I am tempted to break it down into several, but prefer to try to treat it as a single rule, with the complexities in the weightings that determine its salience in a specific case.

> Typicality condition 5: Prefer to use a language that asserts the most advantageous social group membership for you in the proposed interaction.

Assume that both you and your addressee are equally bilingual; that it is a person you have not spoken to before; that there is no third party involved, and that the conversation takes place in a society with at least two groups of uneven power, each with its associated language. If the interaction is between a member of the dominating group and of a dominated group, conditions 1 and 2 suggest that the comfort of the member of the dominating group will be served by using his/her language, unless he/she chooses to accommodate to the other party. Assume, however, a conversation between two members of the dominated group: in such a case, the use of the language of the dominant group will have nothing to do with comfort but will count as a claim to membership of that group and so to an advantageous status in the current situation. The working of conditions like these clearly depends on the ideological values of both people involved and derives from general social values.

We need to be clear about the nature of the model we are proposing for language choice. It is a competence model: a set of rules that underlies the understanding of a competence member of a speech community. In Chomsky's attempt to explain linguistic competence, this person was an idealized monolingual; in a sociolinguistic description, it is of necessity someone who shares not just the community's rules for forming sentences (linguistic competence in its narrowest sense) but its rules for language use (communicative competence). But knowing the rules is of course not the same as using them; there will in practice be cases where mistakes are made, or where knowledge is imperfect. In describing the rules of a speech community, there is another complication in that various members of the community will have different values and apply the same rules differently.

These rules describe for a given speech community its assumptions about appropriate language choice: it sets in other words what Genessee and Bourhis refer to as the situational norm, and what Scotton considers the unmarked case in conventionalized situations. It sets expectations against which an actual performance is judged, and provides an ordered set of hypotheses (like Grice's maxims) to be tested in real life. If someone addresses me in a language I don't know my first (and most charitable) guesses are that he thinks I know it or that he can't speak any other: once I have made clear that the first is wrong, his persistence is judged to be because of the second, and if I later find that this is not so, I move on to a more remote analysis.

But the various conditions themselves obtain their relative weighting in a number of ways. First, there is the question of the relative salience in the situation of the various domains or clusters of role relationships; is this a situation where it is appropriate or valuable to assert a role relationship expressed by choice of a certain language? For example, the foreign-language teacher with a pupil outside class may choose to assert the teacher role by using the foreign language, or the fellow-citizen role by using the native language. It is in this connection that I would prefer to consider the importance of asserting ingroup membership. Second, there is the issue of the status of the language itself, a cluster of attributes arising in part from the functions with which the language is associated and in part from the status of the people who are assumed to use the language. Thirdly, there are the specific and immediate functional claims of the situation, as analyzed by Scotton in her work on negotiation. For instance, in order to obtain a better price, the customer might choose to use the seller's language in contrast to the usual principle that sellers are assumed to accommodate to customers.

In two recent unpublished papers, Moses and Schauber have applied a preference model to analysis of the conditions which account for parents' decisions to raise their children bilingually and to the acquisition of the rules that allow children to judge 'which language to use to whom and when.' They show how the parents' implementation of their own rules provides exemplars according to which the child develops its own set of conditions for judgements about language choice. The preference model thus appears to offer good potential for exploring the complexity of language choice and understanding the system underlying language variation.

6.4. Conclusion

In an article on bilingualism in 1950, Haugen (1950: 272) was able to claim that in the United States, at least, the study of bilingualism was ignored: 'Just as the bilingual himself often was a marginal personality, so the study of his behavior was a marginal scientific pursuit.' In the last 35 years, there has been a marked change in this emphasis, so that just as the study of ethnic minorities has become a central concern of sociology, so the study of the language behavior of the minority person and of any bilingual has become a key issue in sociolinguistics, and one that has clear significance for the field of linguistics as a whole.

REFERENCES

Bailey, C.-J. N. 1974. *Variations and linguistic theory*. Washington: Center for Applied Linguistics.
Beebe, L. M. & Giles, H. 1984. Speech–accommodation theories: a discussion in terms of second-language acquisition. *International Journal of the Sociology of Language* 46: 5–32.
Bell, A. 1984. Language style as audience design. *Language in Society* 13: 145–204.
Blom, J. -P. & Gumperz, J. J. 1972. Social meaning in linguistic structure: code-switching in Norway. In Gumperz & Hymes 1972.
Breitborde, L. B. 1983. Levels of analysis in sociolinguistic explanation: bilingual code switching, social relations, and domain theory. *International Journal for the Sociology of Language* 39: 5–43.
Cooper, R. L. 1982. *Language spread: studies in diffusion and social change*. Bloomington: Indiana University Press, and Washington: Center for Applied Linguistics.
Coupland, N. 1980. Style-shifting in a Cardiff work setting. *Language in Society* 9: 1–12.
Coupland, N. 1984. Accommodation at work: some phonological data and their implications. *International Review of Applied Linguistics* 46: 49–70.
Cummins, J. 1977. Psycholinguistic evidence. In *Bilingual education: current perspectives*, Vol. 4. Arlington: Center for Applied Linguistics.
Cummins, J. 1979. Linguistic interdependence and the educational development of bilingual children. *Review of Educational Research* 49: 222–51.
Cummins, J. 1980. The cross-lingual dimensions of language proficiency: implications for bilingual education and the optimal age issue. *TESOL Quarterly* 14: 175–87.
Cummins, J. 1984a. Wanted: a theoretical framework for relating language proficiency to academic achievement among bilingual students. In C. Rivera (ed.) *Language proficiency and academic achievement*. Clevedon: Multilingual Matters Ltd.
Cummins, J. 1984b. Linguistic minorities and multicultural policy in Canada. In J. Edwards (ed.) *Linguistic minorities, policies, and pluralism*. London: Academic Press.
Edwards, J. R. 1981. The context of bilingual education. *Journal of Multilingual and Multicultural Education* 2: 25–44.
Epstein, N. 1978. *Language, ethnicity and the schools*. Washington: Institute for Educational Leadership.
Fishman, J. A. 1964. Language maintenance and language shift as fields of enquiry. *Linguistics* 9: 32–70.
Fishman, J. A. 1972. Domains and the relationship between micro- and macrosociolinguistics. In Gumperz & Hymes 1972.
Fishman, J. A. 1976. *Bilingual education: an international sociological perspective*. Rowley: Newbury House.
Fishman, J. A. 1978. A graduate program in the sociology of language. Addendum to J. A. Fishman (ed.) *Advances in the study of societal multilingualism*. The Hague: Mouton.
Fishman, J. A., Cooper, R. L. & Conrad, A. W. 1977. *The spread of English: the sociology of English as an additional language*. Rowley: Newbury House.
Fishman, J. A., Cooper, R. L., Ma, R., *et al.* 1971. *Bilingualism in the Barrio*. Indiana University Publications, Language Science Monographs, Vol. 7.
Fishman, J. A., Gartner, M. H., Lowy, E. G. & Milan, K. G. 1985. *The rise and fall of the ethnic revival: perspectives on language and ethnicity*. Berlin: Mouton.
Fortes, M. 1969. *Kinship and the social order*. Chicago: Aldine.
Gal, S. 1979. *Language shift: social determinants of language change in bilingual Austria*. New York: Academic Press.
Genesee, F. & Bourhis, R. Y. 1983. The social psychological significance of code switching in cross-cultural communication. *Journal of Language and Social Psychology* 1: 1–25.
Grosjean, F. 1982. *Life with two languages: an introduction to bilingualism*. Cambridge, MA: Harvard University Press.
Gumperz, J. J. & Hymes, D. (eds.) 1972. *Directions in sociolinguistics*. New York: Holt, Rinehart, & Winston.

Haugen, E. 1950. Problems of bilingualism. *Lingua* 2: 271–90.

Haugen, E. 1956. *Bilingualism in the Americas: a bibliography and research guide*. University of Alabama: Publications of the American Dialect Society.

Haugen, E. 1973. Bilingualism, language contact and immigrant languages in the United States: a research report 1956–1970. In T. A. Sebeok *et al.* (eds.) *Current trends in linguistics*, Vol. 10.

Heath, S. B. 1972. *Telling tongues: language policy in Mexico*. New York: Teachers College Press.

Heath, S. B. & Laprade, R. 1982. Castilian colonization and indigenous languages. Cooper 1982.

Jackendoff, R. 1983. *Semantics and cognition*. Cambridge, MA: MIT Press.

Kachru, B. B. 1978. English in South Asia. In J. A. Fishman (ed.) *Advances in the study of societal multilingualism*. The Hague: Mouton.

Kloss, H. 1966. German–American language maintenance efforts. In J. A. Fishman (ed.) *Language loyalty in the United States*. The Hague: Mouton.

Labov, W. 1972. *Language in the inner city*. Philadelphia: University of Pennsylvania Press.

Leopold, W. F. 1939–1949. *Speech development of a bilingual child*. 4 vols. Evanston: Illinois University Press.

Lewis, E. G. 1972. *Multilingualism in the Soviet Union*. The Hague: Mouton.

Lewis, E. G. 1980. *Bilingualism and bilingual education: a comparative study*. Albuquerque: University of New Mexico Press.

Mackey, W. 1970. A typology of bilingual education. *Foreign Language Annals* 3: 596–608.

Mackey, W. 1972. *Bilingual education in a binational school*. Rowley: Newbury House.

Mackey, W. 1976. *Bilinguisme et contact des langues*. Paris: Klincksieck.

Mackey, W. & Beebe, V. N. 1977. *Bilingual schools for a bicultural community*. Rowley: Newbury House.

Mahmud, U. 1982. Language spread as a wavelike diffusion process: Arabic in the southern Sudan. In Cooper 1982.

Milroy, L. 1980. *Language and social networks*. Oxford: Blackwell.

Moses, R. & Schauber, E. 1982. Bilingual control in families. ms.

Moses, R. & Schauber, E. 1984. Bilingual caretakers and language choice: a preference model analysis. ms.

Paulston, C. B. 1980. *Bilingual education: theories and issues*. Rowley: Newbury House.

Paulston, C. B. 1982. *Swedish research and debate about bilingualism*. Stockholm: National Swedish Board of Education.

Paulston, C. B. 1986. Linguistic consequences of ethnicity and nationalism in multilingual settings. In B. Spolsky (ed.) *Language and education in multilingual settings*. Clevedon: Multilingual Matters Ltd.

Rubin, J. 1968. *National bilingualism in Paraguay*. The Hague: Mouton.

Schauber, E. & Spolsky, E. 1986. *The bounds of interpretation: linguistic theory and literary text*. Stanford: Stanford University Press.

Scotton, C. M. 1980. Explaining linguistic choices as identity negotiations. In H. Giles, P. Robinson & P. Smith (eds.) *Language, social psychological perspectives*. Oxford: Pergamon.

Scotton, C. M. 1983a. Comment. *International Journal of the Sociology of Language* 39: 119–28.

Scotton, C. M. 1983b. The negotiation of identities in conversation: a theory of markedness and code choice. *International Journal of the Sociology of Language* 44: 116–36.

Sebeok, T. A., Abramson, A. S., Hymes, D., Rubenstein, H., Spolsky, B. & Stankiewicz, E. 1974. *Current trends in linguistics*, Vol. 12: *Linguistics and adjacent arts and sciences*. The Hague: Mouton.

Shuy, R. W. 1984. The decade ahead for applied sociolinguistics. *International Journal of the Sociology of Language* 45: 101–11.

Skuttnab-Kangas, T. 1986. Conflicting paradigms in minority education research. In B. Spolsky (ed.) *Language and education in multilingual settings*. Clevedon: Multilingual Matters Ltd.

Spolsky, B. 1974. Linguistics and the language barrier to education. In Sebeok *et al.* 1974.

Spolsky, B. 1976. Bilingualism. In D. Brown and R. Wardhaugh (eds.) *A survey of applied linguistics*. Ann Arbor: University of Michigan Press.

Spolsky, B. 1985. Multilingualism in Jewish Palestine of the first century: an essay in historical sociolinguistics. In J. A. Fishman (ed.) *Readings in the sociology of Jewish languages*. Leiden: Brill.

Spolsky, B. & Cooper, R. L. (eds.) 1978. *Case studies in bilingual education*. Rowley: Newbury House.

Street, R. J., Jr & Giles, H. 1982. Speech accommodation theory: a social and cognitive approach to language and speech behavior. In M. Roloff & C. Berger (eds.) *Social cognition and communication*. Beverly Hills: Sage.

Trudgill, P. (ed.) 1984. *Applied sociolinguistics*. London: Academic Press.

Weinreich, U. 1953. *Languages in contact: findings and problems*. Publications of the Linguistic Circle of New York, 1.

7 Dialectology

Keith Walters

7.0. Introduction

Dialectology is 'the study of dialect and dialects' (Chambers & Trudgill 1980: 3).[1] Not surprisingly, the major issues in the field of dialectology during the century of its existence have been deciding which varieties of language count as dialect and how best to study them. Seen in this light, the history of the discipline can, without too much exaggeration, be characterized as the shift from collecting facts about geographically distributed, (mostly) rural varieties of language to analyzing the distribution of features of (mostly) urban varieties as these features correlate with social and linguistic factors.

This shift in methodology has been accompanied by important changes in the goals of the discipline. Whereas the dialectologists of the late nineteenth century collected data in order to test the contentions of the Neogrammarians about the exceptionless nature of sound change, later researchers, especially those engaged in linguistic atlas projects, collected and studied data mainly as a contribution to the description and history of a particular language. More recently, however, practitioners of urban dialectology, often referred to as sociolinguists or quantitative sociolinguists, have conceived of their work as one of the several 'way(s) of doing linguistics.' As Trudgill puts it, such research

> is concerned to learn more about language, and to investigate topics such as the mechanisms of linguistic change; the nature of linguistic variability; and the structure of linguistic systems. All work in this category . . . is aimed ultimately at improving linguistic theory and at

[1] Special thanks to Susan Davy, Fritz Newmeyer, Suzanne Romaine, Jonathan Tamez, and Peter Trudgill for offering suggestions on earlier drafts of this chapter and to Cindie McLemore for bibliographic assistance. Discussions with Boyd Davis, George Dorrill, Michael Montgomery, Sara Sanders, Ann Sharp, Gary Underwood, and Tony Woodbury have greatly improved my understanding of dialect geography. Studying with John Baugh and Peter Trudgill has shaped many of my ideas about urban dialectology. All are great people, but none can be expected to take responsibility for any errors of fact or interpretation contained herein.

119

developing our understanding of the nature of language . . . (1983: 2–3)

The discipline has thus moved from dialects and their description to dialect and its nature, contending always that variation and 'orderly hetero-geneity' (Weinreich, Labov & Herzog 1968: 100; see also Labov 1982) – not homogeneity – characterize natural language and that any adequate descrip-tion or theory of language must necessarily incorporate this variation (Hud-son 1980: 5–12). This survey of dialectology will consider the two main approaches to the study of dialect and dialects – dialect geography and urban sociolinguistics – and, by examining recent work in each, contrast their goals, methods, and achievements. The discussion of dialect geography takes research in American English as its focus while the treatment of urban sociolinguistics concentrates for the most part on work done in Great Britain.[2]

7.1. Dialect geography

Dialect geography is also sometimes called regional dialectology (e.g. Davis 1983), area linguistics (e.g. Kurath 1972), linguistic geography (e.g. Pederson 1969), and traditional dialectology (e.g. Francis 1983). It has most often been concerned with gathering data for linguistic atlases, which are collections of maps,[3] each showing the geographical distribution of some linguistic variant(s) at the level of phonetics, phonology, morphology,[4] lexicon, or semantics. The patterns of distribution are then compared in order to delineate the boundaries of regional dialects. Data are gathered by a highly trained fieldworker who seeks out appropriate informants in predetermined communities located at more or less equal distances from one another (Atwood 1963: 12). Having located willing and appropriate informants, the fieldworker elicits from them the hundreds of items noted on the question-

---

[2] These choices are not meant to imply that significant research in dialectology and its subfields is not being carried out elsewhere or in languages other than English; they reflect, instead, limitations of time and space as well as the author's assumptions – perhaps incorrect – about his readers, their backgrounds, and their interests. One especially important resource, Wells's (1982) three-volume *Accents of English*, does not fit comfortably into either of the traditions discussed here. The series, however, certainly merits mention, not only because it is the first survey of its kind but also because it offers standardized terminology for many of the phonological processes found in the various accents of the English language. Topics such as lexicography (I. W. Russell 1983), regional speech (Cassidy 1983, 1985–   ), usage (Algeo 1983), proverbs, slang and argot, literary dialect, and onomastics, all of which have often been associated with dialectology and dialectologists, will not be treated here.

[3] Although many dialectologists would agree with Moulton (1972: 198) that there can be no dialect geography without maps showing the distribution of variants, the exorbitant costs of printing such maps has led some projects, e.g. LAMSAS, to resort to publishing responses of informants in list format, keying the number of the response for an item to an informant number on an enclosed map.

[4] While descriptions of atlas projects often speak of the inclusion of grammatical items, most of these, such as the principal parts of irregular verbs, would currently be labeled morphological items. Davis, McDavid and McDavid (1969) offer a compilation of the worksheets from various LAUSC projects.

naire, or worksheet. Responses are recorded in what is perhaps infelicitously referred to as 'impressionistic transcription' (Jaberg 1936: 17, cited in Francis 1983: 92), using complicated systems of notation that vary from one atlas project to the next.

In the United States and Canada, dialect geography is generally associated with the *Linguistic atlas of the United States and Canada* (*LAUSC*), an as yet unrealized effort to produce a linguistic atlas for each of the regions of the two countries.[5] The project was begun in the late 1920s in New England, yielding the *Linguistic atlas of New England* (*LANE*) (Kurath *et al.* 1939–43) and the *Handbook of the linguistic geography of New England* (Kurath *et al.* 1939). None of the other atlas projects has fared so well, with only the *Linguistic atlas of the Upper Midwest* (*LAUM*) (Allen 1973–6) and a few fascicles of the *Linguistic atlas of the Middle and South Atlantic States* (*LAMSAS*) (R. McDavid *et al.* 1980–) reaching publication. With one exception, the remaining atlas projects are somewhere between the stages of initial planning and final editing for publication, all in need of human and financial resources if additional progress is to be made (e.g. R. McDavid 1983).

The single exception is the *Linguistic atlas of the Gulf States* (*LAGS*), under the direction of Lee Pederson (Pederson 1969, 1971, 1974a, 1974b, 1976, 1977b, 1977c, Pederson *et al.* 1974, Pederson, McDaniel & Bassett 1984). LAGS and related projects, such as the Dialect Survey of Rural Georgia, represent both a logical extension of LAUSC, covering for the most part previously unsurveyed areas, and an effort to improve upon the techniques of dialect geography. One improvement is the use of the portable tape-recorder for recording interviews; this practice permits a separation of the tasks of interviewing and transcribing, while preserving the primary data, a part of which can, for the first time, include connected speech (Pederson 1971: 87).[6] Additional innovations in method attempt to overcome the limitations of earlier atlas work, notably the rural bias of the questionnaire (1971: 86) and the failure to interview blacks in sufficient numbers, even in areas in which they constituted a large segment of the population (1971: 82). Pederson, however, remains firmly committed to the basic methodology of the other atlas projects, perhaps the most important concern of which is collecting large amounts of 'comparable' data:

[5] Readers interested in dialect geography in Great Britain may refer to Petyt 1980: 80–100, L. Davis 1983: 43–62, Chambers & Trudgill 1980, Francis 1984, and especially Kirk, Sanderson & Widdowson 1985 for discussions of projects there. For work on languages other than English, see Trudgill 1975 and Malkiel 1984. Additional historical information on the history of LAUSC and the regional atlas projects, especially LANE, is available in McDavid & McDavid 1952, 1956, Atwood 1963, Moulton 1972, Cassidy 1973, Viereck 1973, L. Davis 1983, R. McDavid 1983, and Francis 1984.
[6] Dialect geographers have long used tape-recorders, but LAGS is the first regional dialect survey to give the tape-recorder such a major role. Although earlier projects made records or tapes of informants, these were not part of the basic materials of the survey. In fact, some traditional dialectologists still view anything other than complete transcription during the interview with deep suspicion.

> the LAGS methodology remains squarely in the tradition of
> conventional linguistic geography and . . . all departures from that
> tradition are accretive and supplemental – accretive in that additional
> information is provided and supplemental in that a self-corrective
> capacity is recognized within the project. (1974a:12 and 1974b: 217;
> see also 1974a: 23 and 1977b: 19)

In another departure from earlier projects, Pederson has decided to publish the basic materials of the atlas (e.g. transcripts of tapes, fieldworker notes, etc.) in microform, noting that 'it seems better to publish the basic materials immediately than to suppress them with a promise of later comprehensive analytical description' (1974b: 223), and to make copies of the taped interviews available. Efforts are underway to microfilm the records of other regional atlas projects in order to preserve them from loss[7] and to make the materials available to a larger number of scholars than is currently possible, given the prospects for dissemination in any other form.

Despite the setbacks and problems encountered by the regional atlas projects, the practitioners of dialect geography are quick to point to their achievements in terms of not only the basic field research that has been completed, but also the numerous derivative studies based on atlas field records. The best known of these studies are no doubt Kurath 1949, Atwood 1953, and Kurath & McDavid 1961. The importance of these works and other related studies is surveyed in two well-documented articles, 'Regional dialects 1945–1974' (Allen 1977) and 'Studies of American pronunciation since 1945' (Pederson 1977a), devoted overwhelmingly to work done in the framework of dialect geography.

Yet as this short survey indicates, dialect geography is not as popular as it was, say, before the Second World War. Fewer and fewer students, even among students of language variation, are interested in pursuing work in this area, and funding for projects is almost nonexistent. This situation is obviously bound up with numerous factors, some inherent in dialect geography and others resulting from historical context. Since its beginnings as an outgrowth of philology and historical linguistics, dialect geography has been fiercely proud of the tradition of its methods and goals.[8] Indeed, as the Pederson quotation above illustrates, the methods and goals of LAGS are nearly identical with those of LANE.[9] The LANE project, in turn, had been

---

[7] McDavid (1983) documents the loss of two collections of dialect materials because of administrative 'accidents.'

[8] On the history and development of dialect geography, see Pop 1950, Atwood 1963, Moulton 1972, Cassidy 1973, Chambers & Trudgill 1980, Petyt 1980, Davis 1983, and Francis 1984. Pop 1950, Moulton 1972, and Francis 1984 are especially good sources on the tradition of dialect geography on the Continent.

[9] Pederson (1971: 79) comments, 'Although many summaries of the LAUSC Project include discussions of its aims and methods, the basic statements of Hans Kurath in the *Handbook* . . . (. . . 1939) require no modification in 1970.'

modeled on the Italian linguistic atlas, edited by Jaberg and Jud (1928–40), who had studied with Gilliéron, editor of the French linguistic atlas (Gilliéron & Edmont 1902–10). Thus, the methods of dialect geographers today are not unlike those of their predecessors a century ago. Ironically, the major changes in methodology introduced in the LANE project – the systematic inclusion of urban areas and the systematic sampling of informants from three social levels, both heralded as major advances – became the basis for later criticism by sociologists (Pickford 1956) and even dialect geographers (e.g. Underwood 1976) as too little innovation far too late.

Similarly, the major goal of dialect geography, the description of dialects, has remained unchanged, as have its commitment to describe the speech of elderly informants as a record of the speech patterns from an earlier era and its conviction that work in dialectology can best proceed in additive fashion. Hence, the study of rural dialects has been given priority over the study of urban areas, regional variation has been studied before social variation, and general studies using a detailed, but standardized, questionnaire that may well ignore important aspects of variation, even at the regional level, have been conducted before intensive, localized studies. This research program has repeatedly been justified in the name of providing comparable data and a 'framework' or 'baseline' for later studies (e.g. Kurath 1972).

This tradition of description (and sometimes description alone) has left dialect geography largely out of touch with developments in the study of language, first structuralism and, of course, more recently, work in the generative framework. It was, after all, two decades after Bloomfield's *Language* (1933) before a serious dialogue was undertaken on the relationship between structuralism and dialectology (Weinreich 1954; see also McDavid 1961, Moulton 1968, 1972, G. Sankoff 1973a, Pederson 1977b). This hesitancy, if not refusal, to enter into debate with theoretically oriented colleagues has meant that important data have frequently been ignored,[10] whether out of ignorance or bliss, especially since the results of atlas field-work have remained largely unpublished. Similarly, the rural, geographic,

---

[10] Trudgill (1983: 32) gives two examples of cases in which data from dialect geographers have not been given the consideration they merit. The first involves American syntacticians whose transformational models of English syntax ruled out constructions acceptable in British English. Here, sentences such as *Give it him* – acceptable (not questionable) in many British dialects – could be cited. The second example given by Trudgill concerns the controversy surrounding the origins of American Black English Vernacular (BEV). The controversy over the origins of BEV and the entire issue of the relationship between black and white speech in the United States, whether from a synchronic or diachronic perspective, has often pitted American dialect geographers against American urban dialectologists and their followers. The arguments have extended far beyond questions of BEV to questions of methodology in the study of language variation. Some of the more interesting papers written by those sympathetic to the position of dialect geographers include L. Davis 1969, Pederson 1972, 1977c, R. McDavid & L. Davis 1972, R. McDavid & O'Cain 1973, and L. Davis 1983: 84–127). Fasold (1971) attempts 'an intermediate stance.' Feagin 1979 includes an important summary of many of these issues in addition to presenting significant new data on the topic; see also L. Davis (1983: 121–7) for a dialect geographer's reaction to Feagin's study.

and historical biases of dialect geography have often left it poorly equipped to compete with sociolinguistic projects in urban areas for funding in the study of language variation, as priorities in both the public and private sectors have shifted to issues of language and education in multicultural, urban settings.

Dialect geographers have long been aware of many of these problems. Indeed such biases have been acknowledged from the beginning of the atlas projects (e.g. Kurath *et al.* 1939, R. McDavid 1942). Despite these acknowledgements, however, dialect geographers have continued to make statements that seemingly ignore these professed limitations. Kurath, among others, frequently notes that a particular form does not occur in a given region when he actually means that it did not occur during any of the interviews conducted for atlas research in the region under discussion. More serious, however, as Underwood (1976: 30) points out, are statements such as the following by Kurath in the introduction to his important *A word geography of the Eastern United States*:

> This systematic record of the usage of more than 1,200 persons gives us full information on the geographic and social dissemination of the words and phrases selected for this study. (1949: v)

Even a random sample could not have given 'full information'; a judgement sample of the kind employed for atlas work would have been far less likely to provide such information.

In response to the many critiques of dialectology cited by Underwood (1976) and Trudgill (1983: 31–51), most dialect geographers would probably quote Allen's response to several of Pickford's (1956) criticisms: 'To attack Atlas research because it is not directed at urban groups is something like finding fault with an electric toaster because it cannot fry potatoes' (1977: 229); they would claim that critics had failed to understand or appreciate their goals. And no doubt the critics would retort, 'In an age of microwave ovens, how necessary is a toaster? As for the fried potatoes, who needs the calories or the cholesterol?' Petyt (1980: 116) correctly notes that the findings of dialect geographers are certainly not 'worthless,' as some would claim; they are simply not what many linguists and other social scientists would want.

Despite the valiant and dedicated efforts of scholars like Pederson, few predict a bright future for dialect geography. None of the recent book-length studies of dialectology (Chambers & Trudgill 1980, Petyt 1980, Davis 1983, Francis 1984) is encouraging about the possibilities (but see Kirk, Sanders & Widdowson 1985). In an article entitled 'From Romance philology through dialect geography to sociolinguistics,'[11] Malkiel offers the following prognosis:

---

[11] Although Malkiel is speaking here primarily about Romance dialect geography, his comments are equally applicable to dialect geography in the English-speaking world; by sociolinguistics, he means studies that are labeled 'urban dialectology' or 'quantitative sociolinguistics' in this article.

The title of this article . . . should have been offered in interrogative form. There exist potent ingredients of philology and of traditional dialectology – ingredients that possibly constitute their principal charm and their prime relevance – which do not lend themselves to transmutation into the stuff of sociolinguistics. But a significant part of the older disciplines can, at a certain price and risk, be absorbed into the substance of their younger and more solidly architectured sister, and this possibility of transmission and assimilation remains, in scholarship, the safest guarantee of survival. (1976: 78)

7.2. Urban dialectology

Dialect geography produced several fine studies of variation in urban areas, including R. McDavid's (1948) social analysis of post-vocalic /r/ in South Carolina and DeCamp's (1958, 1959) work in San Francisco. There were also repeated statements by both Kurath (1964) and McDavid (1960) of the necessity of urban studies that would 'naturally call for something like random sampling' (1960: 58). Yet traditional dialectologists could not have predicted the impact of Labov's work when it began to appear in the mid 1960s (Labov 1963, and especially 1966, his work on New York City).

Instead of using the techniques of sampling, interviewing, and analysis of dialect geography for his New York study, Labov did his best to assemble a random sample. He recorded his informants as they engaged in a series of tasks designed to encourage them to pay increasing attention to their language as the interview progressed (cf. Fischer 1958); these tasks included conversation, a reading passage, the reading of word lists, and the reading of lists of minimal pairs. He then analyzed the tapes by calculating the number of occurrences of linguistic variables, which had been determined after a careful study of derivative research from atlas projects and other sources. Finally, Labov correlated the percentage of occurrences of variables during these various tasks with demographic and social variables; the results yielded what he referred to as 'sociolinguistic patterns' of the distribution of variables.

A student of Weinreich, Labov combined his teacher's commitment to analyzing language variation in light of current work in linguistics (cf. Weinreich 1954) with techniques and methods from other social sciences – sociology, anthropology, and psychology – to create new ways of analyzing variation in language. His work, however, should not be seen as merely the source of methodological innovation, but more importantly as a reorientation of the study of linguistic variation, of which dialectology is a part. No doubt most readers are more familiar with Labov's work than with that of any of the dialectologists cited during the discussion of traditional dialectology,

125

an ironic fact since Labov does not see himself as a dialectologist, but as a linguist interested primarily in the structure of linguistic systems, the nature of linguistic variation, and the mechanisms of linguistic change.[12]

Summaries of Labov's major studies (e.g. 1966, 1972a, 1972b) and their impact on the field appear in most surveys of dialectology (G. Sankoff 1973a, Chambers & Trudgill 1980, Petyt 1980, L. Davis 1983, Francis 1984); sociolinguistics (Trudgill 1974a, Wolfram & Fasold 1974, Hudson 1980); and historical linguistics (Bynon 1977). Discussions of recent work done in the Labovian paradigm or extensions of that framework can be found elsewhere in this volume; in the papers collected by Trudgill (1978), Labov (1980b), and Romaine (1982d); and in Romaine 1984b.

It is the extensions of the Labovian tradition that will be the focus of this discussion of the study of dialect and dialects in (mostly) urban settings. As researchers have taken Labov's basic methodology and analytical tools and attempted to apply them in other settings, problems have quite naturally arisen. Coping with these problems has led in some cases to refinements of the methodology, the analytical tools, or the theory of linguistic variation that the methodology and tools represent. In other cases, it has led to their outright rejection. At the risk of oversimplification, these developments may be summarized under the overlapping rubrics of the nature of linguistic variables (7.2.1), the use of mathematical tools in the study of variation (7.2.2), models of the speech community and variation within it (7.2.3), variable rules, variation, and questions of a theory of language (7.2.4) and notions of explanation in the study of language variation (7.2.5).

7.2.1. The nature of linguistic variables

A linguistic variable is 'a linguistic unit with two or more variants involved in covariation with other social and/or linguistic variables' (Chambers & Trudgill 1980:60). A commonly used example is the [ŋ] in the word *fishing* since it can be realized s either [n] or [ŋ], with no change in meaning. Ideally, linguistic variables should occur frequently, they should be structural units, and their distribution should be socially stratified; furthermore, they should be salient, but not so salient that they are consciously manipulated by speakers (Labov 1972b: 8). Elsewhere Labov notes that linguistic variables need to be quantifiable on a linear scale (1966: 49). Their correct analysis, he

---

[12] Labov is also hesitant in accepting the title 'sociolinguist,' fearing that work in quantitative sociolinguistics could degenerate into the production of useless correlational studies. On Labov's 'principles of linguistic methodology,' see Labov 1971, 1982. Weinreich, Labov, & Herzog 1968 outlines the basic relationship Labov sees between his work and earlier work in historical linguistics and dialect geography. Trudgill (1983: 1–7) attempts to locate the work of Labov and those who have been influenced by his work within the broader tradition of sociolinguistics, offering an insightful discussion of the problems of defining the term.

contends, is the 'most important step in sociolinguistic investigation' (1972b: 72). He gives three steps to be followed in defining linguistic variables: enumerating the range of contexts in which the variable occurs; distinguishing as many phonetic variants as is reasonably possible; and assigning each variant a quantitative index (1972b: 71). Researchers following these steps have, however, at times encountered difficulties.

Hudson (1980: 145–6) briefly notes three such problems. Two deal with the enumeration of linguistic contexts for the variable, first, in defining environments, and, second, in deciding which forms can be counted as instances of the variable. Using the example of [h] as a linguistic variable, Hudson asks: if a distinction is to be made between [h] after a word boundary and [h] word internally, what is to be done about words like *greenhouse* and *summer-house*? Do they contain a relevant boundary before the morpheme *house*? Should *hour* be counted as a possible instance of [h]? Even if the example of *hour* strikes many readers as ludicrous, Hudson's point is quite clear: on the basis of what criteria can such decisions be made? J. Milroy (e.g. 1982) has discussed this problem in relation to the choice of underlying forms for lexical items, especially in the study of nonstandard vernacular dialects.

A third problem mentioned by Hudson involves distinguishing a reasonable, accurate, and appropriate number of variants. As Knowles (1978) and Le Page (1980, Le Page *et al.* 1974) illustrate, even individuals trained in phonetics and transcription may disagree on both the best analysis and the identification of tokens as instances of particular variants.

Other problems have arisen with attempts to select and analyze linguistic variables. Several researchers, especially those working with dialects in Britain (e.g. Knowles 1978, J. Milroy 1982) have discussed variables that resist quantification along a linear scale. Unlike previously studied variables, these variables involve variation along several different phonetic parameters. Interestingly, these variables are precisely the ones that seem linked to patterns of sociolinguistic variation in the communities being studied.

A final potential problem relates to the limits of what can serve as a linguistic variable. Given the criteria stated by Labov, it is obvious that phonological variants are excellent choices for linguistic variables; certain aspects of verb morphology and negation are likewise appropriate. Researchers have, however, extended variable rule analysis, and, therefore linguistic variables 'above and beyond phonology,' to the level of syntax, G. Sankoff (1973b) and others working in Montreal being among the first to do so. Lavandera (1978) has noted potential problems with such a step, especially with regard to the selection of variables, because of the different kinds of meaning that phonological and syntactic variants tend to represent. She suggests that functional comparability, not sameness of meaning, be used in determining whether nonphonological forms are, in fact, variants. The debate over appropriate linguistic variants at the syntactic level continues in a series of papers by Labov (1978), Romaine (1981b), and Weiner and Labov (1983); Garcia (1985) reviews many of the issues in the debate, rejecting such efforts as well as all quantitative sociolinguistic studies.

Working in a very different vein, the Tyneside Linguistic Survey (Strang 1967, Pellowe *et al.* 1972, Pellowe 1976, Pellowe & Jones 1978, Local 1982, Jones-Sergent 1983) has attempted to use quantitative methods in order to study intonation, long problematic for linguists of any persuasion.

7.2.2. The use of mathematical tools in the study of variation

As David Sankoff (1978: xiii) points out, most researchers working in the paradigm of urban sociolinguistics are trained as linguists, not as statisticians. Consequently, the mathematical procedures they have used for the analysis of data have not always been especially sophisticated or appropriate for the task. However, great advances have been made in this area since the early research in which frequency counts, implicational scales, and the additive model of the variable rule were the only statistical tools in use.

Undoubtedly, the greatest effort has been devoted to the further refinement of the variable rule as pioneered by Labov (1969). In the years that followed, a series of important papers, including those by Cedergren and D. Sankoff (1974), Kay (1978), Rousseau and D. Sankoff (1978a, 1978b), Kay and McDaniel (1979), and D. Sankoff and Labov (1979), documents the heated discussion surrounding variable rules, their advantages, and their limitations as the mathematical basis of a linguistic model of variation. Since that time, a number of researchers, especially Labov and his followers (e.g. the authors of many of the papers in D. Sankoff 1978 and Labov 1980b), have continued basing their analyses of data on versions of the variable rule or VARBRUL computer program. Similarly, work also continues on refining the variable rule, both as a mathematical and linguistic model of variation.

Two long-term projects, the Tyneside Linguistic Survey alluded to above and the Sociolinguistic Survey of Multilingual Communities (e.g. Le Page 1968, 1972, Le Page *et al.* 1974, Le Page & Tabouret-Keller 1985), however, have chosen to use cluster analysis as their basic mathematical tool. Both projects, believing that the methods of Labov impose too many assumptions on the analysis, have sought mathematical tools that would enable them 'to take nothing for granted about social groups or hierarchies' (Le Page 1980: 340). Pellowe and Jones argue:

> [t]he primary goal must be to find not dimensions which successfully correlate with such things [as socioeconomic class], but dimensions

which are stable for changed samples and which are capable, *in combination*, of eliciting the structure of the variation in those samples. Only when we know enough about such stability and structure will we know what level of thing to look for as correlate. (1978: 121, emphasis in original)

McEntegart and Le Page (1982) offer a sober evaluation of the difficulties of using cluster analysis, and indeed all statistical techniques, observing that '[a] high level of statistical sophistication seems to militate against anything except rather superficial observations' (115), at least in certain kinds of communities (but cf. Labov 1980a, a response to Le Page 1980).

Other statistical models and procedures have been used with varying degrees of success, as exemplified in the papers collected by D. Sankoff (1978), Trudgill (1978), and Romaine (1982d). These studies amply illustrate that quantitative sociolinguists are becoming increasingly aware of the need to understand the appropriate uses and limitations of statistical procedures in order to make additional advances in quantitative analysis of sociolinguistic data.

7.2.3. Models of the speech community and variation in it

Defining the speech community has long been a problem for linguists, but it becomes an issue of special interest for the quantitative sociolinguist because the assumptions that guide the collection of data and the choice of statistical techniques for their analysis are intimately linked with the researcher's conception of the speech community as well as his or her understanding of the nature of linguistic variation and its role in language change. Within the tradition of quantitative approaches to variation, at least three different perspectives on the speech community have emerged, each focussing on a different level of social organization as the starting point for analysis.

The first perspective looks at the speech community as large numbers of people from different socioeconomic classes who happen to live in a single area, usually a large urban area. Labov's work in New York City (1966), Trudgill's study of Norwich (1974b), and other 'classic' studies in quantitative sociolinguistics represent this perspective. As in most work in quantitative sociology, informants are usually categorized according to several socio-demographic parameters, such as sex, age, and socioeconomic class, with great importance being attached to occupation, or, in the case of women, the occupation of the husband.[13]

The statistical procedures used in analyzing the data from these communities take the demographic group (divided according to age, sex, class, etc. or

---

[13] Nichols (1980) is critical of this practice; hers is an excellent discussion of some of the problems inherent in certain kinds of sociological models often used to locate women within speech communities.

some combination of these factors) as the level of analysis; figures on the behavior of individuals are often not reported. This practice is in keeping with Labov's statement of the Saussurian paradox: 'The social aspect of language can be studied through the intuitions of any one individual, while the individual aspect can be studied only by sampling the behavior of an entire population' (1971: 105). Results of such statistical analyses yield the now well-known patterns of Labov 1972b, in which different demographic groups not only use linguistic variables in a similar fashion, although to different degrees, but also evaluate the social prestige of the variables similarly.

This behavior is usually taken as support for the claim that the entire population being sampled shares a single grammar (see Labov 1980a). As Romaine notes, this model of the speech community and language change assumes that social prestige is the most important factor in determining whether or not an innovation spreads. In summarizing this view of change, she states:

> the dominant group affects change by inhibiting it from below, or borrowing from external groups, while the lower social groups initiate change through internal borrowing, either of variants already existing in the group . . . or of the prestige norm of groups higher up, mainly by hypercorrection. (1982c: 21–2)

The second and third perspectives on the speech community focus on the individual rather than the socioeconomic class or group, although each chooses a different level from which to begin analysis. The second looks at social networks, groups of individuals who are linked in any number of ways – as neighbors, as kin, as workmates or colleagues – and who, therefore, interact on a more or less regular basis, while the third looks at the individual him- or herself. Interestingly, researchers who have taken one of these perspectives often refer to the importance of the other in analyzing the results of research (e.g. L. Milroy 1982: 142, J. Russell 1982, and Bortoni-Ricardo 1985: 242–4, which make use of both perspectives).

Influenced by recent work in social anthropology (e.g. Boissevain & Mitchell 1973, Boissevain 1974), studies using the analysis of social networks seek 'to account for variability in *individual* linguistic behavior in communities, which is something a large-scale analysis like Labov's New York City study does not set out to do' (L. Milroy 1980: 21, emphasis in original; cf., however, Labov 1972a: 241–92). Indeed, much of the Milroys' work deals with the role that various kinds of individuals and social networks might play in language change. Their findings have led them to question certain assertions made by Labov about the mechanisms of language change and to refine others (most recently, Milroy & Milroy 1985).

The final perspective concentrates on the individual.[14] It is best represented by the work of Le Page (e.g. 1978, and Le Page & Tabouret-Keller 1985); his work in pidgin- and creole-speaking communities has led him to see linguistic behavior as 'acts of identity.'[15] Briefly, Le Page hypothesizes that 'the individual creates for himself the patterns of his linguistic behavior so as to resemble those of the group or groups with which from time to time he wishes to be identified, or so as to be unlike those from whom he wishes to be distinguished.' The individual's success will be contingent on four constraints:

(1) [he] can identify the groups
(2) [he] has both adequate access to the groups and ability to analyze their behavioural patterns
(3) the motivation to join the groups is sufficiently powerful, and is either reinforced or reversed by feedback from the groups
(4) [he has] the ability to modify [his] behaviour
(Le Page & Tabouret-Keller 1985: 181–2)

An insightful study of the linguistic behavior of British pop singers by Trudgill (1983: 141–60) applies Le Page's theory, demonstrating some of the ramifications of attempting to identify with more than one group at a time, especially when each group has a different pattern of linguistic behavior.

The statistical analyses of data in studies undertaken from these last two perspectives typically include information on individual speakers, both alone and, often, as members of relevant groups to which they belong. Such studies are often limited to a single social class (e.g. the Milroys' work) or group (e.g. J. Russell 1982). Although they lack the statistical generalizability of studies that sample a broader spectrum of the population, the detailed information they offer on the communities they investigate is a necessary complement to the findings of large-scale studies, leading to a richer and no doubt more accurate understanding of the nature of speech communities than any single perspective could supply.

7.2.4. Variable rules, variation, and questions of a theory of language

Despite great advances in variable rule methodology, not all researchers are satisfied with variable rules or with the theory of language variation they

[14] Work by scholars such as Bickerton (e.g. 1973) has focussed on individuals, using implicational scaling to relate the lects of individuals; although it is quantitative in one respect, he would surely not wish his work to be seen as an extension of the Labovian paradigm.

[15] As J. Russell (1982) points out, Le Page's work has a great deal in common with 'accommodation theory,' most often associated with Howard Giles (e.g. Giles & Powesland 1975, Giles & St Clair 1979). The extent to which accommodation theory, which applies to face to face interaction, can be extended to questions of linguistic change is still to be determined (see Trudgill 1986).

represent. Labov's position on this issue is clear: he sees variable rules as a beneficial, even necessary, addition to the generative tradition; furthermore, he sees variable rules as having explanatory power (e.g. D. Sankoff and Labov 1979).

Those who take issue with Labov's position do so for several reasons. First are those who dislike variable rule methodology for its focus on the group at the expense of the individual (e.g. Bickerton 1971, 1973; Berdan 1978; Hudson 1980, and many of the papers in Trudgill 1978 and Romaine 1982d) or for the attention paid to scores for complete variables while the range of scores for the individual variants making up the variable is ignored (Berdan 1975, Hudson 1980). Second, there are those who point out that variable rules, because of their probabilistic nature, stand in a very basic sense in contradiction with the aims of generative grammar as described by Chomsky and practiced by many, if not most, theoretical linguists (e.g. Kay & McDaniel 1979; Chambers & Trudgill 1980; Hudson 1980; Romaine 1981, 1982a, 1984a; Sterelny 1983). Third, there are those who disagree with Labov's contention that variable rules have explanatory power, basing their critiques on arguments from the philosophy of science (Romaine 1981a, 1982a, 1984a; Sterelny 1983).

Yet, as J. Milroy (1982: 46) points out, the issue of the methodological status of variable rules aside, much more faith can be placed in claims based on quantificational techniques, especially when tests of statistical significance are included, than in many of the claims made in linguistics; here he cites the EModE vowel system proposed in *The sound pattern of English* (Chomsky & Halle 1968) or the frequent discussions of rule ordering in some poorly attested dialect. Although an assessment of any such claims is ultimately based on one's own assumptions about how language is best studied, it is clear that the kinds of claims described by Milroy are a significant addition to the data that framers of theories, depending on their goals, might feel compelled to include in a particular theory of language (cf. Kay & McDaniel 1979: 184).

In other words, the issue of the compatibility of variable rules with generative grammar ultimately leads to the issue of the relationship between research done in the quantitative paradigm and that done in theoretical linguistics (e.g. work in syntax in the framework of GB or LFG), or between sociolinguistic theory and linguistic theory as theories of language. Again, Labov's position is quite clear: sociolinguistics *is* linguistics, and research that ignores variation is not worth much. Most sociolinguists would certainly argue for the need of incorporating variation into any viable theory of language, although there would be great disagreement among them as to how this is best done. Some would clearly reject Labov's position and many of his other assumptions, including those he holds about variable rules; they would still, however, acknowledge his contributions to the field. Taking quite the opposite perspective, Sterelny wishes to dismiss the entire Labovian endeavor:

> In my view, Labov has founded an industry rather than proposed a theory of a theoretical programme. For though there is an enormous amount of research along the lines he pioneered, no reason has been given for supposing that the research is more than the collection and display of data. (1983: 66)

Many linguists concerned with theoretical research would no doubt agree with Sterelny's assessment, at least to some degree; after all, variation of the kind studied by most quantitative researchers is by definition ruled out of Chomsky's program for linguistic research.

Yet Romaine reminds us of an obvious, but often overlooked, point: 'If one takes the data Labov typically deals with as the basis for a theory, we certainly arrive at a different theory of language than Chomsky' (1981a: 96). Elsewhere she adds:

> A sociolinguistic theory which is based on descriptions of variability shifts the emphasis away from what Chomsky (1973: 232) has called the fundamental empirical problem of linguistics, namely, to explain how a person can acquire knowledge of a language, to a rediscovery of explaining, as well, how language changes. (1982a: 289)

From this perspective, these two ways of doing linguistics, each with its own priorities and paradigms, will continue to make independent, but not unrelated, contributions to our understanding of the nature of language.

7.2.5. Notions of explanation in the study of linguistic variation

What constitutes an explanation in any branch of linguistics is always a matter of great disagreement; the literature in any field of the discipline is full of criticisms of other researchers who have dared to use the word *explain* when, in fact, according to the critic, all they have done is to describe, define, correlate, or even confound the issue to be explained. In this regard, quantitative sociolinguistics is no different. There is little consensus about when researchers do or do not have the right to claim that they have explained a phenomenon. Such disagreement is probably a sign of the vigor of the field. In spite of this disagreement, it is perhaps possible to delineate four strands in the quantitative study of variation, each of which requires a different kind of explanation and each of which will no doubt lead to productive developments in the future.

The first of these strands is that of Labov and his followers (e.g. the papers in Labov 1980b); they will continue to seek explanations in refinements of the variable rule and other related analytical tools. In characterizing this position as the belief that 'progress in linguistics is dependent on developing new quantitative methodology for analysing variation,' Romaine (1984a: 36) is probably correct. The second of these strands is perhaps best represented by the work of the Milroys (Milroy & Milroy 1977; Milroy & Milroy 1978, 1985; L. Milroy 1980, 1982; L. Milroy & Margrain 1980; J. Milroy 1982) in Belfast and others (e.g. J. Russell 1982; Bortoni-Ricardo 1985) that combine social network analysis and quantitative methods. Such researchers often study communities quite different from 'prototype variable rules communities' (Romaine 1982c: 19) of the sort described by Labov. For a variety of reasons, they find that tools other than the variable rule work best for describing and explaining the kinds of variation found in the communities they study. Romaine sees these researchers as trying 'to break away from the exclusively status-based theory and straightforward correlational methodology of Labov' (1982b: 2). They are concerned with developing both the social and the linguistic aspects of their research.

A third strand is the research of Romaine herself. In a recent article (1984a), she speaks of a 'hermeneutic approach' to the social sciences, including linguistics. From her research thus far (1981a, 1981b, 1982a, 1982c, 1984a, 1984b), it is quite evident that her description of a viable sociolingistic theory and her definition of explanation within that theory, while according an important place to quantitative methods, will be more broadly based than most, attempting to incorporate as completely as possible Hymes's (1974) notion of communicative competence.

The fourth strand is Trudgill's work on geolinguistics, or 'sociolinguistically informed dialectology' (1983: 51). His ideas are most clearly presented in Trudgill 1983 (especially Chapter 3) and in Trudgill 1986. His work is an attempt to combine insights from dialect geography, urban dialectology, and human geography, especially those aspects of human geography which focus on the diffusion of innovations (Hägerstrand 1967). As Trudgill and Chambers state the issue:

> Instead of giving up on the relationship between linguistic orderliness and geographical dispersions [of linguistic innovations and changes], what is required is a richer set of hypotheses about language variation and a more profound understanding of spatial networks and the diffusion of innovations. (1980: 206)

Combining the concept of the linguistic variable with insights, methods, and theories from human geography, he seeks 'to help improve our knowledge of the relationship between language and geography, and of the geographical setting of linguistic change' (1983: 52).

7.3. Conclusion

Although Trudgill's recent work takes dialectology back to questions of geographical diffusion, a concern of dialect geographers (cf. Kurath 1972), his work should not be construed as a return to their methods. As he and Chambers note, the relationship between dialectology as they conceive it and dialect geography is 'largely ancestral rather than theoretical or methodological' (Chambers & Trudgill 1980: 206). Others prefer to see recent developments as the logical progression of earlier work, stretching back to nineteenth-century Germany when Wenker mailed rural schoolmasters his first questionnaire. While the interest in the nature and significance of linguistic variation remains, theories, methodologies, and priorities – as Chambers and Trudgill note – have changed drastically, with the focus of research moving from the description of dialects to the understanding of dialect. This shift in many ways parallels trends in other fields of linguistics and the social sciences in general.

Work will no doubt continue in the tradition of dialect geography, albeit at a slower pace than in times past. Meanwhile, a growing number of people who share the traditional concerns of dialect geographers are incorporating the insights of urban dialectology into their studies (e.g. Feagin 1979). As researchers adapt the research program of urban dialectology to communities of various shapes (J. Milroy 1982) and sizes (e.g. Douglas-Cowie 1978; Clark & Hollett 1984; King 1984), it, too, will undergo changes. In this way, students of dialect and dialects will contribute to our ability to locate language not only in, but also through, time and social – as well as geographical – space.

REFERENCES

Algeo, J. 1983. IV. Usage. *Publications of the American Dialect Society* 71: 36–53.
Allen, H. 1973–6. *Linguistic atlas of the Upper Midwest*, 3 vols. Minneapolis: University of Minnesota Press.
Allen, H. 1977. Regional dialects 1945–1974. *American Speech* 52: 163–261.
Allen, H. & Underwood, G. (eds.) 1971. *Readings in American dialectology*. New York: Appleton-Century-Crofts.
Atwood, E. B. 1953. *A survey of verb forms in the eastern United States*. Ann Arbor: University of Michigan Press.
Atwood, E. B. 1963. The methods of American dialectology. In Allen & Underwood 1971.
Bailey, C.-J. & Shuy, R. (eds.) 1973. *New ways of analyzing variation in English*. Washington: Georgetown University Press.
Berdan, R. 1975. On the nature of linguistic variation. Doctoral dissertation, University of Texas.
Berdan, R. 1978. Multidimensional analysis of vowel variation. In D. Sankoff 1978.
Bickerton, D. 1971. Inherent variability and variable rules. *Foundations of Language* 7: 457–92.
Bickerton, D. 1973. Quantitative versus dynamic paradigms: the case of Montreal *que*. In Bailey & Shuy 1973.
Bloomfield, L. 1933. *Language*. New York: Holt.

Boissevain, J. 1974. *Friends of friends: networks, manipulators, and coalitions*. Oxford: Blackwell.

Boissevain, J. & Mitchell, J. C. (eds.) 1973. *Network analysis: studies in human interaction*. The Hague: Mouton.

Bortoni-Ricardo, S. M. 1985. *The urbanization of rural dialect speakers: a sociolinguistic study in Brazil*. Cambridge: Cambridge University Press.

Bynon, T. 1977. *Historical linguistics*. Cambridge: Cambridge University Press.

Cassidy, F. 1973. Dialect studies, regional and social. *Current trends in linguistics*. Vol. 10. The Hague: Mouton.

Cassidy, F. 1983. III. Regional speech and localisms. *Publications of the American Dialect Society* 71: 32–5.

Cassidy, F. (ed.) 1985– . *Dictionary of American regional English*. Cambridge, MA: Harvard University Press.

Cedergren, H. & Sankoff, D. 1974. Variable rules: performance as a statistical reflection of competence. *Language* 50: 333–55.

Chambers, J. & Trudgill, P. 1980. *Dialectology*. Cambridge: Cambridge University Press.

Chomsky, N. 1973. Conditions on transformations. In S. Anderson & P. Kiparsky (eds.) *A Festschrift for Morris Halle*. New York: Holt, Rinehart and Winston.

Chomsky, N. & Halle, M. 1968. *The sound pattern of English*. New York: Harper.

Clarke, S. & Hollett, R. 1984. Linguistic variation in a small urban context: the St. John's Survey. Paper presented at Methods V. To appear in Warkentyne in press.

Davis, A., McDavid, R., Jr, & McDavid, V. 1969. *A compilation of the work sheets of the Linguistic atlas of the United States and Canada and associated projects*, 2nd edn. Chicago: University of Chicago Press.

Davis, L. 1969. Dialect research: mythology versus reality. *Orbis* 13: 332–7.

Davis, L. 1983. *English dialectology: an introduction*. University: University of Alabama Press.

DeCamp, D. 1958. The pronunciation of English in San Francisco. *Orbis* 7: 372–91.

DeCamp, D. 1959. The pronunciation of English in San Francisco. *Orbis* 8: 54–77.

Douglas-Cowie, E. 1978. Linguistic code-switching in a Northern Irish village: social interaction and social ambition. In Trudgill 1978.

Fasold, R. 1971. The relation between black and white speech in the South. *American Speech* 56: 163–89.

Feagin, C. 1979. *Variation and change in Alabama English: a sociolinguistic study of the white community*. Washington: Georgetown University Press.

Fischer, J. 1958. Social influences on the choice of a linguistic variant. *Word* 14: 47–56.

Francis, W. N. 1984. *Dialectology: an introduction*. London: Longman.

Garcia, E. 1985. Shifting variation. *Lingua* 67: 189–224.

Giles, H. & Powesland, P. E. 1975. *Speech style and social evaluation*. London: Academic Press.

Giles, H. & St Clair, R. (eds.) 1979. *Language and social psychology*. Oxford: Blackwell.

Gilliéron, J. & Edmont, E. 1902–10. *Atlas linguistique de la France*. 13 vols. Paris: Champion.

Hägerstrand, T. 1967. *Innovation diffusion as a spatial process*. Chicago: University of Chicago Press.

Hudson, R. 1980. *Sociolinguistics*. Cambridge: Cambridge University Press.

Hymes, D. 1974. *Foundations in sociolinguistics*. Philadelphia: University of Pennsylvania Press.

Jaberg, K. 1936. *Aspects géographiques du langage (avec 19 cartes). Conférences faites au Collége de France (décembre 1933)* (Société des Publications Romanes et Françaises, XVIII). Paris: Droz.

Jaberg, K. & Jud, J. 1928–40. *Sprach- und Sachatlas Italiens und der Südschweiz*. 8 vols. Zofingen: Ringier.

Jones-Sergent, V. 1983. *Tyne bytes: a computerized sociolinguistic survey of Tyneside*. Frankfurt: Lang.

Kay, P. 1978. Variable rules, community grammar, and linguistic change. In Sankoff 1978.

Kay, P. & McDaniel, C. 1979. On the logic of variable rules. *Language in Society* 8: 151–87.

King, R. 1984. Linguistic variation and language contact: a study of the French spoken in four Newfoundland communities. Paper presented at Methods V. To appear in Warkentyne (in press).

Kirk, J. M., Sanderson, S. & Widdowson, J. D. A. (eds.) 1985. *Studies in linguistic geography; the dialects of English in Britain and Ireland*. London: Croom Helm.

Knowles, G. 1978. The nature of phonological variables in Scouse. In Trudgill 1978.

Kurath, H. 1949. *A word geography of the eastern United States*. Ann Arbor: University of Michigan Press.

Kurath, H. 1964. Interrelation between regional and social dialects. In Allen & Underwood 1971.

Kurath, H. 1972. *Studies in area linguistics*. Bloomington: Indiana University Press.

Kurath, H. & McDavid, R., Jr. 1961. *The pronunciation of English in the Atlantic States*. Ann Arbor: University of Michigan Press.

Kurath, H., Hanson, M. L., Block, J. & Bloch, B. 1939. *Handbook of the linguistic geography of New England*. Providence: American Council of Learned Societies. (2nd edn 1973. New York: AMS Press.)

Kurath, H. *et al*. 1939–43. *Linguistic atlas of New England*. 3 vols. Providence: Brown University Press.

Labov, W. 1963. The social motivation of a sound change. In Labov 1972b.

Labov, W. 1966. *The social stratification of English in New York City*. Washington: Center for Applied Linguistics.

Labov, W. 1969. Contraction, deletion and inherent variability of the English copula. In Labov 1972a.

Labov, W. 1971. Some principles of linguistic methodology. *Language in Society* 1: 97–120.

Labov, W. 1972a. *Language in the inner city*. Philadelphia: University of Pennsylvania Press.

Labov, W. 1972b. *Sociolinguistic patterns*. Philadelphia: University of Pennsylvania Press.

Labov, W. 1978. Where does the linguistic variable stop? *Working Papers in Sociolinguistics* 44. Austin: Southwest Educational Development Laboratory.

Labov, W. 1980a. Is there a creole speech community? In Valdman and Highfield 1980.

Labov, W. (ed.) 1980b. *Locating language in time and space*. New York: Academic Press.

Labov, W. 1982. Building on empirical foundations. In W. Lehmann, & Y. Malkiel (eds.) *Perspectives on historical linguistics*. Amsterdam: Benjamins.

Lavandera, B. 1978. Where does the sociolinguistic variable stop? *Language in Society* 7: 171–82.

Le Page, R. 1972. Preliminary report on the Sociolinguistic Survey of Multilingual Communities. Part I: Survey of Cayo District, British Honduras. *Language in Society* 1: 155–72.

Le Page, R. 1978. 'Projection, focussing, diffusion,' or steps towards a sociolinguistic theory of language, illustrated from the Sociolinguistic Survey of Multilingual Communities, Stages I: Cayo District, Belize (formerly British Honduras) and II: St Lucia. School of Education. St Augustine, Trinidad: Society for Caribbean Linguistics Occasional Paper No. 9. Reprinted in *York Papers in Linguistics* 9 (1980).

Le Page, R. 1980. Theoretical aspects of sociolinguistic studies in pidgin and creole languages. In Valdman & Highfield 1980.

Le Page, R. & Tabouret-Keller, A. 1985. *Acts of identity*. Cambridge: Cambridge University Press.

Le Page, R., Christie, P., Jurdant, B., Weekes, A. J. & Tabouret-Keller, A. 1974. Further report on the Survey of Multilingual Communities. *Language in Society* 3: 1–32.

Local, J. 1982. Modelling intonational variability in children's speech. In Romaine 1982d.

Malkiel, Y. 1976. From Romance philology through dialect geography to sociolinguistics. *Linguistics* 177: 59–84.

Malkiel, Y. 1984. Revisionist dialectology and mainstream linguistics: review article. *Language in Society* 13: 29–66.

McDavid, R., Jr. 1942. Some principles for American dialect study. In McDavid 1979.

McDavid, R., Jr. 1948. Postvocalic /r/ in South Carolina: a social analysis. In McDavid 1979.

McDavid, R., Jr. 1960. The dialectology of an urban society. In McDavid 1979.

McDavid, R., Jr. 1961. Structural linguistics and linguistic geography. In McDavid 1979.

McDavid, R., Jr. 1979. *Dialects in culture: essays in general dialectology*. W. Kretzschmar, Jr. *et al*. (eds.) University: University of Alabama Press.

McDavid, R., Jr. 1983. II. Linguistic geography. *Publications of the American Dialect Society* 71: 4–31.

McDavid, R., Jr. & Davis, L. 1972. The dialects of Negro Americans. In M. E. Smith (ed.) *Studies in linguistics in honor of George L. Trager*. The Hague: Mouton.

McDavid, R., Jr. & McDavid, V. 1952. The *Linguistic Atlas of New England*. In McDavid 1979.

McDavid, R., Jr. & McDavid, V. 1956. Regional linguistic atlases in the United States. In McDavid 1979.

McDavid, R., Jr. & O'Cain, R. 1973. Sociolinguistics and linguistic geography. *Kansas Journal of Sociology* 9: 137–56.

McDavid, R., Jr. *et al.* 1980– . *Linguistic atlas of the Middle and South Atlantic States*. Chicago: University of Chicago Press.

McEntegart, D. & Le Page, R. 1982. An appraisal of the statistical techniques used in the Sociolinguistic Survey of Multilingual Communities. In Romaine 1982d.

Milroy, J. 1982. Probing under the tip of the iceberg: phonological 'normalization' and the shape of speech communities. In Romaine 1982d.

Milroy, J. & Milroy, L. 1978. Belfast: change and variation in an urban vernacular. In Trudgill 1978.

Milroy, J. & Milroy, L. 1985. Linguistic change, social network, and speaker innovation. *Journal of Linguistics* 21: 339–84.

Milroy, L. 1980. *Language and social networks*. Baltimore: University Park Press.

Milroy, L. 1982. Social network and linguistic focusing. In Romaine 1982d.

Milroy, L. & Margrain, S. 1980. Vernacular language loyalty and social network. *Language in Society* 9: 43–70.

Milroy, L. & Milroy, J. 1977. Speech and context in an urban setting. *Belfast Working Papers in Language and Linguistics* 2: 1–85.

Moulton, W. 1968. Structural dialectology. *Language* 44: 451–66.

Moulton, W. 1972. Geographical linguistics. *Current trends in linguistics*, Vol. 9. The Hague: Mouton.

Nichols, P. 1980. Women in their speech communities. In S. McConnell-Ginet, R. Borker & N. Furman (eds.) *Women and language in literature and society*. New York: Praeger.

Pederson, L. 1969. The linguistic atlas of the Gulf States: an interim report. *American Speech* 44: 279–86.

Pederson, L. 1971. Southern speech and the LAGS project. *Orbis* 20: 79–89.

Pederson, L. 1972. Black speech, white speech, and the Al Smith syndrome. In L. Davis (ed.) *Studies in linguistics in honor of Raven I. McDavid, Jr*. University: University of Alabama Press.

Pederson, L. 1974a. Tape/text and analogues. *American Speech* 49: 5–23.

Pederson, L. 1974b. The linguistic atlas of the Gulf States: interim report two. *American Speech* 49: 216–23.

Pederson, L. 1976. The linguistic atlas of the Gulf States: interim report three. *American Speech* 51: 201–7.

Pederson, L. 1977a. Studies of American pronunciation since 1945. *American Speech* 52: 262–327.

Pederson, L. 1977b. Structural description in linguistic geography. In Shores & Hines 1977.

Pederson, L. 1977c. Toward a description of Southern speech. In Shores & Hines 1977.

Pederson, L., McDaniel, S. & Bassett, M. 1984. The LAGS concordance. *American Speech* 59: 332–59.

Pederson, L. *et al.* 1974. *A manual for dialect research in the Southern states*, 2nd edn. University: University of Alabama Press.

Pellowe, J. 1976. The Tyneside Linguistic Survey: aspects of a developing methodology. In Viereck, W. (ed.) *Sprachliches Handeln – soziales Verhalten: ein Reader zur Pragmalinguistik und Soziolinguistik*. Munich: Fink.

Pellowe, J. & Jones, V. 1978. On intonational variability in Tyneside speech. In Trudgill 1978.

Pellow, J. *et al.* 1972. A dynamic modelling of linguistic variation: the urban (Tyneside) linguistic survey. *Lingua* 30: 1–30.

Petyt, K. 1980. *The study of dialect: an introduction to dialectology*. Boulder: Westview Press.

Pickford, G. 1956. American linguistic geography: a sociological appraisal. *Word* 12: 211–33.

Pop, S. 1950. *La dialectologie: aperçu historique et méthodes d'enquêtes linguistiques*, Vol. 1: *Dialectologie romane*. Vol. 2: *Dialectologie non romane*. Louvain: Centre internationale de dialectologie générale.

Romaine, S. 1981a. The status of variable rules in sociolinguistic theory. *Journal of Linguistics* 17: 93–119.

Romaine, S. 1981b. On the problem of syntactic variation. *Working Papers in Sociolinguistics* 82. Austin: Southwest Educational Development Laboratory.

Romaine, S. 1982a. *Socio-historical linguistics*. Cambridge: Cambridge University Press.

Romaine, S. 1982b. Introduction. In Romaine 1982d.

Romaine, S. 1982c. What is a speech community? In Romaine 1982d.

Romaine, S. (ed.) 1982d. *Sociolinguistic variation in speech communities*. London: Arnold.

Romaine, S. 1984a. The status of sociological models and categories in explaining language variation. *Linguistische Berichte* 90: 25–38.

Romaine, S. 1984b. *The language of children and adolescents: the acquisition of communicative competence*. Oxford: Blackwell.

Rousseau, P. & Sankoff, D. 1978a. Advances in variable rule methodology. In D. Sankoff 1978.

Rousseau, P. & Sankoff, D. 1978b. A solution to the problem of grouping speakers. In D. Sankoff 1978.

Russell, I. W. 1983. V. New words. *Publications of the American Dialect Society* 71: 54–9.

Russell, J. 1982. Networks and sociolinguistic variation in an African urban setting. In Romaine 1982d.

Sankoff, D. (ed.) 1978. *Linguistic variation: models and methods*. New York: Academic Press.

Sankoff, D. & Labov, W. 1979. On the uses of variable rules. *Language in Society* 8: 189–222.

Sankoff, G. 1973a. Dialectology. In B. J. Siegel. *et al.* (eds.) *Annual review of anthropology*, Vol. 2. Palo Alto: Annual Reviews, Inc.

Sankoff, G. 1973b. Above and beyond phonology in variable rules. In Bailey & Shuy 1973.

Shores, D. & Hines, C. (eds.) 1977. *Papers in language variation: SAMLA:ADS collection*. University: University of Alabama Press.

Sterelny, K. 1983. Linguistic theory and variable rules. *Language and Communication* 3: 47–69.

Strang, B. 1967. The Tyneside Linguistic Survey. *Zeitschrift für Mundartforschung* 4 (n.s.): 788–94.

Trudgill, P. 1974a. *Sociolinguistics: an introduction*. Harmondsworth: Penguin.

Trudgill, P. 1974b. *The social differentiation of English in Norwich*. Cambridge: Cambridge University Press.

Trudgill, P. 1975. Linguistic geography and geographical linguistics. In C. Board *et al.* (eds.) *Progress in geography: international reviews of current research*, Vol. 7. London: Arnold.

Trudgill, P. (ed.) 1978. *Sociolinguistic patterns in British English*. Baltimore: University Park Press.

Trudgill, P. 1983. *On dialect: social and geographical perspectives*. New York: New York University Press.

Trudgill, P. 1986. *Dialects in contact*. Oxford: Blackwell.

Underwood, G. 1976. American English dialectology: alternatives for the Southwest. *International Journal of the Sociology of Language* 2: 19–40.

Valdman, A. & Highfield, A. (eds.) 1980. *Theoretical orientations in creole studies*. New York: Academic Press.

Viereck, W. 1973. The growth of dialectology. *Journal of English Linguistics* 7: 69–86.

Warkentyne, H. (ed.) in press. *Methods V: Papers from the Fifth International Conference on Methods in Dialectology* (July 1984). University of Victoria: Linguistics Department.

Weiner, E. J. & Labov, W. 1983. Constraints on the agentless passive. *Journal of Linguistics* 19: 29–58.

Weinreich, U. 1954. Is a structural dialectology possible? In Allen & Underwood 1971.

Weinreich, U., Labov, W. & Herzog, M. 1968. Empirical foundations for a theory of language change. In W. P. Lehmann & Y. Malkiel (eds.) *Directions for historical linguistics*. Austin: University of Texas Press.

Wells, J. 1982. *Accents of English*, 3 vols. Cambridge: Cambridge University Press.

Wolfram, W. & Fasold, R. 1974. *The study of social dialects in American English*. Englewood Cliffs: Prentice Hall.

8 Sociolinguistics and syntactic variation*

David Sankoff

In its emergence as a paradigm for the study of language, sociolinguistic variation theory has evolved through simultaneous confrontation with various other ways of viewing language. Along with most other schools of linguistics, it has explicitly taken position against unscientific normative and prescriptive ideologies of language, but it has also carried on a rather subtler rivalry with certain methodologically more rigorous psycholinguistic traditions. Together with other 'hyphenated' branches of linguistics, it has had continuously to situate itself with respect to generative linguistics, but at the same time it has defended its own criteria and methods from attack by antiformalist sociolinguistics. These external debates are reflected in the most important issues within the field; in this chapter I review these highly interrelated isues in what I believe to be a coherent synthesis of the variation theory perspectives on data, method, theory, and the social insertion of linguistic science. I adopt a Habermasian, critical theory approach to understanding:

(i) the social interests underlying linguistic research paradigms
(ii) the origins of variation theory in colonialized and minority language communities
(iii) the type of data that must be accounted for in these communities
(iv) the particular kind of analytical problems and theoretical questions pertinent to these data
(v) the epistemological status of a descriptive–interpretive methodology for dealing with the form–function problem – the central issue in the study of syntactic variation, with ramifications for all of these topics.

* Drafts of various parts of this paper were written independently of each other over a period of several years. A first attempt at a synthesis benefited from a detailed and insightful critique by the late Françoise Gauthier. I am grateful to the following colleagues for discussion and comments on the present version: William Kemp, Anthony Kroch, William Labov, Monique Lemieux, Koula Mellos, Frederick J. Newmeyer, Shana Poplack, Suzanne Romaine, Gillian Sankoff, Pierrette Thibault and Diane Vincent. I also offer much belated thanks to Koula Mellos for her forbearance while imparting the elements of critical theory to an erstwhile intolerant positivist.

In this undertaking I will not be bound by the explicit statements of Labov and other variationists about the scientific status of their endeavor; nor will I follow Habermas in his more recent forays into questions of linguistic methodology (1979: Chapter 1).

The variationist viewpoint on language is determined first by a scientific interest in accounting for grammatical structure *in discourse* – be it spontaneous natural conversation, formal narrative or argumentation, or various written genres – and second by a preoccupation with the polyvalence and apparent instability *in discourse* of linguistic form–function relationships. In emphasizing discourse, we refer to speakers' or writers' sustained and repeated exercise of their linguistic facilities in producing large numbers of sentences (rather than to the influence of discursive context on grammatical structure, or to questions of text coherence, sequencing and coreferentiality). When scientifically accounting for an entire speech sample or corpus, striking and widespread regularities may emerge which pertain solely to the relative frequency of occurrence or cooccurrence of various structures, rather than to their existence or grammaticality. The origin of this interest, and the nature of the preoccupation with form–function polyvalence, explain much of the misunderstanding and controversy about quantitative syntax, variation theory and sociolinguistics.

Despite the mistaken impression (Bickerton 1973; Kay 1978; Downes 1984: Chapter 6) that variationism is fundamentally dependent on some highly formalized notion of 'community grammar,' the internal linguistic conditioning of interest to variationists, and the methods they have developed to study it, can be amply exemplified in the phonology of a single individual (cf. Guy 1979) – even in that of the ideal speaker–hearer postulated in much linguistic argumentation – without regard to social or stylistic factors. This is also true of syntactic variation, though here it is often more difficult to establish empirically than in phonology. Nevertheless, it is of critical importance that the theory and methodology I shall be discussing evolved during research on multispeaker samples from sociologically or ethnographically well-defined speech communities; particularly within the sociolinguistic research paradigm inspired by William Labov. It is in this tradition that we find the origins of the concern for sustained discourse.

It is essential to a critical understanding of why certain topics are studied, which data are used, and which methodologies are applied in scientific investigations, that we attempt to characterize the interest underlying this inquiry. By 'interest' is meant not the intellectual predilections of the individual researcher nor even the explicit or hidden objectives of those who fund research programs, but rather the social and technological projects

141

propelling the historical evolution of societies. Habermas (1972) contrasts two fundamental human projects: the emancipation from material constraints, i.e. achieving mastery of nature, and the emancipation from social constraints, i.e. the identification and dismantling of repressive mechanisms in the social order. The former project is carried out through labor, guided by a positivist science involving controlled experimentation, physical measurement, abstract formulation, and objective criteria for consensus. The latter project is mediated by interaction, and its science is reflexive, interpretive, and antithetical to the constraints involved in controlled experiments and formalized language. It bases its consensus on intersubjective understanding not limited solely to external, 'objective' criteria.

Furthermore, Habermas (1971: Chapter 6) argues that at the current conjuncture of socioeconomic evolution, the dialectic between the two projects involves the extension of positivistic criteria into social science, the methodology of prediction and control of nature being applied to individual and social behavior. This displaces the role of social science in unmasking repression in the social order and replaces it with an opposite orientation reinforcing the ideological justification of existing social, political, and economic configurations.

For present purposes, I distinguish three divergent research paradigms in linguistic science, which I will characterize as introspective–generative, experimental–evaluative, and descriptive–interpretive. In so far as linguistics is an academic discipline, like classics, mathematics, or zoology, research in the field does not evolve solely according to its own inner logic but is also subject to the same types of influence as in other areas: disciplinary vogues and dogma, careers and ambitions, and thematic and strategic programs of universities, foundations, and government agencies, as well as the less obvious processes determining the role of knowledge production and distribution in society. These are common to all three approaches, including the 'ivory tower' introspective–generative school dominating modern linguistics. Each of the other two approaches is specifically inspired by additional influences.

In the case of the experimental–evaluative approach, I will focus on two related types of external impetus for linguistic research, namely first language teaching to speakers of nonstandard dialects, and second language teaching to immigrant speakers of minority languages. There is an explicit, widely accepted goal motivating the kinds of teaching falling under these rubrics: the transmission of linguistic capacities to those who do not have them, but ought to in the view of the dominant society (or, more accurately, the substitution or displacement of one set of linguistic behaviors by another). Such goal-oriented activity is mediated by purposive–rational logic, in Habermas's terms, and inevitably gives rise to research on efficient teaching methods, optimal conditions for learning, and explanations and remedies for learning problems. The methodology for this type of inquiry, in the fields of educational linguistics, psycholinguistics, language evaluation, etc., necessarily involves controlled experimentation, laboratory conditions, questionnaire survey methods, proficiency testing and a conceptual apparatus borrowed from the physical and biological sciences and developed for the prediction and control of natural processes. This apparatus is largely shared with other fields such as neurolinguistics, experimental phonetics and even foreign language teaching, which, however, lack the socially evaluative component characteristic of much educational and psycholinguistic research carried out in working class, immigrant and other minority contexts.

The descriptive–interpretive current which includes variationism also has roots in nonstandard dialects and the language of minorities, but the interests underlying this research are quite different. Its origins are to be found rather in the liberal and other progressive counterattacks of the sixties on racial and cultural stereotypes and on the paternalistic and repressive social policies that these stereotypes serve to justify. (Note that this also distinguishes sociolinguistic variationism from quantitative historical syntax, which is also descriptive–interpretive and which shares many of its analytical tools and formulations.) In making this claim, I do not deny the deep concern and great effort on the part of Labov and other variationists in connection with educational matters (Labov 1967, 1982; Kemp 1981, 1984). In contrast to Dittmar (1974), however, I argue that these matters are peripheral to the question of the roots of variationist linguistics in the history of modern society, to its divergence from dialectology and other related branches of linguistics, and to the internal logic of its development.

That no natural language is superior to another in logical form, coherence, or in aesthetics, has been little questioned in linguistics. This dictum accorded well with the cultural relativity of the anthropologists with whom, and in whose university departments, many linguists worked in the fifties and sixties, including most of those interested in non-Western and unwritten languages. The attack on linguistic stereotypes, then, was not part of any debate within linguistics; rather it formed part of the generalized, if uncoordinated, assault on conventional values and norms, and the social hierarchies they ratify. There was no need within the discipline of linguistics to prove that nonstandard dialects were fully-fledged languages, but there was a social need to demolish linguistic stereotypes through their study in a rigorous, scientific way.

This, in part, is why the florescence of variationism and its emergence as a paradigm distinct from dialectology, ethnolinguistics, traditional pidgin and creole studies, etc., dates from 1969, with the publication of Labov's major study of copula contraction and deletion in Black English, rather than from his earlier work in Martha's Vineyard (1963) or in the Lower East Side (1966), which was not particularly pertinent to any current social movement. It also explains the epistemological rapport among researchers into Black English (Wolfram 1969; Pfaff 1971; Fasold 1972; Labov 1972); Montreal French (D. Sankoff 1978a; Thibault 1979; G. Sankoff 1980; Vincent 1982; Cedergren & Lemieux 1985), pidgins and creoles (Bickerton 1975; G. Sankoff 1980), migrant workers in Germany (Heidelberger Forschungsprojekt 'Pidgin-Deutsch' 1978; Klein & Dittmar 1979), Puerto Ricans in New York (Poplack 1980a, 1980b, 1981, 1983) and with the dialectology of social stratification (Milroy 1981; Naro 1981) rather than with more traditional dialectology (e.g. Bailey 1974).

The descriptive–interpretive approach typically sees the researcher deeply immersed in the speech community and intent on reducing the effects of his or her own role as an expert on and/or native speaker of (a more standard version of) the language under study, and as a (usually petit bourgeois intellectual) member of the wider society, with concomitant preconceived notions about communicative behavior.

This type of research characteristically generates coherent, explicit and compelling critiques of class-based, race-based, or other dominant ideologies of language, with their normativisms, prescriptivisms, and stereotypes about logic, aesthetics, and intelligence. Furthermore, this work inevitably has social repercussions for the wider community, provoking media attention, intellectual debate, and expectedly hostile criticisms from the educational and literary establishment and other professionals of language, thus unmasking an interest in maintaining a repressive *status quo*. It is in engaging in this conflict of ideologies that linguistics may have a socially emancipatory role. Notions that the technically scientific aspects of linguistics may themselves be instrumentally relevant specifically to the working class or minorities are fundamentally mistaken. Technological progress, including a deeper understanding of the structural, psychological, or physiological properties of language, forms part of the project of control over the external world, language being treated as a formal object. As such, it will be appropriated by the classes who generally benefit most from science and technology (cf. Emonds 1976: xii). It is only the critical social-scientific reflection upon language use in its communicative function, with an obligatorily interpretive dimension to its 'method,' which can have a role in an emancipatory project. (I will return to this interpretive component later.) In this sense, the important contribution of linguistics in the court cases concerning Black English in schools (Labov 1982) resides less in its direct effect on particular material or institutional outcomes, and more in its role through national public discussion in awakening and changing consciousness of the issue.

What might be appropriate data for linguistic research with the kind of social orientation we have been discussing? First, introspection by speakers of nonstandard dialects is notoriously unreliable. This is partly because the censure or stigma attached to nonstandard forms suppresses them, whether the speaker is conscious of this or not. It is also partly due to *categorical perception* which works in the opposite direction, the existence of a nonstandard form entailing the perceived exclusion of the standard form from the dialect, though in fact it may be relatively common. It is next to impossible for a speaker in a linguistically stratified community where there are pervasive linguistic norms (whether these are well-formulated or not, realistic or not, accepted or not) systematically to make accurate judgements about which forms belong to which variety – though this same speaker might be an ideal informant when it comes to grammaticality of forms invariant within the community.

Turning to the controlled elicitation and testing methods of psycholinguistics and educational linguistics, these are even less informative about nonstandard usage, given the close association between the test situation and the stigmatization of nonstandard forms versus the approbation attached to the 'correct,' normative answer. In addition, controlled experimentation and questionnaires characteristically require a pre-established inventory of responses, inevitably strongly colored by the contrast between prescribed usages versus deviant or erroneous behavior. This bias is hard to avoid in any work on nonstandard dialects, but the experimental–evaluative approach runs counter to any type of heuristic search for patterns and structures having no direct counterparts in the standard variety. Finally, it is well known that vernacular usage (Labov 1972: Chapter 7) and bilingual or bidialectal behavior (Poplack 1980a) are extremely sensitive to the communicative situation. They tend to be absent from formal interviews and in some cases can be observed only in highly unobtrusive ethnographic work. They are unlikely to be manifested during an examination or a laboratory experiment.

Consideration of the types of data available through the introspective and experimental–evaluation approaches, then, leads to the realization that we can rely neither on how speakers think they behave nor on how they think they ought to behave. For nonstandard, minority or colonialized speech varieties, direct observation of language use is essential, in as natural a communicative interaction as possible. At the very least, we require recordings of relatively lengthy conversations, even if they be between the linguist and the speakers, and they should not take the form of elicitation sessions. It is preferable, of course, for conversation to be between two speakers of the same vernacular, or for the recording to be made of natural interaction, rather than an interview, but the minimum requirement is to obtain some sample of the speaker's actual speech. (For the evolution of the methodology of sociolinguistic corpus development, see Labov 1968: Chapter 7; Labov *et al.* 1968; Shuy, Wolfram & Riley 1968; D. Sankoff & G. Sankoff 1973; Sankoff, Lessard & Nguyen 1978; Poplack 1982; Labov 1984).

The imperative to deal with language use, rather than reflection about language use, as basic data, can now be seen to be derived from the interest in research on nonstandard speech varieties free from the misleading effects of stereotypes, from contamination by the norm and from categorical perception, and designed to be able to detect and handle principles or organization different from those of the standard language. This interest, which must be seen as emancipatory in the social context in which it emerges, contrasts sharply with the interest in control and prediction underlying the experimental–evaluative approach. Sociolinguistics and psycholinguistics thus constitute profoundly different approaches, though superficially they share a number of features: concern with nonstandard dialects, use of non-introspective data and statistical methodology.

In the study of extensive speech samples, or of other types of discourse, what are the substantive grammatical questions that emerge? As with the introspective–generative approach, the presence or absence of certain forms or cooccurrences invite description, generalization, comparisons and explanations. But what is equally important, and often more so, are quantitative patterns of occurrence relatively inaccessible to introspection or even testing methodology. Regular, complex relationships may exist at the quantitative level among a number of structures, but upon introspection, all we can say is that they are all simply 'grammatical.' The quantitative regularities may be vaguely guessed at through introspection, but may not be characterized with anything like the precision with which intuition-based methods can establish categorical relationships.

The quantitative facts are not minor details of linguistic behavior. Universal hierarchies and cooccurrence constraints not manifested in terms of grammaticality versus ungrammaticality for a given language are nonetheless often present in clear and well-developed form in usage frequencies. The classic examples are constraint hierarchies for the expression of certain allophones (or the application of optional phonological and morphophonological rules), but it is also true of syntax, in the study of variable rule order, optional movement or deletion rules, and in preferences among semantically or functionally equivalent phrase structures.

Moreover, it is these variable aspects of grammatical structure which are always the locus of linguistic change. Change virtually always requires a transitional period, often very lengthy, of variability, competition among structures, and divergence within the speech community. The detailed nature of linguistic change and of its synchronic reflex – dialect differentiation – cannot be understood without coming to grips with quantitative relationships.

The tools for studying these relationships are necessarily very different from those used in the introspective–generative paradigm. Frequency counts of forms in contexts are not just quantitative refinements of judgements of grammaticality and have even less to do with acceptability. Counts of 0% are analogous to judgements of ungrammaticality, but not identical to them. Non-occurrence does not necessarily indicate a prohibited form. It may simply be the result of a complex combination of features which could be perfectly grammatical but unlikely to appear in any reasonably sized corpus. Conversely, intuitively ungrammatical forms may appear systematically and at a non-negligible rate in spontaneous speech through the interaction of the grammatical facility with processing constraints (Kroch 1980). Though Labov has introduced methods of 'natural experimentation' to heighten the rate of occurrence of certain complex forms, these techniques are not nearly as easy to use as the generativist's use of intuitions about sets of sentences involving any number of combinations of syntactic features.

The ease with which grammaticality judgements are made may be seen as one of the motivations, or encouragements, for investigating the finer distinctions between syntactic theories. In contrast, the virtual absence from actual linguistic usage of any of the key contexts for resolving them diminishes these issues in importance for the variationist, who has many highly frequent phenomena to account for. These latter phenomena are in turn of no interest to the generativist, who does not encounter frequencies in the course of his or her analyses.

That generativists and variationists focus on different questions about language thus does not derive immediately from differences in the explicitly stated overall goals of the two paradigms, contrary to the argument of Fasold (1986), but rather from the different data each must account for, and the tools that each regards as valid.

Labov (1969), Kroch (1980) and others have at times argued that the key role of variation studies is to shed a new kind of light on specific issues which arise in generative theory. I would contend, however, that the contribution of variationism has this aspect only occasionally. It is rather in the investigation and solution of its own internally generated problems that it has contributed most to the understanding of language.

The classic example is Labov's demonstration of the parallelism of quantitative syntactic constraints on contraction and on deletion of the copula in

Black English (1969). The constraint pattern, which is inexpressible in other than quantitative terms, is consistent with the divergence of black and white varieties of English rather than convergence of Black English from a creole form towards the white vernacular – as recently confirmed by data from an isolated enclave of English speakers in the Dominican Republic, descendants of American blacks who migrated there in the 1820s (Poplack & Sankoff 1984, 1987; Tagliamonte & Poplack 1987). Recent work by Bailey and Maynor (1987) and by Labov's group using a variety of quantitative linguistic indices also supports a pattern of ongoing divergence (Ash & Myhill 1986; Graff, Labov & Harris 1986; Labov & Harris 1986; Myhill & Harris 1986).

Another example is the analysis of the dynamics of acquisition of inversion in *wh*-questions (Labov & Labov 1977). The quantitative aspect enabled the characterization of the complex sequence of phases of this acquisition and of differentiation within the set of *wh*-words.

We also cite G. Sankoff's program (1980: Chapters 10–12) of accounting for the origin of Tok Pisin grammatical structures in the lexical resources of the language and in discourse strategies. By using the variationist techniques of apparent time and real time analysis, she was able to elucidate the mechanisms through which tense and aspect marking, relative clause constructions and the cliticized pronominal apparatus emerged and were grammaticalized over the course of the last century.

We also mention the theory of weak complementarity (to be discussed below) for understanding the discourse mechanisms that lead to the gradual establishment of a syntactic variable (Sankoff & Thibault 1981; D. Sankoff 1982).

A recent example, though drawn from historical syntax rather than sociolinguistics, is Kroch's demonstration (1982) of how, in the emergence of *do*-support in English, several syntactic variables must be considered as essentially a single unitary variable, through his discovery of strict quantitative parallels in their early development.

These are all major insights into the structure of language, how it is used and how it evolves, but they were not motivated by issues in generative theory (nor do they necessarily have much impact on that theory), often despite authors' explicit claims to that effect, but ensued rather from the internal logic of the descriptive–interpretive paradigm in which they were made.

The insistence of descriptive–interpretive research on physical recordings and transcribed speech corpora, on counting occurrences of forms, and on statistical methodology have led some critics to label it, inaccurately, as positivist and/or scientistic. An exclusive dependence on observed facts, on objective evidence, is indeed diagnostic of a positivistic orientation, but the reliance on observation in our case pertains only to linguistic form – as we shall see, there is a strong interpretive component to the analysis of linguistic function. And although we will certainly be concerned with the statistical distribution of forms, this data is not very different from the 'facts' used in both traditional and modern distributional linguistics, aside from being quantitative, and more reliable for the reasons I have discussed.

A critique of positivism in the social sciences and humanities cannot in any case be meaningfully justified simply because of the use of some type of data or analytical technique. Positivist science is better characterized as *excluding* certain types of data or interpretation, such as the subjectivity of participants. In linguistics, this attitude is to be found in approaches which are strictly distributionalist, where all analytical groupings and distinctions must be made on the basis of the sharedness or the complementarity of the observed distribution of surface forms – sounds, particles, words, or syntactic constructions. Thus, in so far as hypotheses about linguistic structure (however arrived at, mechanically, intuitively, or otherwise) must be verified against the grammaticality or ungrammaticality of surface strings of words, and in so far as syntactic and semantic theory is oriented to account for structures thus determined, generative syntax is effectively positivist. That generative linguists use intuitions about grammaticality does not detract from this fact. These 'yes/no' intuitions in no sense constitute interpretive or reflexive science, but simply substitute for external observations of linguists' own behavior as expert 'native speakers.' It is in this sense that generative method is a type of positivist distributionalism.

Scientism is a somewhat vaguer label; it refers to the use of the experimental, mathematical, and quantitative apparatus of physical science to study concepts apparently pertinent to the social sciences or to the humanities, but which are in fact oversimplified, poorly operationalized or of little relevance to the real issues in these domains. In psycholinguistics, this is exemplified by the Bernsteinian paradigm, which sets up categories of behavior qualified as 'restricted' or 'elaborated.' Once this is done, 'scientific' studies of working class versus middle class vernaculars may be undertaken. However the fundamental question of justifying the application of the 'restricted' versus 'elaborated' labels to particular forms is not accessible to quantitative or other formal methodologies, thus the apparently scientific nature of this approach is illusory. Indeed I would argue that, as is typical of research in the experimental–evaluative paradigm, the use of these categories stems from an uncritiqued class-based normativist ideology of language (despite the often explicitly emancipatory aspirations of the practitioners).

The descriptive–interpretive approach cannot be accurately portrayed as positivistic or scientistic. As we shall see, the distribution of forms is only one of the two major types of data in any variationist study, the other being the identification of the linguistic function of each form. Aside from phonological studies, this identification of function has an unmistakably hermeneutic, or interpretive, component which is antithetical to positivist criteria. And as we shall also see, it is the fundamental issues of linguistic change and variation in the speech community which require that we come to grips with the form–function problem and force us into the sociologically critical and essentially non-positivist analysis of function. Were we to content ourselves with the statistical analysis of surface forms, this might justify the term scientistic, but the very fact of counting or using statistics does not, since they are used within the framework of a broader attempt to account for both components of the form–function relationship.

Most variationist work also involves data of an extralinguistic nature and the statistical correlation of these with linguistic data. This too has provoked the label of scientism – incorrectly again, since such correlations are properly used not as explanation or as indication of causality, but in conjunction with other types of analysis – sociological, ethnographic, historical, and critical – in order to understand the processes of linguistic differentiation at the community level.

Macroscopic sociodemographic categories or network-level patterns of relationship do not directly affect the performance of individual speakers; implicit in any correlational study is the existence of mediating processes or intervening mechanisms which lead from extralinguistic factors, through conscious intent and/or unconscious tendencies, to actual behavior. (See Romaine 1984 for a discussion of causality and explanation in sociolinguistics.)

Quantitative, statistical, and probabilistic notions have been introduced into linguistics many times, and they have long been standard in related fields such as lexicology and acoustic phonetics. It is only with Labov's work, however, that they have become widely tolerated, if not whole-heartedly embraced, in phonology and syntax.

The role of statistics in the study of variation has been the subject of much misunderstanding. Most of the critiques are more or less naive attacks on the internal logic of statistical inference itself, despite being phrased in terms of linguistic applications, and have little direct pertinence (e.g. Bickerton 1971, 1973; Kay 1978; Kay & McDaniel 1979; Downes 1984: 101).

There are of course well worked-out philosophical positions which deny the appropriateness of the statistical analysis of human behavior, especially of individual behavior which contains a component of free will; even to the point of excluding all formalized 'method' from the study of human affairs. These may be seen as radical extensions of the position, with which I sympathize, of rejecting strict positivism in the study of communicative behavior. Here I will not defend quantification against these extreme claims, which would willy-nilly exclude statistical or formal treatments from economics, sociology and social psychology, except to refer back to the variationist interest in accounting for large corpora which contain many tokens of a limited number of forms in a variety of comparable contexts. The universal experience in corpus-based research is that the structure of communication in the speech community, the structure of variation and change, is realized through recurrent choices being made at various interactional and grammatical levels by speakers. This is where the form–function problem is originally confronted. Many 'functions' can be carried out by several different 'forms' and the questions of who, when and why become immediately pertinent in accounting for those actually used.

Now, whenever a choice can be perceived as having been made in the course of linguistic performance, and where this choice may have been influenced by factors such as the nature of the grammatical context, discursive function of the utterance, topic, style, interactional context or personal or sociodemographic characteristics of the speaker or other participants, then it is difficult to avoid invoking notions and methods of statistical inference, if only as a heuristic tool to attempt to grasp the interaction of the various components in a complex situation.

It is not a requirement that the choice mechanism itself have any particular linguistic or sociological interpretation. Statistical methods are indifferent to the origin of the variability of the data, whether it be in the grammatical generation of sentences, in processes of production and performance, in the physiology of articulation, in the conscious stylistic decisions of speakers, or even simply as an analytical construct on the part of the linguist. The linguistic significance does of course depend on the nature of the choice process, but this question must be addressed prior to the statistical analysis (in the collection and coding of the data) and/or afterwards, in the interpretation of the results.

(For reviews of the statistical procedures that have been used in the variationist literature, see Cedergren & Sankoff 1974; Rousseau & Sankoff 1978; D. Sankoff 1978a, b; Sankoff & Labov 1979; Sankoff & Rousseau 1979; Naro 1980; D. Sankoff 1982, 1985, 1987.)

Much of the debate over the use of statistics has had to do with the notational representation of statistical regularities within a grammar. Objections to formalisms containing numbers of numerical parameters are often phrased as distaste for the notion of a numerical component in the mental grammatical facility. That mental processes may involve systematic tendencies which are non-categorical even in the most highly specified circumstances is a commonplace, however, and linguistic behavior follows suit, independent of the fact that linguistic competence may also include types of structures which have no counterparts in other domains of mental activity. Furthermore, it is a fallacy to think that numerical parameters at the notational level must correspond to some specific, stored numerical value at the cognitive level, any more than the hierarchical structures of phrase structures must have a neurological representation involving direct counterparts to the lines and nodes of a tree diagram.

Indeed where statistical regularities are found in linguistic performance, they are important as properties of language independent of whether they are consequences of:

> the physiology of articulation, in phonology;
> processing considerations in syntax;
> social or biological universals, as in the competition of tense and aspect inflections with periphrastic constructions based on verbs for standing, sitting, going, etc., or in the competition of modals with verbs for volition, ability, desire, etc.;
> panlinguistic typological tendencies which may or may not be coded in some innate form on the individual level; or
> some punctual actualization of the individual's grammatical facility.

There are many types of causes of statistical regularity, and which one or ones are pertinent to a given linguistic pattern remains an empirical question.

Now that we have compared the distinctive interests underlying the three approaches to the study of language and the types of data they determine, and have alluded to the methodological orientation imposed by the fundamental form–function problem, we turn to how and in what form this problem arises and how it may be approached systematically within the variationist paradigm. This subject has a large and diverse literature, mostly written with a view to affirming or denying the existence of the 'syntactic variable,' but also to documenting the stages and mechanisms of the grammaticalization of lexical or discourse forms. Some important contributions include G. Sankoff 1973; Gazdar 1976; Blanche-Benveniste 1977; Labov 1978; Lavandera 1978; Sankoff & Thibault 1981; Lefebvre 1982; Romaine 1982; Thibault 1983; Lemieux 1985; G. Sankoff & Labov 1985.

In examining a corpus of natural discourse collected in any speech community, it quickly becomes apparent that there are systematic differences among speakers, associated to some extent with one or more of: age, sex, race or ethnicity, geographical origin, education, and class. On the phonological level, this may take the form of two or more different articulations of a given phonological form in the same word or affix, in the same contexts. In the typical case, each speaker will alternate among all the various articulations, and will consistently manifest a pattern of variant frequencies similar to that of other individuals, though overall rates may vary widely among speakers.

These phonological alternations are not generally concomitant with changes in the denotational value (referential meaning) of a lexical item, nor the syntactic function of an affix or particle. The different variants may, however, have different social connotations, being explicitly or implicitly associated with the social or demographic group which uses them most frequently.

Differences among speakers also occur at the syntactic, lexical, and pragmatic levels. These too usually appear to be associated with extralinguistic factors. It would be advantageous to be able to analyze all types of variation within a common framework. There are, however, fundamental distinctions between variation at the phonological level and the other levels we have listed. Syntactic and pragmatic equivalence and lexical synonymy are all controversial concepts, in contrast to the immutability of referential or syntactic function in the presence of phonological variation: variation between two phonological or morphological forms does not entail change of referent or syntactic role, but two different lexical items or structures can almost always have some usages or contexts in which they have different meanings, or functions, and it is even claimed by some that this difference, though it may be subtle, is always pertinent whenever one of the forms is used.

The contrary viewpoint is adopted here, however. While it is indisputable that some difference in connotation may, *upon reflection*, be postulated among so-called synonyms whether in isolation or in context, and that in the case of each one a number of competing syntactic constructions may be acceptable in somewhat different contexts, there is no reason to expect these differences to be pertinent every time one of the variant forms is used. Indeed the hypothesis underlying the study of syntactic variation within a framework similar to that of phonological variation is that for certain identifiable sets of alternations, these distinctions come into play neither in the intentions of the speaker nor in the interpretation of the interlocutor.

Thus we say that *distinctions in referential value or grammatical function among different surface forms can be neutralized in discourse*. Moreover, this is the fundamental discursive mechanism of (nonphonological) variation and change. In what follows, what we exemplify with syntactic variation pertains equally well, and often more so, to lexical variation and variability in discourse structure. (For discourse examples, see Dines 1980; Vincent 1982, 1983; Horvath 1985: Chapter 8; Lemieux, Fontaine &

Sankoff 1986; Schiffrin 1986. For lexical examples see Labov 1973; Sankoff, Thibault & Bérubé 1978).

The systematic study of competing forms requires not only the identification of these forms, but also of the individual contexts in which differences between them are neutralized. It is precisely this which constitutes the interpretive component of variationist methodology. The analyst must in effect be able to infer the meaning or function of each token. In the most favorable situation, he or she does this as an ingroup member familiar with the particular individuals and interaction being studied, drawing on the intersubjective understanding of comembers of the same speech community. In the more usual situation, the linguist has to 'know' enough about the speech variety, and to 'understand' enough about what is transpiring in the particular discourse, to be able to infer speakers' intentions. Thus a basically hermeneutic task is combined with more mechanical distributionalist procedures prior to any statistical analysis. Interpretation of this sort is not new in linguistics, of course, and has more and more methodological stature as we move into historical syntax (cf. Rissanen 1986), into philology, and into analytical literary criticism and exegesis. In variation studies, however, it takes on a particular character, because of its application to large samples of tokens. In sociolinguistic variation theory, moreover, there is yet another important aspect, the sociological implication of judging the function of tokens, some of them socially stigmatized in discourse. I will return to this aspect at the conclusion of this paper.

It is clear that the notion of neutralization-in-discourse is implicit in most work on syntactic variation, and that a purely distributionalist methodology cannot suffice in this field. Since a strict distributionalist would not agree, however, this notion must remain a hypothesis, as must its antithesis – that at every use of a form its full complement of distinctions is somehow brought into play by the speaker and/or hearer. We have no more direct access to speakers' intentions than through their utterances themselves, nor to how hearers decode these than through their responses, particularly in natural situations. Analysts may be motivated by theoretical, normative, or critical considerations to discern intentions, or to deny them, whether or not these interpretations are accurate. Even the speakers themselves may correctly believe or claim, upon reflection, that their linguistic choices were prompted by certain intentions, when these intentions are nothing but *a posteriori* artifacts of linguistic introspection or afterthoughts inspired by linguistic norms. Thus we cannot tell whether one form was used instead of its alternate because of the desire to convey some subtle distinction or whether a free choice was made among two or more equally serviceable alternatives (possibly under a variety of non-deterministic influences).

Let us examine in more detail how this problem arises. Theory, introspection, or an informant suggests a difference in function or a lack of substitutability between two forms; a search is therefore undertaken to tie this distinction systematically to categorical (not statistical) contextual cooccurrences. In those contexts where this fails, either our analytical knowledge of the language and our powers of linguistic argumentation are insufficient, as would claim proponents of unique form–function relationships, or the alternate forms in question are themselves the sole indicators of the proposed functional distinction in the discourse environments in which they are used.

It is in this latter case that the two approaches differ and there might appear to be no methodology acceptable to both for deciding between them, since it is strictly a matter of interpretation of each form with no categorical surface correlates of function available. There is, however, one type of evidence which, in a certain sense, reconciles the two attitudes. Imagine two forms that everyone agrees serve closely related, if not identical, functions in a well-defined range of contexts; suppose that, in analogy to phonological variation, there is a certain 'weak' complementarity of distribution of the forms across the community – one form is frequently used by some speakers and seldom or never by others, while the other form has the opposite distribution. Then either the two forms are fulfilling the same function and any distinction between them is neutralized in discourse, or they retain somewhat different functions but the two functions themselves are in alternation. Some speakers use one form to fulfill one function in the same places where other speakers use the other form to fulfill the other function, the whole form–function complex being in complementary distribution across the community. In this latter case, if the two closely related functions in question are tied to some communicative universal – e.g. expression of past or future time, plurality, genitive case – we are forced to conclude that the distinction between the two alternatives is not germane to the speakers in discourse.

It is clear that in such cases, it is the analysts' concept of function which is the site of disagreement, and not how the alternate forms compete in fulfilling a function, nor the mechanisms of variation and change. (See Sankoff & Thibault 1981; Sankoff 1982 for further discussion and examples.)

The way in which syntactic variation emerges through neutralization of distinctions in discourse is not a process which fits well with current formalisms for synchronic descriptions of syntax. A basic assumption in linguistic theorizing is that the syntactic component of language is in large measure autonomous. It may have certain well-defined input and output interfaces with the phonological, lexical, semantic, or pragmatic components, but otherwise the processes and constraints that constitute syntax interact essentially among themselves without reference to non-syntactic factors in determining the grammatical sentences of the language. Though some students of communicative behavior may criticize this postulate, it would be intellectually counterproductive to pretend that the study of autonomous syntax has not been highly successful in discovering, explaining, and accounting for this complex and subtle aspect of linguistic structure. In accomplishing this, however, modern syntax has excluded from its purview concepts and phenomena that might be (and some have been) considered syntactic in nature, and has consigned them to the lexical, semantic, or pragmatic components of language. These include most of the equivalent-in-discourse relationships of the type we have been discussing. The forms which enter into contextual, stylistic, or social complementarity of distribution do not generally originate as related syntactic structures. Rather, they have something in common on the referential or pragmatic level only and participate in entirely different syntactic structures. This has led to characterizations of syntactic variationism as being technically naive for identifying variants of a variable through their 'having the same meaning' or 'carrying out the same function.' On the contrary, it is only by refusing to limit the range of possible variants to the categories of a particular formalization of autonomous syntax that we can have access to the origins of syntactic variation. If the domain of variability in discourse expands, however, and/or one form tends to displace another in a wide range of contexts, the equivalent-in-discourse relationship must eventually have repercussions at the purely syntactic level – the variation or change in question must be grammaticalized. To understand the origin of this type of syntactic change, then, we must look beyond syntax. During the process of grammaticalization, of course, properly syntactic considerations may predominate more and more, but it is precisely at the blurred margin between the syntactic and the extrasyntactic that the study of syntactic variation is particularly revealing and has the most to contribute.

It is natural within a theory of autonomous syntax to confine syntactic change and variation to small changes in a single feature, condition or parameter. This models the perceived gradualness of change in a way analogous to feature-by-feature phonological change, or to morphological change which affects least 'salient' (Naro 1981) forms or members of a paradigm first. This does occur on the syntactic level too, of course, but in change through neutralization in discourse, gradualness is achieved by the incremental spread of the contexts where the neutralization occurs, while the difference in form generally remains unattenuated.

The forces which drive change and which induce and maintain diversity within the community, whether they derive from natural physiological or cognitive processes, from linguistic ideology, prestige versus solidarity, learning patterns, languages in contact, etc., must all eventually manifest themselves on the level of individual behavior in linguistic interaction. It is the mechanisms which link the extralinguistic with patterned linguistic diversity which are the goals of sociolinguistic understanding.

Starting with the interests underlying the descriptive–interpretive approach to language, I have traced the epistemological imperatives of the study of syntactic variation through data and method to the theoretical preoccupation with form–function polyvalence. I have identified the ultimate locus of all syntactic or sociological claims of a theoretical or methodological nature as being the communicative intentions of a speaker at the moment in discourse where more than one referentially or functionally equivalent structure is accessible. To complete the circle, it remains to situate this 'moment' in a social-scientific critique of linguistic ideologies.

In a theory where 'interaction' is as basic a category as 'work' (Habermas 1972: Chapter 3), the dominant ideology is not merely an epiphenomenon of some mechanistic economic process. Rather it plays a crucial role in the justification of the existing social order and its support by imposing guidelines for individual behavior in interaction. This ideology is itself generated and reinforced in social praxis, i.e. in interaction, where the existing configuration of power, prestige, and wealth appears normal and inevitable according to all the criteria of this same ideology. Positivist science with its predefined categories and rejection of subjectivity is limited to quantifying and formalizing existing relationships. Critical social science, on the other hand, through its focus on the intersubjectivity of participants in interaction and its historical scope, can penetrate the appearances of inevitability and seek the social interests which actually determine both action and ideology.

In linguistic interaction involving variable behavior, an interpretive methodology can establish the functional equivalence of socially stratified forms, where a distributionalist approach will necessarily assume that there is a concomitant differential in function. Working class variants often tend to be syntactically and morphologically reduced, trading off the redundancy and clarity appropriate to the written language and to interaction in formal and technical domains in favor of efficiency and intersubjectivity among (usually intimate) participants, often with compensatory elaboration at the level of discourse mechanisms (cf. Slobin 1979, 'Be clear' versus 'Be quick and easy'). This tendency holds not only for the working class, but for the spoken language in general in familiar and intimate circumstances. Sociolinguistic methodology, however, characteristically succeeds in tapping the vernacular more easily with working class subjects than with middle class or bourgeois speakers. Distributionalism then inevitably infers that working

David Sankoff

class language is functionally reduced. This is also a recurrent tenet in prescriptivist grammatical ideology (Kroch & Small 1978). Not only is positivist methodology ideologically imposed by the same interests which propagate normativism and prescriptivism, thus 'confirming' stereotypes of working class and minority language, but also this ideological basis is hidden behind a 'scientific' rationale which claims universality for positivist criteria. Thus Lavandera (1978), in the name of scientific rigor, criticizes Laberge's (1978) recognition of functional equivalence of second person pronominal forms tu/vous with on in contexts of indefiniteness in French. Laberge had warned against analyses which equated the loss of on with a loss of the corresponding referential distinction. Lavandera dismisses the 'social conviction' behind this warning and calls for more 'empirical' methods for proving that the distinction is not lost, or that if it is lost, then it does not imply reduction at the cognitive level. But this faith in 'empiricism' and refusal of the hermeneutic aspect of the analysis is itself eminently ideological. It is precisely the hermeneutic recognition of equivalence that allows Laberge to avoid the conclusions predetermined by a normative ideology in the guise of a supposedly universally valid positivism.

Given that variationism is not exclusively dedicated to the search for formal structures, it would be incorrect to expect it to develop an axiomatic description of language or of language in society, or to abide by the highly paradigm-bound generative notions of 'theory' and 'explanation.' Such expectations, which recur in the variationist literature (e.g. Naro 1980; Fasold 1986), are perhaps founded in a well-justified admiration for the elegance or complexity of generative formulation, but neglect the fact that the works of Labov (dating at least from Weinreich, Labov & Herzog 1968) and of others, including Naro and Fasold themselves, are rife with what ordinary language, and indeed broader scientific discourse, would characterize as theorizing and explaining. Furthermore this activity, which integrates social and linguistic aspects, has had a cumulative character, with successively more sophisticated analyses leading to a more profound understanding of sociolinguistic process.

REFERENCES

Ash, S. & Myhill, J. 1986. Linguistic correlates of inter-ethnic contact. In D. Sankoff 1986.
Bailey, C.-J. N. 1974. *Variation and linguistic theory*. Arlington: Center for Applied Linguistics.
Bailey, C.-J. N. & Shuy, R. W. 1973. *New ways of analyzing variation in English*. Washington: Georgetown University Press.
Bailey, G. & Maynor, N. 1987. Decreolization? *Language in Society*, to appear.
Bickerton, D. 1971. Inherent variability and variable rules. *Foundations of Language* 7: 457–92.
Bickerton, D. 1973. Quantitative versus dynamic paradigms: the case of Montréal 'que'. In Bailey & Shuy 1973.
Bickerton, D. 1975. *Dynamics of a creole system*. Cambridge: Cambridge University Press.

158

Blanche-Benveniste, C. 1977. L'un chasse l'autre. Le domaine des auxiliaires. *Recherches sur le français parlé* 1: 100–69. Aix-en-Provence: Groupe de recherche en syntaxe.

Cedergren, H. J. & Lemieux, M. 1985. *Les tendances dynamiques du français parlé à Montréal.* Montréal: Office de la langue française.

Cedergren, H. J. & Sankoff, D. 1974. Variable rules: performance as a statistical reflection of competence. *Language* 50: 333–55.

Dines, E. R. 1980. Variation in discourse and stuff like that. *Language in Society* 9: 13–31.

Dittmar, N. 1974. *Sociolinguistics: a critical survey of theory and applications.* London: Arnold.

Downes, W. 1984. *Language and society.* London: Fontana.

Emonds, J. 1976. *A transformational approach to English syntax.* New York: Academic Press.

Fasold, R. 1972. *Tense marking in Black English.* Washington: Center for Applied Linguistics.

Fasold, R. 1986. Linguistic analyses of the three kinds. In D. Sankoff 1986.

Gazdar, G. 1976. Quantifying context. *York Papers in Linguistics* 6: 117–29.

Graff, D., Labov, W. & Harris, W. 1986. Testing listeners' reactions to phonological markers of ethnic identity: a new method for sociolinguistic research. In D. Sankoff 1986.

Guy, G. 1979. Variation in the group and the individual. In W. Labov (ed.) *Locating language in time and space.* New York: Academic Press.

Habermas, J. 1971. *Toward a rational society.* Translated J. J. Shapiro. Boston: Beacon Press.

Habermas, J. 1972. *Knowledge and human interests.* Translated J. J. Shapiro. Boston: Beacon Press.

Habermas, J. 1979. *Communication and the evolution of society.* Translated T. McCarthy. Boston: Beacon Press.

Heidelberger Forschungsprojekt 'Pidgin-Deutsch'. 1978. The acquisition of German syntax by foreign migrant workers. In D. Sankoff 1978a.

Horvath, B. 1985. *Variation in Australian English.* Cambridge: Cambridge University Press.

Kay, P. 1978. Variable rules, community grammar, and linguistic change. In D. Sankoff 1978a.

Kay, P. & McDaniel, C. 1979. On the logic of variable rules. *Language in Society* 8: 151–87.

Kemp, W. 1981. Major sociolinguistic patterns in Montreal French. In Sankoff & Cedergren 1981.

Kemp, W. 1984. Attitudes et pratiques linguistiques: les bénéfices sociaux d'une éducation plus favorable au français québécois. In M. Amyot & G. Bibeau (eds.) *Le statut culturel du français au Québec*, Vol. 2. Québec: Conseil de la langue française.

Klein, W. & Dittmar, N. 1979. *Developing grammars.* Berlin: Springer-Verlag.

Kroch, A. S. 1980. Resumptive pronouns in English relative clauses. Paper presented at the LSA Annual Meeting, San Antonio.

Kroch, A. S. 1982. Function and grammar in the history of English periphrastic DO. In R. Fasold & D. Schiffrin (eds.) *Language variation and change* (to appear).

Kroch, A. S. & Small, C. 1978. Grammatical ideology and its effect on speech. In D. Sankoff 1978a.

Laberge, S. 1978. The changing distribution of indeterminate pronouns in discourse. In R. W. Shuy & A. Shnukal (eds.) *Language use and the uses of language.* Washington: Georgetown University Press.

Labov, W. 1963. The social motivation of sound change. *Word* 19: 273–307.

Labov, W. 1966. *The social stratification of English in New York City.* Washington: Center for Applied Linguistics.

Labov, W. 1967. Some sources of reading problems for Negro speakers of non-standard English. In A. Frazier (ed.) *New directions in elementary English.* Champaign: National Council of Teachers of English.

Labov, W. 1969. Contraction, deletion and inherent variability of the English copula. *Language* 45: 715–62.

Labov, W. 1972. *Language in the inner city.* Philadelphia: University of Pennsylvania Press.

Labov, W. 1973. The meaning of words and their boundaries. In Bailey & Shuy 1973.

Labov, W. 1978. Where does the sociolinguistic variable stop? A reply to B. Lavandera. *Texas Working Papers in Sociolinguistics* 44. Austin: SW Educational Development Laboratory.

Labov, W. 1982. Objectivity and commitment in linguistic science: the case of the Black English trial in Ann Arbor. *Language in Society* 11: 165–202.

Labov, W. 1984. Field methods of the Project on Linguistic Change and Variation. In J. Baugh & J. Sherzer (eds.) *Language in use.* Englewood Cliffs: Prentice-Hall.

David Sankoff

Labov, W., Cohen, P., Robins, C. & Lewis, J. 1968. *A study of the non-standard English of Negro and Puerto Rican speakers in New York City*. Cooperative Research Project 3288. Washington: US Department of Health, Education, and Welfare.

Labov, W. & Harris, W. 1986. De facto segregation of black and white vernaculars. In Sankoff 1986.

Labov, W. & Labov, T. 1977. L'apprentissage de la syntaxe des interrogatives. *Langue Française* 34: 52–88.

Lavandera, B. 1978. Where does the sociolinguistic variable stop? *Language in Society* 7: 171–82.

Lefebvre, C. 1982. Some problems in defining syntactic variables: the case of WH questions in Montreal French. In R. Fasold & D. Schiffrin (eds.) *Language variation and change*, to appear.

Lemieux, M. 1985. *Variation et grammaire*. In H. J. Cedergren & M. Lemieux, *Les tendances dynamiques du français parlé à Montréal*. Montréal: Office de la langue française.

Lemieux, M., Fontaine, C. & Sankoff, D. 1986. Quantificateur et marqueur de discours. In D. Sankoff 1986.

Milroy, L. 1981. The effect of two interacting extra-linguistic variables on patterns of variation in urban vernacular speech. In Sankoff & Cedergren 1981.

Myhill, J. & Harris, W. 1986. The use of the verbal -s inflection in BEV. In Sankoff 1986.

Naro, A. 1980. Review of D. Sankoff 1978a. *Language* 56: 158–70.

Naro, A. 1981. The social and structural dimensions of a syntactic change. *Language* 57: 63–98.

Pfaff, C. 1971. Historical and structural aspects of sociolinguistic variation: the copula in Black English. South West Regional Laboratories. Technical Report 37.

Poplack, S. 1980a. Social structure and syntactic function of code-switching. In R. Duran (ed.) *Latino language and discourse behavior*. New Jersey: Ablex.

Poplack, S. 1980b. Sometimes I'll start a sentence in Spanish Y TERMINO EN ESPAÑOL: toward a typology of code-switching. *Linguistics* 18: 581–618.

Poplack, S. 1981. Bilingualism and the vernacular. In B. Hartford, A. Valdman & C. Foster (eds.) *Issues in international bilingual education: the role of the vernacular*. New York: Plenum.

Poplack, S. 1982. The care and handling of a mega-corpus. In R. Fasold & D. Schiffrin (eds.) *Language variation and change*, to appear.

Poplack, S. 1983. Intergenerational variation in language use and structure in a bilingual context. In C. Rivera (ed.) *An ethnographic sociolinguistic approach to language proficiency assessment*. Avon: Multilingual Matters Ltd.

Poplack, S. & Sankoff, D. 1984. El inglés de Samaná y la hipótesis del origen criollo. *Boletín de la Academia Puertorriqueña de la Lengua Española* 8: 103–21.

Poplack, S. & Sankoff, D. 1987. The Philadelphia story in the Spanish Caribbean. *American Speech*, to appear.

Rissanen, M. 1986. Variation and the study of English historical syntax. In D. Sankoff 1986.

Romaine, S. 1982. *Socio-historical linguistics; its status and methodology*. Cambridge: Cambridge University Press.

Romaine, S. 1984. The status of sociological method and categories in explaining language variation. *Linguistische Berichte* 90: 25–38.

Rousseau, P. & Sankoff, D. 1978. Advances in variable rule methodology. In D. Sankoff 1978a.

Sankoff, D. (ed.) 1978a. *Linguistic variation: models and methods*. New York: Academic Press.

Sankoff, D. 1978b. Probability and linguistic variation. *Synthèse* 37: 217–38.

Sankoff, D. 1982. Sociolinguistic method and linguistic theory. In L. J. Cohen, J. Los, H. Pfeiffer & K. P. Podewski (eds.) *Logic, methodology and philosophy of science*, Vol. 6. Amsterdam: North-Holland & Warsaw: Polish Scientific.

Sankoff, D. 1985. Statistics in linguistics. *Encyclopedia of the statistical sciences*, Vol. 5. New York: Wiley.

Sankoff, D. (ed.) 1986. *Diversity and Diachrony*. Amsterdam: Benjamins.

Sankoff, D. 1987. Variable rules. In U. Ammon, N. Dittmar & K. Mattheier (ed.) *Sociolinguistics. An international handbook of the science of language and society*. Berlin: De Gruyter (to appear).

160

Sankoff, D. & Cedergren, H. J. (eds.) 1981. *Variation omnibus*. Edmonton: Linguistic Research Incorporated.

Sankoff, D. & Labov, W. 1979. On the uses of variable rules. *Language in Society* 8: 189–222.

Sankoff, D., Lessard, R. & Nguyen, B. T. 1978. Computational linguistics and statistics in the analysis of the Montreal French corpus. *Computers and the Humanities* 11: 185–91.

Sankoff, D. & Rousseau, P. 1979. Categorical contexts and variable rules. In S. Jacobson (ed.) *Papers from the Scandinavian symposium on syntactic variation*. Stockholm: Wiksell.

Sankoff, D. & Sankoff, G. 1973. Sample survey methods and computer-assisted analysis in the study of grammatical variation. In R. Darnell (ed.) *Canadian languages in their social context*. Edmonton: Linguistic Research Incorporated.

Sankoff, D. & Thibault, P. 1981. Weak complementarity: tense and aspect in Montreal French. In B. B. Johns & D. R. Strong (eds.) *Syntactic change*. Natural Language Studies 25. University of Michigan.

Sankoff, D., Thibault, P. & Bérubé, H. 1978. Semantic field variability. In D. Sankoff 1978a.

Sankoff, G. 1973. Above and beyond phonology with variable rules. In Bailey & Shuy 1973.

Sankoff, G. 1980. *The social life of language*. Philadelphia: University of Pennsylvania Press.

Sankoff, G. & Labov, W. 1985. Variation theory, XIV Conference on New Ways of Analyzing Variation, to appear.

Schiffrin, D. 1986. Turn-initial variation: structure and function in conversation. In D. Sankoff 1986.

Shuy, R. W., Wolfram, W. A. & Riley, W. K. 1968. *Field techniques in an urban language study*. Washington: Center for Applied Linguistics.

Slobin, D. I. 1979. *Psycholinguistics* (2nd edn). Glenview: Scott, Foresman and Co.

Tagliamonte, S. & Poplack, S. 1987. How Black English PAST got to the present: evidence from Samaná. *Language in Society*, to appear.

Thibault, P. 1979. *Le français parlé: études sociolinguistiques*. Edmonton: Linguistic Research Incorporated.

Thibault, P. 1983. Equivalence et grammaticalisation. Doctoral dissertation. Université de Montréal.

Vincent, D. 1982. Pressions et impressions sur les sacres au Québec. Montréal: Office de la langue française.

Vincent, D. 1983. *Les ponctuants de la langue*. Doctoral dissertation, Université de Montréal.

Weinreich, U., Labov, W. & Herzog, M. 1968. Empirical foundations for a theory of language change. In W. P. Lehmann & Y. Malkiel (eds.) *Directions for historical linguistics*. Austin: University of Texas Press.

Wolfram, W. 1969. *A sociolinguistic description of Detroit Negro speech*. Washington: Center for Applied Linguistics.

9 Language birth: the processes of pidginization and creolization

William A. Foley

9.0. Introduction

Pidgins and creoles have been the center of linguistic controversy for over a century now (Coelho 1880–6; Schuchardt 1883, 1889, 1909) and give no indication of yielding that position today (Bickerton 1981, 1984). Many of the issues of a hundred years ago remain unresolved, and much of current discussion was anticipated by Schuchardt in his many articles. Even standard definitions of pidginization and creolization have not been accepted by all scholars concerned with the field (see, for example, the conflicting definitions in Hymes 1971 and Andersen 1983). For my purposes I will adopt the following definitions. A pidgin is a contract language which is an amalgam of linguistic elements of two or more languages and which arises in social and economic transactions between at least two groups speaking different languages, by a process of restriction and simplification of one of the languages of these groups, usually that in a socially superior position. This process of restriction and simplification is termed pidginization. By definition a pidgin is no one's native language. A creole is a pidgin which has become the native language of a speech community. In the process of becoming nativized, the pidgin undergoes extension and elaboration, i.e. it becomes creolized. Consequently, creoles are normally contrasted with pidgins by their greater functional and structural complexity and their stability in usage.

9.1. Pidgins and pidginization

As defined above, pidginization occurs in a multilingual contact situation to aid communication between groups. In any multilingual contact situation, a number of language choices may occur, of which a pidgin is only one. In other cases, the native language of one of the groups in contact may be used, as with English in Australia; or a language not native to any of the groups in contact may function as a *lingua franca*, for example, English in

162

India or Koine Greek in the eastern Mediterranean in ancient times; or stable reciprocal multilingualism may persist, as in Kupwar village in India, described by Gumperz and Wilson (1971). What determines whether a pidgin will arise in a contact situation, rather than one of the alternatives, is a complex interaction of social and linguistic factors. At least two languages must be involved in the genesis of a pidgin: that which supplies the bulk of the pidgin language's vocabulary and is spoken by a socially superior group (the superstrate language) and that which contributes less obviously and is spoken by a socially inferior group (the substrate language). There is normally only a single superstrate language, but commonly multiple substrate languages. In the classical cases of pidgins, those which arose in the plantation areas of the Atlantic, Pacific and Indian oceans, a very wide social gulf existed between the speakers of the superstrate and substrate languages, and this has sometimes been seen as a necessary social condition for the development of pidgins. But as we shall see below, the cases of indigenous pidgins developed in New Guinea show this not to be the case. A simple asymmetry of social and economic roles is sufficient.

Pidgins grow out of economic necessity. Because of economic relations of trade or enforced labor, it becomes imperative for groups in these contact situations to find a common language. There is a socioeconomic asymmetry in that the language of the dominant group is not easily made available to the members of the subordinate group(s). For this reason the language of the prestige group cannot function as the contact language, and the possibility of a language from the subordinate group(s) functioning in this role is blocked by its very association with perceived social inferiors. The social reasons for the unavailability of the prestigious language are varied. Demography may be important if the number of speakers of the superstrate language is very small in comparison to that of the substrate speakers; few models for the superstrate language would be around. This probably played an important role in the development of Tok Pisin (New Guinea Pidgin English: Mühlhäusler 1979, 1983). Another important factor may be the attitude of the superstrate speakers toward their language. They may believe that it is an important badge of their distinctive cultural identity or is too difficult for speakers of other languages to learn. Thus, they may withhold their true language as a model for the substrate speakers, producing a kind of 'foreigner talk' (Ferguson & DeBose 1977; Ferguson 1982), consisting of a simplified version of the language and specialized for use in contact situations with speakers of other languages.

Such language attitudes seem to have been central in the genesis of Police Motu and Chinook Jargon. Dutton 1985 reports how the Motu deliberately withheld knowledge of their real language in dealing with foreigners, but produced a kind of simplified Motu foreigner talk. This foreigner talk probably first developed historically through their intensive trading networks with their neighbors speaking the unrelated Koita language. Dutton 1985 reports that the first Christian missionary to the area immediately set to learning Motu and thought that he was learning the real language. But in fact he was only taught the foreigner talk by the Motu men and only discovered this deception from his young son who learned the real language from his playmates in the village.

Hymes (1980) points out the haughty attitude of the Chinook toward their language, even within their own speech community. He also mentions that other Indian tribes of the area regarded true Chinook as being the most difficult language to learn. A simplified version of Chinook, a precursor of Chinook Jargon, would fit both Chinook and non-Chinook attitudes to the language. Because of their possessive and exclusive attitude toward their own language, the Chinooks believed that non-Chinooks should not properly learn true Chinook. On the other hand it was the non-Chinook view that true Chinook was impossible to learn and the best to hope for was a simplified Chinook jargon. The existence of a precontact foreigner talk for Chinook is probably impossible to verify, but given these attitudes and Chinook economic and trade domination of their neighbors (Hymes 1980), as well as the presence of non-Chinook slaves in Chinook villages, it would almost seem a foregone conclusion that such must have existed.

Foreigner talk, then, may play a very central role in pidginization. Because pidgins arise in a restricted (and restricting) social context, typically laboring or trading situations, they have a much reduced range of linguistic functions to perform, in comparison with native languages (see Mühlhäusler 1980; Halliday 1974 on the functions of language). Pidgins largely function to get people to perform desired actions within a plantation or trading context (directive function), or to describe a concrete situation to bring about a desired end (referential function). They are not generally used to promote social cohesion (interactional function), to express abstract ideas and inner states (expressive function), to talk about language (metalinguistic function) or to create language based art forms (poetic function). Much of the complexity of native languages is associated with the expression of these latter functions; some examples are stylistic variation to express social or aesthetic meanings in complex lexical alternatives such as *eat/dine*, *eye-doctor/optometrist*; allomorphic variations as sociolinguistic markers, for example *-in* versus *-ing* (Shopen & Wald 1980); complex subordinating discourse styles (elaborated codes) versus simpler linear coordinating styles (restricted codes: Bernstein 1971); politeness phenomena, realized both morphologically and syntactically (Brown & Levinson 1978); metaphors, puns, and other conscious forms of language manipulation and play. All of these features of language are involved

Table 1. *Linguistic simplification*

More complex or unsimplified linguistic structure	Simpler or simplified linguistic structure
Lexicon	
Larger vocabulary in a given domain or overall	Smaller vocabulary, generic terms rather than specific
Compounds and morphologically complex words	Monomorphemic words, paraphrases of complex words
Syntax	
Subordinate clauses	No subordinate clauses, parataxis
Variable word order, conditioned by syntax (e.g. negation)	Invariable word order
Presence of copula, pronouns, function words	Absence of copula, pronouns, function words
Morphology	
Extensive inflectional systems	Heavily reduced or no inflections
Allomorphy, including of stems	No allomorphy, invariant stems (e.g. full forms as opposed to contractions)
Phonology	
Consonant clusters	CV monosyllables and CVCV disyllables
Polysyllabic words	

largely with functions other than the directive and referential. As only these latter two functions are germane typically to a pidgin, such languages do not present the same structural complexities common in other languages, complexities which are the formal realizations of their richer variety of functions. Pidgins represent a restriction in linguistic functions associated with a simplification of linguistic form.

The next question is an obvious one: what is the nature of this simplification and how does it come about? This is where Ferguson's work on foreigner talk (Ferguson 1971, 1982; Ferguson & DeBose 1977) becomes critical. Ferguson points out that it is part of the communicative competence of adult speakers in many speech communities to know how to simplify their language to aid comprehension by nonfluent speakers (for recent studies of this, see Meisel 1977; Snow, van Eeden & Muysken 1981). How to talk simply is part of our linguistic knowledge, and further, the application of this knowledge to languages of diverse structure seems to result in remarkably similar outputs. Table 1 (from Ferguson 1982: 60) displays the features of simplified language forms in contrast with those of the source language.

To summarize these changes, the basic principle seems to be to maximize invariance in the language code; in other words, the relationship between form and meaning should be as transparent as possible. The restriction of words to generic terms, the elimination of allomorphy, the use of parataxis rather than embedding, and the adoption of invariant word order for grammatical relations all ease the processing load of the hearer. There is no need to cope with variations and irregularities. This is not surprising, for in foreigner talk it is the hearer who is the nonfluent speaker. Furthermore, the loss of inflections and function words and their replacement by full lexemes maximizes that area of the language easiest for the foreigner to acquire – the lexicon. A number of writers (Silverstein 1972; Mühlhäusler 1979) have noted how early, unstable pidgins consist of no more than a reduced lexicon put through the grammatical rules of one's native language.

Some of these linguistic simplifications are directly relatable to the loss of certain language functions, as found in pidgins. To take one example: as Nichols (1980) indicates, the loss of subordination in favor of a paratactic coordinating style reflects a tendency to minimize presupposition in favor of assertion. As pidgins (and, presumably, foreigner talk) are largely used in the directive and referential functions, functions in which assertion is paramount, it is to be expected that structural features which do not express assertions will be subject to loss. The likelihood of loss would no doubt be increased with more complex morphological and syntactic subordinating devices in the source language.

Ferguson's (1982) list of the features of simplified language forms corresponds very closely to the universal features of pidgins *vis à vis* their source languages, and this would suggest a close historical connection, as I will indeed argue. I suggest that a pidgin is a version of a foreigner talk of a superstrate community that has been conventionalized and accepted, most importantly by speakers of the substrate language(s). It is conceded that some pidgins may have had a different historical origin, but this does seem to be the general case. Thus, the first motivation for a pidgin comes from the speakers of the superstrate language, whose language is withheld, possibly because of the reasons discussed earlier. They, perhaps unwittingly, propagate a simplified version of their language, a foreigner talk. This, in turn, is taken up by the speakers of the substrate language(s) and conventionalized and extended. During the process of conventionalization, some features of the substrate languages may find their way into the developing pidgin, as with Tolai words in Tok Pisin. Many of these transfers from or continuities with the substrate languages during the process of conventionalization may themselves result in seeming simplifications from the superstrate language. It is the speakers of the substrate languages who ultimately set the form of the pidgin, because it is they who control the process of conventionalization. Pidgins weakly conventionalized correspond to Mühlhäusler's (1979) jargon phase, which is referentially impoverished, has little grammatical integrity – often just a vocabulary with grammatical rules drawn from the speaker's native language – and shows high variation from speaker to speaker. More strongly conventionalized pidgins correspond to Mühlhäusler's (1979) stable pidgin phase, which is referentially more adequate, has a coherent grammatical structure of its own, distinct from superstrate and substrate languages, and shows relatively little variation across speakers. The process of conventionalization is greatly facilitated by high linguistic diversity in the substrate speakers. In such situations the incipient pidgin will be immediately seized upon for communication across linguistic boundaries, and its early stability will determine its effectiveness. The very rapid stabilization/conventionalization of Tok Pisin between 1880 and 1890 (Mühlhäusler 1983) is no doubt due to its quick adoption as an intertribal *lingua franca*. Similar developments must have occurred in the Caribbean and Indian Ocean plantation islands. It has been claimed by Whinnom (1971) that a multilingual substrate community is necessary for pidginization to occur (his 'tertiary hybridization'). As we shall see, while this is a common ingredient of pidginization contexts, it is not a necessary feature. Rather such substrate communities simply favor rapid conventionalization and stabilization of the incipient pidgin. Pidginization can occur in simple bilingual contact situations, and I will now turn to the study of one such case.

9.2. Indigenous pidgins in New Guinea

New Guinea, with about a thousand languages, is the most linguistically complex area in the world, and within New Guinea itself the most complex area is the Sepik-Ramu basin with somewhere around 300 languages. The Sepik-Ramu basin is just as highly fragmented culturally as linguistically. The basic cultural unit is the hamlet or village. Kinship links are the primary basis of social structure. Each village or hamlet is viewed as the center of the social world, and outside it other communities are regarded as increasingly different with geographical distance. There is no sense of intercommunity solidarity based on shared linguistic allegiance; many villages form closer economic and social ties with neighboring villages speaking a different language than with those speaking the same language.

Within this complex picture the paramount cultural theme is exchange and trade. Sepik societies have been described as 'importing cultures' (Mead 1938), and this indeed is the overriding cultural concern. Gewertz 1983 is a detailed study of the middle Sepik area. Here the primary trading pattern is sago, the carbohydrate staple, exchanged for fish. Trading contacts of this sort are not sporadic, but are sustained and often passed down in clans from generation to generation (Harrison 1986). A status differential also marks these exchanges. As Gewertz (1983) makes clear, the fish suppliers occupy a superior position socially and economically *vis à vis* the sago suppliers. Thus we have the scenario set for the development of a pidgin in these trading networks, with the fish suppliers speaking the superstrate language and the sago suppliers the substrate.

A pidgin has indeed grown up in at least one of these trading networks, that between the Yimas and the Arafundi groups of the Karawari river area, although further research in the Sepik area will probably turn up many more (the Sepik area is still very poorly known linguistically). The Yimas are the fish suppliers, and the Arafundi the sago suppliers. Other goods besides fish and sago are exchanged between the Yimas and the Arafundi, but in almost all cases it is the Yimas who provide the prestige trade items. As expected, then, the pidgin is based largely on Yimas. Pidginized Yimas is a relatively stable pidgin; native speakers of both Yimas and Arafundi speak it much the same (the major differences being phonological). Structurally it is a radically simplified version of Yimas proper, with some mixture of Arafundi. Yimas proper is a highly complex polysynthetic language; Yimas Pidgin is morphologically simple, of an almost isolating structure. Over 80% of the vocabulary of Yimas Pidgin is Yimas in origin. The rest is Arafundi or unplaced. Consider the sample list of words in Table 2. As these show, the vocabulary of Yimas Pidgin is drawn from both languages. The sample, however, gives a somewhat distorted view of the relative lexical proportions, since to document adequately the Arafundi presence, I have selected a rather large number of pidgin words with Arafundi sources. A more complete sample would reduce the Arafundi percentage to under 20% overall. For example, not a single verb root is Arafundi in origin. One interesting feature of the pidgin's lexicon is that the words for major trade items are generally those of the importing group. Thus, *tupwi* 'sago' and

Table 2. *Vocabulary sources in Yimas Pidgin*

	Yimas proper	Yimas Pidgin	Arafundi
man	payum	payum	
man		nuŋgum	nuŋgum
woman	ŋaykum	aykum	nam
pig	numbran	numbrayn	ya
cassowary	awa	karima	karima
dog	yura	tam	taum
yesterday	ŋariŋ	ariŋ	nay
betelnut	patn	patn	kumwɨ
sun	tɨmal	tim	kom
village	num	kumbut	kumbuk
water	arɨm	yim	yem
one	mban	mban	kapunta
two	tɨmbal	kundamwin	Kɨndamuɲ
talk	malak-	mariawk-	yaŋ-
hear	andɨ-	andɨ-	eik-

numbrayn 'pig' are Yimas, but *yamban* 'basket' and *kambam* 'catfish' are Arafundi.

Yimas proper is a highly complex language morphologically, with extensive allomorphy and suppletion and a great plethora of bound forms, especially in the verbal system. Yimas Pidgin is derived from this by massive reduction, by eliminating all allomorphy and suppletion and almost all bound forms, and by drastically cutting most distinctions in any category. For example, while Yimas proper makes seven tense distinctions, Yimas Pidgin only makes two. There is also a small admixture of Arafundi forms in the grammar of Yimas pidgin.

I will illustrate this process of simplification in a number of areas of Yimas grammar. Consider first the pronouns of Yimas and the pidgin in Table 3.

Table 3. *Pronouns in Yimas and Yimas Pidgin*

		Yimas	Yimas Pidgin
SG	1	ama	ama
	2	mi	mi
	3	mɨn	mɨn
DL	1	kapa	kapa
	2	kapwa	mi kundamwin
	3	mɨrɨm	mɨn kundamwin
PC	1	paŋgɨt	paŋgɨt
	2	paŋgɨt	
	3	miŋgɨt	
PL	1	ipa	paŋgɨt
	2	ipwa	mi asɨŋ
	3	mum	mɨn manba

Note that while Yimas proper distinguishes four numbers in its pronouns, singular, dual, paucal and plural, Yimas Pidgin distinguishes only three, lacking a paucal (in this feature Yimas Pidgin parallels Arafundi, which also distinguishes only three numbers). While the first person monomorphemic forms are preserved in the pidgin, in the second and third persons, the non-singular forms are analyzed into their component parts, person plus number: e.g. *mi kundamwin* 2 two 'you(DL)' and *mɨn manba* 3 many 'they(PL)' (*kundamwin* 'two' and *manba* 'many' are both from Arafundi). Here is an example of the tendency in language simplification toward transparent relations between form and meaning to aid hearer processing: forms which are semantically complex (i.e. person and number), but morphologically simplex in Yimas proper become morphologically complex in Yimas Pidgin. Each unit of meaning has a corresponding formal realization.

169

Other examples of morphological simplification involve massive morphological loss between Yimas and the pidgin. I will consider two examples, one in the nominal system and another in the verbal. Yimas proper has complex nominal inflection: it distinguishes three numbers and over a dozen noun classes. Nominal modifiers like adjectives and possessives agree in number and class with their head nouns. These are marked by bound affixes, underlined in the examples in (1):

(1) a. Pat*n*   ama-na-*kin*   k*i*pa-*n*   a*n*ak
        betelnut v SG   1SG-POSS-V SG   big-v SG   cop v SG
        'My betelnut is big'

     b. Par*i*ŋgat   ama-na-*ra*   k*i*pa-*ra*   arak
        betelnut v PL   1SG-POSS-V PL   big-v PL   COP v SG
        'My betelnuts are big'

     c. Tr*i*ŋ   ama-na-*ŋ*   k*i*pa-*ŋ*   ak*i*k
        tooth VI SG   1SG-POSS-VI SG   big-VI SG   COP VI SG
        'My tooth is big'

     d. Tr*i*ŋgi   ama-na-*ŋgi*   k*i*pa-*ŋgi*   akiak
        tooth VI PL   1SG-POSS-VI PL   big-VI PL   COP VI PL
        'My teeth are big'

     e. Tan*i*m   ama-na-*m*   k*i*pa-*m*   ap*i*k
        bone VII SG   1SG-POSS-VII SG   big-VII SG   COP VII SG
        'My bone is big'

Yimas Pidgin loses all inflection for number and class. Number of a noun is marked by *kundamwin* 'two' or *manba* 'many,' placed after it. The forms for class v singular (the unmarked class in Yimas with the largest membership) are extended to cover all nouns, as in (2):

(2) a. SG: Patn ⎫
                Tr*i*ŋ ⎬ ama-nak*i*n   kipan   anak
                Tan*i*m ⎭ 1SG-POSS   big   COP

     b. PL: Patn ⎫
                Tr*i*ŋ ⎬ manba   ama-nak*i*n   k*i*pan   anak
                Tan*i*m ⎭ many   1SG-POSS   big   COP

The pervasive allomorphy of number marking conditioned by class for nouns and nominal adjuncts is completely eliminated in Yimas Pidgin, again increasing the transparency of the form–meaning correlation and easing the hearer's processing load.

Yimas verbs exhibit extensive cross-referencing for core grammatical relations. Subject, direct object and indirect object are all marked on the verb, indicating their person, number, and, if inanimate, their class. Consider the examples in (3):

(3) a. Na-   ka- tupul
       3SG DO-1SG s-hit
       'I hit him'

  b. Tupuk   ku-   n-   ŋa- ŋa- ndut
     sago XI SG XI SG DO- 3SG S-1SG IO-give-RM PAST
     'He gave me sago long ago'

  c. Pia- ka-   i- kɨr- umbun
     words-1SG S-say-RM FUT-3PL IO
     'I will tell them after tomorrow'

It is the presence of these verbal affixes which indicates grammatical relations in Yimas, as word order of nominals is free and there is no core nominal case marking.

All cross-referencing is eliminated in Yimas Pidgin. Nominal word order is still free, but indirect objects are now marked by a postposition *namban* 'toward.' This postposition is extended optionally to mark animate direct objects, cases in which ambiguity would result from indeterminacy between subject and object, as in (4a):

(4) a. Ama mɨn namban kratɨkɨ-nan
       1SG 3SG   toward   hit-NON FUT
       'I hit him'

  b. Mɨn tupwi ama namban asa-nan
     3SG sago   1SG   toward   give-NON FUT
     'He gave me sago'

  c. Ama mɨn manba namban mariawkɨn anak
     1SG 3SG many   toward   talk   FUT
     'I will tell them'

This simplification is again one which eases the processing task of the hearer. Yimas verbs, with their multiple *unstressed* affixes bearing crucial information regarding grammatical relations (not just the functions themselves, but the person, number and class of the nominals filling those functions), present a probable processing overload. By dropping these affixes in favor of stressed pronouns and nouns and a stressed postposition, Yimas Pidgin makes the hearer's task that much less daunting.

As a final example let me consider a feature of Yimas proper that Yimas Pidgin not only simplifies, but also regularizes. Aspect in Yimas proper is indicated in a number of different ways. Some aspectual inflections occupy the final position of the tense suffixes, as (5) illustrates:

(5) Amdra   ya-   ka- am-ɨt
    food V PL V PL DO-1SG S-eat-PERF
    'I have eaten the food'

In other cases, aspect is indicated by incorporated adverbials preceding the main verb stem:

(6) Pu-   yakal-tau-and<del>i</del>-ndut
   3PL S-PROG- sit- hear-RM PAST
   'They were waiting and listening'

In Yimas Pidgin these aspectual contrasts are expressed by the auxiliary verbs *ta-* PROG and *mind<del>i</del>k-* PERF (from Yimas *mind<del>i</del>k-* 'finish'), following a verb marked with the dependent suffix -*mbi*. The auxiliary verbs take the tense suffixes, as in (7):

(7) a. Ama mi namban and<del>i</del>-mbi mind<del>i</del>k-nan
      ISG 2SG toward hear-DEP PERF-NON FUT
      'I heard you already'
   b. Ama mi   namban and<del>i</del>-mbi ta-nan
      ISG 2SG toward hear-DEP PROG-NON FUT
      'I am listening to you'

This simplification results in the removal of the syntagmatic equivalent of allomorphy. Whereas allomorphy is the paradigmatic alternation in form of a base morpheme in differing environments, the aspectual system of Yimas proper illustrates the same basic grammatical category parcelled out in a number of different syntagmatic positions. Given that the elimination of allomorphy is a pervasive feature of language simplification, the removal of its syntagmatic equivalent is something one might expect.

Yimas Pidgin has not expanded beyond its sphere of use between Yimas and Arafundi speakers and will probably die out in the next 25 years or so, as its function has now been preempted by Tok Pisin. I now turn to a case of an indigenous New Guinea pidgin which has successfully extended its domain of use and is now one of the three national languages of Papua New Guinea. This language is called Police Motu, and its history has recently been documented in great detail in Dutton 1985, whose findings I will summarize here. I will largely be concerned with the social process of pidginization in the case of Police Motu, since the strictly linguistic effects of pidginization were highlighted in the discussion of Yimas.

Police Motu is essentially a pidginized version of Motu, the native language of the Port Moresby area. Because Motu proper is a much simpler language morphologically than Yimas, Police Motu does not present as radical a departure from its source language as does Yimas Pidgin. In fact, Police Motu exists in two forms, one more simplified and less Motu-like than the other. The more complex, more Motu-like form is spoken by native speakers of Austronesian languages closely related to Motu, while the simpler form is used by speakers of Papuan languages unrelated to Motu.

In precontact times the Motu were engaged in a number of extensive trading networks. The most spectacular of these were the *hiri* trading voyages to the Gulf of Papua, a dangerous journey of some 400 km. The Motu traded pots and received sago and lumber in return. In these trading contacts pidginized versions of the Papuan languages of the peoples of the Gulf of Papua were used as *lingue franche*. These are discussed in an important paper by Dutton (1983). In the vicinity of their own territory, the Motu engaged in extensive and probably constant trade with their Papuan speaking Koita neighbors. The Koita and the Motu were closely integrated socially and economically, engaging in a symbiotic trading in which the Koita provided game and bush products and the Motu pots and sea products.

It is not known what language the Motu used in their contacts with the Koita, but, given their attitudes toward their language discussed earlier, it is highly unlikely it was Motu proper. In any case, with the arrival of the first Europeans in the Port Moresby area in 1874, we have reports of a simplified Motu used in talking to foreigners. It is most implausible that this grew up with the appearance of Europeans, but rather it seems probable that this was the continuation of an indigenous tradition, such as a contact language for the Koita. As it was a kind of foreigner talk, Simplified Motu was not a distinct language from Motu, but rather a special register used in dealings with non-Motu speakers. The features in which Simplified Motu differed from Motu proper are closely in line with those suggested by Ferguson (1982) (see Table 1). Quite likely, Simplified Motu varied significantly from speaker to speaker and over time and place. In other words, it was very weakly conventionalized.

With the advent of Europeans, this precontact situation began to shift dramatically. Not only did Europeans of different ethnic and linguistic background arrive in the Port Moresby area, but also Pacific Islanders, Chinese, and Malay Indonesians soon appeared. These arrivals were interested in evangelizing or trade, and for both these functions a common language was needed. Because of conscious Church policy, Motu proper quickly became the target language of the mission, but Motu attitudes toward their language insured that the immigrant traders would learn Simplified Motu. As these immigrants to the Port Moresby area came from diverse linguistic backgrounds, Simplified Motu would have been the only language in common, and it quickly assumed the role of contact language between immigrants, as well as between Motu and immigrant. This is Whinnom's (1971) 'tertiary hybridization,' the use of an incipient pidgin between speakers of different substrate languages. This would no doubt have rapidly increased the speed at which Simplified Motu became conventionalized as a pidgin. By the time the Colony of British New Guinea was declared in 1888, Simplified Motu was probably already heavily conventionalized and well on its way to becoming a stable pidgin, Police Motu (Dutton 1985). This is a sufficient time span for conventionalization and stabilization to occur: remember Tok Pisin conventionalized from a jargon to a stable pidgin in approximately 10 years (Mühlhäusler 1983).

With colonial status now established, it became imperative to extend administrative control of Papua beyond the Port Moresby area. At first, police were recruited for this job from Fiji and the Solomon Islands. Although these recruits spoke Pidgin English, their native languages were Austronesian languages related to Motu. As Simplified Motu was already well established in the Port Moresby area as the *lingua franca*, these men could not help but learn it in their dealings with the locals. They would no doubt have been encouraged in this by the similarity of the Simplified Motu vocabulary to that of their own native languages.

It was the police who played a major role in propagating Police Motu (hence its name) throughout Papua. Over the years the foreign police recruits were replaced by Papuans, but Police Motu remained intimately associated with the force. By opening up and pacifying new administrative areas, the force introduced it throughout Papua. Leaders of headhunting raids and other offenders were brought back to jail in Port Moresby for some months, where they were taught Police Motu and some Pidgin English. They were then released back in their native villages. As these offenders were commonly men of high standing in their community, their knowledge of Police Motu conferred high prestige on the language, resulting in its further propagation. Police Motu was the *de facto* language of the Government in remote areas, and by the turn of the century it was a thoroughly conventionalized and stable pidgin, quite distinct from its source language, Motu proper (Dutton 1985).

The rest of the story of Police Motu parallels that of Tok Pisin and many other pidgins. After 1900, workers from other areas of Papua began to be recruited for labor on plantations in the Port Moresby area and elsewhere. As Police Motu was already well established as a contact language, these labor recruits soon learned it, and, when repatriated to their areas of origin, they spread it into yet new territories. By the Second World War the language was well entrenched in many areas of Papua. With the independence of Papua New Guinea in 1975, it was proclaimed one of the three national languages (the other two being Tok Pisin and English).

The histories of Yimas Pidgin and Police Motu provide an interesting contrast. Both originally arose as contact languages in a trading network with speakers of another language. Both show extensive simplification from their source languages in line with the generalizations of Table 1. But Yimas Pidgin never extended beyond this role; it is doomed to extinction in the next 25 years, its role being usurped by Tok Pisin. The necessary social conditions for it to function as an extensive *lingua franca* never obtained. Economic development and social integration at the extravillage level came hand in hand in the area with Tok Pisin, and it was this language which assumed the linguistic functions associated with these changes. When economic development and extravillage social integration began to occur with the arrival of the immigrants in the Port Moresby area in the 1870s, there was no ready made language for these changes. Simplified Motu, already used as trade jargon, simply stepped in to fill this gap. The language then became intimately associated with economic development and national integration, and when it was spread throughout Papua in the manner outlined above, it was naturally accepted as the language of these changes, as was Tok Pisin in the Sepik region.

These New Guinea case studies bear crucially on an important question in pidgin studies – that of their monogenesis (Whinnom 1965, 1977; Voorhoeve 1973). This theory argues that all European-language based pidgins and creoles descend from a fifteenth-century Portuguese based pidgin. Evidence for this theory comes from the highly similar structure of all these European based pidgins and a stock of words of Portuguese ancestry in pidgins and creoles of other European language sources, in both the Atlantic and Pacific. The English, French, Spanish and Dutch based pidgins and creoles are said to derive from relexification of the Portuguese based pidgin by words from the respective source language. This latter possibility is not as far-fetched as it sounds: Muysken (1981) has convincingly documented the existence of an Andean contact language which is formed by relexifying Quechua structures with Spanish words.

Yimas Pidgin and Police Motu show many of the same simplifications *vis à vis* their source language as do the European based pidgins (compare, for example, the Yimas Pidgin pronouns with those of Tok Pisin). This suggests that similar processes have been operative in the development of them all, in particular, the conscious simplification of the superstrate language. Given that the European source languages were already more similar to each other than to Yimas or Motu, very similar results of this process of simplification would be expected. Hence, the overall similarity of structure of European based pidgins is no argument for their common origin. As to the Portuguese words common in many of these pidgins, a common knowledge of a Portuguese based pidgin by sailors and traders in the fifteenth and sixteenth centuries seems well attested. It is plausible that European based pidgins of different stocks developed independently as sketched above, but that words from the widely known Portuguese based pidgin partly relexified them. There are also present in many pidgins and creoles a few words derived from nautical jargon, and the Portuguese vocabulary could have entered in much the same way as these did: sailors seem to have been the first disseminators of European based pidgins in much of the world.

9.3. Creolization: expansion and elaboration

As defined in 9.0, a creole is a pidgin which has become the native language of a community. In being nativized the language must expand to fill a much larger range of linguistic functions, such as promoting social cohesion, expressing abstract ideas and feelings, producing language art, etc. To cope with these increased functional demands, creoles are generally more elaborated structurally than pidgins. But, the expansion of a pidgin and its creolization may be two separate processes. A pidgin may develop and become structurally elaborated and yet not creolize, as long as its social role has expanded beyond being a mere contact language. Mühlhäusler (1980) presents the following life history of a pidgin: unstable jargon → stable pidgin → expanded pidgin → creole.

Tok Pisin is an example of an expanded pidgin. While there is a small, but increasing, number of first language creole speakers of Tok Pisin, research (Sankoff & Laberge 1974; Mühlhäusler 1979; Sankoff 1979) has shown that the differences in language use and structure between creole and expanded pidgin speakers are not great. Tok Pisin has had a greater role in New Guinea than a simple contact language for a long time. Consider Mead's (1931) description of its linguistic position in the Sepik area in the early 1930s:

> In the Mandated Territory of New Guinea a strange, widely flung culture is growing up, a new culture bred of the contact of the white man and the native, a culture that is breaking down barriers hundreds, perhaps thousands, of years old . . . It is a strange culture; almost all those affected by it are males between the ages of twelve and thirty; their homes are scattered far and wide . . . but they speak a common language, pidgin English . . . Pidgin English, especially a knowledge of the names of the strange objects used by the white man, is the most important key to this world of adventure. In the back villages where a white man is seen perhaps twice a year, five and six year old boys go about muttering long pidgin phrases to themselves, learning pronunciation and cadence long before they learn the meaning of words. By the time they are . . . twelve or thirteen, they can converse easily in this new language, and even have time to school the smaller boys by the hour.

These are not the attitudes expected to be associated with a make-do contact language. Rather, the language is already viewed in the 1930s as being of high prestige, allied with the rich and open culture (as locally perceived) of the outside. As has been amply documented, Tok Pisin is often used today within a village, to fellow villagers speaking the same native language. It is the language of the outside world, the world of government, power and money, and carries these connotations in intravillage use (Sankoff 1977).

Tok Pisin began to acquire its status as an expanded pidgin after the First World War, and, as Mead (1931) demonstrates, by the 1930s it was no longer being learned only by adult laborers on plantations, but also by children as a second language within the village. Tok Pisin is acquired in many villages of rural New Guinea today even earlier, so that many speakers must really be regarded as being natively bilingual. It is in this context that Tok Pisin's expansion must be considered; it is called upon to perform virtually every function that the vernaculars do. Consequently, in the last 60 years it has undergone a continual process of lexical enrichment and grammatical change, reflecting its new roles.

Mühlhäusler (1979) reports that a number of new patterns of lexical formation have developed in Tok Pisin in the last 50 years, greatly increasing the stylistic variation in the language. Whereas in the earlier stabilized pidgin we found circumlocutions such as (8):

(8) a. man bilong les 'lazy fellow'
    b. man bilong save 'expert'
    c. meri bilong hambak 'promiscuous woman,'

in the expanded pidgin the compounds of (9) are also possible and even favored:

(9) a. lesman 'lazy fellow'
    b. saveman 'expert'
    c. hambakmeri 'promiscuous/troublesome women'

In the stabilized pidgin stage only the following complex predications in (10) were grammatical:

(10) a. Ai bilong mi i laik slip 'I'm sleepy'
     b. Yau bilong em i pas 'He's deaf'
     c. Gras bilong mi i wait pinis 'I've got grey hair'

But in the expanded pidgin we also find (11), in which compounds function as predicates:

(11) a. Mi aislip nau 'I'm sleepy'
     b. Em i yaupas 'He's deaf'
     c. Mi waitgras pinis 'I've got grey hair'

Note that this change from circumlocutions to compounds is beginning to undo the effects of the simplification/pidginization process, in which transparency of the form–meaning relation is favored. The circumlocutions have a separate word for each concept; the compounds are a single word realizing multiple concepts.

In the expanded phase of Tok Pisin, productive morphology also begins to appear. Mühlhäusler (1980) points out that in the stabilized stage causatives were formed periphrastically by using an auxiliary verb *mekim*, as in (12):

(12) a. Yu mekim sam wara i boil 'You boil water'
     b. Mi mekim kabora i drai 'I dried the copra'

But in the expanded pidgin phase there are also synthetic causatives, formed with the transitive verbal suffix -*im*:

(13) a. Yu boil-*im* wara 'You boil water'
     b. Mi bagarap-*im* haus 'I ruined the house'

Other developments of incipient morphology come from syntactic compression. Jargons or early stabilized pidgins tend to be spoken slowly with relatively equal stress on all words. In expanded pidgins and creoles, function words and auxiliaries may become unstressed, with the result that they become contracted, cliticized or even bound morphemes. In earlier stages of Tok Pisin habitual actions were expressed by placing the verb *save* 'know' before the main verb (14):

(14) Mipela save wokim haus olsem 'We usually build houses like this'

But for perhaps most modern speakers of Tok Pisin, the habitual is expressed by a preverbal particle *se*, a contraction from *save*, as in (15):

(15) Mipela se wokim haus olsem 'We usually build houses like this'

The *se* is probably best analyzed as a proclitic, for it never receives full stress.

Sankoff and Laberge (1974) have demonstrated the evolution of a future tense marker in Tok Pisin from adverb to proclitic. In earlier stages of the language (Clark 1979) *baimbai* from English *by and by* functioned as an adverbial to express future time. As with most adverbs, its position was rather free, although it tended to occur initially. In modern expanded Tok Pisin this form has been nearly totally replaced by the contraction *bai* (16):

(16) Bai mi kam long haus 'I will come to the house'

As Sankoff and Laberge (1974) show, for most speakers *bai* now occurs immediately before the main verb and often receives less than full stress, so that it appears to have been reanalyzed as a verbal proclitic, much like *se*. Compare (17):

(17) Mi bai kam long haus 'I will come to the house'

The development of morphology in the expanded pidgin is again one which reverses the simplification process of the pidginization stage. Single words now express a complex amalgam of semantic concepts, some of these concepts indicated in less prominent, reduced and unstressed syllables. This reflects the greater fluency with which the language is learned and used, as a result of the wider contexts in which it is spoken.

Finally, I wish to consider changes in the syntactic/discourse structures of expanded Tok Pisin. As pointed out in 9.1, pidgins typically have little in the way of embedded structures, making do with weakly linked conjoined clauses strung together. This is the result of their limited communicative functions, those associated with assertions and commands. But with the extension of its functions, a pidgin needs to be able to express background information and presuppositions. Structural methods for subordination then become necessary. Sankoff and Brown (1976) have shown how embedded relative clauses rather than a simple juxtaposition of clauses are recent innovations in Tok Pisin. Woolford (1979) documents the development of the complementizer system in Tok Pisin. In earlier periods and optionally today in the expanded pidgin, there were no embedded complements; two sentences were merely juxtaposed, as in (18):

(18) Mi no save. Ol i wokim dispela haus
   'I didn't know. They had built this house'

But in expanded Tok Pisin the second sentence can be embedded with the complementizer *olsem*, homophonous with an adverb meaning 'thus,' as in (19):

(19) Mi no save olsem ol i wokim dispela haus
   'I didn't know that they built this house'

Other complements are introduced with *long*, which in its other uses is the general all purpose preposition. Consider (20):

(20) Mi no save long wokim haus 'I don't know how to build a house'

In a recent letter (April 1986) from Yimas village from a fluent second language speaker of expanded Tok Pisin, I found an example of a nominalized complement introduced by *long* (21):

(21) Mi toksave long yu *long i go bilong mi* long wok
   'I'm advising you of my going to work'

The predicative marker *i* before *go* clearly identifies it as a verb, but the possessive *bilong* marking the actor indicates a noun. The whole nominalization is introduced by *long*. As nominalized complements are the normal form in Yimas, this sentence could represent substrate influence. On the other hand it could also represent the extension of the complement system to include a new type.

As mentioned earlier, there are no great differences in the Tok Pisin of expanded pidgin speakers and creole speakers. There are, however, a few interesting innovations. Sankoff and Laberge (1974) report that creole speakers tend to unstress the preverbal particles more, reducing their vowels, so that the predicate complex tends to take on the appearance of a single word with stem and bound affixes. Mühlhäusler (1979) shows that in some forms of creolized Tok Pisin much of the sharper categorial information of bases in the stabilized and expanded stages is obscured. For example, in (22), utterances from speakers of creolized Tok Pisin taken from Mühlhäusler (1979), verbs are freely used as abstract nouns, including those with the overt transitive verbal suffix *-im*:

(22) a. I gat planti *harim* bilong tok pisin
  'There are many dialects of Tok Pisin'
 b. *Dilem* bilong yu i no stret
  'Your way of dealing cards is not correct'
 c. No ken gat *sot* bilong wara
  'There won't be a shortage of water'
 d. I gat planti kain *kolim* bilongen
  'There are many different names for it'

These changes result in an increase in the opacity in the grammar. Whereas in expanded Tok Pisin, *sot* 'short' is uniquely a verb lexically and *-im* is uniquely a marker of transitive verbs, this is no longer true in this creolized version.

These facts would seem to call into question Bickerton's (1981, 1984) claims that children acquiring a creole always arrive at the most 'natural' grammar, determined largely by the bioprogram, the innate neurological prewiring for language structure (see also his chapter in Volume II of this series). In terms of categorial information it would seem that this creole version of Tok Pisin is less 'natural' than that of the expanded pidgin. It could be that these creole speakers were already presented with a stable model, the expanded pidgin, and could thereby freely elaborate on it. But the question still remains why would they deviate from a maximally 'natural' system, one clearly exhibiting many features associated with Bickerton's bioprogram. Rather these findings suggest that it is part of the normal process of language acquisition to build more and more complex and elaborate structures. In most language communities these tendencies are held in check by the necessity to acquire the target language, the stable language of the adult members. But in creolizing communities, where these constraints are weak or non-existent, these innovative, elaborating tendencies are given freer rein. The whole process of pidgin expansion and creolization indicates that complex structures are highly favored linguistically, for the varied resources they make available in the performance of diverse linguistic functions.

Having discussed in some detail the strictly linguistic effects of creolization, let me turn now to the social factors for this process. In the paradigmatic cases of creolization, the plantation areas of the Caribbean and the Indian Ocean, two factors were critical: (1) the fact that the slaves were drawn from a wide range of linguistic and cultural backgrounds, and (2) that the slaves enormously outnumbered the white colonial speakers of the European languages. The first factor insured that a *lingua franca* would be needed among the slaves and the second insured that it would not be the European language of the masters. For there would have been too few models of the European language for the slaves to emulate, and, in any case, the social conventions of these slave colonies decreed a very wide social distance between master and slave. Children growing up in such environments would have need of a language to communicate to their peers and parents, and any pidgin used as a *lingua franca* would quickly creolize, as there simply was no alternative to it.

But these paradigmatic cases will not explain all cases of creolization, and specifically some cases of creolization of Tok Pisin in Papua New Guinea. Fundamentally there are two different situations of creolization of Tok Pisin: urban creolization and rural creolization. Urban creolization may profitably be viewed as simply an extension of the paradigmatic case above. In the urban context of modern Papua New Guinea, children often grow up in households where the parents speak different languages, or even more commonly, interact in a social environment with peers who share no common language but Tok Pisin. It is an obvious outcome that the language would creolize in these situations.

Rural creolization is a different and much more complex matter, for here creolization may occur in a previously monolingual village. Occasionally rural creolization occurs on an individual basis in children who have parents speaking different languages because of a case of an exogamous marriage arrangement. But more commonly rural creolization occurs with a significant proportion of a generation. Normally creolization happens first with a generation of boys, and only later spreads to girls. This is the case with the creolizing communities of the Sepik region. Part of the explanation for this development is sociological: Tok Pisin, as the earlier quote from Mead (1931) demonstrated, has long been viewed in these areas as a language of high prestige, connected with the goods and money of the outside world. Because of this association, parents are very keen to have their male children learn Tok Pisin and often speak it to them in preference to the local vernacular. Children grow up learning this as their primary language, and it is the language of choice in interacting with their peers. But more strictly linguistic factors may be at work in the creolization process as well. In a number of language communities in which Tok Pisin is gradually supplanting the local language, the language being usurped is of a quite complex morphological type (Yimas is one of these communities), and I have commonly observed that bilingual children are often able to express an idea in perfectly grammatical Tok Pisin long before they can manage it in the vernacular. As a result the children come to lean much more heavily on Tok Pisin, and the vernacular cedes more and more of its function to it. The end result of the process is the complete creolization of Tok Pisin and the death of the vernacular. These examples of rural creolization again demonstrate the subtle interplay of social factors and strictly linguistic ones in the processes of pidginization and creolization.

REFERENCES

Andersen, R. W. 1983. *Pidginization and creolization as language acquisition.* Rowley: Newbury House.
Bernstein, B. 1971. *Class, codes and control.* New York: Schoken.
Bickerton, D. 1981. *Roots of language.* Ann Arbor: Karoma.
Bickerton, D. 1984. The language bioprogram hypothesis. *Behavioral and Brain Sciences* 7: 173–221.
Brown, P. & Levinson, S. 1978. Universals in language usage: politeness phenomena. In E. Goody (ed.) *Questions and politeness.* Cambridge: Cambridge University Press.
Clark, R. 1979. In search of Beach-La-Mar: towards a history of Pacific Pidgin English. University of Auckland ms.
Coelho, A. 1880–6. Os dialectos romanicos ou neo-latinos na Africa, Asia e America. *Lisboa* 2: 129–96; 3: 451–78; 6: 705–55.
Dutton, T. 1983. Birds of a feather: a pair of rare pidgins from the Gulf of Papua. In E. Woolford & W. Washabaugh (eds.) *The social context of creolization.* Ann Arbor: Karoma.
Dutton, T. 1985. *Police Motu: iena sivarai (its story).* Port Moresby: University of Papua New Guinea Press.
Ferguson, C. 1971. Absence of copula and the notion of simplicity: a study of normal speech, baby talk, foreigner talk and pidgins. In Hymes 1971.
Ferguson, C. 1982. Simplified registers and linguistic theory. In L. Obler & L. Wise (eds.) *Exceptional language and linguistics.* New York: Academic Press.
Ferguson, C. & DeBose, C. 1977. Simplified registers, broken language and pidginization. In Valdman & Highfield 1977.
Gewertz, D. 1983. *Sepik river societies.* New Haven: Yale University Press.
Gumperz, J. & Wilson, R. 1971. Convergence and creolization: a case from the Indo-Aryan/Dravidian border. In Hymes 1971.
Halliday, M. 1974. *Explorations in the functions of language.* London: Arnold.
Harrison, S. 1986. Cultural efflorescence and political evolution on the Sepik River. Paper presented at the Wenner-Gren Symposium 101: Sepik culture history: variation and synthesis. Mijas, Spain, February.
Hill, K. (ed.) 1979. *The genesis of language.* Ann Arbor: Karoma.
Hymes, D. (ed.) 1971. *Pidginization and creolization of languages.* Cambridge: Cambridge University Press.
Hymes, D. 1980. Commentary. In A. Valdman and A. Highfield (eds.) *Theoretical orientations in language studies.* New York: Academic Press.
Mead, M. 1931. Talk-boy. *Asia* 31: 141–51.
Mead, M. 1938. The Mountain Arapesh: an importing culture. *American Museum of Natural History Anthropological Papers* 36: 139–349.

Meisel, J. 1977. Linguistic simplification: a study of an immigrant worker's speech and foreigner talk. In S. Pit Corder & E. Roulet (eds.) *The notion of simplification, interlanguages and pidgins and their relations to second language pedagogy.* Geneva: Droz.

Mühlhäusler, P. 1979. Growth and structure of the lexicon in New Guinea Pidgin. *Pacific Linguistics* C52.

Mühlhäusler, P. 1980. Structural expansion and the process of creolization. In A. Valdman & A. Highfield (eds.) *Theoretical orientations in creole studies.* New York: Academic Press.

Mühlhäusler, P. 1983. Samoan Plantation Pidgin English and the origin of New Guinea Pidgin. In E. Woolford & W. Washabaugh (eds.) *The social context of creolization.* Ann Arbor: Karoma.

Muysken, P. 1981. Halfway between Quechua and Spanish: the case for relexification. In A. Highfield & A. Valdman (eds.) *Historicity and variation in creole studies.* Ann Arbor: Karoma.

Nichols, J. 1980. Pidginization and foreigner talk: Chinese Pidgin Russian. In E. Traugott (ed.) *Papers from the Fourth International Conference on Historical Linguistics.* Amsterdam: Benjamins.

Sankoff, G. 1977. Multilingualism in Papua New Guinea. *Pacific Linguistics* C40: 265–307.

Sankoff, G. 1979. The genesis of a language. In Hill 1979.

Sankoff, G. & Brown, P. 1976. The origin of syntax in discourse: a case study of Tok Pisin relatives. *Language* 52: 631–66.

Sankoff, G. & Laberge, S. 1974. On the acquisition of native speakers by a language. In D. DeCamp & I. Hancock (eds.) *Pidgins and creoles: current trends and prospects.* Washington: Georgetown University Press.

Schuchardt, H. 1883. Uber das Melaneso-Englische. *Sitzungsberichte der Wienische Akademie von Wissenschaften* 105: 131–61.

Schuchardt, H. 1889. Allgemeineres über das Indoportugiesische. *Zeitschrift für Romanische Philologie* 13: 476–576.

Schuchardt, H. 1909. Die Lingua Franca. *Zeitschrift für Romanische Philologie* 33: 441–61.

Shopen, T. & Wald, B. 1980. A researcher's guide to the sociolinguistic variable (ING). In T. Shopen & J. Williams (eds.) *Style and variables in English.* Cambridge, MA: Winthrop.

Silverstein, M. 1972. Chinook Jargon: language contact and the problem of multilevel generative systems. *Language* 48: 378–406, 596–625.

Snow, C., van Eeden, R. & Muysken, P. 1981. The interactional origins of foreigner talk: municipal employees and foreign workers. *International Journal of the Sociology of Language* 28: 81–92.

Valdman, A. & Highfield, A. (eds.) 1977. *Pidgin and creole linguistics.* Bloomington: Indiana University Press.

Voorhoeve, J. 1973. Historical and linguistic evidence in favour of the relexification theory in the formation of creoles. *Language in Society* 2: 133–45.

Whinnom, K. 1965. The origin of the European based creoles and pidgins. *Orbis* 14: 509–27.

Whinnom, K. 1971. Linguistic hybridization and the 'special case' of pidgins and creoles. In Hymes 1971.

Whinnom, K. 1977. Lingua franca: historical problems. In Valdman & Highfield 1977.

Woolford, E. 1979. The developing complementizer system of Tok Pisin: syntactic change in progress. In Hill 1979.

10 Language death

Wolfgang U. Dressler

10.0. Introduction

Language death occurs in unstable bilingual or multilingual speech communities as a result of language shift from a regressive minority language to a dominant majority language. Language shift typically involves a gradual transition from unstable bilingualism to monolingualism, that is the loss or 'death' of the recessive language. There are two other ways in which a language may perish that are not typically referred to as 'language death.' One is a result of its having been transformed into a daughter language, as, for example, the replacement of standard Latin by standard Spanish. Thus a 'dead language' (e.g. Latin) does not necessarily arise through 'language death.' The other is where an entire speech community has died, as happened with Tasmanian and the Californian language Yaki (Swadesh 1948: 226ff.).

This chapter, following most work on the topic, will focus primarily on the phenomena of language decay that lead or seem to lead to language death. The most important of these are those structural and functional changes that appear to be irreversible, particularly those which cannot be halted in spite of efforts to preserve the dying form or usage. Ideally, one would wish for a comprehensive theory which would predict and explain such irreversible changes. While a deductive theory of language decay and death does not yet exist, I can nevertheless propose a partial theory which explains a certain amount of the data and which addresses both structural and functional decay.

10.1. Lexical and grammatical aspects of language death

Any purist would cite the massive interference in one language by another as a sign of language decay. But interference is not a sufficient criterion for decay, since it can be reversed. (If interference were in general irreversible, then there would be nothing for the purist to do!) And in any event, borrowing is a sign as much of the enrichment of a language as of its decay. Consider English, for example, the most dominant language of today, which freely borrows words from other languages (though many more loans go in the opposite direction).

We can, however, identify several phenomena which accompany the moribundity of a language. The first involves massive lexical loans from the dominant into the recessive language, while those in the other direction are sporadic and involve only words designating cultural items of folkloric interest which do not exist outside the recessive language's culture (see Dorian 1982b; Fasold 1984). This asymmetry of interference reflects the general social, sociopsychological, socioeconomic, and political subordination of the recessive speech community to the dominant one (for discussion of the effects of such 'linguistic colonialism,' see Calvet 1974).

In the terminal stages of language decay, words loaned from the dominant language tend to be treated as citation words, with little phonological and no morphological integration (much as English speakers treat the German word *Weltanschauung*). Yet, at the same time, they are still *used* like normal words of the recessive language (for example, see Dressler & Wodak 1977a; Hill & Hill 1977; Knab & Hasson de Knab 1979; Dorian 1981a; Dressler 1982). Thus these loaned words, not being integrated, do not enrich the recessive language, but simply replace indigenous words. This substitution has been called 'relexification' by Hill & Hill (1977) and reflects another property of linguistic colonization: the substitution of indigenous by nonindigenous concepts. Similarly, the borrowing of morphological suffixes is a symptom of decay if the synonymous indigenous suffixes become completely unproductive at the same time. Thus the dying Australian language Dyirbal is replacing its ergative construction by English-type word order rules (Schmidt 1985).

A more complex accompaniment of language decay and death is that word-formation rules (WFRS) cease to be productive (Dressler 1977, 1981, 1982; Schlieben-Lange 1977; Hill & Hill 1978; Knab & Hasson de Knab 1979; Williamson, van Eerde & Williamson 1983).[1] The ceasing of speakers of recessive languages to create new words from native rules results from the fact that the language of technology, culture, fashion, etc. has changed from the recessive to the dominant language, at least for the vanguard of speakers most likely to be responsible for creating, adapting, and sanctioning neologisms. Likewise, at least for semi-speakers (as Dorian 1973 first called the imperfect speakers of a dying language), the cognitive function of

---

[1] The primary functions of WFRs are lexical enrichment through neologisms, thereby serving the communicative and cognitive functions of language, and the easing of memory loads through morphosemantic and morphotactic motivation of existing complex word forms. Dressler 1985 gives an account of WFRs in terms of natural morphology and Aronoff 1976 distinguishes the generative function of WFRs and their function as redundancy rules.

language in these areas becomes supported by the dominant, rather than the recessive, language (Denison 1982). In other words, form follows function. To cite a concrete example, in the nineteenth century, Bretons translated the newly invented French *batt-euse* 'threshing machine' by *dorn-erez*; however, in the twentieth century, the newly invented French *mois-sonneus–batteuse* 'combined harvester' was taken over as such. This is an example of the shift from indigenous neologisms (via WFRS) in the recessive language to systematic borrowing of all neologisms from the dominant language.

The loss of WFRS is typically accompanied by the increasing morphotactic transparency of existing complex forms. So in Breton *di-blegañ* 'to unfold,' where the prefix *di-* lenites the initial /p/ of *plegañ* 'to fold,' has largely been substituted by *dis-plegañ*, with no rule diminishing morphotactic transparency. Still, the difficulty of semi-speakers in relating derived words to their bases appears to be a characteristic feature of language decay (Dressler 1977).

Other structural losses in dying languages cannot be directly attributed to the model of the dominant language. Rankin (1978), for example, documented the reduction of the phonemic system of Qupaw, which did not occur in the direction of dominant English. And in Dressler 1972a I studied the decay and loss of Breton initial consonant mutations that have no counterpart in French. Let us briefly compare the fate of three mutations, each of which applies after different grammatical words. First, consider the mutations themselves:

(1) Spirantization. Word-initial /p,t,k/ to /f,z,h/, e.g. *penn* 'head'>*va/ma fenn* 'my head'.
(2) Fortition. /b,d,g/ to /p,t,k/, e.g. *bara* 'bread'>*o para* 'your bread'.
(3) Lenition. /p,t,k,b,d,g,m/ to /b,d,g,v,z,h,v/, e.g. *e benn, e vara* 'his head/bread'.

Decay proceeds in the following direction:

(1) Decay of spirantization precedes decay of fortition or lenition, and spirantization is largely replaced by lenition, e.g. *va fenn*>*va benn*.
(2) The consonants subject to lenition are reduced to /p,t,k/, thus *e benn, e bara*.
(3) Fortition is lost before and largely replaced by lenition, thus *o bara* or *o vara* instead of *o para*.
(4) The number of grammatical and lexical words triggering mutations is slowly reduced (I referred to this process as 'lexical fading' in Dressler 1972b).

If the claim were simply that the dying Breton dialects acculturated to

French, we could account for the decay and loss of these mutations, but not the hierarchy and order of decay. However, these aspects do admit of explanation. For example, lenition is best preserved (as it was in related Cornish just before its death) because it is triggered by the largest number of grammatical words, compounding, and by syntactic conditions, and applies to the largest number of consonants. It is, so to speak, the 'default' mutation, on which semi-speakers fall back.[2] Also, it seems to be the phonologically most natural mutation rules (or part thereof) that are best preserved, i.e. those which change only one phonological feature. Thus fortition and especially the regular part of lenition (/p,t,k/>/b,d,g/), are best preserved.

Likewise, the direction and hierarchy of decay of inflectional morphology cannot be attributed directly to interfering structures from the dominating language. A striking example can be found in Dorian's (1981a) account of the decay of the case system in East Sutherland Gaelic. There the vocative is much better preserved than the genitive, although dominant English has a genitive, but no vocative. For other examples, see Schmidt's study (1985) of the reduction of allomorphy in dying Australian languages and Dressler's (1981) of the decay of Breton plural allomorphs, which, incidentally, fits well into a model of natural morphology.

As far as syntactic phenomena typical of dying languages are concerned, many have called attention to the decay of subordinate clauses (Hill 1973, 1978; Voegelin & Voegelin 1977; Knab & Hasson de Knab 1979; Dorian 1982c; Tsitsipis 1984; Schmidt 1985). This may be reflected in a simple decrease in use or a total loss of certain types. Syntactic subordination is perhaps the most efficient means of conveying backgrounding and semantic relations between propositions, and it is therefore used extensively in many languages in argumentative and narrative texts. Thus if subordination is lost in a recessive language, the dominant language must be used for the same purpose. In fact, the shift of communication and cognition to the dominant language undoubtedly causes the loss of (certain) subordinate clauses in the recessive language; the resultant lack of performance must lead to noncompetence, at least in the next generation.

A morphosyntactic change observed in dying languages is the replacement of synthetic by analytic constructions (Dorian 1977, 1978, 1981a; Trudgill 1977). Thus Breton has both a synthetic and an analytic present tense construction. Most semi-speakers use only the latter construction and have lost the former, which expresses infinitive and person synthetically.

It is a commonplace observation that the replacement of synthetic by analytic constructions occur in 'normal' language change, as well as the reverse process (consider the development of future 'I'll sing' from Latin to

---

[2] The notion 'default' has found its place in natural morphology (see Dressler 1981, 1985).

French: *canta+b+o>(ego) cantare habeo>je chanter+ai>je vais chanter).*
But interestingly, the replacement of analytic by synthetic constructions has
never been observed in language decay. This may be due to the lack of
phonological change in language decay.

It is worth raising the question whether the phenomena cited above
illustrate diachronic 'simplification' or 'reduction.' In normal language
change, simplifications in some part of a linguistic system (however these are
defined within the particular linguistic model) are compensated for by complications or enrichments in other parts. Thus in the development of the
modern Romance languages and English, the case systems of Latin and Old
English were simplified by loss of case forms, categories, and finally, the
entire system, but in compensation, prepositional constructions flourished,
word order became more rigid, and obligatory articles were introduced.

However, we have seen examples of structural loss without compensation. This accompanied the recessive language becoming partly dysfunctional
– lack of compensation through structural enrichment entailed a functional
shift toward the dominant language. Thus there is an interdependency (not a
unidirectional causation) between gradual functional shift and gradual structural decay. Perhaps such a gradual interdependent change could be
cybernetically modeled as a self-regulating system.

10.2. Sociolinguistic aspects of language death

One sociological symptom of terminal decay is the lack of puristic reactions
against the massive interference from the dominant language (Denison
1982). The resultant semi-speakers fail to notice such 'corruptions,' while
older fluent speakers tend to give up correcting them. This reflects a change in
language attitude: the recessive, decaying language is considered worthless,
not worthy of being properly transmitted (for discussion, see Ryan 1979).
Such attitudinal change produces a relaxation of social, sociolinguistic, and
linguistic norms, and thus permits nonintegration of loans.

An early sign of language decay is the cessation of giving and using
proper names in the recessive language, particularly in oral ingroup interac-
tios (Dressler & Wodak 1977b; Dressler 1982; Williamson *et al.* 1983).[3]
Thus in earlier years Bretons who were officially named *François* were still
called *Fañch* in intimate conversation. Nowadays, however, even lower
class Bretons may always be called *François*.

Terminal language decay seems to show a tendency towards monostylism (Dressler 1972a; Dressler & Wodak 1977a, b; Dorian 1977; Giacalone
Ramat 1983). That is, recessive languages are more and more used in casual

---

[3] This does not necessarily hold for the upper classes, where foreign fashions of naming may easily
penetrate and where revivalists may easily resuscitate indigenous proper names.

styles only, for example, those which are appropriate for intimate routine interactions at home. This stylistic change is yet another dysfunctional change in so far as the recessive language becomes inadequate for certain speech situations, domains, and functions. Moreover, it implies loss of sociolinguistic norms governing stylistic choice (for concrete examples drawn from Breton phonology, see Dressler 1974; for general discussion, Dressler & Wodak 1982).

Interestingly, monostylism is also a property of pidgin languages, as are reduced grammar and lexicon, and total or near total lack of subordination, synthetic constructions, inflectional morphology,[4] and WFRs. Moreover, pidgins are clearly dysfunctional languages in so far as they are adequate only for certain speech situations, domains, and functions. Can one therefore say that language death is the 'reverse' of language birth, in so far as normal languages arise from pidgins (for discussion of this question, see Dressler & Wodak 1977a, b; Trudgill 1977; Dorian 1978, 1981a; Dressler 1981, 1982; Gal 1983; Giacalone Ramat 1983; Schmidt 1985)?

Despite the many parallels, it must be noted that there are many differences between dying languages and pidgins. First, the speech situations, domains, and functions of the two are different, as are the attitudes of the speakers. Second, the mode of acquisition of pidgins is generally quite different from that of the acquisition of dying languages (see Trudgill 1977; Dorian 1981b, 1982b; Dressler 1981; Szemerényi 1981; Williamson *et al.* 1983). Third, dying languages, much more so than pidgins, are characterized by great variation, as represented by massive occurrences of free allophones (see Jackson 1955; Miller 1971; Dressler 1972b; Dressler & Wodak 1977a, b; Kieffer 1977; Trudgill 1977; Denison 1979; Dorian 1982b; Giacalone Ramat 1983). This variation is due to increasing lack of performance in the recessive language and the accompanying relaxation of sociolinguistic norms in general. Fourth, while code-switching, that is, switching between the dominant and recessive languages even within the same sentence, is found in dying languages, and is typical in stable bilingualism as well, it is not characteristic of pidgin interactions. (For discussion of code-switching in dying language situations, see Trudgill 1977; Gal 1979; Dorian 1981a; Williamson *et al.* 1983).

A theoretically important finding of Dorian's (1981a, 1982a, b c) is that semi-speakers may have a very restricted grammatical and lexical competence in the recessive language (i.e. in comparison with older fluent speakers), but an excellent sociolinguistic or communicative competence. Thus their meager grammatical and lexical competence might not be noticed. Dorian also notes that semi-speakers are much better understanders

---

[4] But dying languages, even in their last stages, have more morphology than pidgins (see Dorian 1978, Schmidt 1985).

than producers. She concludes (correctly, in my opinion) that the definition of a speech (or language) community must not be based on the notion of 'grammatical competence.' In other words, Dorian provides another argument against Saussure's social (homogeneous) definition of *langue* and another reason to doubt seriously the possibility of any social basis of the notion 'ideal speaker–hearer' (for more discussion, see Dressler 1981).

10.3. Towards an explanation of language death

How, then, is language death to be explained? As we have seen, we may safely conclude that many phenomena of language decay cannot be sufficiently accounted for by assuming acculturation of the recessive language in the narrow sense of a structural alignment with the structures of the dominant language. Not only do structures *fail* to align in many instances, but purely structural explanations miss the point that in language decay it is often the case (as we have seen) that 'form follows function' (for further elaboration of this point in functionalist and in sociolinguistic theory, see Dressler 1985 and Dressler & Wodak 1982 respectively).

It stands to reason, then, that there are inherent principles of language change that affect the way that languages decay and die, partially irrespective of the structures (rules, constraints, representations, etc.) of the dominant language. As a first approximation, the way that a recessive language dies is a consequence of (1) the principles of language death in general and (2) intervening variables, both structural (i.e. the structural differences between the recessive and the dominant language), and social, such as functional shift and changes of attitude toward the two languages.

Unfortunately, grossly simplified 'explanations' of language death are only too common. Knab and Hasson de Knab, for example, citing a Mexican example, argue 'that the process of language replacement and its ultimate end, language death, are the result of changing relationships between the capitalist national economy of Mexico and indigenous communities' and deride 'such ephemeral things as language attitudes, prestige, identification, and solidarity' (1979: 481). Nobody would deny that socioeconomic and political changes may be seen as the deepest causes of language shift (the necessary, but insufficient precondition of language death), nor that Knab and Hasson de Knab did an excellent job of identifying phases of socioeconomic change in the Aztec-speaking valley of Puebla. But developments in capitalist economy are neither sufficient nor necessary causes of language death, since many languages are dying in countries with socialist economies. Furthermore, microsociological variables must be connected with, but cannot be reduced to, macrosociological factors; indeed, any correlationist sociolinguistics that directly correlates economic or socioeconomic variables with linguistic variables and interprets correlations between them causally is doomed to failure, because the 'causal chain' necessarily comprises the attitudes, interpretations, identifications, and actions of the speakers. Only by accounting for these (independent) socio-psychological factors of language death and by modeling bridge theories between all the disciplines involved may we hope to approach a satisfactory explanation of language death.

REFERENCES

Aronoff, M. 1976. *Word formation in Generative Grammar.* Cambridge, MA: MIT Press.
Breitborde, L. B. 1983. Levels of analysis in sociolinguistic explanation: bilingual code switching, social relations and domain theory. *International Journal of the Sociology of Language* 39: 5–43, 161–77.
Calvet, L.-J. 1974. *Linguistique et colonialisme: petit traité de glottophagie.* Paris: Payot.
Denison, N. 1979. Zur Triglossie in der Zahre. In P. S. Ureland (ed.) *Standardsprache und Dialekte in mehrsprachigen Gebieten Europas.* Tübingen: Niemeyer.
Denison, N. 1982. A linguistic ecology for Europe? *Folia Linguistica* 16: 5–16.
Dorian, N. C. 1973. Grammatical change in a dying dialect. *Language* 49: 413–38.
Dorian, N. C. 1977. The problem of the semi-speaker in language death. *International Journal of the Sociology of Language* 12: 23–32.
Dorian, N. C. 1978. The fate of morphological complexity in language death. *Language* 54: 590–609.
Dorian, N. C. 1981a. *Language death: the life cycle of a Scottish Gaelic dialect.* Philadelphia: University of Pennsylvania Press.
Dorian, N. C. 1981b. The valuation of Gaelic by different mother-tongue groups resident in the Highlands. *Scottish Gaelic Studies* 13. 2: 169–82.
Dorian, N. C. 1982a. Defining the speech community to include its working margins. In S. Romaine (ed.) *Sociolinguistic variation in speech communities.* London: Arnold.
Dorian, N. C. 1982b. Language loss and maintenance in language contact situations. In R. D. Lambert & B. F. Freed (eds.) *The loss of language skills.* New York: Rowley.
Dorian, N. C. 1982c. Linguistic models and language death evidence. In L. K. Obler & L. Menn (eds.) *Exceptional language and linguistics.* New York: Academic Press.
Dressler, W. 1972a. *Allegroregeln rechtfertigen Lentoregeln: sekundäre Phoneme des Bretonischen.* Innsbruck: Institut für Sprachwissenschaft.
Dressler, W. 1972b. On the phonology of language death. *Papers of the Chicago Linguistic Society* 8: 448–57.
Dressler, W. 1974. Essai sur la stylistique phonologique du breton: les débits rapides. *Etudes Celtiques* 14: 99–120.
Dressler, W. 1977. Wortbildung bei Sprachverfall. In H. Brekel & D. Kastovsky (eds.) *Perspektiven der Wortbildungsforschung.* Bonn: Bouvier.
Dressler, W. 1981. Language shift and language death – a Protean challenge for the linguist. *Folia Linguistica* 15: 5–28.
Dressler, W. 1982. Acceleration, retardation and reversal in language decay? In R. Cooper (ed.) *Language spread.* Bloomington: Indiana University Press.
Dressler, W. 1985. *Morphonology.* Ann Arbor: Karoma.
Dressler, W. & Wodak, R. 1982. Sociophonological methods in the study of sociolinguistic variation in Viennese German. *Language in Society* 11: 339–70.
Dressler, W. & Wodak-Leodolter, R. (eds.) 1977a. Language death. *Journal of the Sociology of Language* 12 (=*Linguistics* 19.1).
Dressler, W. & Wodak-Leodolter, R. 1977b. Language preservation and language death in Brittany. *International Journal of the Sociology of Language* 12: 33–44.
Fasold, R. 1984. *The sociolinguistics of society.* Oxford: Blackwell.

Gal, S. 1979. *Language shift: social determinants of linguistic change in bilingual Austria.* New York: Academic Press.

Gal, S. 1983. 'Comment' to Breitborde 1983. *International Journal of the Sociology of Language* 39: 63–72.

Giacalone Ramat, A. 1983. Language shift and language death. *Folia Linguistica* 17: 495–507.

Hill, J. H. 1973. Subordinate clause density and language function. In C. Corum *et al.* (eds.) *Papers from the Comparative Syntax Festival.* Chicago Linguistic Society.

Hill, J. 1978. Language death, language contact and language evolution. In W. C. McCormack & S. A. Wurm (eds.) *Approaches to language. Anthropological issues.* The Hague: Mouton.

Hill, J. & Hill, K. 1977. Language death and relexification in Tlaxcalan Nahuatl. *International Journal of the Sociology of Language* 12: 55–69.

Hill, J. & Hill, K. 1978. Honorific usage in modern Nahuatl. *Language* 54: 123–55.

Jackson, K. 1955. *Contributions to the study of Manx phonology.* Edinburgh: Nelson.

Kieffer, C. 1977. The approaching end of the relict Southeast Iranian languages *Ormuṛi* and *Parāči* in Afghanistan. *International Journal of the Sociology of Language* 12: 71–100.

Knab, T. & Hasson de Knab, L. 1979. Language death in the valley of Puebla: a sociogeographic approach. *Proceedings of the Berkeley Linguistic Society* 5: 471–83.

Miller, W. 1971. The death of language or serendipity among the Shoshoni. *Anthropological Linguistics* 13: 114–120.

Rankin, R. L. 1978. The unmarking of Quapaw phonology: a study of language death. *Kansas Working Papers in Linguistics* 3: 45–52.

Ryan, E. B. 1979. Why do low-prestige language varieties persist? In H. Giles & R. St Clair (eds.) *Language and social psychology.* Oxford: Blackwell.

Schlieben-Lange, B. 1977. The language situation in southern France. *International Journal of the Sociology of Language* 12: 101–8.

Schmidt, A. (1985) The fate of ergativity in dying Dyirbal. *Language* 61: 378–96.

Swadesh, M. 1948. Sociologic notes on obsolescent languages. *International Journal of the Sociology of Language* 14: 226–35.

Szemerényi, O. 1981. Sprachverfall und Sprachtod besonders im Lichte indogermanischer Sprachen. In Y. L. Arbeitman & A. R. Bomhard (eds.) *Bono homini donum: essays in historical linguistics in Memory of J. A. Kerns.* Amsterdam: Benjamins.

Trudgill, P. 1977. Creolization in reverse: reduction and simplification in the Albanian dialects of Greece. *Transactions of the Philological Society*: 32–50.

Tsitsipis, L. D. 1984. Functional restriction and grammatical reduction in Albanian language in Greece. *Zeitschrift für Balkanologie* 20: 122–31.

Voegelin, C. F. & Voegelin, F. M. 1977. Is Tübatulabal de-acquisition relevant to theories of language acquisition? *International Journal of American Linguistics* 43: 333–8.

Williamson, R. C., van Eerde, J. A. & Williamson, V. 1983. Language maintenance and shift in a Breton and Welsh sample. *Word* 34. 2: 67–88.

11 Language planning: the view from linguistics*

Donna Christian

11.0. Introduction

Languages offer their speakers a rich array of expressive possibilities. In a given situation, speakers 'choose their words' carefully in an attempt to communicate as closely as possible what they want others to understand. On a variety of levels (referential, emotive, social), these choices convey meaning. In English, for example, we say 'lemme' when we assess the situation as less formal, 'let me' when more formal; we indicate sarcasm with a particular intonation pattern; we demonstrate the relationship we perceive with an interlocutor by the form of address we use (Ms Jones, Susan, or a nickname). When distinct varieties of language, or different languages, are available within a community's linguistic repertoire, the resources for expression are increased still further, since the use of one language variety rather than another in a given situation conveys meaning as well, by demonstrating identification with a particular group, loyalty to a heritage language, attitude toward an interlocutor, and so on.

Since language alternatives typically carry social import, it is not surprising that attempts are made to influence the way in which language is used. As Fasold (1984: 246) observes, 'The existence of alternatives makes planning possible.' These alternatives exist at all levels of language use, but not all levels are equally susceptible targets for language planning. Planning is typically directed toward uses of language in official or public functions rather than in casual everyday communication, where the choices are left up to the natural sociopsychological factors governing the situation. The goal of planning may be actual legislation to prescribe what language(s) may fill what functions (official, national, medium of education, and so on), or other formulations of official policy. It is important to bear in mind that language fills not only communication, but also symbolic functions within a society. In many cases, the policy decisions relate as much to the symbolic value of

* I would like to express my sincere thanks to Walt Wolfram, Carol Eastman, and G. Richard Tucker for their thought-provoking comments and helpful suggestions on earlier versions of this paper.

language as a unifying or separatist force in a community (Garvin & Mathiot 1956) as to real communication needs. As a result, political, social, and economic concerns typically far outweigh linguistic considerations in language planning.

Language problems (or sociopolitical problems involving language) that require attention are wide-ranging, from the naming of a national language to the selection of terminology for advanced technology. Whatever the problem, language planning allows for the making of reasoned choices, based (ideally) on an analysis of the available information within a framework developed out of prior experience. The nature of planning attempts varies as widely as the alternatives, however. A few examples illustrate the range of possibilities.

India's population contains groups of people who speak hundreds of different languages natively (as 'mother tongues'). Prior to the country's independence from Great Britain, this linguistic heterogeneity was subsumed within a policy naming English as the official language. At the time of independence, however, the country's leaders were faced with the problem of deciding whether to keep the colonial language, English, as the official language, or name one of the indigenous languages to take its place. To underscore the new national identity, Hindi was chosen to be the official language. One form of language planning, then, is found in such governmental policy formulations when they assign official status to one or more languages.

In Israel, the choice of an official language (or languages) at the time of the nation's creation posed a different sort of problem. With a population which came from many parts of the world, speaking many languages natively, the decision was an especially sensitive one. Policy-makers felt it was important to give Hebrew (along with Arabic) official status, since it was a language which had high symbolic importance to the people, even though it was not a language of wider use. This meant that effort needed to be put into expanding the functions which Hebrew could fill (Cooper in press), so that its role as an official language would not remain primarily symbolic. Choosing to revive a language not in wide use is another form of planning, one which then typically requires further consideration of how to make the language fully functional.

In eastern Africa, Swahili developed as a language of wider communication in the late nineteenth century. The colonial power, Great Britain, formulated an educational policy after the First World War which recognized the position of Swahili and called for its use. However, Swahili existed in many forms, and a commission was appointed to choose a dialect to standardize. The Zanzibar dialect was selected, and activities to promote standardization were undertaken. These efforts were most successful in written forms of the language. Swahili later became an official language in a number of independent East African nations, including Tanzania (Ansre 1971). Choice among varieties of a language as well as development of a standard form of the language are thus further areas for intervention.

Examples of direct attempts to shape language and its use could go on for many pages, through script reform for Chinese, movement toward a bilingual policy in Canada, and attempts to arrive at a compromise position among dialects in Norway. The point here is not to catalog instances of planning (although in many ways the term is defined by its instantiations), but rather to examine the framework within which language planning operates. It is important to remember that 'language problems cannot be solved by attention to language alone' (Neustupny 1983: 2) since language alternatives are embedded in the social, economic, and political context in which they function. A reasonable approach to language planning provides a way of assessing the forces at work in a situation, linguistic and otherwise, along with the goals that have been set, to determine what goals are realistic and how they may be achieved in the given context. This can be thought of as an 'empirical' approach, since it relies heavily on an analysis of the actual situation.

The development of an empirical framework for language planning, and the contribution that linguistics[1] can make, will be taken up in later sections. First we will consider what is meant by language planning and what factors contribute to success in that endeavor. Throughout the discussion, special attention will be paid to the contributions that linguistics and language study can make to language planning.

11.1. Toward a definition of language planning

11.1.1. Scope

The practice of language planning has not yet reached a point where its boundaries have been well defined. Its practitioners and researchers differ widely in the activities they would group under that label. For Haugen, language planning concerns work toward changes within a language, as 'the normative work of language academies and committees, all forms of what is commonly known as language cultivation . . . and all proposals for language

---

[1] Language planning is usually categorized as a *sociolinguistic* concern (Eastman, for example, discusses how in some ways, language planning can be thought of as 'applied sociolinguistics': 1983: 4). It is certainly true that language planning deals with issues central to sociolinguistics, namely the relationship of language forms and uses to social structures and behaviors. However, it is also true that planning draws on other areas of linguistics as well, as it relies on information from language description, psycholinguistic approaches to attitudes, and so on. Thus, this paper examines the role of linguistics, from a broad perspective, in language planning, while acknowledging that the field is most often specifically associated with sociolinguistics.

reform or standardization' (1969: 287). Das Gupta considers a scope beyond a single language, calling language planning 'a set of deliberate activities systematically designed to organize and develop the language resources of the community in an ordered schedule of time' (1973: 157). Fishman takes a still broader view, using the term to refer to 'the organized pursuit of solutions to language problems, typically at the national level' (1973: 23–4). As Eastman (1983: Chapter 4) observes, the definitions offered have evolved as emphases and trends in language planning have changed and developed. Such a historical perspective is helpful not only in tracing the evolution of the field, but also in moving toward a characterization which reflects but is not constrained by current emphases.

Other terms are also found in use to designate activities that may be considered within the language planning umbrella. Alisjahbana (1961), for example, discusses 'language engineering' in Indonesia as purposeful attempts to influence the development of the language. Other scholars write about language 'development' and 'determination,' (Jernudd 1973), 'cultivation,' 'formation,' 'modernization,' and so on. These references can be seen as particular directions in which language planning can be taken, if a broad definition of the more general term is assumed.

A current approach to defining language planning views it from an even wider perspective of language problems and correction in general (Neustupny 1983). In this view, 'language problems' cover a continuum from a speaker's mis-statement in discourse to the choice of official languages in a multilingual nation. Following this, 'correction' is the removal of problems, which may be accomplished very simply, through a clarification issued shortly after a problem in discourse, or in a much more complicated way, through a process of careful consideration of alternatives. In this model, 'language planning becomes one kind of language correction, done in a conscious, planned manner by groups authorized to carry out the change' (Rubin 1984: 139) and it is grounded in a language planning theory, making it 'systematic, theoretical, rational (in other words "rigorous") and future-oriented' (Neustupny 1983: 2). The concern for the development of a theoretical framework has been voiced on a number of occasions recently (Neustupny 1983; Nahir 1984) and progress is being made in this direction.

11.1.2. Key components

Many scholars agree on the use of language planning in a more inclusive way, to cover a range of activities which have in common that they are 'purposeful' and that they aim toward particular goals with respect to language use and usage in a community. Fasold provides perhaps the least restrictive statement of that position: 'Language planning is usually seen as an explicit choice among alternatives. This, in turn, implies that there has been an evaluation of alternatives with the one that is chosen having been evaluated as the best' (1984: 246).

A review of case descriptions and definitions points to a number of key features. Language planning is:

Intervention. Above all, language planning takes on the task of intervening in the normal course of events to influence future language use or usage. It attempts to cause 'deliberate language change' (Rubin 1984: 138) through measures designed to implement choices made.

Explicit. Language planning deals with conscious and deliberate attempts to manipulate language use and usage. The end result might be what would have taken place apart from the intervention, but planning necessarily implies some deliberate effort to structure the course of progress on a conscious level. It is *proactive* rather than *reactive*.

Goal-oriented. The motivation for language planning attempts must be clearly understood and kept in mind throughout the process. A 'future orientation' (Rubin 1984: 138) or objective in terms of eventual outcome is a central feature. Political, social, and economic concerns are most often responsible for decisions to undertake language planning, and the goals are typically seen as progress in those areas.

Systematic. Language planning takes an approach to problems which is systematic and based on the accumulated experiences of the field. It requires a careful analysis of the existing situation and desired outcomes to design and coordinate a sequence of activities that will address the problem.

Choice among alternatives. As pointed out earlier, planning is possible only if there are alternatives to choose among. These alternatives must be identified and a reasoned choice among them made. Again, the choice is often based purely on sociopolitical grounds, but evaluation of alternatives needs to take all available information into account.

Institutionalization. Finally, although attention may be given to language problems at many levels, language planning refers primarily to institutionally organized efforts involving public policy. This is often national, but may extend to provincial, state, or local jurisdictions. Further, many individuals may play a role in language planning, but the results will be effective only if those with authority to implement decisions take part, that is, the policy-makers.

Using these key features, we can suggest the following definition: language planning is an explicit and systematic effort to resolve language problems and achieve related goals through institutionally organized intervention in the use and usage of languages.

11.2. The role of lingustics in the process of language planning

Historically, linguistics was concerned primarily with the formal aspects of language, the code. In current approaches, however, the scope of lingustic concern has broadened considerably, to include both form and function. The social dynamics of language use are being studied within the field along with the formal properties of languages. In addition, for many linguists over the years, monolingualism was considered the norm, despite the fact that most communities in the world had a multilingual character (Kachru 1982: 6). In this area as well, linguistics appears to have broadened its view, so that accounts of language use in multilingual situations (and considerations of code descriptions for multilingual speakers) are welcomed as part of the knowledge base of the field. The development of sociolinguistics as a major orientation within language study has contributed significantly to this expansion.

As a result, new avenues have opened up for the involvement of linguistics in language planning, which focusses more on language as behavior than on the language code, and typically operates within multilingual situations. Sociolinguists have in particular turned their attention to language use in multilingual communities. Sociopolitical concerns will remain in the forefront of language planning efforts, but linguistic work need not be isolated from those issues any longer.

However, a caution should be kept in mind:

> It took at least two decades to realize that language policy decisions
> require a robust common sense, and, above all, a sympathetic
> understanding of the linguistic context. One has to appreciate various
> social, attitudinal, and political pulls and pushes. Unfortunately, such
> non-linguistic contexts are not always visible to a linguist's analytic
> eye. One soon realizes that linguistic solutions to language planning
> go only so far; indeed, perhaps not very far at all.   (Kachru 1982: 5)

Support for the validity of this caution can readily be found.

We can consider, for example, the proposed solution to the world communication problem, Esperanto. This language, created in the late 1800s by Zamenhof, is promoted as a step toward world peace through better communication by the Universal Esperanto Association's over 30,000 members worldwide (Weinstein 1983: 164). This language planning effort aims to provide a language that will be used on a worldwide basis between speakers who do not share the same native language. In this way, all speakers would have equal access to the international language. It is claimed that the language is 'neutral,' since it is not used natively by any national community and thus no group has any particular advantage.

Despite considerable efforts on the part of proponents (including an Australian ambassador to the United Nations who recommended adoption of Esperanto as the official international language: see Weinstein 1983: 164), however, the movement has thus far failed. This would appear to be a case of a purely linguistic solution that ignores the social aspects of the situation. The approach focusses on the code to the exclusion of crucial language behavior variables. In international dealings, power and prestige are important determinants of language choice. Throughout history, the languages of the world powers have assumed the role of languages of diplomacy and trade. In addition, even though Esperanto may be linguistically neutral (it actually is not even that, since it is said to be very European in nature), it cannot be sociolinguistically neutral, since social inequalities will remain to affect communication. Thus, the failure of Esperanto to achieve its goals can be attributed to its inability to address the nonlinguistic issues.

Where, then, can linguistics and language study fit into the process of language planning? If we operate within the problem-solving framework suggested earlier, we can think in terms of three components to the process. First, the problem to be addressed must be identified. Second, a solution to that problem must be developed and implemented. Third, the results must be monitored to determine if they conform to what was expected. We can consider each of these phases in turn and the role that linguistic work might play.

11.2.1. Identification of the problem

The identification of a language problem is often a response to the articulation of more general goals. These goals are typically political, social, economic, or religious – and *not* linguistic (although those involved may believe otherwise). When people say that a problem is linguistic, they are usually speaking of language as the manifestation of culture, a symbolic behavioral function. Further, solution of the language problem may constitute only a part of the achievement of the broader goals. For example, in a multilingual country, a political and social goal may be to promote greater national unity. Because there is a widely held belief that having a single official language unifies a nation, policy makers will view establishment of an official language as a problem that needs to be addressed. Lack of a mutually intelligible means of communication among citizens is seen as a barrier to unity. This language choice, a planning problem, responds to a broader political goal. As discussed earlier, India made Hindi the official language for this reason. Kenya opted for a single national language to promote unity, but chose Swahili largely for economic reasons. Swahili had become the language of wider communication in East Africa and was valued as the language of the work force (Mazrui & Zirimu 1978).

Alternatively, a language in wide use within a region may face the problem of a need for vocabulary expansion to accommodate technological developments of the modern world. Here the wider goal may again be social or economic (in the quest to make the language functional in a wider variety of situations), but the choices fall within a language rather than across languages. Users of Bengali in Bangladesh and West Bengal faced such a situation after the Second World War and decolonization of the Indian Empire, when the language was expected to take over the functions that English had fulfilled. Bengali planners have focussed on, and continue to give attention to, providing terminology to meet the needs of speakers through government commissions that have been established. Borrowing from English has been one source of new terms, with mixed results in terms of acceptability (Musa 1984).

Linguistic input can be important at this stage in clarifying the goals and defining the role that language planning can play. An understanding of the interaction of language attitudes with the characterizations of problems offered by those close to the situation may be crucial. Policy-makers without linguistic expertise may not be able to separate their attitudes as speakers of a language from their decisions about that language. Further, a realistic assessment of the contribution of language to a problem (e.g. mutual intelligibility) and accompanying expectations about possible results depend on the involvement of individuals who are knowledgeable about language. Identifying the lack of a common language as the source of conflict between two groups without considering other social or religious differences may lead, for example, to an overly simplistic view of the problem to be addressed. On the other hand, it is also important to bear in mind that when the goals extend beyond language matters, then expertise in other areas is also required.

11.2.2. Plan development and implementation

The second stage, the actual development of a plan or policy and its implementation, can benefit greatly from linguistic input. Rubin (1971) identifies four phases in the work of the language planner, three of which relate to developing and implementing the plan:

(1) fact-finding – gathering information about the situation;
(2) planning – formulating goals, the means to achieve them, and the expected outcomes; and
(3) implementation – putting the plan into action.

(The fourth step, feedback, will be discussed shortly). It should be clear that linguistic expertise will be valuable in all of these activities, particularly the first two.

In order to describe the situation accurately, judgements about what information will be useful and how to go about getting it must be made. The experience of linguists (especially sociolinguists) brings valuable insight on both counts. In choosing a language to serve as the medium of instruction in early education, for example, it is important to assess the attitudes of the community toward the various choices. It is also important to determine the relationships among the varieties of language involved, to find out if, on purely formal grounds, one choice might be more accessible to speakers of other varieties. In both cases, a nonlinguist might not recognize the value of such information on structural and social dimensions. In addition, the methodology for compiling these data would be available from linguistics (for a discussion of the use of linguistic methodologies in language planning processes, see Eastman 1983: 76–82).

In the actual formulation of plans, similar considerations are relevant. If the goals that have been set are to be achieved, it makes sense to design a plan that makes best use of natural linguistic and sociolinguistic tendencies.[2] As Bailey points out, for example, 'the study of implicational universals . . . has improved the linguist–planner's hopes of not promoting incompatible phenomena in a language,' as has the consideration of naturalness in language (1975: 156). In other words, if a sociolinguist can examine a proposed change in light of what would be more natural for speakers, rather than less, in terms of linguistic structure, this would be very useful information in deciding whether or not to attempt to implement the change. Likewise, investigations of the role of various factors, such as motivation, in the learning of languages (Paulston 1974; Gardner 1985); on the patterns of language choice, maintenance and shift at both individual and group levels (Fishman 1966; Herman 1968; Gal 1979; Li 1982); on the role of education, mass media, and legislation in the spread of linguistic innovation (Spolsky 1972; Karam 1974; Cooper 1982) have all added to the knowledge base a linguist can draw on. These areas, among others, are important considerations in effective language planning.

The implementation phase may or may not depend on further input from linguistics. Typically, however, there are details to be worked out as a plan is put into place, as well as minor revisions to be made as reactions to the plan become evident. In such cases, continuing consultation with linguists about the evolving plan should prove helpful.[3]

---

[2] This observation is not as uncontroversial as it might seem at first glance. It is a premise of what is being offered here as the 'empirical' approach (which is similar to what Fasold calls the 'socio-linguistic' approach: 1984: 250).

[3] In this discussion, the assumption is that linguists are not likely to be those who are actually running the

11.2.3. Evaluation

The third stage leads us to evaluation of the effectiveness of the plan. As Rubin (1971) argues convincingly, evaluation is an ongoing process that should inform all stages of planning, as alternative goals and strategies are assessed and priorities are analyzed. After a plan is put into effect, however, during the 'feedback' phase (Rubin 1971: 481), the planner compares actual results with the original goals, to judge how successful the plan has been and whether or not revised strategies are called for. Linguistic input is clearly required in the development of criteria to measure success when language is the object of measurement (for example, to determine what structural changes, if any, are taking place). The question of why particular strategies have not worked as anticipated will depend on the insight of the linguist into the functioning of language within various social contexts, as well as for the examination of intervening variables which arose. In addition, any restructuring of the approach to the problem will again involve linguistic concerns.

It is important at this point, in light of the preceding discussion, to consider once again the fact that linguistics often plays a very small role in language planning problems and solutions. Since language is involved, however, the input that linguistics can provide is likely to be very beneficial, particularly as language is considered in its broader context. This context encompasses the nonlinguistic domains – political, social, economic – which contain the decisive influences.

11.3. Dimensions of language planning

Many investigators have noted that there are two primary directions that language planning may take. The first involves choosing among languages or varieties of a language for particular purposes. The second is concerned with the development of a single language or variety of a language. These two directions have been referred to as 'language status planning' and 'language corpus planning,' respectively (Kloss 1969). By looking at specific cases of each type of planning, we can gain insight into the processes and the factors that affect the success of such efforts.

11.3.1. Status planning

Status planning refers to cases in which the attributed status of a language or variety is altered. That is, a language is given or denied official language

planning operation, but instead are serving in a consulting capacity of some type. This assumption is based on the fact that most planning efforts are generated from governmental or other social agencies where linguists are not as likely to be found in advance. Naturally, continuing and close involvement of linguists is most desirable.

status; a variety is mandated or prohibited as the medium of instruction for education; or a language is added or deleted on the list of those permitted in some context. In all cases, an agency or institution with the power to do so assigns the new status and often prescribes other measures to back up the decision.

A good example of the blend of historical, social, and pragmatic factors in such decisions can be seen in Singapore (Christian 1984). There are four official languages in Singapore – Malay, Tamil, Mandarin (dialect of Chinese), and English – reflecting the multicultural nature of the island nation. Despite periodic language planning efforts to the contrary, English has become the dominant working language in Singapore, functioning as the primary language in the educational system, in the government, in business, and in all phases of public activity. However, only about 2% of the people of this nation have English as their native language.

Ethnically, Singapore is made up of roughly 76% people of Chinese ancestry, 15% Malays, and 7% Indians (many of whom, but not all, speak Tamil) (Kuo 1980). This cultural make-up accounts for three of the four official languages and illustrates the important symbolic function attached to status designations. Most of the population speak a Chinese dialect natively; however, less than 1% have Mandarin as their native tongue. Mandarin was the dialect chosen for official status, however, to underscore the strong ties felt with China, through a prestige dialect. Tamil was included to indicate that the Indians are a valued, if small, minority.

Geographical and historical factors explain special considerations given to Malay. After independence was received from Great Britain, Singapore joined for a time with Malaysia (Singapore became fully independent in 1965). During the period of strong allegiance with Malaysia, there was a campaign to promote the use of the Malay language, and even after independence, Malay was given the special status of national language to reinforce the close ties that remained with Malaysia. However, except among the Malays, the language functions largely for ceremonial purposes only (for example, the national anthem is in Malay).

The dominance of English can be traced back to Singapore's earlier status as a British colony. In the late 1970s and early 1980s, a 'Speak Mandarin' campaign was mounted by the government, in an effort to preserve Chinese cultural values and stem the tide of Western influence on society that accompanied the growing role of the English language. In this case, language became the focus for desired social change (or resistance to it) and planning was used as an instrument in the effort. The concern for Chinese maintenance, however, seems to have lessened, with a later policy decision which made English the sole language of education at all levels, effective in 1987.

Thus, Singapore represents a multilingual nation which has directed its language planning efforts toward reflection of the diversity of its population. However, it has, for the most part, accepted the social, economic, and political forces which are responsible for actual language use patterns in the country. The nation recognizes the diverse population by giving official status to four major languages and promotes the use of all languages through the mass media and education. Policy-makers have also apparently recognized the strong role that English plays, both as a unifying force across groups and as a tool for international communication, and they have not devoted major effort to blocking that language's growth.[4]

Another example of status planning which shows clearly the relationship between language policy and nonlanguage factors can be found in Canada, as described by Weinstein (1983: 45–56). As French-speaking residents of Quebec moved toward strong separatist feelings, the central government was sensitive to the pivotal role played by language. In 1969, both French and English were named official languages of Canada, a development which recognized the political as well as the linguistic reality of the situation. Later, in 1974 and 1977, Quebec went further with its language policy by making French the official language of the province, so that government communications, education, and other aspects of public life would be in French. Provisions for further development of the French language were included, along with the establishment of an 'Office de la Langue Française' (OLF) to monitor compliance with the law. This was not only an expression of support for the French language; it was also a strong political statement, and the political struggle continues to be heavily aligned with language differences. Although it is highly oversimplified, this picture of the linguistic and political situation in Canada illustrates further the way in which language planning activities often respond to nonlanguage factors.

Not all status planning attempts are successes, of course. Attempts to revive Irish as a language of general communication in Ireland, after the language had been almost completely replaced by English, have not been successful. Irish is designated as the national, and, along with English, an official language. As such, it does succeed in filling an important symbolic function for the nation. However, despite educational requirements for the study of Irish, relatively few people know the language well enough to use it (Fasold 1984: 278–85).

---

[4] There are, of course, drawbacks to the position that reinforces diversity, as well. As Banton points out (cited in Wardhaugh 1986), Singaporean policies emphasize the difference between groups and seem to deny the development of a common culture, which appears to be emerging in conjunction with the wide use of English.

11.3.2. Corpus planning

Other planning efforts concentrate on developing a language in some way, by expanding the domains in which it can be used or by standardizing its usage. This type of planning often accompanies status planning, when a language variety chosen to fill official functions needs additional resources in order to do so. For example, once the decision was made to revive Irish as a national language, a number of steps were taken to modernize and standardize the language, so that it could be taught and would be functional.

Ferguson (1968) suggests that there are three basic types of corpus planning: graphization, modernization, and standardization. Graphization refers to activities which establish and/or refine the writing system of a language. In 1972, the Australian government changed its policy and gave Aboriginal children the right to a primary education in their native language; until then, primary education had been available only in English (Sandefur 1985). A widely used creole, which was given the name Kriol, was recognized as a medium of instruction, but there were a number of areas of the language which needed elaboration in order to make it fully suitable for educational functions. A first task was to develop a written form of the language, a way to represent the spoken forms orthographically. Many programs that promote native language literacy face such a problem, when the language in question does not have a written mode. Such cases represent the need for graphization corpus planning.

In other instances of graphization, a written mode exists but changes or refinements are deemed necessary. For example, after the Russian revolution, non-Russian languages in the Soviet Union (which had been previously ignored) were put into use in the education system. The Uzbek language was at that time written in a Roman alphabet. However, a shift to Cyrillic for Uzbek was undertaken in the 1930s in order to promote a common writing system in the country (Weinstein 1983: 45). Corpus planning was required to make the shift between alphabets. The creation of a phonetic alphabet for Chinese ('pinyin') as an alternative to the traditional character-based writing system (DeFrancis 1967) is another instance of a graphization planning attempt.

Modernization is undertaken when a language needs to expand its resources in order to meet the demands of the modern world (also called 'elaboration' by Haugen 1983). A prototypical example of this planning type involves a language which changes in status (following independence from a colonial power or a change in governmental policy concerning language in education, for example). Often, vocabulary expansion is needed to provide the terminology associated with new domains of discourse. The case of Bengali was mentioned in section 11.2.1. Similar situations have been encountered with Hebrew in Israel, where its revival meant that many terminological gaps needed to be filled, since the language had, up to that point, functioned in fairly restricted domains. A number of committees were convened in response to this problem, including, for example, a 'Committee on the Terminology of Librarianship' (Fellman & Fishman 1977), to make recommendations. One area of debate centered on the choice between indigenous constructions (molded from Hebrew elements) and international terms (based on borrowings). Likewise, the development of Navaho in the southwestern United States required expansion of vocabulary among other processes of modernization (Spolsky & Boomer 1983).

Finally, standardization is probably the most familiar form of corpus planning. Ray describes the process in two stages: 'first the creation of a model for imitation, and second, promotion of this model over rival models' (1968: 760). Language academies have sought to determine what is acceptable as standard for a number of languages, including French, Spanish, and Hebrew, with varying degrees of success. They rule on points of grammar, set the policy for accepting foreign borrowings and, in some cases, consider pronunciation issues as well. In the case of the Shona language in Rhodesia (now Zimbabwe), planners in the 1930s sought to establish a standard from among the numerous distinct dialects. The decision was made to create a standard reflecting the major dialects rather than to choose one and make it the standard. However, the efforts were confined to the writing system and were aimed at creating a literary form for educational and governmental purposes (Ansre 1971: 688–91). While these efforts turned out not to be very far-reaching, a standard written form has evolved for Shona, largely as a result of its usage in the educational system.

Other standardization activities affect more restricted areas of language use. Strevens and Weeks (1985), for instance, report on the development of 'Seaspeak' which is 'a regularized, simplified subset of English for use principally in intership and ship-to-shore speech communications' (1985: 1). The need for standardization is quite obvious here, as it is in aviation English, for very practical reasons, and so the success rate in efforts of this type would be expected to be quite high. This is not the case for many standardization attempts in natural languages where the effects of planning on actual behavior may be very small.

11.4. An empirical framework for language planning

Although language planning discussions tend to be primarily problem-oriented, there has also been some concern for the development of a theoretical framework for the field (Haugen 1983; Neustupny 1983). As mentioned earlier, a promising direction that can be traced through a number of recent writings looks at language planning through an analysis of all the relevant factors in a situation. Language is set in its full socio-cultural and political context and decision-making procedures are designed to take all relevant factors into account, and 'there is now a much better understanding of the linguistic, political, sociological, and attitudinal constraints on language policy formation' (Kachru 1982: 2). The evolving paradigm recognizes the 'close relationship between socioeconomic, communication and language problems' and calls for 'the identification of socioeconomic determinants and consequences of language problems by language planners and their active contribution to the solution of such problems' (Neustupny 1983: 2).

Current approaches also draw on models from other fields that turn out to be highly relevant when the full scope of language problems and solutions is realized. In particular, concepts from economic and political theory have been helpful: cost–benefit analysis has been offered as a model for the evaluation of proposed plans (Fasold 1984: 254–6); diffusion of innovation and other marketing concepts have been suggested as useful tools in the implementation of language planning decisions (Cooper 1985a). Haugen opens his discussion of implementation in corpus planning with the observation, 'This topic is basically one that ought to be handled by either a political scientist or a PR man' (1983: 269). Again, this points to the growing acceptance of the reality that language issues are only one part of the total language planning picture.

Despite the acknowledged priority of sociopolitical concerns in most language planning efforts, however, the study of language factors can make important contributions. The expansion of linguistics to include functional and social concerns aligns the field with the movement in planning toward an empirical framework. As Bailey argues, new paradigms in linguistics, including dynamic models which incorporate variation and change into a unified account of language, bring a better understanding of how language works to the task of language planning. 'The linguist can only go so far in what is a vaster political strategy. But at least he can now be equipped with a better theory in a better framework to go as far as he can in his limited role in language planning' (Bailey 1975: 157).

Further, an empirical approach treats the full cycle of language planning, as outlined above, from identification of the problem through plan development/implementation to evaluation (with feedback leading to possible revisions). There are relatively few case studies available which document the full planning cycle, however. This is an important area for further work so that relationships among stages, as well as the influence of individual factors, linguistic and otherwise, throughout the process, can be better understood.

The evolving empirical framework, then, is a trend in language planning toward active consideration of language variables embedded in the socio-cultural context along with the full range of issues that must be brought to bear in formulating and implementing solutions to language problems. A systematic approach developed on this basis promises to give planners a solid foundation for designing effective responses to problems.

11.5. Conclusion

Language planning, as an explicit effort to influence language use and usage, must respond to a variety of demands. The desired outcomes are most often political, social, or economic in character, and language is a means to these ends. The developing empirical framework for language planning considers these issues in their socio-cultural context, so that fully informed language choices can be made. The priority of nonlanguage factors is accepted as a natural reflection of the broader situation.

However, the fact that language planning is not primarily a linguistic activity does not mean that there is no role for linguists. A linguist who understands the socio-cultural context of language behavior is in fact better informed to make recommendations concerning the direction and implementation of changes that will lead to political or social outcomes than those who focus on the outcomes alone.

REFERENCES

Alisjahbana, S. T. 1961. Language engineering molds Indonesian language. *The Linguistic Reporter* 3. 3: 1.

Ansre, G. 1971. Language standardization in sub-Saharan Africa. In J. Fishman (ed.) *Advances in language planning*. The Hague: Mouton.

Bailey, C.-J. N. 1975. The new linguistic framework and language planning. *International Journal of the Sociology of Language* 4: 153–7.

Christian, D. 1984. Country Status Report: Singapore. Language/Area Reference Center Report. Washington: Center for Applied Linguistics.

Cobarrubias, J. & Fishman J. (eds.) 1983. *Progress in language planning: international perspectives*. The Hague: Mouton.

Cooper, R. (ed.) 1982. *Language spread: studies in diffusion and social change*. Bloomington: Indiana University Press.

Cooper, R. 1985. Selling language reform. Paper presented at Georgetown University Roundtable on Languages and Linguistics.

Cooper, R. in press. Hebrew as a national language. In F. Coulmas (ed.) *With forked tongues: what are national languages good for?* Ann Arbor: Karoma.

Das Gupta, J. 1973. Language planning and public policy: analytical outline of the policy process related to language planning in India. In R. Shuy (ed.) *Georgetown University roundtable on languages and linguistics*. Washington: Georgetown University Press.

DeFrancis, J. 1967. Language and script reform. *Current Trends in Linguistics* 2: 130–50.

Eastman, C. M. 1983. *Language planning: an introduction*. San Francisco: Chandler and Sharp Publishers, Inc.

Fasold, R. 1984. *The sociolinguistics of society*. Oxford: Blackwell.

Fellman, J. & Fishman, J. 1977. Language planning in Israel: solving terminological problems. In J. Rubin *et al.* (eds.) *Language planning processes*. The Hague: Mouton.

Ferguson, C. 1968. Language development. In J. Fishman, C. Ferguson & J. Das Gupta (eds.) *Language problems of developing nations*. New York: Wiley.

Fishman, J. (ed.) 1966. *Language loyalty in the United States*. The Hague: Mouton.

Fishman, J. (ed.) 1968. *Readings in the sociology of language*. The Hague: Mouton.

Fishman, J. 1973. Language modernization and planning in comparison with other types of national modernization and planning. *Language in Society* 2. 1: 23–42.

Gal, S. 1979. *Language shift: social determinants of linguistic change in bilingual Austria*. New York: Academic Press.

Gardner, R. 1985. *Social psychology and second language learning: the role of attitudes and motivation*. London: Arnold.

Garvin, P. & Mathiot, M. 1956. The urbanization of the Guarani language. In Fishman 1968.

Haugen, E. 1969. Language planning, theory and practice. Reprinted in A. Dil (ed.) *The ecology of language*. Stanford: Stanford University Press.

Haugen, E. 1983. The implementation of corpus planning: theory and practice. In Cobarrubias & Fishman 1983.

Herman, S. 1968. Explorations in the social psychology of language choice. In Fishman 1968.

Jernudd, B. 1973. Language planning as a type of language treatment. In J. Rubin & R. W. Shuy (eds.) *Language planning: current issues and research*. Washington: Georgetown University Press.

Kachru, B. 1982. An overview of language policy and planning. In R. Kaplan (ed.) *Annual review of applied linguistics*. Rowley: Newbury House.

Karam, F. X. 1974. Toward a definition of language planning. In J. Fishman (ed.) *Advances in language planning*. The Hague: Mouton.

Kloss, H. 1969. *Research possibilities on group bilingualism: a report*. Quebec: International Center for Research on Bilingualism.

Kuo, E. C. Y. 1980. Language planning in Singapore. *Language Planning Newsletter* 6. 2: 1–5.

Li, W. L. 1982. The language shift of Chinese–Americans. *International Journal of the Sociology of Language* 28: 109–24.

Mazrui, A. A. & Zirimu, P. 1978. Church, state, and marketplace in the spread of Kiswahili: comparative educational implications. In B. Spolsky & R. L. Cooper (eds.) *Case studies in bilingual education*. Rowley: Newbury House.

Musa, M. 1984. Issues of term planning for Bengali. *Language Planning Newsletter* 10. 2: 1–5.

Nahir, M. 1984. Language planning goals: a classification. *Language Problems and Language Planning* 8. 3: 294–327.

Neustupny, J. V. 1983. Toward a paradigm for language planning. *Language Planning Newsletter* 9. 4: 1–4.

Paulston, C. B. 1974. *Implications of language learning theory for language planning: concerns in bilingual education*. Washington: Center for Applied Linguistics.

Ray, P. 1968. Language standardization. In Fishman 1968.

Rubin, J. 1971. Evaluation and language planning. In J. Rubin & B. Jernudd (eds.) *Can language be planned?* Honolulu: The University Press of Hawaii.

Rubin, J. 1984. Review of *Language planning: an introduction*. *Language in Society* 14. 1: 137–41.

Sandefur, J. 1985. Language planning and the development of an Australian aboriginal creole. *Language Planning Newsletter* 11. 1: 1–4.

Spolsky, B. (ed.) 1972. *The language education of minority children*. Rowley: Newbury House.

Spolsky, B. & Boomer, L. 1983. The modernization of Navaho. In Cobarrubias & Fishman 1983.

Strevens, P. & Weeks, F. 1985. The creation of a regularized subset of English for mandatory use in maritime communications: SEASPEAK. *Language Planning Newsletter* 11. 2: 1–6.

Wardhaugh, R. 1986. *An introduction to sociolinguistics*. Oxford: Blackwell.

Weinstein, B. 1983. *The civic tongue: political consequences of language choices*. New York: Longman.

12 Ethnography of speaking: toward a linguistics of the praxis*

Alessandro Duranti

12.0. Introduction

The ethnography of speaking (henceforth ES) studies language use as displayed in the daily life of particular speech communities. Its method is ethnography, supplemented by techniques developed in other areas of study such as developmental pragmatics, conversation analysis, poetics, and history.[1] Its theoretical contributions are centered around the study of *situated discourse*, that is, linguistic performance as the locus of the relationship between language and the socio-cultural order.[2]

From the point of view of the *content* of daily verbal interaction, ES is interested in the relationship between language use and local systems of knowledge and social conduct. ES views discourse as one of the main loci for the (re)creation and transmission of cultural patterns of knowledge and social action. More specifically, ES studies what is accomplished through speaking and how speech is related to and is constructed by particular aspects of social organization and speakers' assumptions, values, and beliefs about the world. The meaning of speech for particular speakers in specific social activities is thus a central concern for ES. Some typical questions asked by ethnographers of speaking in analyzing a particular strip of verbal interaction are: what is the goal of speech in this case? Which attributes of the linguistic code warrant its use in this context? What is the relation of this interaction to other, similar acts performed by the same actors or to other events observed in the same community?

With respect to the *form* of daily language use, ES has been focussing on

* Several friends and colleagues provided comments on earlier drafts of this chapter. In particular, I would like to thank for their helpful criticism Richard Bauman, Donald Brenneis, Charles Goodwin, Frederick J. Newmeyer, Bambi Schieffelin, and Joel Sherzer. During the writing of this chapter, I also benefited from conversations with Emanuel Schegloff on the notion of context and its relevance to the analysis of talk.

[1] See, for instance, Bauman 1977; Shenkein 1978; Ochs & Schieffelin 1979; Hymes 1981; Bauman 1983; Heath 1983.

[2] For a general discussion and overview of the ethnographic approach to the study of language use, see Hymes 1974; Bauman & Sherzer 1975; Coulthard 1977: Chapter 3; Sherzer 1977; Hymes 1982b; Saville-Troike 1982; Sherzer 1983: 11–20; Duranti 1985.

patterns of variation across socio-cultural contexts, both within and across societies, with particular emphasis on the interrelation of the emergent and the culturally predictable structure of verbal performance in the conduct of social life.

The question often arises, whether explicitly or not, as to the relationship between ES and the supposedly wider area of sociolinguistics.

If we understand sociolinguistics as the systematic study of language use in social life, there should then be no doubts that ES should be considered a subfield of sociolinguistics. Such an inclusion of ES within the larger spectrum of sociolinguistic research could only benefit ES, which has often been criticized for its limited typology of actually analyzed linguistic phenomena (e.g. too much emphasis on ritualized speech or formal events) (Bloch 1976) and for its lack of concern for more explicit indications about its relevance for other branches of linguistics and anthropology (Leach 1976).

There are, however, peculiarities both in the methods and in the very object of inquiry of ES that make it related to, but distinct from, much of sociolinguistic research. Such differences, both at the methodological and at the theoretical level, accompanied by an abundance of new and stimulating research in some of the areas comprised by Hymes's notion of *communicative competence* (see below), have made more and more apparent the need to keep expanding the range of data and theoretical discussion within the ES approach before merging it with other fields of inquiry.

12.1. Language use

Like sociolinguists in general, ethnographers of speaking are interested in language *use*. A distinction must be drawn, however, between the commonly accepted sense of this term within linguistics at large and that meant by ES. Formal grammarians, historians of linguistics, and even sociolinguists at times interpret 'language use' in a narrow sense, namely as the actual employment of particular utterances, words, or sound by particular speakers at a given time and place, as linguistic 'tokens,' in other words, as opposed to 'types' (Lyons 1972). *Use* is thus often identified with *parole* as opposed to *langue* (cf. Saussure 1916). The sociolinguist's goal is thus to infer patterns of variation on the basis of the systematic sampling of more or less controlled 'uses' (or *actes de parole*). This notion of language use is strictly related to the view of sociolinguistics as merely a different *methodology*, a different way of obtaining data from that usually practiced by formal grammarians (Labov 1972: 259). In this view, the sociolinguist is depicted as someone who refuses to accept or test linguistic intuitions and prefers to them a tape-recorder with which to gather data from actual speech. Although formal grammarians have accepted the *social* significance of sociolinguistic research, many of them are still unable to see its significance from the point of view of *grammatical theory* (Chomsky 1977: 55).[3] What is missing here is both the realization by the formal grammarians, and the ability to convince by the sociolinguists, that mere structural descriptions of linguistic forms are useful and interesting but consistently lacking some essential feature of what makes language so precious to the human species, namely, its ability to function *in context* as an instrument of both reflection and action upon the world. So-called 'cognitive models' rely on the assumption that it is possible – and in fact mandatory in order to have a *theory* – to account for human behavior by means of context-independent rules. But we know now that decontextualized features pick out objects and provide analyses that are qualitatively different from those handled by social actors (Bourdieu 1977; Dreyfus 1983; Dreyfus & Dreyfus 1986). The use of 'intuitions' in linguistic as well as in metalinguistic behavior can be seen as an individual ability to rely upon or reconstruct (intrapsychologically) contextual information.

Thus, for ethnographers of speaking, as well as for many other researchers in the social sciences, *language use* must be interpreted as *the use of the linguistic code(s) in the conduct of social life.* ES accepts Wittgenstein's (1958) claim that the unity of '(a) language' is an illusion and one should rather look at specific contexts of use (or 'language games') in order to explain how linguistic signs can do the work they do. The interaction between speech and social action is so important that the methodologies and notations developed to study the referential (or denotational) uses of speech may be inadequate to study its *social* uses (Silverstein 1977, 1979). The term *speaking* was introduced by Hymes to stress the active, praxis-oriented aspect of the linguistic code, as opposed to the more contemplative, static notion of 'language' as seen and described by structural (synchronic) linguistics. Speaking must thus be thought of as a form of *human labor*, the phylogenetically and ontogenetically most powerful form of cooperative behavior (Vygotsky 1978; Leontyev 1981; Rossi-Landi 1983).

The concern with language use is thus not only a methodological commitment toward getting what speakers *really* say in a variety of contexts but also a consequence of the interest in what speakers *do* with language, whether willingly or unwillingly, consciously or unconsciously, directly or obliquely. In particular, ethnographers of speaking have been concerned

---

[3] For Chomsky, to 'incorporate nonlinguistic factors into grammar: beliefs, attitudes, etc.' would amount 'to a rejection of the initial idealization of language, as an object of study'; it would mean that 'language is a chaos that is not worth studying' (Chomsky 1977: 152–3). This attitude has produced a culturally extremely impoverished object of inquiry ('core grammar'). To think that such an 'object' bears some relationship to 'language' is an interesting and provoking hypothesis, but to give it the theoretical status of a phylogenetically defined organ and claim that it is the only object worth of study still seems, to many of us, at least unwarranted by the data.

with the work done by and through language in (1) establishing, challenging, and recreating social identities and social relationships, (2) explaining to others as well as to ourselves why the world is the way it is and what could or should be done to change it; (3) providing frames for events at the societal as well as individual level; (4) breaking, or more often sustaining, physical, political, and cultural barriers. Some of these areas of inquiry have also been studied within *pragmatics* (Gazdar 1979; Levinson 1983). What usually distinguishes the ethnographic approach from pragmatic analysis is a stronger concern for the socio-cultural context of the use of language, with the specific relationship between language and local systems of knowledge and social order, and a lesser commitment to the relevance of logical notation to the strategic use of speech in social interaction.

12.2. Communicative competence

The ethnographic study of language use aims at describing the knowledge that participants in verbal interaction need and display in order to communicate successfully with one another. *Communicative competence* is the term Hymes (1972b) used for this kind of complex expertise, which includes but goes beyond Chomsky's (1965) *competence* (Hymes 1982b).

> We have . . . to account for the fact that a normal child acquires
> knowledge of sentences, not only as grammatical, but also as
> appropriate. He or she acquires competence as to when to speak,
> when not, and as to what to talk about with whom, when, where, in
> what manner. In short, a child becomes able to accomplish a
> repertoire of speech acts, to take part in speech events, and to
> evaluate their accomplishment by others. This competence,
> moreover, is integral with attitudes, values, and motivations
> concerning language, its features and uses, and integral with
> competence for, and attitudes toward, the interrelation of language,
> with the other codes of communicative conduct.
>
> (Hymes 1972b: 277–8)

Within ES and sociolinguistics, the discussion of communicative competence versus linguistic (or grammatical) competence usually centers around two issues: (1) the need to accompany grammatical description with conditions of appropriateness; (2) the complementarity of the grammatical (or linguistic) code with other aspects of cooccurring rule-governed behavior (e.g. gestures, eye-gaze) (Hymes 1982b).

In fact, a crucial difference between Chomsky's notion of *competence* and Hymes's notion is that the former relies on the assumption that knowledge can be studied separately from performance, meant as the implementation of that knowledge in language use, whereas for Hymes, participation, performance, and intersubjective knowledge are all essential features of the ability to 'know a language.' Furthermore, Chomsky presents the hypothesis of autonomous grammar as a prerequisite to maintaining 'order' in the object of study (see note 3). The very possibility of 'doing science' on linguistic phenomena is tied to the researchers' ability to construct hypotheses about linguistic forms without having to make reference to nonlinguistic factors such as beliefs and attitudes (Chomsky 1977).

But the assumption that grammar of an idealized language is necessarily *orderly*, whereas patterns of actual verbal communication are *chaotic*, can hardly be supported by empirical investigation. Anyone who has ever engaged in grammatical analysis of the 'idealized' sort knows that disagreement among speakers on sentence acceptability is common; and anyone who has ever read any study on linguistic variation and linguistic performance knows that there are a lot of people out there finding 'order' in the apparent 'chaos' of language use. Although these are not sufficient reasons either for rejecting the use of introspection and idealization or for claiming full understanding of linguistic performance, they are arguments in favor of wanting to keep under a common roof – the notion of *communicative competence*, that is – the variety of phenomena that speakers must be able to handle in order to be considered 'competent.'

We all know that a large part of the work done by Chomsky and his students is based on their ability to find (i.e. imagine) appropriate contexts for the uttering of certain utterance-types. Despite the theoretical assumption of the innateness of certain aspects of grammar as pure cognitive/ biological endowment, the actual definition of such aspects rests on the possibility of matching sentences with possible worlds, which are, in turn, constructed on the basis of the experience linguists have of the world in which they live. Criticism of such a methodology by ES and other approaches is not a rejection of abstraction or idealization, but rather a fundamental skepticism about the uncritical use of what phenomenological sociology calls 'preunderstanding' of the world (Garfinkel 1967; Bleicher 1982). In the case of linguistic research, it is the preunderstanding of the relationship between linguistic and nonlinguistic behavior that is usually ignored by formal grammarians. The same criticism drawn by Husserl toward objectivism in psychology applies here:

> The psychologists simply fail to see that they too [like physicists] study neither themselves nor the scientists who are doing the investigating nor their own vital environing world [*Umwelt*]. They do not see that from the very beginning they necessarily presuppose

themselves as a group of men belonging to their own environing world and historical period. (Husserl 1965: 186–7)

Within ES, the explicit discussion of the relationship between the researchers' expectations and norms and the system they try to describe has become a major concern for the study of language acquisition and socialization. Ochs & Schieffelin (1984) have taken 'the descriptions of caregiving in the psychological literature as ethnographic descriptions' (1984: 283) and compared them with other accounts provided by members of other societies on how children acquire language and develop into competent members of their society. What is taken for granted by linguists and psychologists describing language development to other members of their own society is thus unveiled by a process of estrangement:

> using an ethnographic perspective, we will recast selected behaviors of white middle-class caregivers and young children as pieces of one 'developmental story.' The white middle-class developmental story . . . will be compared with two other developmental stories from societies that are strikingly different: Kaluli (Papua New Guinea) and Western Samoan. (Ochs & Schieffelin 1984: 285)

The result is a new discussion of the relationship between the process of acquiring language and the process of becoming a competent member of a society. An understanding of the ways in which the two processes are interwoven provides the necessary perspective for assessing the relevance of local theories of self and of knowledge for members' linguistic behavior on the one hand and our description of it on the other.

Ultimately, any attempt at relating linguistic forms to their *content* depends on the ability that both members and researchers have to utilize the *context* of speech as a resource for achieving understanding and getting things done.

12.3. Context

In formal linguistic analysis, context is usually brought in when difficulties or doubts arise with respect to the interpretation or acceptability of certain linguistic expressions. Although context is in fact crucial for imagining possible alternative interpretations of structurally ambiguous sentences, its use and role are not officially recognized in formal models of linguistic competence. The ethnographer's job, on the other hand, crucially relies on the ability skilfully and explicitly to relate patterns of behavior, speech included, to their immediate as well as broader sociocultural context. It is not by accident then that it was Malinowski, the father of modern ethnography, who first stressed the need to interpret speech in its *context of situation*, 'an expression which indicates on the one hand that the conception of *context* has to be broadened and on the other that the *situation* in which words are uttered can never be passed over as irrelevant to the linguistic expression' (1923: 306).

Although Malinowski originally thought that the need to keep speech and context tied to one another was restricted to the study of 'primitive people,' for whom language 'is a mode of action and not an instrument of reflection' (1923: 312), he later reformulated his views to include the importance of context in the interpretation of all languages, across all kinds of uses, literacy included (Malinowski 1935, Vol. 2: Part iv):[4]

> Our definition of meaning forces us to a new, a richer and wider type of observation. In order to show the meaning of words we must not merely give sound of utterance and equivalence of significance. We must above all give the pragmatic context in which they are uttered, the correlation of sound to context, to action and to technical apparatus; and incidentally, in a full linguistic description, it would be necessary also to show the types of drills or conditioning or education by which words acquire meaning. (1935, Vol. 2: 60)

Behavioristic tones aside, this passage expresses concerns and assumptions that were, thirty years later, at the heart of Hymes's call for an *ethnography of speaking* (Hymes 1964a, b).

In the last twenty years or so the term *context* has been broken down and variedly redefined to include the range of actual or potential speakers, the spatio-temporal dimensions of the interaction, the participants' goals. Three notions have been adopted and discussed within ES and related approaches: *speech community*, *speech event*, *speech act*.

12.3.1. Speech community

The widest context of verbal interaction for ES as well as for sociolinguistic research is usually taken to be the *speech community*, defined as a group of people who share the rules for interpreting and using at least one language

---

[4] Here is the official statement that sanctions Malinowski's 'turn': 'in one of my previous writings, I opposed civilised and scientific to primitive speech, and argued as if the theoretical uses of words in modern philosophic and scientific writing were completely detached from their pragmatic sources. This was an error, and a serious error at that. Between the savage use of words and the most abstract and theoretical one there is only a difference of degree. Ultimately all the meaning of all words is derived from bodily (sic!) experience' (Malinowski 1935, Vol. 2: 58).

(Gumperz 1972: 16) or linguistic variety (Hymes 1972a: 54). One of the reasons for taking the speech community as the starting point for linguistic research was to avoid the assumption that the sharing of the same 'language' implies shared understanding of its use and meaning in various contexts (Hymes 1972a, b).

It has been shown that the notion of speech community should not be simply equated with linguistic homogeneity of a well-defined set of features (Hudson 1980; Hymes 1982b). In the Norwegian community studied by Blom and Gumperz (1972), for instance, individual speakers who were born and raised in the community exhibited fundamental differences in terms of the uses of code-switching, of its interpretation and its value. One way of accounting for such diversity is to claim that it is characteristic of the very use of linguistic communication in social life:

> When studied in sufficient detail, with field methods designed to elicit speech in significant contexts, all speech communities are linguistically diverse and it can be shown that this diversity serves important communicative functions in signaling interspeaker attitudes and in providing information about speakers' social identities.
>
> (Gumperz 1972: 13)

Another way to deal with the kind of diversity documented by Gumperz and others is to propose that in fact speech communities do not exist except as 'prototypes' in people's minds (Hudson 1980: 30). To test such a hypothesis, it would be necessary to show that there is a psychological reality of some prototypical or 'ideal' core features of language use within a certain group of people. Some of Labov's (1972) findings on the uniformity of overt types of evaluative behavior could be used in such an argument. At the same time, his detailed work on *patterns* of variation in phonological and lexical domains points to a different, if not opposite, hypothesis, namely, the idea that the 'types' or regularities to be found are not in anyone's head but rather somewhere *out there*, in the (real) world of performance.

Any notion of speech community (and this would be also true for defining 'dialect' or 'vernacular') will thus depend on two sets of phenomena: (1) patterns of variation in a group of speakers also definable on grounds other than linguistic homogeneity (e.g. speakers of this town tend to drop post-vocalic /r/ in the following contexts) and (2) emergent and cooperatively achieved aspects of human behavior as strategies for establishing comembership in the conduct of social life. The ability to explain (1) ultimately relies on our success in understanding (2).

Alessandro Duranti

12.3.2. **Speech event**

In contrast to sociolinguists, researchers in ES tend to start their analyses of speech behavior from the loci of use of speech rather than from the surveying of a particular set of norms for a particular range of social actors. The notion of *speech event* is the analytical tool for such a research program. The basic assumption of a speech-event analysis of language use is that an understanding of the form and content of everyday talk in its various manifestations implies an understanding of the social activities in which speaking takes place (Hymes 1964a, 1972a; Levinson 1979; Duranti 1985). Such activities, however, are not simply 'accompanied' by verbal interaction, they are also *shaped* by it: there are many ways, that is, in which speech has a role in the constitution of a social event. The most obvious cases are perhaps gossip sessions and telephone conversations, neither of which could take place if talk were not exchanged. But even the most physically oriented activities such as sport events or hunting expeditions rely heavily on verbal communication for the participants' successful coordination around some common task.

How is one to face the formidable task of isolating and describing event-units? Hymes (1964a) proposed a preliminary list of features or components of communicative events. The idea was to provide 'a useful guide in terms of which relevant features can be discerned – a provisional phonetics, as it were, not an *a priori* phonemics, of the communicative event' (Hymes 1964a: 13). The first list was later extended to include 16 components, grouped under 8 main entries, to be remembered with the acronym SPEAKING (Hymes 1972a): S (situation: setting and scene); P (participants: speaker/sender, addressor, hearer/receiver/audience, addressee); E (ends: outcomes, goals); A (act sequence: message form and message content); K (key); I (instrumentalities: channel, forms of speech); N (norms: norms of interaction and interpretation); G (genres). (See also Saville-Troike 1982; Duranti 1985).

In the last ten years or so, the speech-event unit has become a useful tool for the analysis of language use within and across societies. Many of the most recent contributions to the understanding of the constitutive role of speaking in political arenas, child-rearing practices, literacy activities, and counseling, have made use, whether explicitly or not, of the notion of speech event (Duranti 1981; Scollon & Scollon 1981; Heath 1983; Philips 1983; Anderson & Stokes 1984; Brenneis & Myers 1984; Schieffelin & Ochs 1986; Watson-Gegeo & White in preparation). For many researchers, the speech event still represents a level of analysis that has the advantage of preserving information about the social system as a whole while at the same

218

time allowing the researcher to get into the details of personal acts (Duranti to appear).

The Speaking model also represents a basic difference between ES and other branches of linguistics: the grid, in its various versions, has always maintained an *etic* status and was never accompanied by a (general) theory of the possible relationships among the various components. Such a theoretical discussion, in Hymes's program, seemed to be possible only at the *local* level (i.e. with respect to particular communities) and not within a more global, comparative framework. This entails that, within ES, there has never been an attempt at formulating a *general phonemics* of communicative events. The relationship among the components of the model are each time shown to be meaningful within a particular society – as an *emic* description, that is, – but do not necessarily exemplify any universal principle of the relation between speech and context in *societies* in general. The few attempts to draw general principles, such as Irvine 1979 are in fact discussions of how one should *not* infer universal features from what a given group chooses to do in a particular type of speech event; that is, what is 'formal' in one context need not be formal in another. (The only exceptions here are some attempts at elucidating general *areal* patterns where there are enough local studies to allow for it, e.g. Roberts & Forman 1972; Abrahams 1983.)

Is this tendency simply a reflection of the cultural relativism that ES shares with most of modern anthropology? It might well be the case. But most importantly, I think, the care for specific *emic* accounts and the reluctance to posit universal principles (with the exception of Brown & Levinson 1978) is strongly related to the fundamental anti-Universalism that characterizes ES as originally defined by Hymes. If some kind of universal claim is ever accepted by ES, it will be similar to what Merleau-Ponty (1964) called *lateral universal*, that is, the universality of the intersubjective enterprise rather than of the structures. To understand this, we must reflect again on the goals of ES. Differently from other approaches within linguistics, ES is concerned with language use as a link to and as an instrument of social life. This means that ethnographers of speaking, through a number of subjective, objective, and intersubjective methods (e.g. intuitions, audio-recording, transcription, interviews, participation in the life of the 'subjects'), get involved in studying an 'object' which is more complex and multiform than that typically studied in other branches of linguistics. One of the goals of ES is to maintain the complexity of *language as praxis* rather than reduce it to abstract, independent principles. In other words, the kind of universality ES is interested in cannot be the abstract kind of generative grammar or of conversational maxims. In the latter cases (i.e. for Chomsky and Grice), many aspects of the context must be removed in order to 'see' the principles at work. The researcher must create a vacuum wherein to show that certain structures or constraints are operating 'under' or 'above' what is going on. Once this is achieved, the researcher's work is over: the pieces are left on the ground. The whole is not put together again. Ethnographers, on the other hand – like the people they study – struggle to both capture and maintain the whole of the interaction at hand. The elements of one level (e.g. phonological register, lexical choice, discourse strategies) must be related to the elements of another level (e.g. social identities, values) – which, in turn, is further defined and constituted by those elements. In this process, ethnographers act as the linking elements between different levels and systems of communication. In so doing, they act in a similar fashion to those psychologists who study learning and cognitive development by consciously creating functional environments where behavior can be observed without destroying elements of the 'whole task' (Luria 1979; Griffin, Cole & Newman 1982; LCHC 1984).

A possible criticism of speech-event analysis is that it tends to select strips of interaction that are labeled by a culture, but it may overlook those interactions which are not recognized as units of some sort by the members. It should be mentioned here that, although the presence of a lexical term for a given activity or 'strip of interaction' is only one level of local organization of experience – perhaps the most obviously ideological – the lack of a term for any given such 'strip' is an interesting clue for fieldworkers.[5]

There is nothing, however, in the Speaking model or in the very idea of speech event that invites research on one kind of activity over another. Although ethnographers take native taxonomies seriously (Abrahams & Bauman 1971; Gossen 1972), what they end up studying is a by-product of what members of the culture describe as relevant or important and what

---

[5] The lack of native labeling for certain kinds of often unbounded activities may however be a problem for the necessary coordination between participants and observer. Those who are being observed might feel that they need to be 'doing something' in order for someone to be observing them. When Elinor Ochs, Martha Platt and I were collecting data on language use and language acquisition in a western Samoan village, for instance, we recorded and studied different kinds of events. While I mostly concentrated on conversations among adults and formal meetings of the village council, Ochs and Platt documented household interaction between young children and their caretakers (older siblings, parents, or grandparents). Whereas participants almost immediately accepted the intrusion of my tape-recorder during conversations and important meetings without any major or lasting shift in the nature of their interaction, the people who were home with their younger children kept trying, during the first weeks, to frame their interaction with each other and with the reseachers as 'doing school' (*fai le 'aaoga*). It was only after the startling realization that the researcher had nothing to teach and in fact wanted to learn something from them that people stopped performing school routines and body postures and accepted the intrusion of the researcher with the tape-recorder. The asymmetry between these contexts – the conversations and meeting on the one hand and the household interaction on the other – interestingly correlates with the presence versus absence of native labels for the activity at hand: whereas there are local labels for 'conversation' (*talanoaga*) and 'meeting' (*fono*), there is no native category for staying home with the kids. It would seem then that by reframing the interaction as 'doing school,' participants tried to create a context that could be reportable and perhaps valuable, within the local range of known and admissible activities.

they are expected to document as practitioners of a particular research tradition.

12.3.3. Speech act

The notion of speech *act* stresses the pragmatic force of speech, its ability not only to describe the world but to change it by relying on public, shared conventions (Austin 1975). Historically, the importance of Austin's work was to provide a philosophically sophisticated discussion of meaning in language that did not solely rely on the notion of truth (Levinson 1983). In order to explain the *illocutionary* force of an utterance one must be able to relate the *locution* – i.e. the words used – with its context. Thus, the sentence *I don't like to watch tv* can be used to do different things according to when it is used, by whom, etc. The different *uses* of such an utterance may all share the same linguistic *form* – actually, some abstraction of it – but they will serve different *functions* – e.g. to justify the absence of a tv set in my house, to object to an evening at home, to explain why I can't follow a conversation about tv programs. The same utterance can thus be used to different ends, by relying on different shared understanding of the social event in which speech occurs. The analyst's task is to explain the relationship between the speaker's subjective reality, the linguistic form chosen, and the audience response: 'The level of speech acts mediates immediately between the usual levels of grammar and the rest of a speech event or situation in that it implicates both linguistic form and social norms' (Hymes 1972a: 57).

The acceptance of the notion of speech act does not necessarily imply the acceptance of the epistemological foundations or underlying ideology (Pratt 1981) of speech-act theory. In particular, such a theory has been said to give too much prominence to the speaker's intentions for the definition of the utterance meaning. A number of researchers have lately shown that the role assigned to the speaker's intentions in the interpretation of speech actually varies across cultures and contexts (Streeck 1980; Ochs 1982; Rosaldo 1982; Kochman 1983; Duranti 1984). In the cases of verbal dueling among Blacks discussed by Kochman (1983), for instance, a speech act cannot be defined as insult until the receiver has chosen to interpret it as such. In the Samoan *fono* – a traditional politico-judiciary arena – the speaker's original intentions and understanding of certain events at the time of the speech act seem at times irrelevant for those who interpret his words and assess his responsibility (Duranti 1984). As demonstrated by analysts of conversation, however, even within American white middle class society, the emergent model of verbal interaction is much more dialogical than is usually recognized by the dominant ideology (Streeck 1980; Goodwin 1981; Schegloff 1982).

More generally, ES is interested in the relationship between the Austinian notion of speech act and various aspects of the local theories of communication and interpretation, including (1) the relationship between modes of production and modes of interpretation, as for instance found in the local organization of task accomplishment (Duranti & Ochs 1986); (2) the notion of self and the speaker's ability to control the interpretation of his or her own words (Rosaldo 1982; Shore 1982; Holquist 1983); (3) the local ontology of interpretation (e.g. whether it involves the ability to be in someone else's place or mind) (Ochs 1984); (4) the relevance of 'sincerity' for the performance of any speech act (Rosaldo 1982).

12.4. Other approaches: conversation analysis

By no means do the three kinds of context discussed above exhaust the possible or the existing levels of study of talk in social interaction (see for instance the papers in van Dijk 1985; Schiffrin 1984). Let me mention here another approach that shares with ES some important concerns and goals. The approach I have in mind is conversation analysis (CA). The relationship between CA and ES over the last ten or fifteen years has been a complex one, with moments of great unity (see Gumperz & Hymes 1972) and moments of separation and misunderstanding. Some recent developments in terms of both theoretical pronouncements and participation in conferences and symposia seem to indicate the possibility of a fruitful osmosis between the two schools. Although their methodologies are quite distinct, ES and CA do share some important assumptions and concerns (see the relevant papers and their introductions in Gumperz & Hymes 1972). In particular, both ES and CA tend to stress the role of speech in *creating* context, the need to take the participants' perspective in the analysis of their interaction, the cooperative nature of verbal communication – the latest feature being related, but not identical, to the claim of the emergent nature of (some aspects of) the social order.

There are at least two sources of apparent disagreement between CA and ES: (1) a different notion of what constitutes 'context'; (2) the issue of the universality of the turn-taking system and its correlates. A brief discussion of these issues should help clarify some possible misunderstandings.

12.4.1. Context

CA looks at talk-in-interaction, claiming the independence of the turn-taking system from various aspects of the socio-cultural context of speech such as the socioeconomic status of ethnic identity of the speakers (e.g. American white middle class, American working class, Thai peasants); the speech acts that are being performed (e.g. threats, promises, apologies); or the particular social occasion that has brought the participants together (e.g. a birthday party, waiting for the bus, calling the police). According to CA, the relevance of these contextual features should be used by the analyst only when the participants themselves explicitly evoke such features (Schegloff & Sacks 1973; Schegloff 1986a). On the other hand, certain principles such as 'one speaker at a time' and notions like 'prior speaker,' 'current speaker,' and 'recipient' are instead said to be always relevant, regardless of the specific occasion on which conversation takes place (Sacks, Schegloff & Jefferson 1974; Moerman 1977; Schegloff, Jefferson & Sacks 1977; Schegloff 1986a, 1986b). CA has thus defined an area of study in which the 'problems' and the 'solutions' speakers encounter in conversation can be described without referring to aspects of what ES researchers would define as crucial elements of the socio-cultural context. In so doing, CA shares something with the 'autonomous' trends within contemporary formal linguistics. Both CA and generative grammar, for instance, claim to be dealing with a level of structural relationships and dependencies among speech forms which can be studied separately from the occasion in which they are produced (unless we consider 'conversation' a kind of occasion). CA, however, makes no claim as to the innate nature of the turn-taking mechanisms and, more importantly, shares with ES (and ethnomethodology) the concern for the participants' point of view (or 'orientation'). The methods for arriving at defining the participants' perspective, however, may differ. For CA, what is found in the interaction (on a transcript, for instance) is the only legitimate source of knowledge for inferring the participants' concern. For ES, on the other hand, certain aspects of the social identity of the speakers as well as their past history are important. Furthermore, ethnographers routinely rely on members' accounts and explanation of what they (or others) were doing and meaning in a given verbal interaction. Those accounts, however, cannot by themselves constitute the only evidence of certain notions or practices. The researcher must search for both direct and indirect evidence of certain patterns of behavior. Let me give an example from my own work. In Samoan society, members can often articulate their expectations about particular social actors' duties and rights *vis à vis* different contexts. When I analyzed the speech of chiefs and orators participating in village council meetings (*fono*), those expectations seemed important for both me and the Samoan research assistants in interpreting the interaction. Despite the fact that participants' verbal behavior during the meetings was clearly part of the *stuff* that members of the society use to define certain people as 'chiefs' and others as 'orators,' native competent speakers were continuously trying to match the recorded performance with some ideal notion of what was appropriate for a given actor in a particular situation. Given the importance of the interplay between projected and actual behaviors in the interpretation of talk, it would seem to be a logical error to accept certain role notions only in their emergent versions, and not as part of people's guidelines for explaining how social order could or should be achieved in particular contexts.

12.4.2. Universality

Although, as far as I know, CA has never officially claimed the universality of the English turn-taking system and its corollaries across societies and languages, such a claim has been taken to be implicit in their practice.[6] A few studies, some of which are in the ES tradition, have challenged the universality of certain aspects of the turn-taking mechanisms (Philips 1976; Godard 1977; Philips 1983; Wolfson 1983). As discussed by Schegloff (1986b), however, the issue is not really resolved by simply concentrating on variation and differences. We would not gain very much insight into the phenomena being described by simply lining up – *à la* Popper – a set of apparent counterexamples to what is claimed by CA for English. The issue is at least twofold: (1) what is in common beyond (or despite) the differences (Schegloff 1986b); and (2) how are those differences related to *other differences* – a point recently recognized by Schegloff (in press a) in discussing cross-linguistic work on repair mechanisms. In fact, even if the universal nature of the phenomena described by CA were to be further corroborated by a wide range of cross-cultural data, the 'autonomous' level of the discoveries about conversational interaction would still leave open the question of the *meaning* of those 'problems' and 'solutions' for different cultures. Silence is a typical example of a phenomenon that, differently distributed across cultures, can acquire different meanings (Basso 1970; Reisman 1974; Bauman 1983). More generally, what appears identical on a transcript (e.g. a sequence, a set of words or interruptions, a pause) might be quite different in people's lives or in their minds. For this reason, I believe that both CA and ES are needed to help clarify the mechanisms and meaning of daily verbal interaction.

12.5. Conclusions

Speaking or its absence seem significant in most, if not all, human interac-

---

[6] Again, perhaps paradoxically, CA finds itself aligned with traditional generative grammarians, who claim that the in-depth study of one language, viz. English, might be sufficient for making interesting hypotheses about Universal Grammar.

tions. The very moment we start looking at a sequence of talk, we realize that the accompanying interaction could have not been the same without it. Even in its most phatic or seemingly redundant uses, talk is always *constitutive of* some portion of reality: it either makes something already existing *present* to (or for) the participants or creates something anew.

ES's fundamental theoretical contribution, beyond description of communicative patterns within and across societies, is the discussion of the role of speaking in the shaping of people's lives. It is thus the true *semantics* of human language. Without necessarily rejecting formal or structural accounts of language use, ES remains an important element in establishing a linguistics of human praxis, a field of study in which the analysts do not lose track of the sociohistorical context of speech, while trying to bridge the gap between linguistic form and linguistic content. In its attempts to describe what other subfields of linguistics leave out or take for granted, ES stays within the tradition of what Luria (1978) called 'romantic science.' Its goal is not to strive for simplicity measures or one-dimensional patterns, but rather to capture, through ethnography and linguistic analysis, the inherent 'heteroglossia' of any (one) language (Bakhtin 1981), the complexity of the human experience as defined and revealed in everyday discourse.

REFERENCES

Abrahams, R. D. 1983. *The man-of-words in the West Indies: performance and the emergence of creole culture.* Baltimore: John Hopkins University Press.
Abrahams, R. D. & Bauman, R. 1971. Sense and nonsense in St. Vincent: speech behavior decorum in a Caribbean community. *American Anthropologist* 73: 262–72.
Anderson, A. B. & Stokes, S. J. 1984. *Social and institutional influences on the development and practice of literacy.* In H. Goelman, A. Oberg & F. Smith (eds.) *Awakening to literacy.* London: Heinemann.
Austin, J. L. 1975. *How to do things with words*, 2nd edn., ed. J. O. Urmson & M. Sbisa. Cambridge, MA: Harvard University Press.
Bakhtin, M. M. 1981. *The dialogic imagination.* Ed. M. Holquist, trans. by C. Emerson & M. Holquist. Austin: University of Texas Press.
Basso, K. 1970. 'To give up on words': silence in western Apache culture. *Southwestern Journal of Anthropology* 26: 213–30.
Bauman, R. 1977. *Verbal art as performance.* Rowley: Newbury House.
Bauman, R. 1983. *Let your words be few: symbolism of speaking and silence among seventeenth-century Quakers.* Cambridge: Cambridge University Press.
Bauman, R. & Sherzer, J. 1975. The ethnography of speaking. *Annual Review of Anthropology* 4: 95–119.
Bleicher, J. 1982. *The hermeneutic imagination: outline of a positive critique of scientism and sociology.* London: Routledge & Kegan Paul.
Bloch, M. 1976. Review of R. Bauman & J. Sherzer (eds.) *Explorations in the ethnography of speaking. Language in Society* 5: 229–34.
Blom, J.-P. & Gumperz, J. J. 1972. Social meaning in linguistic structures: code-switching in Norway. In Gumperz & Hymes 1972.
Bourdieu, P. 1977. *Outline of a theory of practice.* Cambridge: Cambridge University Press.
Brenneis, D. & Myers, F. (eds.) 1984. *Dangerous words: language and politics in the Pacific.* New York: New York University Press.

Brown, P. & Levinson, S. 1978. Universals in language usage: politeness phenomena. In E. Goody (ed.) *Questions and politeness: strategies in social interaction.* Cambridge: Cambridge University Press.

Chomsky, N. 1965. *Aspects of the theory of syntax.* Cambridge, MA: MIT Press.

Chomsky, N. 1977. *Language and responsibility. Based on conversation with Mitsou Ronat.* Trans. by J. Viertel. New York: Pantheon.

Coulthard, M. 1977. *An introduction to discourse analysis.* London: Longman.

Dijk, T. A. van (ed.) 1985. *Handbook of discourse analysis,* 4 vols. New York: Academic Press.

Dreyfus, H. 1983. Why current studies of human capacities can never be scientific. Berkeley: Berkeley Cognitive Science Report No. 11.

Dreyfus, H. & Dreyfus, S. 1986. *Mind over machine: the power of human intuition and expertise in the era of the computer.* London: Macmillan/The Free Press.

Duranti, A. 1981. *The Samoan fono: a sociolinguistic study. Pacific Linguistics* B80. Canberra: The Australian National University.

Duranti, A. 1984. Intentions, self, and local theories of meaning: words and social action in a Samoan context. Technical Report No. 122. San Diego: University of California Center for Human Information Processing.

Duranti, A. 1985. Sociocultural dimensions of discourse. In van Dijk 1985, Vol. 1: *Disciplines of Discourse.*

Duranti, A. to appear. Doing things with words: conflict, understanding, and change in a Samoan *fono.* In Watson-Gegeo & White in preparation.

Duranti, A. & Ochs, E. 1986. Literacy instruction in a Samoan village. In B. B. Schieffelin & P. Gilmore (eds.) *Acquisition of literacy: ethnographic perspectives.* Norwood: Ablex.

Gazdar, G. 1979. *Pragmatics: implicature, presupposition, and logical form.* London: Academic Press.

Godard, D. 1977. Same setting, different norms: phone call beginnings in France and the United States. *Language in Society* 6: 209–19.

Goodwin, C. 1981. *Conversation organization: interaction between speakers and hearers.* New York: Academic Press.

Gossen, G. 1972. Chamula genres of verbal behavior. In A. Paredes & R. Bauman (eds.) *Toward new perspectives in folklore.* Austin: University of Texas Press.

Griffin, P., Cole, M. & Newman, D. 1982. Locating tasks in psychology and education. *Discourse Processes* 5: 111–25.

Gumperz, J. J. 1972. Introduction. In Gumperz & Hymes 1972.

Gumperz, J. J. & Hymes, D. (eds.) 1972. *Directions in sociolinguistics: the ethnography of communication.* New York: Holt.

Heath, S. 1983. *Ways with words: language, life, and work in communities and classrooms.* Cambridge: Cambridge University Press.

Holquist, M. 1983. The politics of representation. *The Quarterly Newsletter of the Laboratory of Comparative Human Cognition* 5: 2–9.

Hudson, R. 1980. *Sociolinguistics.* Cambridge: Cambridge University Press.

Husserl, E. 1965. Philosophy and the crisis of European man. In *Phenomenology and the crisis of philosophy,* trans. with an introduction by Q. Lauer. New York: Harper & Row.

Hymes, D. 1964a. Introduction: toward ethnographies of communication. In *American Anthropologist* 66, *Special publication*: J. J. Gumperz & D. Hymes (eds.) *The ethnography of communication.*

Hymes, D. (ed.) 1964b. *Language in culture and society: a reader in linguistics and anthropology.* New York: Harper & Row.

Hymes, D. 1972a. Models for the interaction of language and social life. In Gumperz & Hymes 1972.

Hymes, D. 1972b. On communicative competence. In J. B. Pride & J. Holmes (eds.) *Sociolinguistics.* Harmondsworth: Penguin.

Hymes, D. 1974. *Foundations in sociolinguistics.* Philadelphia: University of Pennsylvania Press.

Hymes, D. 1981. *'In vain I tried to tell you'. Essays in native American ethnopoetics.* Philadelphia: University of Pennsylvania Press.

Hymes, D. 1982a. *Vers la compétence de communication.* Trans. by F. Mugler. Paris: Hatier-Credif.

Hymes, D. 1982b. Postface. In Hymes 1982a.

Irvine, J. T. 1979. Formality and informality in communicative events. *American Anthropologist* 81: 773–90.

Kochman, T. 1983. The boundary between play and nonplay in Black verbal dueling. *Language in Society* 12: 329–37.

LCHC. 1983. Re-mediation, diagnosis and remediation. San Diego: University of California, Laboratory of Comparative Human Cognition.

Labov, W. 1972. *Sociolinguistic patterns*. Philadelphia: University of Pennsylvania Press.

Leach, E. 1976. Social geography and linguistic performance. *Semiotica* 16: 87–97.

Leontyev, A. N. 1981. *Problems of the development of the mind*. Moscow: Progress Publishers.

Levinson, S. 1979. Activity types and language. *Linguistics* 17: 365–99.

Levinson, S. 1983. *Pragmatics*. Cambridge: Cambridge University Press.

Luria, A. R. 1978. *The making of mind: a personal account of Soviet psychology*, ed. M. Cole & S. Cole. Cambridge, MA: Harvard University Press.

Lyons, J. 1972. Human language. In R. A. Hinde (ed.) *Non-verbal communication*. Cambridge: Cambridge University Press.

Malinowski, B. 1923. The problem of meaning in primitive languages. In C. K. Ogden & I. A. Richards (eds.) *The meaning of meaning*. New York: Harcourt, Brace & World.

Malinowski, B. 1935. *Coral gardens and their magic*, 2 vols. New York: American Book Company. (Republished 1961 by Dover Publications, New York.)

Merleau-Ponty, M. 1964. *Signs*. Trans. with an introduction by R. C. McCleary. Evanston: Northwestern University Press.

Moerman, M. 1977. The preference for self-correction in a Tai conversational corpus. *Language* 53: 872–82.

Ochs, E. 1982. Talking to children in Western Samoa. *Language in Society* 11: 77–104.

Ochs, E. 1984. Clarification and culture. In D. Schiffrin (ed.) *Georgetown University Round Table on Languages and Linguistics 1984*. Washington: Georgetown University Press.

Ochs, E. & Schieffelin, B. (eds.) 1979. *Developmental pragmatics*. New York: Cambridge University Press.

Ochs, E. & Schieffelin, B. 1984. Language acquisition and socialization: three developmental stories. In R. Schweder & R. Levine (eds.) *Culture theory*. Cambridge: Cambridge University Press.

Philips, S. U. 1976. Some sources of cultural variability in the regulation of talk. *Language in Society* 5: 81–95.

Philips, S. U. 1983. *The invisible culture: communication in classroom and community on the Warm Spring Indian Reservation*. New York: Longman.

Pratt, M. L. 1981. The ideology of speech-act theory. *Centrum* New Series 1: 5–18.

Reisman, K. 1974. Contrapuntal conversations in an Antiguan village. In R. Bauman & J. Sherzer (eds.) *Explorations in the ethnography of speaking*. Cambridge: Cambridge University Press.

Roberts, J. & Forman, M. 1972. Riddles: expressive models of interrogation. In Gumperz & Hymes 1972.

Rosaldo, S. 1982. The things we do with words: Ilongot speech acts and speech act theory in philosophy. *Language in Society* 11: 203–37.

Rossi-Landi, F. 1983. *The language of work and trade: a semiotic homology for linguistics and economics*. Trans. by M. Adams & others. South Hadley: Bergin & Garvey.

Sacks, H., Schegloff, E. & Jefferson, G. 1974. A simplest systematics for the organization of turn-taking for conversation. *Language* 50: 696–735.

Saussure, F. de 1916. *Cours de linguistique générale*. Lausanne: Payot.

Saville-Troike, M. 1982. *The ethnography of communication: an introduction*. Oxford: Blackwell.

Schegloff, E. 1982. Discourse as an interactional achievement: Some uses of 'uh huh' and other things that come between sentences. In D. Tannen (ed.) *Georgetown University Round-table on Languages and Linguistics 1981*. Washington: Georgetown University Press.

Schegloff, E. 1986a. Between macro and micro: contexts and other connections. In J. Alexander, B. Giesen, R. Munch & N. Smelser (eds.) *The micro–macro link*. Berkeley and Los Angeles: University of California Press.

Schegloff, E. 1986b. The routine as achievement. *Human Studies*. 9: 111–51.

Schegloff, E., Jefferson, G. & Sacks, H. 1977. The preference for self-correction in the organization of repair in conversation. *Language* 53: 361–82.
Schegloff, E. & Sacks, H. 1973. Opening up closings. *Semiotica* 8: 289–327.
Schenkein, J. 1978. *Studies in the organization of conversational interaction*. New York: Academic Press.
Schieffelin, B. & Ochs, E. (eds.) 1987. *Language socialization across cultures*. Cambridge: Cambridge University Press.
Schiffrin, D. (ed.) 1984. *Georgetown University Round Table on Languages and Linguistics 1984: Meaning, form, and use in context: linguistic application*. Washington: Georgetown University Press.
Scollon, R. & Scollon, S. K. 1981. *Narrative, literacy, and face in interethnic communication*. Norwood: Ablex.
Sherzer, J. 1977. The ethnography of speaking: a critical appraisal. In M. Saville-Troike (ed.) *Georgetown University Round Table on Languages and Linguistics 1977*. Washington: Georgetown University Press.
Sherzer, J. 1983. *Kuna ways of speaking*. Austin: Texas University Press.
Shore, B. 1982. *Sala'ilua: a Samoan mystery*. Columbia University Press.
Silverstein, M. 1977. Cultural prerequisites to grammatical analysis. In M. Saville-Troike (ed.) *Linguistics and anthropology*. Washington: Georgetown University Press.
Silverstein, M. 1979. Language structure and linguistic ideology. In P. R. Clyne, W. F. Hanks & C. L. Hofbauer (eds.) *The elements: a parasession on linguistic units and levels*. Chicago: Chicago Linguistic Society.
Streeck, J. 1980. Speech acts in interaction: a critique of Searle. *Discourse Processes* 3: 133–54.
Vygotsky, L. S. 1978. *Mind in society*. Cambridge, MA: Harvard University Press.
Watson-Gegeo, K. & White, G. (eds.) in preparation. *Disentangling: the discourse of conflict and therapy in the Pacific*.
Wittgenstein, L. 1958. *Philosophical investigations*, 3rd edn. trans. by G. E. M. Abscombe. New York: MacMillan.
Wolfson, N. 1983. Rules of speaking. In J. C. Richards & R. W. Schmidt (eds.) *Language and communication*. New York: Longman.

13 The organization of discourse*

Diane Blakemore

13.0. Introduction

The study of discourse belongs to the study of language in use, which means that it is concerned not just with the properties of linguistic representations but also with the nonlinguistic factors that determine what message is conveyed by the use of a linguistic form and whether it counts as an acceptable contribution to the communicative enterprise.[1] While the linguistic properties of an utterance may determine a range of possible interpretations, the actual message recovered by the hearer depends on its nonlinguistic properties. Consider, for example, the exchange in (1):

(1) A: You're not eating.
    B: It's too hot.

A grammar that pairs phonetic and semantic representations of sentences cannot determine the reference of *you* or *it*, what meaning of *hot* is intended, or what it is too hot for. Moreover, it is not evident from the linguistic properties of A's utterance whether he is informing the hearer that she is to refrain from eating, asking the hearer to confirm that she is not eating, or expressing his disapproval of the fact that the hearer is not eating. The hearer is expected to recover a specific message on the basis of nonlinguistic or contextual information.

Some writers, recognizing that the interpretation of an utterance is not fully determined by its linguistic properties as they are defined by a traditional sentence grammar, have argued that the grammar should be extended to include a pragmatic component that assigns interpretations to sentence–context pairs. This strategy means that we could speak, as, for example, Gazdar (1979) does, of a language 'having' a pragmatics in exactly the same

* I would like to thank Deirdre Wilson for her advice during the preparation of this chapter. She is not, of course, to be held responsible for any mistakes it contains.

[1] It should be noted at the outset that the approach to discourse adopted here contrasts, but is not necessarily inconsistent, with the social interaction approach adopted by conversational analysts. For an introduction to this approach see Levinson 1983.

way that it 'has' a syntax or a phonology. In this chapter I shall be less concerned with Gazdar's formal pragmatics than with the view adopted, for example, by van Dijk (1977), that the notion of a grammar should be extended so that it can account for the well-formedness of discourse or, in other words, so that it can predict whether a given utterance is an acceptable contribution to a text (written or spoken). Nevertheless it may, perhaps, be worth indicating why the objections that I have to this view are fundamentally objections to any approach which treats the principles which constrain the interpretation of utterances (as opposed to sentences) as a part of a grammar.

The claim that we 'know' a language has generated considerable controversy, especially where 'language' refers not to a set of sentences but to the internalized rules and representations used to generate those sentences.[2] This controversy aside, it is clear that the 'knowledge' which constitutes our grammatical competence is not the same kind of knowledge that hearers bring to bear on the interpretation of utterances. Unlike real-world or nonlinguistic knowledge, linguistic knowledge is not knowledge of or about anything, and hence cannot be said to be true or false. In other words, grammatical representations do not have what philosophers call semantic (or 'intensional') properties. To include a pragmatic component in the grammar would be to include a component with intensional properties along with a purely formal component. The modular approach to cognitive psychology (cf. Fodor 1983; Newmeyer 1983; Carston in Volume III of this series) depends for its coherence on individuating separate modules by virtue of their computational properties. If we regard grammatical knowledge as a 'module,' it is difficult to see why one bit of it should have a set of computational properties (e.g. intensional ones) lacking in the other bit.

Even if we did allow grammatical computations to take nonlinguistic knowledge as input, we would still have to address the question of how hearers decide which of all the knowledge accessible to them they should bring to bear on the interpretation of a given utterance. In principle, hearers could bring any of their beliefs to bear on utterance interpretation, which means that, in principle, they could recover any interpretation. A theory which aims to explain how hearers understand utterances in context must include an account of the principles by which the actual context for interpretation is selected from the range of logically possible contexts. As we shall see, the hearer's choice of context is constrained by principles which govern not

---

[2] Chomsky (1986) distinguishes between E Languages (external languages or sets of sentences) and I Languages (internalized grammars). It is clear that Gazdar's (1979) program proceeds from an interest in the former rather than the latter. However, Chomsky argues that it is impossible to study an E language without making some assumption about the I language underlying it. Given that the E language that Gazdar is interested in is natural language, this means that his purely formalist methodology is inappropriate. For further discussion of the nature of grammatical knowledge see Chomsky 1980.

just verbal communication but all types of communication, verbal and nonverbal. It is difficult to see why such general-purpose cognitive principles should be included in a theory whose domain is restricted to language use.

13.1. Coherence and cohesion in discourse

Much recent work on the interpretation of discourse has adopted the view that the way that hearers recover messages from utterances is governed by their assumption that in discourse, contiguous linguistic strings are meant to be interpreted as being connected, or, in other words, that discourse is coherent. These connections are not always made explicit: hearers are expected to fill them in on the basis of their background or contextual assumptions. Indeed, unless they can recognize that the segments of the discourse cohere in some way, they will not be able to recover any kind of message and the discourse will be ill-formed.

The idea that the elements of a well-formed discourse are bound together by principles of connectivity of textual unity is fundamental to the work of a number of authors – for example, van Dijk (1977), Halliday and Hasan (1976), and Hobbs (1978, 1979). However, not all these authors agree about the source of the unity. For example, Halliday and Hasan's book is a detailed exploration of the view that a text is created by cohesive relationships within and between sentences – that is, by the use of cohesive devices available in the language. Thus in (2a) the 'texture' is created by the use of the pronoun *her* and the ellipse in the second sentence; in (2b), apart from the anaphoric relationship between *he* and *his*, there is a cohesive relation expressed by *so*; and in (2c) the use of *then* points to a relation of temporal sequence:

(2) a. My neighbor asked me if I would like to go to her son's school play. I told her I couldn't.
   b. There was $4 in his wallet. So he hadn't spent all the money.
   c. I cooked myself an omelette and then spent the evening marking essays.

Halliday and Hasan are careful to point out that a text is a unit of language in use and as such does not consist of sentences. Nevertheless they claim that the meaning relations within a text are encoded in or realized by sentences: 'Cohesion is part of the system of language. The potential for cohesion lies in the systematic resources of reference, ellipsis and so on that are built into the language itself' (1976: 5). However, it is not clear that these meaning relations must be realized explicitly in order for a discourse to have coherence. Both the 'causal' relation expressed in (2b) and the temporal relation in (2c) could have been conveyed implicitly.[3] Moreover, the relation

[3] This point is also made by Brown and Yule (1983).

indicated by a cohesive device is not always a relation between linguistically realized meanings. If I arrive laden with parcels, you may appropriately produce the utterance in (3):

(3) So you've spent all your money.

It is not clear that a theory of discourse interpretation ought to distinguish this use of *so* from the one in (2b).[4]

Even when two sentences are related by a cohesive tie, hearers have to go beyond their linguistic resources in order to recover an interpretation. For example, Hobbs (1979) points out that in (4), *he* could in principle refer to either John or Bill:

(4) John can open Bill's safe. He knows the combination.

Brown and Yule (1983) suggest that Halliday and Hasan were not attempting to explain how texts are understood but were instead concerned with the linguistic resources available in English for marking relationships within a text. It is certainly true that a theory of linguistic meaning must take account of those expressions which contribute to the structure and organization of discourse. However, such an account must be grounded in a psychologically adequate theory of the principles by which discourse is organized and understood.

This might suggest that we need to turn to the semantic or conceptual relations that may be realized by cohesive ties, or, in other words, to connectivity of semantic content. Some writers (see van Dijk 1977 and Hobbs 1978, 1979) assume that coherence of content can be explicated in terms of coherence relations between propositions. However, Johnson-Laird (1981, 1983) argues that there are two levels of representation for discourse: 'a superficial propositional format close to linguistic form, and a mental model that is close to the structure of the events or states of affairs that are described in the discourse' (1983: 377). Coherence relations, he claims, hold between the latter rather than the former. I cannot do justice to Johnson-Laird's arguments for mental models here. However, even without the details of these arguments it seems clear that coherence relations are intended to play the same role in the construction of mental models as the one that, for example, Hobbs attributes to them in the recovery of propositional representations. According to Johnson-Laird, words in a sentence are 'cues to build a familiar mental model' (1981: 122). However, like propositions, mental models are only partially determined by the linguistic properties of

---

[4] Although Halliday and Hasan refer to the connection expressed by *so* as a causal connection, it seems more accurate to characterize it in inferential terms: see section 13.2 below. However, notice that *therefore*, which seems to express the same inferential connection as *so*, cannot be used without a linguistic antecedent.

utterances. Hearers must use nonlinguistic or contextual assumptions in order to construct their model of the state of affairs/event described. The question is, to what extent is the hearers' choice of context, and hence their actual interpretation, determined by their aim of establishing coherence relations?

According to Hobbs, the coherence of a text or discourse is defined in terms of a set of structural binary relations between the segments of a text, which depend on their propositional content. Speakers who wish their utterance to be understood must ensure that it stands in one of these relations to the preceding text, and the recognition of the particular relation it bears is essential for its successful comprehension. This approach seems to assume a menu of discourse connections, the speaker's task being to select a connection, and the hearer's task being to identify the speaker's choice. For example, one of the items on Hobbs's menu is the relation of 'Elaboration' which subsumes 'trivial' moves like pure repetitions, repairs, and tag questions as well as those cases in which the speaker conveys 'the same message from two different perspectives' (1978: 25). It is the recognition of this relation, claims Hobbs, that accounts for the fact that the hearer of (4) above interprets the pronoun *he* as referring to John rather than Bill.

Now, obviously, discourse is not an arbitrary sequence of utterances. Moreover, hearers are able to identify specific connections between utterances, connections which, as Halliday and Hasan have recognized, may be coded in the language. However, it is clear that a speaker may not use just any coherence relation in order to continue the discourse. Each of the utterances in (5) stands in a coherence relation to the preceding one, and yet the result is nonsense:

(5) John was late. The station clock had struck nine. It was time for Susan to start work. She took the first essay from the pile. It was by Mary Jones. Mary had not been well for weeks. The doctor told her to take a holiday. The problem was that she couldn't afford one. Living in London is now very expensive. All central government subsidies to the Greater London Council have been abolished. Paradoxically, this might be seen to follow from the premises of Libertarian Anarchism. The minor premise might be difficult for the reader to discern. Our theorem-proving program does this using a 'crossed-syllogism' technique.

Moreover, as Blass (1985) shows, a text that is appropriate in one context may be inappropriate in another. The second sentence of (6) can be understood as an elaboration of the first. While it is appropriate as part of an autobiography, it is inappropriate as part of a *curriculum vitae*:

(6) I was born in Lower Hutt, New Zealand. It used to be a dormitory suburb of Wellington, but is now a busy town with high-rise office blocks.   (adapted from Blass 1985)

This suggests that a theory of discourse organization cannot consist simply of a taxonomy of coherence relations. It must also include the principles which constrain the speaker's choice of utterance, or, in other words, an account of the appropriateness of utterances in discourse.

As I mentioned earlier, some writers have taken this to mean that the notion of a grammar must be extended to cover not just the well-formedness of sentences, but also the well-formedness of discourse. For example, van Dijk (1977) suggests that in order to account for the well-formedness of discourse we need to include in our grammar a 'pragmatic component' with rules relating sentence–context pairs to interpretations at a global level of semantic description or 'macro-structure' (1977: 6–7). According to this view, the problem with a sequence like (5) is that although each sentence is linked to the next by a coherence relation, there is no unifying topic, or, in other words, no level of representation at which the meaning of each sentence defines the meaning of the discourse as a whole.

The notion of topic of discourse (or topic of conversation) is often appealed to, but rarely defined. In his analysis of an example of written text, van Dijk proposes that its topic can be represented as a proposition that is nontrivially and jointly entailed by the ordered sequence of propositions expressed by the sequence of sentences in a text. However, this assumes that hearers are able to identify the proposition expressed by each sentence in the text. As we have seen, the propositional content of an utterance is only partially determined by its linguistic properties: the actual interpretation recovered by hearers depends on the nonlinguistic or contextual knowledge they bring to bear. Presumably, hearers' choice of context, and hence their interpretation, is constrained by the requirement that each proposition recovered must be relevant to the topic of the discourse. The problem is that the identification of the discourse topic itself depends on the hearer's ability to recognize the proposition underlying each sentence of the text.

Moreover, as van Dijk himself points out, the context is involved in the recognition of the entailment relations in terms of which the topic of discourse is defined. That is, the topic representation is entailed by the joint set of propositions expressed by the sentences in the text only given certain items of real-world knowledge. There is no space to give the details of his analysis here. However, the context dependence of the relations which contribute towards the macro-structure of the text may be illustrated by just one of the inferences that the reader is expected to make:

(7) [town(a) & prosperous(a)]$\longleftrightarrow$[have(a,c) & industry(c) &
   lucrative(c)]

In other words, once we know a town is prosperous, we may expect the
information that it has lucrative industry. Hence the well-formedness of the
sequence in (8):

(8) In the past it [the town of Fairview] had been a go-ahead, prosperous
   little town, and its two large factories, specializing in hand-tools, had
   been a lucrative source of wealth.   (1977: 132)

In accounting for such inferences van Dijk appeals to the notion of a
frame, that is, a representation of the knowledge people have of stereotypical
events and situations.[5] For example, the inference in (7) is part of the reader's
knowledge of a stereotypical economic phenomenon. It is generally accepted
that our knowledge of the world is organized into chunks. Moreover, it seems
reasonable to suppose that hearers access chunks of information rather than
individual propositions for the interpretation of utterances. However, given
the assumptions of van Dijk's discourse grammar, it is difficult to see how
frames could play any useful role in the organization and interpretation of
discourse.

   In the first place, not all the knowledge used in discourse interpretation is
stereotypical. The following utterance was produced at breakfast during a
linguistics conference:[6]

(9) If I'd known it was going to be fish, I would have put my contact
   lenses in.

This utterance could have been interpreted on the basis of stereotypical
information about fish – in particular, the information that fish have bones
that are difficult to see – together with stereotypical knowledge of contact
lenses – in particular, that their use provides normal vision for people who
would otherwise be without it. However, there is another interpretation, the
one which was in fact intended, which is based on stereotypical knowledge of
contact lenses – specifically, the knowledge that putting them in is time
consuming – together with non-stereotypical information about the speaker –

---

[5] This notion was originally developed in the field of artificial intelligence as an attempt to deal with the
organization of memory. Another related proposal in AI appeals to the notion of a 'script' which is
defined in terms of a network of conceptual dependencies (see, for example, Samet & Schank 1984).
while psychologists investigating the role of stereotypic knowledge in discourse interpretation have
developed the notions of scenarios and schemata. For a clear introduction to all these approaches see
Brown & Yule 1983. For a critical evaluation of the contribution of AI to discourse understanding see
Dresher & Hornstein 1976.
[6] I am grateful to Doug Arnold for this example.

that is, the information that he doesn't like fish. Obviously, the speaker of (9) would not have intended this interpretation if he did not have grounds for thinking that the hearer was able to access this information.

This example illustrates a further difficulty for this approach to discourse interpretation. As we have seen, a contact lens frame could include both the information that they enable people to see and the information that inserting them is time consuming. However, each of the two interpretations mentioned above involves only one of these items. Similarly, stereotypical knowledge of fish includes not only the information that they have bones, but also the information that they swim, that they have fins, etc., etc., but it is only the first proposition that would be considered relevant for the interpretation of (9). This leaves us with the question of how hearers select from their total knowledge chunk the particular information that they bring to bear in the interpretation process.

The need for some kind of constraint on context selection follows additionally from the fact that a text can in principle give the hearer access to a number of knowledge chunks not all of which are actually used. For example, it is not clear from van Dijk's account of the excerpt in (8) why the hearer is not expected to access a 'town frame,' or a 'hand-tools frame,' or a 'factory frame.' If there are rules for determining whether a particular utterance is an appropriate continuation of the discourse, then there must be rules for selecting the contextual information used in establishing the required relationships.

In a coherence based account of utterance interpretation the role of the context is restricted to establishing coherence relations. However, as Blass (1985) has pointed out, hearers do not always use contextual information in order to maintain coherence relations. She demonstrates this point by appealing to the distinction between the mention and use of language:

(10) A: What did Susan say?
     B: You've dropped your purse.

B's response can be construed either as a report of an assertion made by Susan or as an assertion by B that A has dropped her purse. According to the coherence approach, only the former (coherent) interpretation should be possible. However, it is not difficult to imagine circumstances in which the other non-coherent interpretation would be recovered.

In fact, discourse is full of utterances which do not exhibit coherence relations and which are nevertheless perfectly understandable given the appropriate contextual information. For example, in England, (11), written on a piece of paper attached to an empty milk bottle placed outside someone's front door, will be understood as a request for three pints of milk:

(11) Three bottles today.

In another context the same piece of paper could convey quite a different message. In other words, the fact that an utterance is neither preceded nor followed by another utterance does not mean that it cannot be understood in isolation from the context. Indeed, as we have seen in (3) above, it is possible that an apparently discourse-initial utterance may be understood only in terms of the specific relationship that it bears to information outside the text or discourse. As Blass says, it is not clear why the principles that constrain the selection and use of contextual information in the interpretation of an utterance that is part of a text should be different from the ones that govern its use in the interpretation of an isolated utterance.

Blass's arguments suggest that all discourse, whether it consists of a sequence of utterances or a single utterance, must be interpreted by the same principles, and that the notion of coherence is derivable from some more general theory of discourse interpretation. In the next section I shall outline the theory which, according to Blass, provides a more integrated account of the selection and use of contextual information in the interpretation of discourse.

13.2. Relevance in discourse

The view that there is a grammar of discourse, a set of rules for producing and interpreting utterances, is in direct conflict with the view of discourse advocated by H. P. Grice in his 1967 William James Lectures (see Grice 1975). His basic idea was that in communicating, speakers aim to meet certain general standards, and that hearers interpret utterances with these standards in mind. On this approach, utterance interpretation is not a matter of decoding messages, but rather involves taking the meaning of the sentence uttered together with contextual information, inference rules, and working out what the speaker meant on the basis of the assumption that the utterance conforms to very general principles of communication. The main advantage of this approach from Grice's point of view was that it provided a nonsemantic (or, in other words, pragmatic) explanation for a wide range of phenomena which had posed serious problems for traditional theories of meaning. However, although a number of theorists have seen the advantages of this approach for simplifying theories of linguistic semantics, until recently it has not been shown how it could be developed into a complete and psychologically adequate pragmatic theory.[7]

---

[7] For example of Gricean analyses of non-truth-conditional phenomena see Gazdar 1979, Kempson 1975, Levinson 1983, Wilson 1975. For an account of the shortcomings of Grice's proposals as a basis for a complete pragmatic theory see Wilson and Sperber 1981, Sperber and Wilson 1986.

Sperber & Wilson (1986) have shown that Grice's insight has much wider implications than most Gricean accounts suggest. The basic idea underlying their theory is that in processing information, people generally aim to bring about the greatest improvement to their overall representation of the world for the least cost in processing. That is, they try to balance costs and rewards. Obviously, not every addition of information counts as an improvement: a hearer's representation of the world will not necessarily be improved by the presentation of information which it already contains. Nor is it improved by the presentation of information that is unrelated to any of the information it contains. The hearer's aim is to integrate new information with old, or in other words, to recover information that is relevant. Notice, too, that hearers are not just interested in obtaining more information about the world. They are also aiming to obtain better evidence for their existing beliefs and assumptions. Indeed, an improvement of a hearer's representation of the world may result from the elimination of false assumptions.

In every case, the effect achieved is a result of processing new information in a context of existing assumptions. This suggests that the relationship between a newly presented item of information and the context can be viewed from two different perspectives: on the one hand, it can be seen in terms of the way in which the context is affected by the presentation of a new item of information, while on the other, it can be viewed in terms of the role that contextual assumptions play in assessing this effect. As we shall see, both types of relationship play a part in a relevance-based account of textual relationships.

In this theory, computing the effect of a proposition crucially involves deduction. That is, the role of contextual assumptions is to combine with the content of an utterance as premises in an argument. There is no space here to outline the model of the inferential abilities that Sperber and Wilson believe to be involved in utterance interpretation. However, it is worth emphasizing that in this account propositions are treated not just as logical objects but as psychological representations, and that deductive inferences are psychological computations performed over those representations. Basically, their claim is that assumptions about the world come with varying degrees of strength, and that logical computations assign strength to conclusions on the basis of the strength of the premises from which they are derived.

There are three ways in which an inference system plays a role in assessing the impact of a new item of information on an existing representation of the world. First, since an inference system can be used to test for inconsistencies in the propositions submitted to it, it can play a role in the hearer's decision to abandon an existing assumption. Second, the fact that conclusions inherit their values from the premises from which they are derived means that inference rules can be used to assess the extent to which an existing assumption is confirmed or justified by a new item of information. Finally, since the propositions which are taken as premises may be derived from the hearer's existing representation of the world, an inference system may play a role in the identification of what Sperber and Wilson call the contextual implications of a given proposition. That is, it enables hearers to add to their representation of the world by processing new information in a context of old information.

According to this view, interpreting an utterance is not just a matter of identifying the proposition that it expresses: it also involves working out the consequences of adding it to a set of existing assumptions. Indeed, there seems to be little point in hearers' being able to identify the proposition expressed by an utterance unless they can also see its consequence for what they believe already. By the same token, there is little point in speakers offering hearers information unless they have grounds for thinking that it will have some effect on their existing assumptions. For example, although it is probable that you can identify the proposition expressed by (12), it is unlikely that you will be able to see the point of my utterance given the contextual assumptions you have in mind at the moment:

(12) My brother lives in New Zealand.

It is not enough for you to recover an item of information that you didn't have before: you must be able to relate this information to assumptions you have already. That is, your aim is to establish that it is relevant.

While it is unlikely that you can relate the proposition in (12) to the contextual assumptions at the forefront of your attention, it is equally unlikely that you cannot access some context in which it has some impact. For example, on the basis of the assumption in (13a), you will be able to derive the contextual implication in (13b):

(13) a. New Zealand is in the southern hemisphere.
     b. The author's brother lives in the southern hemisphere.

The problem is that in principle, any of the hearer's accessible assumptions might be brought to bear in establishing the relevance of a proposition, which means that in principle, he or she could interpret any utterances as having relevance. However, hearers do not interpret utterances in just any context. Nor do speakers produce just any utterance. The fact that successful communication occurs, and hearers interpret utterances in the way that they are expected to, suggests that the hearer's choice of context is one that can be exploited and manipulated by the speaker.

According to Sperber and Wilson, what the speaker manipulates is the hearer's search for relevance. Intuitively, it is clear that the more contextual implications a proposition yields the greater its relevance. On the other hand, accessing contextual assumptions and using them to derive contextual implications involves a cost, and the cost of deriving contextual implications from a small, easily accessible context will be less than the cost of obtaining them from a larger, less accessible context. A hearer who is searching for relevance will process each new item of information in the context that yields a maximum contextual effect for the minimum cost in processing. Obviously, it is in the interests of a hearer who is searching for relevance that the speaker should produce an utterance whose interpretation calls for less processing effort than any other utterance he or she could have made. But equally, given that the speaker wishes to communicate with the hearer, it is in his interests to make the utterance as easily understood as possible. This means that the hearer is entitled to interpret every utterance on the assumption that the speaker has tried to give him or her adequate contextual effects in return for the minimum necessary processing. Sperber and Wilson call the principle that gives rise to this assumption the Principle of Relevance.[8]

It is important to recognize that in this theory, relevance is a property of propositions rather than of utterances. The point is that a proposition may be relevant whether or not it has been deliberately communicated. For example, it does not matter whether I discover the fact that I have just mis-spelt the word *relevance* or whether I am told that I have mis-spelt it. Either way the information is relevant to me. This is not to say that we cannot talk of the relevance of an utterance. However, this is a derivative notion: an utterance is relevant only in the sense that it conveys relevant information.[9]

It is equally important to recognize that a context in this theory is not characterized as the co-text of discourse, but as a set of assumptions stored in memory. That is, whereas coherence is defined as a relation between linguistic units (that is, utterances, segments of a text), relevance is a relation between propositions. This is not to say that the contextual assumptions used in interpreting an utterance may not have been made available by the preceding discourse. Indeed, as we shall see, this is what characterizes a coherent text. However, they may also be made accessible through the observation of a non-communicative event. For example, the utterance in (14) would have a rather different import in the event of an electricity cut than it would in the situation in which the hearer is preparing to decorate the Christmas tree:

---

[8] See the Kempson chapter ('Grammar and conversational principles') in Volume II of this series for further discussion of the principle of relevance.

[9] Notice that the relevance of an utterance does not always lie in its content, but sometimes lies in the fact of its being made. For example, although in the following dialogue the proposition expressed by the pupil's reply is unlikely to be relevant to the teacher, the fact that the pupil was able to answer the question is likely to be highly relevant:

> Teacher: What is the capital of France?
> Pupil: Paris.

(14) There's a packet of candles in the kitchen.

If the speaker has grounds for thinking that the hearer has observed that the lights have gone off, then that speaker will have grounds for thinking that the hearer has access to contextual premises which, combined with assumptions made accessible by the utterance, yield some contextual effect.

Of course, the observation that the lights have gone off could give the hearer access to all sorts of further assumptions which might, in principle, be brought to bear on the interpretation of (14). For example, it might give access to the assumption that the deep freeze will have stopped working. Similarly, the proposition expressed by (14) could give the hearer access to a whole range of contextual assumptions about candles or, indeed, the kitchen. For example, it could give access to the assumption that candles are made of wax. The fact that neither of these assumptions is likely to play a role in the interpretation of (14) can be explained in terms of the Principle of Relevance. The hearer is entitled to interpret the utterance in the smallest and most accessible context that yields a contextual effect. If the hearer can establish a connection between the proposition expressed by (14) and the proposition that the lights have gone off without accessing these assumptions, then there is no point in adding them to the context for the interpretation of the utterance.

This example shows that the appropriateness of an utterance in discourse depends on the possibility of establishing not a connection between it and a preceding utterance, but a connection between the proposition it expresses and the most recently processed proposition. However, as Blass has shown (in example 10 above), the most relevant interpretation for an utterance is not always the one that is established in the context of the most recently processed proposition. Unplanned discourse is full of interruptions and sudden changes of direction. To take another example from Blass, suppose you have met a friend in the street and she asks you if you have time for coffee. If as she speaks you see someone who is apparently about to snatch her bag, then, clearly, it is more relevant, and hence more appropriate, to warn her about this than it is to answer her question.

On the other hand, Blass points out, within a planned discourse there is continuity of context. That is, information made accessible by the interpretation of the first utterance is used in establishing the relevance of the second; the interpretation of that utterance makes information available for the interpretation of the third, and so on. In this way discourse provides the hearer with a continually changing background against which new propositions are processed. If the preceding discourse does not make contextual assumptions accessible for a new utterance, then the hearer will not be able to see any connection, and the discourse will seem incoherent.

Notice that seeing the connection between one utterance and the next is not always a matter of seeing that the interpretation of the first gives access to assumptions that can be combined with the proposition expressed by the second for the deduction of contextual implications. Consider, for example, the sequence in (15):

(15) The electricity isn't on. We will have to light candles.

In this case, the interpretation of the first utterance is expected to give the hearer access to contextual premises which allow him or her to derive the proposition expressed by the second as a consequence. In other words, the hearer is expected to establish that the second utterance is relevant as a specification of the relevance of the first. Clearly, it is possible that the hearer has already worked out this consequence. However, since there is a whole range of consequences that the hearer might have derived, the speaker may be justified in drawing attention to this particular one. This is not to say that the second utterance doesn't have contextual effects of its own. Indeed, there is little point in drawing the hearer's attention to a particular contextual implication of a remark unless there are grounds for thinking that this information is relevant.

Hearers may also find it relevant to have their attention drawn to a premise that licenses the deduction of a given proposition. For example, the fact that John can open Bill's safe could be a consequence of a whole range of facts – for example, the fact that he is a professional thief, the fact that Bill has given him permission, etc., etc. Given that it is possible that the production of the first utterance in Hobbs's example in (4) could raise in the hearer's mind the question of which of these possibilities is in fact the case, the speaker may be justified in telling him. That is, the second utterance of this example may be relevant by virtue of providing an explanation for the state of affairs described in the first.

It will be recalled that in Sperber and Wilson's framework inference rules are not just used for deriving new information that is added to the hearer's existing representation of the world. The fact that a conclusion inherits its strength from the strength of the premises from which it is derived means that they also provide a means for establishing the extent to which new information provides further evidence for an existing assumption. Thus if the hearer has immediate access to a context in which a newly presented proposition licenses the deduction of the proposition expressed by the preceding utterance, then he or she might have grounds for thinking that it was offered as evidence or proof. In other words, the second utterance in (4) could also be relevant by virtue of providing evidence for the assertion made in the first.

A deduction may also result in a contradiction. A hearer who is presented with a proposition which licenses the deduction of a proposition that is inconsistent with an assumption that he or she already holds will either have to reject the new information or abandon the existing assumption. This means that an utterance may be relevant by virtue of being a denial of a preceding utterance. Thus for example, given the appropriate contextual assumptions, B's utterance in (16) can be construed as a denial of the assertion made by A:

(16) A: Susan's not at work today.
     B: I just saw her in her office.

In all of these cases the relevance of one utterance lies in the way its content interacts with the contextual assumptions made available by the preceding one, and its coherence is a by-product of the way it is relevant. Given the role that deduction plays in the assessment of contextual effects, it is not surprising that these relationships can be characterized in inferential terms. However, it seems that coherence does not always arise in this way. Consider, for example, the conjoined sequences in (17) and (18):

(17) He ran over to the cliff and jumped.
(18) Bill insulted Mary and she left.

It is well known that the temporal and causal connotations of utterances like these cannot be due to the meaning of *and*, since they are conveyed even when it is replaced by a period. However, this should not be taken to mean that these connotations cannot be analyzed as part of the proposition expressed. Indeed, the fact that they fall under the scope of logical operators suggests that they must.[10] Hearers are rarely able to identify the proposition expressed by an utterance on the basis of its linguistic properties alone. For example, while the meaning of a pronoun like *she* determines a range of possible referents, the actual referent is chosen on the basis of the context. Similarly, hearers are able to identify the proposition expressed by fragmentary utterances like 'Telephone' or 'Not now' only in context. As we have seen, the context for the interpretation of an utterance may be made immediately accessible through the interpretation of the preceding discourse. This means that the Principle of Relevance entitles a hearer to use the information made available through the interpretation of one segment of text in the identification of the proposition expressed by the next. Thus the interpretation of the first conjunct of (18) provides the hearer with the context for the interpretation of the pronoun in the second.

According to this view, coreference relations in discourse are a conse-

[10] For examples that demonstrate this point see Cohen 1971 and Carston forthcoming. These examples were used by Cohen to argue against Grice's (1975) pragmatic account of the temporal and causal connotations of conjoined utterances. However, Carston shows that they should instead be construed as evidence for a pragmatic account at the level of propositional content. See Kempson's chapter in Volume II of this series for further discussion.

quence of the hearer's aim of recovering the proposition that satisfies the Principle of Relevance.[11] Recently, Carston (1985) has proposed that the Principle of Relevance plays a similar role in the interpretation of temporal and causal relations. An utterance describing an event is normally understood as expressing a proposition which contains a value for a time index. Hearers will interpret an utterance as conveying a temporal relation between its conjuncts if their search for the maximally relevant proposition leads them to base the value of the index in the second of the value of the index in the first. Obviously, the fact that an event occurred does not entail that it had a cause. Nevertheless the most relevant proposition expressed by (18) may be the one represented in (19):

(19) [Bill insulted Mary$_i$]$_j$ and as a result of that$_j$ she$_i$ left.

Equally, the fact that someone jumped does not entail that they jumped over the cliff. Yet this is what would be understood by the utterance in (17).

The suggestion, then, is that there are two types of coherence in discourse. On the one hand, there is the coherence that arises from the role that one utterance plays in determining the relevance of another, while on the other, there is the coherence that arises from the role that one utterance plays in determining the content of another. However, in both cases the connection is established only by establishing a relationship between the propositions that are expressed, a task which, as we have seen, may require the hearer to supply contextual assumptions that have not been made explicit. Moreover, in both cases the fact that the connection is established is a consequence of the hearer's search for relevance.

However, as the example in (5) was designed to show, the fact that a discourse exhibits coherence relations does not necessarily mean that it is well-formed. Nor is it true that every utterance in a well-formed discourse is connected to a preceding utterance: discourse-initial utterances are the most obvious examples. The point is that hearers cannot be expected to establish a coherence relation unless it is relevant for them to do so. Now whereas in unplanned discourse the speakers' goal is simply to make each utterance relevant, in a planned discourse it seems that their aim is to maximize relevance over the discourse as a whole. If an utterance produced in an

---

[11] I do not wish to suggest that the grammar plays no role at all in the interpretation of anaphoric expressions. The point is that in many cases the grammar does not fully determine the interpretation of referential expressions even when their antecedents are made available in the preceding discourse. For example, a generative grammar could not account for the correct (i.e. normal) interpretation of *it* in (i) or its two occurrences in (ii):

    (i) The butterfly wing fell on the table and it broke.
    (ii) A: Have you heard Periah's recording of the Moonlight Sonata?
        B: Yes, it made me realize I'd never be able to play it.

For further discussion of this point see Kempson's chapter in Volume II of this series.

unplanned discourse is interpreted as being connected to the preceding one, it is because the hearer finds it the most relevant way of interpreting that utterance. In contrast, if an utterance in a planned discourse is interpreted as being connected to the preceding one it is because the hearer has grounds for thinking that the contextual effects thus achieved are the ones that would have been intended by a speaker who was aiming to maximize relevance over the discourse as a whole. The problem in (5) is that the speaker makes available information whose contribution to the discourse as a whole is never made clear by the interpretation of subsequent utterances. Thus for example, while the ninth utterance in (5) (repeated in 21) might be interpreted as an explanation for the proposition expressed by the eighth (repeated in 20), it is not clear even by the end of the text what the relevance of this explanation is meant to be:

(20) The problem was that she couldn't afford one.
(21) Living in London is very expensive.

13.3. Grammar and discourse

A sentence grammar is a code for pairing phonetic and semantic representations. It cannot deal with the nonlinguistic properties of utterances which hearers must take into account if they are to discover what speakers are trying to convey or how it relates to what has been conveyed already. This has been taken to suggest that in order to account for the interpretation of utterances in discourse, we need to extend the grammar to include a pragmatic component with rules which relate sentence–context pairs to interpretations in such a way that the connections that characterize a well-formed discourse can be maintained. In the previous section it was argued that this approach to the interpretation of discourse is mistaken, and that all discourse, whether it consists of a sequence of connected remarks or an isolated utterance, is governed by a general constraint that applies to all forms of communication. However, in rejecting the idea that the notion of a grammar be extended to the analysis of discourse I am not necessarily rejecting the idea that there are links between linguistic form and the interpretation of utterances. Indeed, given the relevance-based framework just described, it is possible to provide a principled account of the relationship between linguistic form and pragmatic interpretation.

It will be recalled that Grice's main aim in his theory of conversation (Grice 1975) was to show how the fact that speakers can convey more than the truth-conditional content of their utterances can be explained in terms of a set of general communicative principles, and hence falls outside the domain of linguistic theory. However, Grice also recognized that the non-truth-condi-

245

tional (or implicit) content of utterances could be determined by particular lexical items or linguistic constructions. For example, he claimed that the use of *therefore* in (22) indicates that his being brave is a consequence of his being an Englishman, but that the utterance would not be false should the consequence in question fail to hold:

(22) He is an Englishman; he is, therefore, brave.

Grice's notion of 'conventional implicature' has been applied to a number of other expressions which resist analysis within a truth-conditional semantics.[12] However, without a coherent theory of verbal communication this term is simply a synonym for 'non-truth-conditional.' In this section I shall briefly outline how a relevance-based theory suggests an approach which not only sheds light on a wide range of phenomena recognized to be on the borderline between semantics and pragmatics, but also has interesting implications for the role of grammar in the organization of discourse.

The term 'consequence' can refer either to a causal effect or to a logical conclusion. However, it seems clear that what Grice meant in his analysis of (22) was not that *therefore* indicates that his being brave was caused by his being an Englishman, but that it indicates that the fact he is an Englishman is a reason for believing that he is brave. In other words, *therefore* signals an inferential connection between the two propositions in (22) in much the same way as *after all* signals an inferential connection between the two propositions in (23):

(23) He is brave; he is, after all, an Englishman.

In this case, of course, it is the first proposition which is understood to be the consequence. That is, whereas *therefore* introduces a proposition which is understood to be proven or justified by the preceding one, *after all* introduces a proposition which is understood as proof of the preceding one.

Given the role of deduction in the assessment of contextual effects, it should not be surprising that an expression whose use is associated with evidence or proof should be analyzed as an inferential connective. However, it will be recalled that deduction does not always serve as a means for assessing new information as evidence for an existing assumption. We might also expect to find an inferential connective which is used to indicate that the proposition it introduces is a contextual implication of the one expressed in the preceding utterance. This is the role of *so* in (24):

(24) The electricity isn't on. So we'll have to light candles.

Equally, we might expect to find an expression which expresses the same

---

[12] See e.g. Karttunen & Peters 1979.

inferential connection as *after all*, but which is used to signal that the proposition it introduces is relevant as an explanation. This is the role played by *you see* in (25):

(25) John can open Bill's safe. You see, he knows the combination.

It will be recognized that the differences between these expressions mirror some of the differences between the ways in which an utterance may make available information for use in assessing the relevance of the next. That is, their function is to constrain the relevance of the proposition they introduce by indicating that it stands in a particular relation to the one most recently processed. In this respect they must be distinguished from the cohesive devices in (26) and (27) which indicate how the information made available through the interpretation of the first utterance must be used in determining the content of the second:[13]

(26) We had lunch at the Lamb. Afterwards, Mary read while we played tennis.
(27) Mary hurt her ankle. As a result she couldn't play tennis.

I do not wish to suggest here that these are the only inferential connectives in English. For example, it seems that the connections expressed by *moreover* in (28) and *but* in (29) can be analyzed in inferential terms:

(28) John is a socialist. Moreover, he's a member of the Communist Party.
(29) John is a member of the Communist Party, but he's not supporting the strike.

The relevance of the proposition introduced by *moreover* will be understood to lie in the fact that it is additional evidence for whatever conclusion is expected to be drawn from the first, while the proposition introduced by *but* is relevant as a denial of a proposition which is expected to have been derived from the first.[14]

Nor do I wish to suggest that inferential connectives are the only type of linguistic constraints on relevance. Notice that in each of the cases in (22)–(25) the prescribed connection can be established only against a background of contextual assumptions. Thus for example, the second proposition of (22) is deducible from the first only given the assumption in (30):

(30) All Englishman are brave.

This suggests that the effect of using one of these expressions in an utterance is to constrain the hearer's choice of context for its interpretation. However,

---

[13] This distinction seems to correspond closely to Halliday and Hasan's distinction between external and internal cohesive relations (1976: 240–1).
[14] For a more detailed treatment of these expressions see Blakemore forthcoming.

languages also have devices which constrain the hearer's choice of context for the interpretation of the utterances that contain them in a more direct fashion. In particular, they have devices which constrain the hearer's choice of context by highlighting or focussing particular constituents. Consider, for example, the difference between (31) and (32):

(31) a. It was Bill who insulted Mary.
    b. BILL insulted Mary.
(32) a. It was Mary whom Bill insulted.
    b. Bill insulted MARY.
    (Capitalization indicates focal stress).

Intuitively, it is clear that whereas the relevance of (31) lies in the identity of the person who insulted Mary, in (32) it lies in the identity of the person Bill insulted. Since they both have the same propositional content (they are true under the same conditions), this difference must be due to the fact that they are processed for relevance in different contexts. As is well known, focal structure plays an important cohesive role. For instance, B's response in (33) is anomalous because its focal structure is inappropriate in the context of A's utterance:

(33) A: Whom did Bill insult?
    B: BILL insulted Mary.

Questions surrounding focus are discussed by Sperber & Wilson (1986; cf. Wilson & Sperber 1979), and research on these issues is currently in progress within their relevance-based framework (Blakemore 1985b, 1987).

It should be clear that although all research into linguistic constraints on relevance falls within the domain of linguistic theory, it must be grounded in a theory of the role of context in utterance interpretation. On the other hand, it may not be clear how this research is compatible with the approach to discourse interpretation outlined in the last section. In particular, it may not be clear how the existence of such linguistic constraints can be reconciled with the view that all discourse is governed by a single general pragmatic principle. The point here is that the Principle of Relevance entitles the bearer to interpret every utterance in the smallest and most accessible context which yields an adequately relevant interpretation. This means that if speakers wish to constrain the interpretation that hearers recover, then they must constrain their choice of context by making the necessary assumptions immediately accessible to them thus ensuring their selection under the principle of relevance. That is, they must direct hearers to a particular set of assumptions.

In some cases it seems that speakers constrain hearers' interpretation of their utterances by increasing their processing costs. For example, the indirect answer given by B in (34) entails more processing than the direct one would have. Yet B may exploit the hearer's assumption that the reply conforms to the Principle of Relevance in order to convey the information in (35):

(34) A: Is Susan rich? B: All lawyers are rich.
(35) Susan is rich.

This is a nonlinguistic means of constraining relevance. In order to preserve the assumption that B was conforming to the Principle of Relevance, the hearer must supply the contextual assumption in (36):

(36) Susan is a lawyer.

The fact that the B has forced the hearer to access this assumption in order to derive (35) as a contextual implication may be explained if the processing effort these steps require is offset by the recovery of contextual implications that would not have been derivable from the direct answer. In other words, the extra information he gives must have some relevance of its own.

By contrast, since the linguistic devices we have been considering in this section do not contribute to the content of the utterances that contain them, their use could not be said to add any extra information. Instead their use minimizes the hearer's processing costs by guaranteeing that the information conveyed by the utterance that contains them is relevant in a specific context. Thus, for example, the use of *therefore* in Grice's example in (22) indicates that the hearer is expected to process the utterance in a context in which the first proposition can be construed as evidence for the second. In other words, these expressions provide the speaker with an effective means of constraining the interpretation of utterances in discourse in accordance with the Principle of Relevance.

REFERENCES

Blakemore, D. L. 1985. Non-inferential constraints on relevance: an analysis of also. Paper presented at the International Pragmatics Conference, Viareggio.
Blakemore, D. L. 1987. *Semantic constraints on relevance.* Oxford: Blackwell.
Blakemore, D. L. forthcoming. So as a constraint on relevance. In Kempson forthcoming.
Blass, R. 1985. Cohesion, coherence and relevance. University College London. ms.
Brown, G. & Yule, G. 1983. *Discourse analysis.* Cambridge: Cambridge University Press.
Carston, R. 1985. Saying and implicating. In Kempson forthcoming.
Chomsky, N. 1980. *Rules and representations.* Oxford: Blackwell.
Chomsky, N. 1986. *Knowledge of language: its nature, origins and use.* New York: Praeger.
Cohen, J. 1971. Some remarks on Grice's views about the logical connectives of natural language. In Y. Bar-Hillel (ed.) *Pragmatics of natural languages.* Dordrecht: Reidel.
Dijk, T. van. *Text and context.* London: Longman.
Dresher, B. E. & Hornstein, N. H. 1976. On some supposed contributions of artificial intelligence to the scientific study of language. *Cognition* 4: 321–98.
Fodor, J. A. 1983. *The modularity of mind.* Cambridge, MA: MIT Press.

Gazdar, G. 1979. *Pragmatics: implicature, presupposition and logical form.* New York: Academic Press.

Grice, H. P. 1975. Logic and conversation. In P. Cole & J. Morgan (eds.) *Syntax and semantics 3: speech acts.* New York: Academic Press.

Halliday, M. A. K. & Hasan, R. 1976. *Cohesion in English.* London: Longman.

Hobbs, J. R. 1978. Why is discourse coherent? Technical note, SRI Projects 5844, 7500 & 7910.

Hobbs, J. R. 1979. Coherence and co-reference. *Cognitive Science* 3: 67–90.

Johnson-Laird, P. N. 1980. Mental models in cognitive science. *Cognitive Science* 4: 71–115.

Johnson-Laird, P. N. 1983. *Mental models.* Cambridge: Cambridge University Press.

Karttunen, L. & Peters, S. 1975. Conventional implicature in Montague grammar. Paper presented at the First Annual Meeting of the Berkeley Linguistics Society.

Kempson, R. 1975. *Presuppositions and the delimitation of semantics.* Cambridge: Cambridge University Press.

Kempson, R. (ed.) forthcoming. *Mental representations: the interface between language and reality.* Cambridge: Cambridge University Press.

Levinson, S. C. 1983. *Pragmatics.* Cambridge: Cambridge University Press.

Newmeyer, F. J. 1983. *Grammatical theory: its limits and possibilities.* Chicago: University of Chicago Press.

Samet, J. & Schank, R. 1984. Coherence and connectivity. *Linguistics and philosophy* 7. 1: 57–82.

Sperber, D. & Wilson, D. 1986. *Relevance: communication and cognition.* Oxford: Blackwell.

Wilson, D. 1975. *Presupposition and non-truth-conditional semantics.* London: Academic Press.

Wilson, D. & Sperber, D. 1979. Ordered entailments: an alternative to presuppositional theories. In C. K. Oh & D. A. Dineen (eds.) *Syntax and semantics 11: presupposition.* New York: Academic Press.

Wilson, D. & Sperber, D. 1981. On Grice's theory of conversation. In P. Werth (ed.) *Conversation and discourse.* London: Croom Helm.

14 Conversation analysis
Deborah Schiffrin

14.0. Introduction

Some of the very same qualities that make conversation an important topic for linguistic attention also make conversation a difficult topic for linguistic analysis. First, in having a conversation – something which we all do virtually every day – we draw upon our communicative competence (Hymes 1972): our tacit knowledge of the abstract rules of a language, which is required both to produce sound/meaning correspondences within grammatical sentences and to use those correspondences between sound, meaning, and form in socially and culturally appropriate ways. Such competence includes 'the knowledge of linguistic and related communicative conventions that speakers must have to create and sustain conversational cooperation' (Gumperz 1982a: 209). Despite the ubiquity of our communicative competence, however, neither the nature of that knowledge, nor the ways in which it can be put to use for social and expressive purposes, is readily accessible to our own introspection. Rather, such knowledge has to be inferred through the analysis of structures and patterns in that which it is able to produce, i.e. in conversation. The fact that inferences about what is *causing* a particular phenomenon have to be made through observation of its *outcome* is one reason why conversation is a difficult topic for linguistic analysis. (This dilemma is faced not just by those who analyze conversation, but by those who analyze language in general; this makes it no less a source of difficulty for conversation analysts.)

The pervasiveness of conversation in our everyday lives suggests a second reason why it is both important and difficult to study: conversation is a more basic, unmarked mode of communication than other communicative genres. For example, conversation has been said to be the genre in which 'the most straightforward principles of pragmatics' can be discovered such that 'other types of discourse can be usefully described in terms of their deviation from such a base' (Fillmore 1981: 165). And from a diachronic perspective, Lyons (1977: 638) states, 'there is much in the structure of

251

languages that can only be explained on the assumption that they have developed for communication in face-to-face interaction.' For example, the communicative processes underlying conversation have been shown to guide the emergence and development of syntactic structures in language over both historical time (e.g. Sankoff & Brown 1976; Givón 1979; Sankoff 1984) and developmental time (Bates & MacWhinney 1979, 1982; Ochs & Schieffelin 1979). Thus it is the fact that conversation is a basic form of communication – and from here, the fact that it impinges upon both diachronic processes and synchronic structures – that makes conversation both important and difficult to study.

Third, conversation displays more than speaker/hearers' communicative competence: conversation also displays many of the tacit procedures and common sense understandings out of which social order is constituted (Garfinkel 1967; Schutz 1970). This social reflexiveness not only complicates efforts to specify the communicative competence underlying conversation, but also implies that conversational structures and regularities need not be the product of *linguistic* structures and regularities alone. Rather, they may instead be (or also be) the product of more general social processes and norms of interaction through which people's interpersonal goals, selves, and relationships are negotiated, and out of which a sense of social order is created. The difficulty for conversation analysts, then, is to integrate the contribution which language makes to conversation with the contribution of non-linguistic social processes. More generally, conversation analysis forces one to test the limits of linguistic analysis, and therefore to examine the interface between linguistic methods, concepts, models, and paradigms, and those from other fields.

Despite its importance (and perhaps because of the difficulties sketched above), conversation analysis is a fairly recent development in linguistics and many of its guiding assumptions originate in other fields (sociology, anthropology, philosophy). In this paper, I define conversation analysis (describing both the focus of inquiry and methods of analysis, 14.1); review some of the linguistic problems which have faced conversation analysts and some of the ways that scholars have addressed these problems, 14.2; and compare how different conversation-analytic approaches have focussed on two specific phenomenon (turn-taking, dialogic pairs, 14.3). It is my hope that these topics will reveal the assumptions, concepts, methods, and findings of conversation analysis. My conclusion suggests some general directions for further research, 14.4.

14.1. Defining conversation analysis

Although conversation analysis may be seen as a subfield of discourse analysis (Levinson 1983: 286–94), it is important to differentiate the two areas for two reasons: first, there *are* some issues specific to conversation analysis, and second, even problems that seem initially parallel turn out to receive different solutions.

Let us begin by defining discourse as any unit of language beyond the sentence, and conversation as any discourse which is produced by more than one person. Discourse, then, includes both dialogic and monologic forms in either spoken or written modes; conversation includes just spoken dialogue.

There are three important caveats to this definition. First, although 'spoken' and 'written' are convenient ways of labeling different features and patterns that tend to cluster together in the two modalities, they are potentially misleading generalizations: some spoken dialogues (e.g. formal debates) may be more 'written' in style, and some written monologues (e.g. letters to home) may be more 'spoken' in style (Tannen 1982). Second, the definition of conversation as spoken dialogue does not capture the way that ordinary speakers and hearers might define conversation (see Goffman 1981: 14 for suggestions along these lines). Third, defining conversation as spoken dialogue should not imply that forms of talk that seem monologic – simply because they are produced at length by one speaker – are not also phenomena with conversational importance. Many features of everyday stories, for example, are designed precisely because such stories are told to audiences (Polanyi 1985), and many features of rhetorical argument can be understood only if we define arguments as talk which is basically dialogic in intent (Schiffrin 1985a). Similarly, even a verbalization that occupies *less* than a full turn at talk (and thus might not be seen as a contribution to conversation) can have a conversational function. As Schegloff (1982) argues, for example, a back-channel *uhhuh* from a potential next speaker allows a current speaker to continue talking; thus, since a continuation may be contingent on the placement of another's verbalization, we would not want it defined merely as monologue. In short, even if it is not openly designed for a recipient, whatever occurs in the presence of another is potentially communicative (Goffman 1967: 3), and potentially functional in the achievement of coordinated talk.

In addition to the written/spoken, monologue/dialogue difference, another difference between discourse and conversation analysis concerns data. Although many discourse analysts *do* focus on actual (rather than imagined) texts, the focus on actual spoken dialogue is critically important to all conversation analysts. The reasons for such a focus vary in detail, but conversation analysts in general agree that the use of actual talk is both *methodologically* and *theoretically* motivated.

From a *methodological* standpoint, it is only through analysis of actual interactions between speakers that one can find *internal evidence* for the function of a particular conversational device. For example, one can argue that the word *well* or *okay* from a current speaker allows the introduction of an unfinished topic into conversation prior to its closing (Schegloff & Sacks 1973). But it is only through repeated observations of such a pattern in conversation that one gains evidence that speakers and hearers also treat the expression in the way proposed by an outside analyst's perspective. Or, if one is arguing that speakers from one social group utilize a particular intonation to indicate that their remarks should be taken in a joking way – and that members of other social groups do not share knowledge of the contextualizing function of that intonation – then actual misunderstandings of the meaning of that intonation would provide internal evidence of such an analysis (e.g. Gumperz 1982b).

Gathering such evidence is not only methodologically strategic for conversation analysts, but also *theoretically* important: it is speakers and hearers whose conversational procedures are the focus of inquiry and the analyst's perspective should aim to replicate the language user's perspective. In fact, one group of conversation analysts (ethnomethodologists, see 14.3) argue that conversationalists are *themselves* analysts – or else they would not be able to make sense out of talk. Thus, outside analysts have no choice but to use precisely that data to which conversationalists have access (and *only* that data) if they wish to discover the procedures which conversationalists use to make sense of talk. In short, what one is trying to account for are speaker/hearers' own procedures for constructing talk, and there is simply no way to do this without having access to their actual construction of talk.

The focus on actual spoken dialogue raises inevitable questions of transcription. As can be attested by the generations of linguists who have proposed systems of phonetic and phonemic transcription, all transcription systems are necessarily selective, and no system for transforming spoken speech into written form is without broader ramifications. For conversation analysts, devising transcription systems requires decisions about phenomena such as false starts, intonation, pacing, laughter, and nonverbal gestures, which may or may not turn out to be analytically important (Ochs 1979). The problem, of course, is that it is later analysis which reveals what is important, but that such analysis cannot proceed without as narrow a transcription as possible.

Thus far, I have suggested that conversation analysts agree on two issues: the use of actual spoken dialogue as data, and the importance of transcription. Analysts disagree, however, on the details of a transcription system (compare the systems in Atkinson & Heritage 1984 and Tannen 1984). There is still less agreement on what constitutes an adequate corpus for analysis. We can isolate two general approaches. A *sequentially account-able* approach focusses on a few sequences of talk and aims to account for the way in which each utterance fits into its text (e.g. Labov & Fanshel 1977; Schiffrin 1984b). A *distributionally accountable* approach focusses on multiple sequences and aims to account for why a particular feature occurs in texts in general (e.g. Schiffrin 1980; Heritage 1984).

Different motivations underlie analysts' choice of these strategies of corpus selection. For example, some who take the former approach wish to be able to explain the particularities of every utterance: why this? why here? (e.g. Labov & Fanshel 1977: 24). Others who also adopt a sequentially accountable approach are quite differently motivated. Gumperz (1982a, b), for example, views conversation as a multichanneled accomplishment, such that particular features from one channel cannot be assumed to operate independently of features from another channel, and thus cannot be analyzed as isolated occurrences across many different conversations. As Gumperz (1982b: 30) states, 'we cannot extricate one element and seek its isolated role in accounting for observed differences in behavior.' In other words, it may be misleading to analyze the function of a single feature in many different sequences. Rather:

> The analyst's task is to make an in depth study of selected instances of verbal interaction, observe whether or not actors understand each other, elicit participants' interpretations of what goes on, and then (a) deduce the social assumptions that speakers must have made in order to act as they do, and (b) determine empirically how linguistic signs communicate in the interpretation process. (Gumperz 1982a: 35–6)

Yet, a similar reluctance to assign too much functional weight to a single, recurring linguistic form has led other analysts away from an approach which relies too heavily upon either sequential or distributional accountability. Ethnomethodologists, for example, argue against focussing on particular linguistic items wherever they occur, 'for in so doing there is always a danger of presuming in advance that some particular word or nonlexical response will invariably have the same interactional implications wherever and whenever it occurs' (Atkinson & Heritage 1984: 298). But instead of focussing detailed attention on a limited number of sequences, ethnomethodologists usually search for the ways in which a particular task (e.g. turn transition, Sacks, Schegloff & Jefferson 1974; disagreement, Pomerantz 1984) is accomplished across a wide range of sequences. Thus, although they do not seek generalizations about the function of a particular form, they do seek generalizations about how a particular function is fulfilled by a diversity of forms. And it is this goal which leads them away from reliance on either a detailed analysis of a limited number of sequences, or a distributional analysis of a particular form across many sequences.[1]

In sum, we have seen that conversation analysis focusses on spoken dialogues which actually occur. We have also seen that decisions about transcription and corpus selection are important issues both methodologically and theoretically, but that they are not uniformly resolved.

14.2. Linguistic issues in conversation analysis

I noted above that although some linguistic problems addressed by conversation analysts are also addressed by discourse analysts, they receive different solutions because of the focus of conversation analysts on spoken dialogue. I begin with such an issue: the search for textual structures (14.2.1). Still other issues arise simply because of conversation analysts' focus on spoken dialogue. I consider two such issues: the creation of joint meanings and situated actions (14.2.2), and whether conversation is a linguistic unit (14.2.3).

14.2.1. Structures

Harris (1952) defined the goal of discourse analysis as the systematic differentiation of a random list of sentences from a text. Many discourse analysts now equate those principles defining 'text' with an explanation of those qualities creating 'coherence' (e.g. Stubbs 1983: 15), and this shift in focus has greatly expanded the analytic importance of semantics and pragmatics in the definition of text (14.2.2). However, such a focus was not intended in Harris's initial procedure. Rather, Harris attempted to extend the methods of structural linguistics into discourse analysis: the structure of a text was expected to result from recurrent patterns of morphemes independent of either their meaning or their relationship with non-textual factors.

Although the search for structure *per se* does continue in conversation analysis, the types of structures identified have not been those envisioned by Harris. First, the constituents in conversational structures may be pragmatic or interactional units (e.g. actions, turns at talk) rather than strictly linguistic units of morphemes or sentences. As we will see, even conversational pairs which *might* be defined linguistically are viewed in terms of their consequences for the unfolding interaction between speaker and hearer; for example, even though a question/answer pair may be defined as a semantic sequence in which an incomplete proposition presented by one speaker is completed by another, such a definition is not relevant to the concerns of many conversation analysts (14.3.2).

---

[1] Schiffrin (1987a) describes these approaches as having different, but complementary, goals. An effort to combine both approaches in the analysis of discourse markers is Schiffrin 1987b.

Second, although analysts may agree that conversation has a structure, they disagree on which unit is considered the 'minimal' constituent of such structures: units as varied as the sentence, the utterance, the tone unit, the message unit, the turn at talk, and the move have been suggested (Schiffrin 1987b: Chapter 2). This lack of unanimity not only reveals a fundamental disagreement as to what conversation is composed of (complicating discussion of higher level structures as well), but it also reflects different analytical perspectives and methods, ranging from those in which verbal displays are seen as reflections of speakers' intentions and strategies to those whose sole focus on verbal displays precludes any attempt to discover underlying interactional intentions and strategies (see discussion in 14.2.2, 14.3).

Third, the external boundaries between constituents of conversation are considerably more fluid than those between smaller, more familiar linguistic constituents. For example, although stories are units of talk which may be studied as discrete entities with linguistic structure (Labov 1972a; G. Prince 1973; Rumelhart 1975; Calfee 1982; Fillmore 1982), many conversation analysts have observed that opening and closing a story during conversation – both tasks which are clearly critical to the emergence of the story as a structure – depends on coordination between story teller and audience (Sacks 1971; Jefferson 1978; Polanyi 1985; Schiffrin 1984b). Because such coordination often has to be negotiated, e.g. when hearers do not realize that a speaker wishes to begin a story, the boundary between the story and some prior conversational unit is not as rigid as is the boundary between the two lower level linguistic constituents. (But see Goodwin 1981 and Schegloff 1979 for proposals that sentences are also interactionally constructed, and thus not rigidly bound.)

Fourth, the fact that conversation is created by the interaction between two different people greatly expands its structural possibilities. One reason for this expansion is that when two people interact, each person's contribution creates an additional environment – an additional context – in which his or her utterances can make sense (Gazdar 1979: 4–5). One consequence of this continual expansion of contexts is that it is almost impossible to identify a structure which is categorically prohibited. This does not mean, however, that some structures are not less marked than others. For example, the greeting sequences in (1) are listed in a decreasing order of frequency and distribution. (1a)–(1c) are all telephone greetings which would follow a prior exchange in which the ringing telephone is a summons from the caller, and 'hello' from the called is an answer (Schegloff 1972).

(1)   Caller: [Telephone rings]
         Called: Hello.
    a. A. Caller: Hi.
       B. Called: Hi.

    b. A. Caller: How are you?
        B. Called: Hi.
    c. A. Caller: Hi.
        B. Called: Thank you.

(1a) is easily understood as a well-formed greeting structure, and it may occur in a wide range of telephone openings (although the particular pairing of *hi* and *hi* without self-identification suggests a context in which caller and called are acquainted and can identify each other). (1b) can also be understood as well-formed, but because B is not a response to the syntactic question posed by A, such an understanding requires us to view the relationship between A and B slightly differently: rather than B being a response to A, both *how are you* and *hi* respond to the situation of increased contact between A and B. Thus, understanding why (1b) is a well-formed structure requires that we view A and B not as question and answer, but as interchangeable elements in an access ritual (Goffman 1963, 1981: 47). Understanding (1c) as well-formed requires still more specification of context and attention to the underlying relationships between A and B. Since (1c) actually occurred, let me detail the circumstance: after receiving a message that someone had called me, I returned the phone call within five minutes. In (1c), the called's *thank you* marks appreciation that I returned the phone call so quickly. Thus, B is a response not to my *hi*, but to the phone call in general, and more precisely, to its timing (closing following the initial call).[2] The point here is not just that seemingly deviant conversational sequences such as (1b) and (1c) can be contextualized into well-formedness – that two adjacent utterances can be given a context in which their linear order is predicted and well-formed – but that different degrees of context specificity may need to be included in an explanation of why some sequences are well-formed structures. This is important because it is the process of specifying our contextual descriptions which allows us to see a greater range of conversational sequences as well-formed. And it is precisely this task of context specification that conversation forces us to do – simply because each person's contribution goes one step further in defining a context in which a next contribution can be understood.

    Finally, there are several different levels at which conversation analysts have identified structure, ranging from the ways in which entire encounters are framed and bracketed from each other both at their initiation (Schegloff 1972; Goffman 1974; Schiffrin 1974, 1977; Godard 1977; Corsaro 1979; Collett 1983; Hall & Spencer-Hall 1983) and termination (Schegloff & Sacks 1973), to the ways in which single turns at talk are sequenced (Sacks,

---

[2] Another way of describing the transition from (1a) to (1c) is that (1a) requires no more than application of a rule of 'local interpretation,' i.e. use of a minimal context in the search for interpretation, whereas (1c) requires considerably more than such a rule (Brown & Yule 1983: 58–63).

Schegloff & Jefferson 1974; see also 14.3.1). Included between these extremes is a focus on topic structures (Kennan & Schieffelin 1976; Brown & Yule 1983: Chapter 3; Button & Casey 1984; Jefferson 1984), and dialogic pairs (such as question/answer pairs; see discussion in 14.3.2). Because units such as encounters, topics, dialogic pairs, and turns are so different from each other in substance, however, it is not at all clear that they form the sort of hierarchical structures to which linguists are accustomed at other levels of analysis.

In sum, conversation analysts may join other linguists and discourse analysts in their search for structure, but the structures that they have found are not like those usually discussed at lower levels of linguistic analysis. Thus, Stubbs (1983) suggests that conversational discourse exhibits a structure in which functionally differentiated units are syntagmatically chained into predictable linear sequences, but that this structure is not a linguistic structure *per se*. I return to this issue in 14.2.3.

14.2.2. Joint meaning and situated action

Another issue facing conversation analysts is to identify, describe, and explain the processes through which conversationalists create joint meanings and perform situated actions. Note that the way I have defined this issue narrows it from a more general interest in textual meanings and cohesion of discourse (Halliday & Hasan 1976), because it focusses solely on those meanings which are established and become shared through the work of both speaker and hearer, i.e. meanings which are intended by a speaker and recognized as so intended by a hearer (Grice 1957). My definition also separates the analysis of action from the analysis of unsituated, sentence-level speech acts focussed upon by many philosophers and linguists (Austin 1962; Searle 1969; Cole & Morgan 1975; Bach & Harnish 1982). Thus, I will focus in this section only on scholarship which considers how meanings and actions are jointly constructed and situated in conversation.

Many scholars have observed that an analysis of what a speaker says does not provide an exhaustive account of what a speaker intends to communicate or what a speaker does. Three different strands of research have offered ways of supplementing semantic meaning to arrive at an understanding of how hearers interpret speakers' intended meaning. Although these approaches differ in detail, each proposes a way of contextualizing what is actually said in order to arrive at a fuller interpretation of what is being communicated.

In pragmatic approaches to conversation influenced by Grice (1975), the semantics of a proposition supplies its truth-conditional meaning, and added information about speaker's communicative intention is inferable through both parties' use of a set of jointly held maxims concerning the quality, quantity, relevance, and manner of information presentation. Thus, a speaker who says (2a) may be taken to intend to communicate (2b):

(2) a. Sue finished her PhD.
      She got a job teaching linguistics.
   b. Sue finished her PhD.
      Then she got a job teaching linguistics.

Such an understanding would be conveyed (in Grice's terms 'implicated') because speakers and hearers jointly assume the operation of a submaxim of manner 'be orderly,' which includes an assumption that (unless stated otherwise) events will be reported in the order in which they occurred (Kempson 1975: 198–9). This approach provides a powerful and wide-ranging mechanism to account for how speakers convey considerably more than the stable semantic core of their words: in fact, understanding what a speaker intends to communicate actually *requires* a hearer to modify (e.g. add to, override) the semantic content of a message with the help of very general assumptions about cooperation.[3]

Whereas the pragmatic approach allows one to avoid the effort to map what is said directly to what is meant (an effort argued by Levinson, 1981, to be futile), other scholars propose multiple mapping relationships linking utterances into sequences, and linking what is said to what is meant and done. Labov (1972b; Labov & Fanshel 1977: 25), for example, suggests that conversational sequencing rules presuppose a prior set of rules mapping speakers' underlying meanings and actions to their utterances. Furthermore, it is not the surface utterances (not the output of the mappings) but the underlying meanings and actions (the input to the mappings) which are the basis of coherent sequencing between adjacent utterances in conversation. Another way of saying this is that coherent connections between utterances hold only if one understands the underlying meanings and actions realized through those utterances.

Still other scholars propose that the process of conveying meaning requires speaker and hearer to share underlying interpretive schemata whose relevance for the interpretation of a particular message is signaled through the use of specific verbal and nonverbal devices. Gumperz (1982a) suggests that communicative meaning is achieved through a process of situated interpretation in which hearers infer speakers' underlying strategies and intentions by interpreting the linguistic cues which contextualize their messages. Crucial to Gumperz's framework is the idea that such contextualization cues do not merely signal, but *create* interpretive contexts through which a

---

[3] There is a vast literature in pragmatics which applies Grice's insights. Levinson 1983: Chapter 3 is a helpful summary; see also Leech 1983 for a revision of some of Grice's basic ideas.

speaker's underlying communicative intention can be inferred. Thus, communicative meaning depends upon shared access to (culturally defined) repertoires of verbal and nonverbal devices which guide a hearer to the interpretive schema within which a message is to be understood.

Despite the differences among these three approaches, each is an attempt to derive communicative meaning – meaning which is intended by a speaker and received by a hearer – by supplementing semantic meaning with contextualizing factors. What differ are the contextualizing factors: for Grice, they are cooperative maxims; for Labov, underlying actions; for Gumperz, interpretive schemata.

Once we turn our attention to actions, however, we will see that few conversation analysts maintain that the interpretation of an utterance as the performance of a particular action is achieved through contextualizing factors which *supplement* semantic meaning. Rather, analysts suggest quite the opposite: the performance and understanding of utterances as actions depends on their context.[4]

Labov & Fanshel (1977) offer one version of this view of speech as situated action. Their analysis of the discourse of a single patient during a therapeutic interview uncovers layers of speech actions, revealed only through their knowledge of the complex web of social relationships and beliefs of the patient. An approach which depends less upon the contribution to understanding made by the specific identities of particular speakers, and more upon the contribution of the immediate conversational context, is the ethnomethodological approach. Schegloff (1984), for example, suggests that utterances are understood as actions primarily because of where they are placed in a sequence of other utterances. Furthermore, the functional ambiguities discussed by many philosophers and linguists (e.g. whether *can you pass the salt?* is a question about ability and/or a request for the salt) never arise in actual conversation, for participants encounter utterances in 'detailed single scenarios embedded in fine-grained context' (1984: 51). In short, different levels of contextual information – background knowledge about the speaker, what has just occurred during an exchange of talk – play a more critical role in allowing the recognition of an utterance as an action than the set of static, mutually known preconditions typically focussed upon by speech-act theorists.

Consider, finally, that the issue discussed in this section – the nature of conversational meaning and action – is related to the issue posed in the previous section – the attempt to differentiate discourse from a random sequence of sentences. What this section suggests is that it may not be structure *per se* which is the essence of a conversation, but the achievement of

---

[4] The boundary between meaning and action in traditional speech-act theory is not always as clear as I may have implied here.

communicative meaning and concerted action. If so, then we have greatly expanded the role of semantics and pragmatics in conversation analysis, at the same time that we have reduced the role of the sort of formalistic analysis envisioned by Harris for discourse analysis in general. In addition, we may have begun to resolve a question posed earlier about the basic constituents of conversation analysis, and to suggest that although discourse may contrast with a random sequence of sentences, conversation is orderly not because of order among its sentences, but because of the ways in which speakers and hearers coordinate their joint productions of meanings and actions. This view, however, takes us further away from a purely linguistic approach to conversation, and this is the issue I address in the next section.

14.2.3. Conversation as a linguistic unit

Much of my discussion thus far has suggested that conversation is not a discourse which can be considered solely as a linguistic unit. Two further characteristics of conversation also complicate efforts to understand conversation in purely linguistic terms: conversation is inherently contextual (14.2.3.1); conversation is constructed through social interaction (14.2.3.2).

14.2.3.1. Contexts

We have already seen that each utterance in a conversation creates an ever-expanding context for a next utterance, and that this greatly complicates efforts to differentiate well-formed discourse structures from random sequences. But there are still other reasons to consider conversation as inherently contextual, and these reasons are potentially more troublesome for attempts to characterize conversation in purely linguistic terms.

Let us start by briefly reopening the search for well-formed conversational sequences. We will see that social and cultural knowledge can be pivotal in differentiating appropriate from inappropriate sequences, and that it is thus misleading to consider conversational sequences in isolation from these *contexts of understanding*.

Compare (3a) and (3b); each is a potential service encounter between a shopkeeper and a customer (Merrit 1976):

(3) a. Customer: You have coffee to go?
      Server: Cream and sugar?
      Customer: Yes please.
      Server: That'll be 50 cents.
      Customer: (pays 50 cents)

(3) b. Customer: You have 1986 Corvettes?
       Server: Convertibles?
       Customer: Yes please.
       Server: That'll be 30 thousand dollars.
       Customer: (pays 30 thousand dollars)

Why is (3a) appropriate, but not (3b)? Consider, first, that several underlying actions and understandings are implicit in (3a):

(3) a'. Customer: You have coffee to
                  go?   1A. [Request for information]
        Server: Yes.   1B. [Information]
        Customer: I would like some.   2A. [Request for action]
        Server: Okay.   2B. [Acknowledgement]
                   Cream and sugar?   2B' [Request for information
                                                 about compliance with 2A]
        Customer: Yes please.   2B" [Information]
        Server: (gives coffee)   2C. [Compliance with 2A]
                   That'll be 50 cents.   3A. [Request for action]
        Customer: (pays 50 cents)   3C. [Compliance with 3A]

What is implicit in (3a) is the following: the request for information [1A] is a pre-request (Heringer 1977) such that the provision of information [1B] allows the request in [2A] to be issued; the request [2A] and its acknowledgement [2B]; the nonverbal actions of giving coffee [2C] and paying 50 cents [3C]. These implicit contingencies and actions allow us to understand why (3a) is well-formed: its structure is dependent on the underlying meanings and actions expanded above. But what is also critical is that we have the social and cultural knowledge allowing us to understand that (3a) can be expanded to (3a'), and that (3b) is not subject to an analogous expansion. More specifically, we understand that a yes/no question about coffee, but not about 1986 Corvettes, is a pre-request, and that a positive answer to the question about coffee, but not 1986 Corvettes, licenses a request. The point, then, is not just that an expansion of underlying meanings and actions can explain the well-formedness of (3a), but that the expansion itself is allowed by our social and cultural knowledge. In short, our social and cultural knowledge provides an interpretive context which allows us to discover reasons for the underlying well-formedness of conversation – and this is one reason for considering conversation to be inherently contextual.

Consider, next, that many conversation analysts question the importance of the boundary between verbal and nonverbal moves in conversation. One reason is that verbal and nonverbal moves may work together to comprise an encounter. Our expansion of (3a), for example, contained two nonverbal

263

moves which did not have to be accompanied by talk: the server gave the coffee, and the customer paid 50 cents. Another reason is that a move in one modality can be functionally equivalent to a move in another: in (3a), the server's acknowledgement could just as easily be performed nonverbally (by pouring the coffee) as by saying *okay*.

There are also very general reasons to question the verbal/nonverbal boundary. Not only are the schemata in which communicative meaning is interpretable (14.2.2) created by both verbal and nonverbal modalities, but there are many nonverbal devices which are as instrumental in creating a sense of overall interactional coherence as verbal devices, e.g. rhythmic synchrony (Erickson & Schultz 1981; Scollon 1981). Thus, as Goffman (1981: 71) observes:

> Words are the great device for fetching speaker and hearer into the same focus of attention and into the same interpretation schema that applies to what is thus attended. But that words are the best means to this end does not mean that words are the only one or that the resulting social organization is intrinsically verbal in character. Indeed, it is when a set of individuals have joined together to maintain a state of talk that nonlinguistic events can most easily function as moves in a conversation.

Considerations such as these suggest that the linguistic form and content of conversation does not occur in a matrix of more general communicative behavior which is *independent* of what is said. Nor does such a matrix provide an *external context* for talk: although (as we saw before) talk creates its own context, it now seems that such a context is comprised of more than just talk, and that what remains cannot easily be disentangled from what is said. Observations such as these imply that context is always part of an analysis of conversation – simply because it is always part of conversation – rather than something to be appealed to only if other attempts at understanding fail.

Still another way that conversation is inherently contextual is that conversational patterns can become a resource by which participants understand and become familiar with the many different facets of the social world in which talk occurs. Not only are conversational patterns (e.g. action sequences, turn-taking patterns, question/answer formats) associated with particular institutional arrangements, but such patterns help to constitute – or at the very least reinforce – those arrangements (West 1984). Similarly, particular conversational styles (e.g. in pacing, selection of topics, use of narratives) can become indicative of different social types, such that individuals may respond to a constellation of linguistic features as they would to a person from a particular region or social group, or to a person who is assumed to have a certain kind of personality (Tannen 1981, 1984). In short, conversational patterns can have very broad symbolic meanings for participants: they can become an index to the larger social worlds (the social contexts of self, other, and situation) in which talk occurs. This is still another reason to consider conversation as inherently contextual, and another reason why an approach which focusses on conversation as only a linguistic phenomenon may not be the most revealing.

4.2.3.2. Social interaction

Because conversation is produced by more than one individual, understanding its construction requires an examination of how efforts from different individuals are coordinated. Clark (1985: 3) suggests that

> the most basic type of coordination . . . is between what the speaker means and what his addresses understand him to mean. All other types of coordination – as in turn taking, choice of conversational topics, and course of narration – are really in service of the more basic coordination between meaning and understanding.

Clark goes on to suggest, however, that coordination is also required at semantic and syntactic levels of language use. Studies of the information structure of sentences, for example, suggest that speakers begin with the information assumed to be most salient (familiar, given, thematic) for their listeners and progress toward information assumed to be less salient (Mathesius 1924; Firbas 1964; Halliday 1967; Chafe 1977; Prince 1981), thus coordinating their productive syntactic efforts with their listeners' need for interpretation of information. And as Slobin (1975) suggests, the various pressures to which language is subject serve the speaker and/or hearer's need for communication. For example, the tremendous amount of redundancy in language is designed to ease the comprehension process and thus to aid the recipient's end of the process of coordinating communicative meaning (also Leech 1983: 64–70).

Despite the fact that a general coordinative effort is required for all language use, the dependency of conversation on coordination has been explained not only in linguistic terms, but in terms of the nature of conversation as *social interaction*. Sociologists such as Mead (1962) and Cooley (1902) proposed that the self is constructed through social interaction; one learns to see oneself through the eyes of the other's actions, which are in turn, in response to one's own actions. The construction of the self provides a powerful motivation for the coordinative work of conversation, for, as Goffman states:

> The individual must rely on others to complete the picture of him of which he himself is allowed to paint only certain parts. Each

individual is responsible for the demeanor image of himself and the deference image of others, so that for a complete man to be expressed, individuals must hold hands in a chain of ceremony, each giving deferentially with proper demeanor to the one on the right what will be received deferentially from the one on the left. (1967: 84)

In short, whatever it is that one attempts to mean through one's individual efforts at expression cannot alone create a self; those expressive meanings have to be understood and acted upon by the one to whom they are directed.

Although not all explanations for conversational coordination are dependent on sociological views of the self, several others do suggest that pressures towards coordination are exerted by individuals' efforts to balance their social with their individual needs (Lakoff 1973; Brown & Levinson 1978; Tannen 1984). And from a somewhat different perspective, Grice's (1975) cooperative principle assumes the underlying importance of a particular social belief – shared rationality – for the meaning and understanding achieved in conversation.

My discussion thus far has proposed that conversation is orderly because of the ways in which speakers and hearers coordinate their joint productions of meanings and actions in continually emergent contexts of social interaction. This is a view of conversation which moves us away from a purely linguistic approach to either theories about, or methods for studying, conversation. Although I have presented this as a view generally shared by all conversation analysts, I have also tried to point out subtle differences in the specific details of such a view. In the next section, I focus more on the differences among conversation analysts, by describing how several phenomena have been analyzed in different perspectives.

14.3. Different approaches to conversation analysis

The analysis of conversation draws its theories, models, concepts, and methods from a variety of fields; in fact, the scholars discussed above have included sociologists (e.g. Goffman), linguists (e.g. Labov), anthropologists (e.g. Gumperz), and philosophers (e.g. Grice). Rather than explicitly compare the contribution of specific fields to conversation analysis (see van Dijk 1985 for comparison among sociological, linguistic, and anthropological perspectives) I will focus here on two phenomena which have been treated from different perspectives: turn-taking (14.3.1) and dialogic pairs (14.3.2). Because ethnomethodologists have drawn analysts' attention to each of these phenomena, however, I will first provide some background on this particular sociological perspective toward conversation (cf. Levinson 1983: Chapter 6; Zimmerman & West 1983).

One of the basic assumptions of ethnomethodology is that 'properties of social life which seem objective, factual, and transformational, are actually managed accomplishments or achievements of local processes' (Zimmerman 1978: 11). Such properties include institutional arrangements (Maynard 1982, 1983), status and role (Cicourel 1972) and knowledge structures (Coulter 1979), as well as conversation. A key part of the ethnomethodological approach to conversation, then, is a focus on the local organization of talk as it is accomplished by interactants, i.e. the minute step by step details by which talk is constructed, rather than the underlying interpretive schemata, speaker intentions, or social norms which provide more general interactional strategies. Such constructional details are seen as methodical solutions to the underlying technical problems posed by talk, e.g. how is turn transition accomplished? how is relevance noted? how are topics changed? It is solutions to these problems which create interactants' sense of stability and regularity, and thus, it is the description of these solutions which is the task of the ethnomethodologist. Note, however, that it is only those procedural details which participants themselves display, and to which they themselves orient, which are seen as relevant to their construction of talk. It is for this reason, as I noted earlier (section 14.2) that the outside analyst limits him/herself only to that data to which interactants themselves have access. Thus, it is only if interactants themselves are seen to orient to contextual categories as diverse as cultural, gender, or social class identity, institutional setting, or another's interactional goal, that such categories warrant inclusion in an ethnomethodological account of the construction of talk. I turn now to two of the organizational problems of talk for which ethnomethodologists have proposed local solutions.

14.3.1. Turn-taking

One of the basic problems in conversation is the coordination of turn-taking: how do individuals alternate turns at talking? Two specific facets of this problem are defined by Sacks, Schegloff and Jefferson (1974): first, how turns are exchanged with minimal gap (one person usually starts talking soon after another has stopped) and minimal overlap (turn exchange usually provides for one person speaking at a time); second, how conversational turn exchange is locally achieved, i.e. on a turn by turn basis. (Compare debates and press conferences in which turn exchange is prearranged.) Sacks, Schegloff and Jefferson (1974) propose that conversationalists address these problems through a set of rules whose ordered options operate on a turn by turn basis. The rules apply at various transition-relevance places in a current speaker's turn (places which are defined both intonationally and syntactically as possible completion points), and they provide, first, for current speaker's selection of next speaker, second, for next speaker's self-selection, and third, for possible continuation of current speaker. The rules reapply, in the same order, at each transition-relevance place.

There are two potentially important features of turn transition for which the rule based account does not provide. First is the informational content of what is said in current and/or next turn. Schiffrin (1986) finds, for example, that incoming turns are differently placed relative to prior turns depending upon the semantic content of their initiating word: turns initiated with *but* are more likely to occur at non-transition relevance places than turns initiated with either *so* or *and*. If turn transition is sensitive in still other ways to the informational content of what is said, then the turn-exchange rules may need to be calibrated to the content of both current and next turn. Also ignored by the ethnomethodological framework is the fact that overlaps occur with different frequencies for, and are differently evaluated by, members of different social groups. Tannen (1983, 1984), for example, demonstrates that members of some ethnic groups interpret overlaps as evidence of cooperative involvement and enthusiasm (see also Schiffrin 1984a). Such an observation is important, for it changes the definition of the conversational problem which the turn-taking system is designed to resolve: if a system with overlap is desirable, then the turn-exchange rules (which are designed to avoid overlap) may not succeed in providing for the current solution at each juncture.

In sum, the ethnomethodological analysis of turn-taking proposes that an ordered set of rules operates locally and recursively at each turn transition place to resolve recurrent problems of turn transition. Other analyses suggest that the content and social meaning of turn transitions are important in achieving orderly transition, and thus, that these factors should figure in accounts of the production and interpretation of turns at talk.

14.3.2. Dialogic pairs

Another local organization focussed upon by ethnomethodologists is the adjacency pair: a sequentially constrained pair of turns at talk in which the occurrence of a first-pair-part creates a slot for the occurrence of a second-pair-part (a conditional relevance), such that the nonoccurrence of the second part is heard as an official absence (Schegloff & Sacks 1973). Examples are question/answer pairs and compliment/response pairs. Evidence for the constraining influence of the first part comes from observations about the interactional consequences of an absent second part: first parts are repeated, delayed second parts are accompanied with explanations for the delay (Schegloff 1972). Note, again, the ethnomethodological focus on interactants' own displays of relevancies: adjacency pairs are seen as sequentially implicative because this is how they are treated in talk. Similarly, it is proposed that the prime location for the display of a relationship between utterances is in the next turn at talk, especially (it would seem) one whose relevance to a prior turn has already been proposed:

> There is one generic place where you need not include information as to which utterance you're intending to relate an utterance to . . . and that is if you are in Next Position to an utterance. Which is to say that for adjacently placed utterances, where a next intends to relate to a first, no other means than positioning are necessary in order to locate which utterance you're intending to deal with. (Sacks 1971)

Finally, adjacency pairs exhibit dialogic structure (14.2.1) not only because they strongly constrain linear sequencing, but because they provide a basis for formal modifications (e.g. insertion sequences, Schegloff 1972), and because they have an internal relationship that binds them together apart from whatever other connections are present in their containing conversation.

A general critique of the ethnomethodological emphasis on adjacency pairs is Goffman 1981. Goffman (1981: 31–4) notes that the tendency to focus on the adjacency pair *out of context* from the rest of conversation parallels the context-independent approach taken by syntacticians toward isolated sentences. Such a focus can lead one to overemphasize the role of the adjacency pair as the conversational mechanism by which relevance between initiating references and follow-up responses is displayed:

> our basic model for talk perhaps ought not to be dialogic couplets and their chaining, but rather a sequence of response moves with each in the series carving out its own reference. . . . In the right setting, a person next in line to speak can elect to deny the dialogic frame, accept it, or carve out such a format when none is apparent. This formulation would finally allow us to give proper credit to the flexibility of talk – a property distinguishing talk, for example, from the interaction of moves occurring in formal games – and to see why so much interrupting, nonanswering, restarting, and overlapping occurs in it. (Goffman 1981: 52)

Thus, the conversational relevance said to be provided by the adjacency pair format may actually be part of a more general set of linkages between *reference and response* which is not dialogic in format. Schiffrin's (1985b) analysis of the use of *well* supports the idea that participants orient to reference/response linkages other than those provided by adjacency pairs: although *well* is used in dialogic pairs (when answers do not fulfill the options for propositional completion opened by prior questions), it is also used in non-compliances with requests, requests, embedded reference/response pairs, and self-responses. Thus, if conversationalists' own use of a particular word is oriented to a range of reference/response pairs, then perhaps the dialogic format captured by adjacency pairs is not the best basis for a model of talk.

Another reason to downplay the role of dialogic pairs in a model of conversation is that adjacency pairs may themselves be motivated by a very general set of system and ritual conditions (Goffman 1981: 14–21) which have to be fulfilled for conversation to occur:

> Given a speaker's need to know whether his message has been received, and if so, whether or not it has been passably understood, and given a recipient's need to show that he has received the message and correctly – given these very fundamental requirements of talk as a communication system – we have the essential rationale for the very existence of adjacency pairs. (Goffman 1981: 12)

In short, the general sequential implicativeness of adjacency pairs may actually be motivated by the deeper functional requirements of talk as a communicative system. Similarly, the constraint that a question imposes on the next conversational slot may be motivated by general semantic and pragmatic properties which questions *share* with other initial conversational moves. For example, questions are incomplete propositions which are presented to another person for completion through an answer. Thus, question/answer pairs may be seen as a paradigm example of the interactional effort toward the achievement of textual cohesion and joint meanings (14.2.2). Questions are also frequently used to perform requests for information or action with which the addressee is expected to comply. Individuals may orient their next conversational move toward a question, then, because of a more general constraint to show understanding of a felicitous speech act (although not necessarily compliance with the request). But because there are different syntactic formats through which such requests are performed, this would mean that question/answer pairs are no more privileged a dialogic pair than other syntactic forms which enact the same acts (including declarative sentences in which indirect requests are issued), and that the reason for their sequential implicativeness is participants' understanding of the felicity conditions underlying their acts.[5]

In sum, the dialogic format highlighted by a focus on adjacency pairs may overemphasize the role of two-part sequences of adjacent utterances in talk. Not only do the sources for conversational linkages go beyond the immediate chains created by adjacency pairs, but the motivation for these chains may be

[5] Viewing question/answer pairs as request/compliance pairs suggests the need for some kind of mapping procedure between syntactic form and pragmatic function. See discussion in 14.2.2.

more general functional pressures on conversation as a communication system, and the more general semantic and pragmatic properties of the first and second parts of adjacency pairs.

In this section, I have suggested that two aspects of conversation – turn-taking and adjacency pairs – focussed upon by ethnomethodologists as the product of a local management system may actually be more generally motivated by semantic meanings, pragmatic understandings, culturally relative interactional strategies, and functional constraints on conversation as a communication system. Through these suggestions, I hope to have highlighted some of the different perspectives used to analyze the same conversational phenomenon, and more generally, to show how seemingly subtle differences actually have fairly wide consequences for our overall view of how conversation is achieved.

14.4. Conclusion

Despite differences in assumptions, perspectives, and methodologies, there seems to be a general consensus that conversation is orderly because of the ways in which speakers and hearers coordinate their joint productions of meanings and actions in continually emergent contexts of social interaction. One problem with this view, however, is that it is difficult to disagree with or test – simply because it is so generally formulated. Thus, one very general need in conversation analysis is the formulation of specific and empirically testable propositions about conversation. For example, many conversation analysts assume that particular ways of saying something, e.g. certain expressions, ways of ending or beginning a turn, are used in conversation because of the functions that they serve. Yet, functionalist perspectives in general require specification of an overall *system* within which functions are defined (Halliday 1973). The specification of such systems might not only help conversation analysts formulate testable hypotheses about the functions of particular items, but might also allow a precise description of how *different systems* are integrated in conversation and why particular items and constructions therefore seem to have *multiple functions* in talk (Schegloff 1980; Schiffrin 1985c, 1987b).

Directions for further research also rest on the resolution of some nagging methodological issues. For example, there is no guarantee that the recurring regularities which one finds in a corpus of spoken dialogue provide the sort of internal evidence of conversational functions for which analysts hope. One obvious problem is that one does not really know what prompts an interlocutor to respond in a certain way, and conversely, one cannot be sure just what is meant by a *lack* of response. And how does one judge whether a pattern occurs with *enough* regularity? Although quantitative analyses have aided such judgements in many other areas of linguistics, not all conversation analysts are willing to use such methods, in part because they require analysts to view linguistic tokens in isolation from the multiple channels and contexts in which they occur, and to differentiate such tokens into mutually exclusive categories. Other remaining methodological questions concern data. From whom should data be collected? Can open-ended interviews among strangers provide access to the same range of conversational phenomena as chats among friends? How much information about participants' identities is needed for analysis? What is the role of the analysts' *own* interpretation of 'what is going on,' and should the analyst also be a participant in the conversation?

Although the directions for further research which I have already mentioned have fairly broad theoretical ramifications, there is a very general theoretical issue remaining: the relationship between conversation as language and conversation as social interaction. There are two sides to this issue. The first concerns the way that the language used in conversation – the particular expressions and constructions – provide the overall sense of order and coherence which characterizes a conversation. Since words and constructions do not create a conversation outside of a continually emerging set of social and interpretive contexts, the challenge is to characterize how linguistic and nonlinguistic understandings work together to create conversation. To this end, a synthesis between conversation analysis and pragmatics would be helpful.

The second issue concerns the way that conversation is both a linguistic unit of analysis, and a vehicle through which selves, relationships, and situations are socially constructed. What does this dualism reveal about the relationship between language and society in general? I suggest that the fact that conversation is intertwined with social life be treated not as an impediment to, but as a resource for, a wider sociolinguistic theory. That is, perhaps it can lead us toward a more general theory about language and society which defines not only texts, but language in general, as both a social and a linguistic product. To this end, a synthesis between conversation analysis and other work in sociolinguistics (e.g. variation analysis) would be helpful.

In sum, I suggested initially that some of the same qualities that make conversation an important topic for linguistic attention also make conversation a difficult topic for linguistic analysis. Those qualities included a methodological difficulty: inferences about what is causing conversation have to be made through observation of its outcome. They also included two theoretical difficulties. One centered around the relationship between conversation as language and conversation as social process: what is displayed in conversation is not only speaker/hearers' communicative competence, but their procedures for constructing social order. The other centred around the relationship between conversation and language in general: conversation is a basic mode of communication with effects on diachronic processes and synchronic structures of language. It is my hope that this paper has provided a deeper understanding of why these issues are both important and difficult, and that it will encourage analysts to overcome the difficulties not only to gain insights into an important domain of linguistics, but to better understand an important part of human life.

REFERENCES

Atkinson, M. & Heritage, J. 1984. Introduction. In Atkinson & Heritage 1984.
Atkinson, M. & Heritage J. (eds.) *Structures of social action: studies in conversation analysis.* Cambridge: Cambridge University Press.
Austin, J. L. 1962. *How to do things with words.* Cambridge, MA: MIT Press.
Bach, K. & Harnish, R. M. 1979. *Linguistic communication and speech acts.* Cambridge, MA: MIT Press.
Bates, E. & MacWhinney, B. 1979. A functionalist approach to the acquisition of grammar. In E. Ochs & B. B. Schieffelin (eds.) *Developmental pragmatics.* New York: Academic Press.
Brown, G. & Yule, G. 1983. *Discourse analysis.* Cambridge: Cambridge University Press.
Brown, P. & Levinson, S. 1978. Universals in language use: politeness phenomena. In E. Goody (ed.) *Questions and politeness: strategies in social interaction.* Cambridge: Cambridge University Press.
Button, G. & Casey, N. 1984. Generating topic: the use of topic initial elicitors. In Atkinson & Heritage 1984.
Calfee, R. 1982. Some theoretical and practical ramifications of story grammars. *Journal of Pragmatics* 6: 441–50.
Chafe, W. 1977. Creativity in verbalization and its implications for the nature of stored knowledge. In R. Freedle (ed.) *Discourse production and comprehension.* Norwood: Ablex.
Cicourel, A. 1972. Basic and normative rules in the negotiation of status and role. In D. Sudnow (ed.) *Studies in social interaction.* New York: Free Press.
Clark, H. 1985. Language use and language users. In G. Lindzet & E. Aronson (eds.), *Handbook of social psychology*, 3rd edn. Reading, MA: Addison-Wesley.
Cole, P. & Morgan J. L. (eds.) 1975. *Syntax and semantics*, Vol. 3: *Speech acts.* New York: Academic Press.
Collett, P. 1983. Mossi salutations. *Semiotica* 45.3/4: 191–248.
Cooley, C. H. 1902. *Human nature and the social order.* New York: Charles Scribner's Sons.
Corsaro, W. A. 1979. 'We're friends, right?': children's use of access rituals in a nursery school. *Language in Society* 8: 315–36.
Coulter, J. 1979. *The social construction of mind: studies in ethnomethodology and phenomenology.* Totawa: Rowman and Littlefield.
Dijk, T. van. 1985. Introduction: dialogue as discourse and interaction. In T. van Dijk (ed.) *Handbook of discourse analysis*, Vol. 3: *Discourse and dialogue.* London: Academic Press.
Erickson, F. & Schultz, J. 1982. *The counselor as gatekeeper: social interaction in interviews.* New York: Academic Press.
Fillmore, C. J. 1981. Pragmatics and the description of discourse. In P. Cole (ed.) *Radical pragmatics.* New York: Academic Press.
Fillmore, C. J. 1982. Story grammars and sentence grammars. *Journal of Pragmatics* 6: 451–4.
Firbas, J. 1964. On defining the theme in functional sentence analysis. *Travaux Linguistiques de Prague* 1: 267–80.
Garfinkel, H. 1967. *Studies in ethnomethodology.* Englewood Cliffs: Prentice Hall.
Gazdar, G. 1979. *Pragmatics: implicature, presupposition, and logical form.* New York: Academic Press.
Givón, T. 1979. *On understanding grammar.* New York: Academic Press.

Godard, D. 1977. Same setting, different norms: phone call beginnings in France and the United States. *Language in Society* 6: 209–19.

Goffman, E. 1963. *Behavior in public places*. New York: Free Press.

Goffman, E. 1967. The nature of deference and demeanor. In *Interaction ritual*. New York: Anchor Books.

Goffman, E. 1974. *Frame analysis*. New York: Harper & Row.

Goffman, E. 1981. Replies and responses. In *Forms of talk*. Philadelphia: University of Pennsylvania Press. (Originally published 1976 in *Language in society* 5: 257–313.)

Goodwin, C. 1981. *Conversational organization: interaction between speakers and hearers*. New York: Academic Press.

Grice, H. P. 1957. Meaning. *Philosophical Review* 67: 377–88.

Grice, H. P. 1975. Logic and conversation. In Cole & Morgan 1975.

Gumperz, J. 1982a. *Discourse strategies*. Cambridge: Cambridge University Press.

Gumperz, J. 1982b. *Language and social identity*. Cambridge: Cambridge University Press.

Hall, P. H. & Spencer-Hall, D. A. 1983. The handshake as interaction. *Semiotica* 45.3/4: 249–64.

Halliday, M. A. K. 1967. Notes on transitivity and theme in English. *Journal of Linguistics* 3: 37–81, 199–244.

Halliday, M. A. K. 1973. *Explorations in the functions of language*. London: Arnold.

Halliday, M. A. K. & Hasan, R. 1976. *Cohesion in English*. London: Longman.

Harris, Z. 1952. Discourse analysis. *Language* 28: 1–30.

Heringer, J. T. 1977. Pre-sequences and indirect speech acts. In E. O. Keenan & T. L. Bennett (eds.) *Discourse across time and space*. University of Southern California: Southern California Occasional Papers in Linguistics 5.

Heritage, J. 1984. A change-of-state token and aspects of its sequential placement. In J. Atkinson & J. Heritage (eds.) *Structures of social action: studies in conversation analysis*. Cambridge: Cambridge University Press.

Hymes, D. 1972. Toward ethnographies of communication: the analysis of communicative events. In P. Giglioli (ed.), *Language and social context*. Harmondsworth: Penguin. (Originally published 1964 in *American Anthropologist* 66.)

Jefferson, G. 1978. Sequential aspects of storytelling in conversation. In J. Schenkein (ed.) *Studies in the organization of conversational interaction*. New York: Academic Press.

Jefferson, G. 1984. On the organization of laughter in talk about troubles. In Atkinson & Heritage 1984.

Keenen, E. O. & Schieffelin, B. B. 1976. Topic as a discourse notion: a study of topic in the conversation of children and adults. In C. N. Li (ed.) *Subject and topic*. New York: Academic Press.

Kempson, R. 1975. *Presupposition and the delimitation of semantics*. Cambridge: Cambridge University Press.

Labov, W. 1972a. The transformation of experience in narrative syntax. In *Language in the inner city*. Philadelphia: University of Pennsylvania Press.

Labov, W. 1972b. Rules for ritual insults. In D. Sudnow (ed.) *Studies in social interaction*. New York: Free Press.

Labov, W. & Fanshel, D. 1977. *Therapeutic discourse: psycho-therapy as conversation*. New York: Academic Press.

Lakoff, R. 1973. The logic of politeness, or minding your p's and q's. In C. Corum, T. Smith-Stark & A. Werser (eds.) *Papers from the Ninth Regional Meeting of the Chicago Linguistics Society*.

Leech, G. 1983. *Principles of pragmatics*. New York: Longman.

Levinson, S. C. 1981. The essential inadequacies of speech act models of dialogue. In H. Parret, M. Sbisa & J. Verschueren (eds.) *Possibilities and limitations of pragmatics: proceedings of the conference on pragmatics at Urbino*. Amsterdam: Benjamins.

Levinson, S. C. 1983. *Pragmatics*. Cambridge: Cambridge University Press.

Lyons, J. 1977. *Semantics*, 2 vols. Cambridge: Cambridge University Press.

Mathesius, V. 1924. Some notes on the function of the subject in modern English. *Časopis pro Moderni Filologii* 10: 1–6.

Maynard, D. 1982. Aspects of sequential organization in plea bargaining discourse. *Human Studies* 5: 319–44.

Maynard, D. 1983. Social order and plea bargaining in the courtroom. *Sociological Quarterly* 24: 233–52.

Mead, G. H. 1962. *Mind, self and society*. Chicago: University of Chicago Press.

Merritt, M. 1976. On questions following questions (in service encounters). *Language in Society* 5: 315–57.

Ochs, E. 1979. Transcription as theory. In Ochs & Schieffelin 1979.

Ochs, E. & Schieffelin, B. B. (eds.) 1979. *Developmental pragmatics*. New York: Academic Press.

Polanyi, L. 1985. Conversational storytelling. In T. van Dijk (ed.) *Handbook of discourse analysis*, Vol. 3: *Discourse and dialogue*. London: Academic Press.

Pomerantz, A. 1984. Pursuing a response. In Atkinson & Heritage 1984.

Prince, E. 1981. Towards a taxonomy of given-new information. In P. Cole (ed.) *Radical pragmatics*. New York: Academic Press.

Prince, G. 1973. *A grammar for stories*. The Hague: Mouton.

Rumelhart, D. 1975. Notes on a schema for stories. In D. Bubrow & A. Collins (eds.) *Representation and understanding: studies in cognitive science*. New York: Academic Press.

Sacks, H. 1971. Lecture notes. School of Social Science, University of California at Irvine.

Sacks, H., Schegloff, E. & Jefferson, G. 1974. A simplest systematics for the organization of turn-taking in conversation. *Language* 50: 696–735.

Sankoff, G. 1984. Substrate and universals in the Tok Pisin verb phrase. In D. Schiffrin (ed.) *Meaning, form, and use in context: linguistic applications (Georgetown University Round Table on Languages and Linguistics)* Washington: Georgetown University Press.

Sankoff, G. & Brown, P. 1976. The origins of syntax in discourse. *Language* 52: 631–66.

Schegloff, E. 1972. Sequencing in conversational openings. In J. Gumperz & D. Hymes (eds.) *Directions in sociolinguistics*. New York: Holt, Rinehart, and Winston.

Schegloff, E. 1979. The relevance of repair to syntax for conversation. In T. Givón (ed.) *Syntax and semantics*, Vol. 12: *Discourse and syntax*. New York: Academic Press.

Schegloff, E. 1980. Preliminaries to preliminaries: 'Can I ask you a question?' *Sociological Inquiry* 50: 104–52.

Schegloff, E. 1982. Discourse as an interactional achievement: Some uses of 'uh huh' and other things that come between sentences. In D. Tannen (ed.) *Georgetown University Roundtable on Languages and Linguistics* 93. Washington: Georgetown University Press.

Schegloff, E. 1984. On some questions and ambiguities in conversation. In Atkinson & Heritage 1984.

Schegloff, E. & Sacks, H. 1973. Opening up closings. *Semiotica* 7: 289–327.

Schiffrin, D. 1974. Handwork as ceremony: the case of the handshake. *Semiotica* 12–13: 189–202. Reprinted in A. Kendon (ed.) *Nonverbal communication, interaction and gesture*, 1981. New York: Moulton.

Schiffrin, D. 1977. Opening encounters. *American Sociological Review* 42: 671–91.

Schiffrin, D. 1980. Meta-talk: organizational and evaluative brackets in discourse. In D. Zimmerman & C. West (eds.) *Language and social interaction*. Special edition of *Sociological Inquiry* 50: 199–236.

Schiffrin, D. 1983. Turn initial variation. Paper presented at New Ways of Analyzing Variation, 12. Montreal, Canada.

Schiffrin, D. 1984a. Jewish argument as sociability. *Language in Society* 13: 311–35.

Schiffrin, D. 1984b. How a story says what it means and does. *Text* 4: 313–46.

Schiffrin, D. 1985a. Everyday argument: the organization of diversity in talk. In T. van Dijk (ed.) *Handbook of discourse analysis*, Vol. 3: *Discourse and dialogue*. London: Academic Press.

Schiffrin, D. 1985b. Multiple constraints on discourse options: a quantitative analysis of casual sequences. *Discourse Processes* 8: 281–303.

Schiffrin, D. 1985c. Conversational coherence: the role of *well*. *Language* 61: 640–67.

Schiffrin, D. 1986. Turn-initial variation: structure and function in conversation. In D. Sankoff (ed.) *Diversity and diachrony*. Current Issues in Linguistic Theory 53. Amsterdam: Benjamins.

Schiffrin, D. 1987a. Discovering the context of an utterance. In N. Dittmar (ed.) *Linguistics*, special volume on variation and discourse, to appear.

Schiffrin, D. 1987b. *Discourse markers*. Cambridge: Cambridge University Press.

Schutz, A. 1979. *Alfred Schutz: on phenomenology and social relations*. Chicago: University of Chicago Press.

Scollon, R. 1981. The rhythmic integration of ordinary talk. In D. Tannen (ed.) *Georgetown University Roundtable on Languages and Linguistics*. Washington: Georgetown University Press.

Searle, J. R. 1969. *Speech acts*. Cambridge: Cambridge University Press.

Slobin, D. 1975. The more it changes . . . On understanding language by watching it move through time. *Papers and reports on child language development*. Berkeley: University at California at Berkeley.

Stubbs, M. 1983. *Discourse analysis: the sociolinguistic analysis of natural language*. Chicago: University of Chicago Press.

Tannen, D. 1981. New York Jewish conversational style. *International Journal of the Sociology of Language* 30: 133–9.

Tannen, D. 1982. Therapeutic discourse: psychotherapy and conversation. *Language* 57: 481–6.

Tannen, D. 1983. When is an overlap not an interruption? In R. DiPietro, W. Frawley & A. Wedel (eds.) *The first Delaware symposium on language studies*. Newark: University of Delaware Press.

Tannen, D. 1984. *Conversational style: analyzing talk among friends*. Norwood: Ablex.

West, C. 1984. *Routine complications: troubles with talk between doctors and patients*. Indiana: Indiana University Press.

Zimmerman, D. 1978. Ethnomethodology. *American Sociologist* 13: 6–15.

Zimmerman, D. & West, C. 1983. Conversation analysis. In K. R. Scherer & P. Eckman (eds.) *Handbook of methods in nonverbal behavior research*. Cambridge: Cambridge University Press.

Index of names

Index of names

Index of subjects

Aboriginal children, education in native language 205
Abstract thinking, literacy and 68–71
Academies, language 195, 206
Accents of English (Wells) 120 n. 2
Acceptability judgements 82–3
Accommodation theory (Giles) 108–9, 110–11, 131 n. 5
Acquisition: creole 180; language 24, 69; of dying languages 189; and socialization 215
Acrolectal speakers, *see* English, standard
Action, situated, joint meaning and 259–62
Address, sexual politics of 86
Africa, East 194–5, 200
Afro-Americans 49
Age, in communicative situation 8, 9
Aguaruna 27
Allomorphic variations, as sociolinguistic markers 164
Allomorphy: elimination of in simplification 172; reduction of in language decay 187
Amazon Indians 82
Ambiguities, functional, in conversation 261
American Black English Vernacular (BEV) 123 n. 10
American English 21, 31, 120; women's language 82–3
Amerindian 82
Andean contact language 175
Animacy hierarchies 18–20
Anthropology 14–15, 75, 125, 211, 266, *see also* social anthropology; cognitive 30–1; linguistic 17; and world view 25–6
Apache 25
Appropriateness of utterances in discourse 234, 241
Arabic 102, 112, 194; Sudanese 28–9
Arafundi 168
Area linguistics, *see* dialect geography
Artificial intelligence 235 n. 5

Atlantic Ocean, plantation areas 163
Atlases, linguistic 119, 120–5
Attitudes, gender and 86–96
Attitudes, language: and development of pidgins 163–4; in language decay 188, 189, 190; and planning 200, 201
Audience design 105, 109–12
Australia 20, 43–4, 185, 187, 205; English in 162; intonational change 59
Austria 108
Austronesian languages 172
Autonomy of syntax 1, 17, 156, 214
Aviation English 206
Aymaran language 27
Aztec-speaking people 190

Bangladesh 200
Belfast vernacular maintenance study 54, 108, 134
Bengali 200, 205
BEV, *see* American Black English Vernacular
Bilingualism 3, 100–18; definitions 100–1; review of literature 100
Bioprogram, in creole acquisition 180
Birth, language 3, 162–83
Black English 49, 53, 144, 148
Black vernacular English 70, 72; *see also* American Black English Vernacular
Blacks: genetic fallacy 65–7; middle class women 83; verbal dueling 221
Borrowing 185–6; from English 200
Brasilia 46
Brazil 54
Breton 186–7, 188, 189
British pop singers 131
Burmese 25, 26

CA, *see* conversation analysis
California 184
Canada 195, 204; dialect geography 121
Canewalk study 47–8
Capitalism 18, 40–1, 47, 190

283

Index of subjects

Semi-speakers 185, 189
Sentence grammar 245
Sepik area, New Guinea 167–75, 176–7, 181
Sequencing rules, in conversation 260
Sex difference 8, 9: and class 37, 48–9; cultural construction of 77; *see also* gender
Sexist language 86–7
Sexual politics, of address 86; of language 76
Sexuality, theory and politics of 94
Shift, language 101, 105, 184
Shona language 206
Silence, meaning of 224
Simplification, in pidgins 162, 165–7 (Table 1)
Sinama of Mindanao 22
Singapore 203–4
Slave colonies, creolization in 181
Slave societies 47
Social action: language as a map for 14; meaning and 88; and speech 212–13; theory of 11
Social anthropology 130
Social class, language and 37–63
Social context 9–10; language change and 102
Social function 1, 4
Social interaction, in conversation analysis 222–4, 229 n. 1, 265–6
Social interests, in linguistic research 140, 141–5
Social network, and language choice 108
Social network analysis 130, 134
Social order, theory of (Goffman) 2
Social psychology 106, 108–9
Social reflexiveness in conversation 252
Social science 142, 157
Social stratification 42–4; dialectology of 144; fine 43–4; sharp 43–4; functional equivalence of linguistic forms 157–8; gender and 78; race and 72; *see also* class
Social stratification of English in New York City (SSENYC) (Labov) 6, 42–4, 45–6, 50, 52–3, 57, 125, 129, 130
Social stratification studies 52–4
Social theory, need for 6–7
Socialism 190
Society, language and 272–3
Socio-cultural context 1–13
Socioeconomic asymmetry, and development of pidgin 163
Socioeconomic class (SEC) 42, 50, 129
Socioeconomic status 8; and conversation analysis 223
Sociolects 60

Sociolinguistic Survey of Multilingual Communities 128
Sociolinguistic theory 132–3
Sociolinguistics 1, 6, 9, 11, 126; applied 195 n. 1; and ethnography of speaking 211–13; goals of 3–4; in language planning 198; macro- 3; quantitative, *see* quantitative sociolinguistics; and syntactic variation 140–61
Sociology 38, 102, 106, 125, 265, 266
Sound pattern of English, The (Chomsky and Halle) 132
South America 103
South Asian varieties of English 103
South Carolina 125
Soviet Union, *see* Union of Soviet Socialist Republics
Spanish 16, 18, 103, 107, 175, 184; standardization 206
Spanish–Guarani bilingualism 106
Speakers: gender of 79–80, 84; meaning of speech for 210–28
Speaking: ethnography of, *see* ethnography of speaking; as human labour 212
Speech act theory 221–2, 259–62
Speech community 7, 60: definitions 8 n. 5, 45–6, 49–52, 190, 216–17; density of communication 49–50; groups within 8, 64–5; models of, and variation studies 129–31; shared norms 50–1
Speech event analysis 218–21
Spirantization 186
Spoken dialogues 253
Spread, language 101–3; definition 102
SSENYC, see Social stratification of English in New York City
Standard English, IQ and 67–71
Standard language, class and 40, 44
Standardization 46, 196, 205, 206
Statistics, role in variation studies 150–2
Status 10, 37; class and 41–4; of language 115; change in 205–6
Status planning 202–4
Stereotyped knowledge in discourse 235–6
Stereotypes: gender 80–1, 83; language, working class and minority 158; linguistic, attack on 143–4
Strategies (Gumperz) 6
Structural linguistics, and conversation analysis 256–9
Structuralism 123
Structure, social and linguistic 9
'Studies of American pronunciation since 1945' (Pederson) 122
Style, in communicative situation 8
Style design 111–12
Style shifting 50, 109–10

290

Index of subjects

Variation theory:
origins 140, 142–4;
sociolinguistic 140–61
Verb morphology 127
Verb 'to be' 68, 70
Verbs, feminine conjugations of 80
Vernacular: death of 182; sociolinguistics and the 157–8; usage 145
Vision, language, knowledge and 20
Vocabulary, expansion, to accommodate technological development 200

Wales 112
Wave theory 102
Weltanschauung, see world view
West Bengal 200
West Futunese 27
Western languages 20
Whorf hypothesis 14–16, 28
Wintu 17
WL, *see* women's language
Women: black middle class 83; linguistic alienation of 91; marginalization of 93–4; in speech communities 129 n. 13

Women and Language 78
Women's language (WL) 80, 81–5; evaluation of 88–9
Word formation rules (WFRs) 185–6
World geography of the Eastern United States, A (Kurath) 124
Words, meaning in context 216
Working class 149: codes 54–5; role in linguistic innovation 46, 57–9; variants 157
World view: anthropology and 25–6; gender and 91; language, culture and 14–36
Written mode: difference from speech 68–9, 71; languages without 205
Written monologues 253

Yaki 184
Yana 79
Yimas 168–72
Yimas Pidgin 168–72, 174–5
Yimas village 179, 182

Zimbabwe 204

Contents of Volumes I, II, and III

Volume III   Language: psychological and biological aspects